DEBATING HUMAN RIGHTS

Human rights have become a central concern of the post-Cold War world.
The United States, as the only remaining superpower, became more assertive,
and several Asian governments, in response, challenged Western hegemony,
asserting their own cultural values. However, there are more than two sides
to this debate (East and West), and the agendas that inform it include issues
of history and power as well as values.

Debating Human Rights brings together a very broad range of scholars and
activists from Asia and the United States to discuss the problems that so
frequently cause division. It includes four opening chapters that cover the
broad issues in dispute, such as the impact of globalization and Asian values.
There are also separate sections on human rights in China, women's rights,
and international relations and human rights. The book concludes with a
section that critiques the role of China, Japan and the US in contemporary
human rights diplomacy.

This volume breaks new ground by bringing together such a diverse group
of contributors with controversial views. It will also be welcomed for its pragmatic attempt to reconcile at least some of their differences in an effort to
find common ground.

Peter Van Ness is associate professor at the Graduate School of International
Studies, University of Denver, and research associate, Contemporary China
Centre, Australian National University.

ASIA'S TRANSFORMATIONS
Edited by Mark Selden
Binghamton and Cornell Universities

DEBATING HUMAN RIGHTS

Critical essays from the United States and Asia

Edited by

Peter Van Ness

with contributions by
*Nikhil Aziz, Linda Butenhoff, Radhika Coomaraswamy,
Manisha Desai, Edward Friedman, Hoshino Eiichi,
Kishore Mahbubani, Chandra Muzaffar, Shih Chih-yu,
Michael J. Sullivan, Daniel Wessner and Zhu Feng*

London and New York

First published 1999 by Routledge
11 New Fetter Lane, London EC4P 4EE

Simultaneously published in the USA and Canada
by Routledge
29 West 35th Street, New York, NY 10001

Typeset in Baskerville by The Florence Group, Stoodleigh, Devon
Printed and bound in Great Britain by
MPG Books Ltd, Bodmin, Cornwall

British Library Cataloguing in Publication Data
A catalogue record for this book is available from the British Library

Library of Congress Cataloging in Publication Data
A catalog record for this book has been requested

ISBN 0–415–18506–8 (hbk)
ISBN 0–415–18507–6 (pbk)

This book is
dedicated with love
to Steve, Tom, and Harry –
pioneers into the
twenty-first century

CONTENTS

CONTRIBUTORS

Nikhil Aziz is a PhD candidate in the Graduate School of International Studies, University of Denver <nhemmady@du.edu>.

Linda Butenhoff is Assistant Professor in the Department of Political Science at St Cloud State University in Minnesota <lbutenho@calpoly.edu>.

Radhika Coomaraswamy is Director of the International Centre for Ethnic Studies in Colombo, Sri Lanka, and Special Rapporteur on Violence against Women for the United Nations Human Rights Commission <radhika@cmb.ices.ac.lk>.

Manisha Desai is Associate Professor of Sociology at Hobart and William Smith Colleges, in Geneva, New York <DESAI@hws.edu>.

Edward Friedman is Hawkins Professor of Political Science at the University of Wisconsin, Madison <friedman@polisci.wisc.edu>.

Hoshino Eiichi is Associate Professor of International Relations in the College of Law and Letters at the University of the Ryukyus in Okinawa <ehoshino@ll.u-ryukyu.ac.jp>.

Kishore Mahbubani is Permanent Secretary in the Ministry of Foreign Affairs in Singapore.

Chandra Muzaffar is President of the International Movement for a Just World (JUST), and director of the Centre for Civilizational Dialogue at the University of Malaysia, Kuala Lumpur <muza@po.jaring.my>.

Shih Chih-yu is Professor of Political Science at the Department and the Graduate Institute of Political Science, National Taiwan University <cyshih@ms.cc.ntu.edu.tw>.

CONTRIBUTORS

Michael J. Sullivan is a Visiting Fellow at the Center for International Studies, University of Wisconsin-Milwaukee <sull@csd.uwm.edu>.

Peter Van Ness is Associate Professor in the Graduate School of International Studies, University of Denver, and a research associate in the Contemporary China Centre at Australian National University <pvan@coombs.anu.edu.au>.

Daniel Wessner is a PhD candidate in the Graduate School of International Studies, University of Denver, and an SSRC–MacArthur Foundation Fellow in Vietnam <dwessner@du.edu>.

Zhu Feng is Associate Professor in the School of International Studies at Peking University in China <zhufeng@pku.edu.cn>.

ACKNOWLEDGMENTS

Over seven years in the making of this book, I have enjoyed moral and material support from many people and institutions. Most important, I want to thank each of the contributors for their thoughtful and provocative essays. I would like also to thank the Department of International Relations and the Contemporary China Centre at Australian National University, the Center on Rights Development and the Graduate School of International Studies at the University of Denver, and the Fulbright–Hays program for their financial and intellectual sustenance, as well as the Woodrow Wilson International Center for Scholars in Washington, DC, where some of these ideas first began to take shape many years ago. The hospitality of Renmin University in Beijing and Keio University in Tokyo was vital to the success of the project.

Many people supported this project in different ways. In addition to the contributors and on their behalf, I would especially like to thank Hilary Charlesworth, Chen Mumin, Bill and Nancy Doub, Greg Fry, John Girling, Anne Gunn, Samuel S. Kim, John McCamant, Jim Richardson, Mark Selden, George Shepherd Jr, Victoria Smith, Tsuneishi Kei-ichi, Yamada Tatsuo, Zhang Xiaojin, and Zhang Yan. However, exclusive responsibility for what we have written of course rests with the contributors and myself.

Finally, the chapters by Aziz, Butenhoff, Coomaraswamy, Muzaffar, Sullivan and Wessner originally appeared in two special issues of the *Bulletin of Concerned Asian Scholars* (vol. 27, no. 4, October/December 1995; vol. 28, no. 2, April/June 1996) that I edited; and Manisha Desai's chapter was first published in *New Political Science* (no. 35, 1996). We are grateful to both publications for permission to reprint.

Peter Van Ness
July 1998

INTRODUCTION

Peter Van Ness

Often it is difficult, looking back, to remember the exact moment when the idea for a book occurred to you. But I remember well the conception of this book. It was an autumn evening in 1991 at Keio University in Tokyo when Professor Yamada Tatsuo, who had invited me to give a seminar on my human rights research, opened the question period after my initial presentation, asking me a series of questions that I could not answer.

My research in Japan as a visitor at Keio focused on trying to understand the hesitant Japanese reaction to Tiananmen. My wife, Anne Gunn, and I had by chance been working in China during the entire period of the student-led demonstrations of spring 1989, and, horrified by the slaughter in Beijing in June, after leaving China, we joined our colleagues at Australian National University, where we were both working at the time, to attempt to document in detail what had happened in China during those weeks.[1] A specialist on Chinese foreign policy, I had decided to focus on researching the impact of human rights issues on the international relations of the region. I was studying the reaction of the various countries to the Beijing massacre, and a Fulbright grant had given me the opportunity to do interviews in Japan on Tokyo's response.

My assessment that autumn evening at Keio University was quite critical of Japan's reaction to the events in China. Adopting an Amnesty International perspective on Tiananmen, I had criticized both Japan's reluctance to condemn the killing in Beijing and Washington's hypocrisy in condemning the Chinese government in public while secretly sending high-level envoys to assure paramount leader Deng Xiaoping that President George Bush nonetheless wanted to maintain a close and cooperative relationship. From my perspective, both Washington and Tokyo should have taken a consistent and principled stand against such an atrocious violation of human rights. Today, I still believe that.

Professor Yamada is a friend and colleague, dating back to 1978 when I had taught at Keio for a year. In attendance that evening were also several of my former students from that time, and the atmosphere that evening was for me one of trust and well-being. Yamada did not ask his questions in

1

anger or irritation, but rather in the fashion of a colleague trying to prompt his friend to understand some things that any intelligent person should know.

How, Yamada asked, can the West criticize others for human rights abuse after what the West did to Asia in the nineteenth and twentieth centuries? In Sino-American relations, isn't the American emphasis on human rights really an effort to subvert the Chinese social system (to overthrow communist rule by "peaceful evolution" as the Chinese allege), as the West has already success-fully subverted the Soviet Union? And, finally, aren't Amnesty International's human rights principles simply Western values that people in the West, once again, are trying to impose on others?

That evening, I replied making a case for the universality of human rights, how I thought arguments asserting a cultural relativist position were often simply smokescreens attempting to cover up government abuse of human rights, and so on. But I was not happy with my own replies. The more I thought about Yamada's questions, the more I felt that there were important perspectives on human rights in Asia that I knew nothing about. History, power, race . . . all seemed to be involved. This was not just a debate about values. Certainly it was true for Japan: evidence the Japanese government's struggle to come to terms with its own World War II past, especially in China and Korea (e.g. the Nanjing Massacre, the "comfort women," Unit 731 that experimented on human subjects, and the Japanese textbook controversies).[2]

About that time China launched its own human rights diplomacy, and a debate began to take shape around the argument that "Asian values" were somehow different than those in the West. I could see how self-serving were the various positions on human rights taken by *all of the governments* involved (e.g. China, Japan, and the United States), but behind the governmental rhetoric, I thought that I could discern serious disagreements among acade-mics and activists (some having government connections but most not). Many of these people were searching for common ground with their colleagues East and West, South and North, but they were not prepared to accept an imposed orthodoxy.

THE CONTRIBUTORS

This book is a collection of essays by the people that I found – in Asia and in America. From their many different perspectives, each in his/her own way is searching for common ground: a way to connect and cooperate to help better protect the essentials of our common humanity. But first there was much to be addressed, researched, and debated. On the basis of what kinds of understandings about fundamental issues might common ground be found, and consensus be built?

I traveled to Penang to meet Chandra Muzaffar, and to Singapore to talk with Kishore Mahbubani. Shih Chih-yu came to Denver to give a paper that I immediately wanted to include in the collection. I had read Zhu Feng's work before a visit to China, and we met for the first time in Beijing. I organized panels for academic meetings in Hong Kong, Denver, and under the auspices of the Association for Asian Studies in Washington, DC, where Edward Friedman, Nikhil Aziz, Linda Butenhoff, Hoshino Eiichi, Michael Sullivan, and Daniel Wessner at different times presented papers. Other contributors were suggested to me by friends and colleagues, and two, Radhika Coomaraswamy and Manisha Desai, I have not yet had a chance to meet in person. Several of the authors contributed to two special issues of the *Bulletin of Concerned Asian Scholars* on "Debating Human Rights" that I edited.

From time to time, I would check in with Yamada Tatsuo to see if I had come any closer to answering his questions. I urged him to write a Conclusion for this volume, but in the meantime, his colleagues had reelected him Dean of the Faculty of Law at Keio, so unfortunately the responsibilities of running the university intervened.

I have selected these particular essays for two reasons: because to my mind they represent the real debate about international human rights, and because in my opinion the authors are engaged in a serious search for common ground. The contributors are academics and activists from the United States and from seven countries in Asia, prominent senior analysts as well as younger scholars, two of whom are still working on their PhD dissertations. Each addresses a different topic that s/he feels is central to the international human rights debate, but they often differ quite sharply on fundamental issues.

Our objective here is to examine the roots of the international debate in this collection of differing interpretations. The heart of the matter, as I see it, has mainly to do with values, history, and power – not a modest agenda. The international debate was prompted in part by the assertion by some governments and scholars that "Asian values" are fundamentally different from Western understandings of human rights, and deserving of equal priority and consideration. Moreover, the 500-year history of Western expansion and domination of the non-Western world has set the scene for the contemporary debate, where power continues to shape practice and even principle. So, we are not simply discussing right and wrong but also talking about the legacy of the past and the problem that too often "might makes right."

The international debate emerged following the collapse of the Soviet Union, partly as a result of an assertive new US role (as the sole remaining superpower triumphant in the Western victory over Communism), partly as an attempt by abusive governments to defend themselves from international condemnation (e.g. China and Burma), and partly as a determination by Asians to assert their own standards and to reject Western hegemony in deliberations about what is most fundamental to humanity.[3] The essays in Part 1 of the book by Chandra Muzaffar, Nikhil Aziz, Edward Friedman, and Kishore Mahbubani examine these issues in detail, laying out some of the general parameters of the debate.

There are not simply two sides in this debate, but many different understandings and interpretations. In this volume, our intention is to demonstrate the intellectual significance of that diversity of paradigms and perspectives. In Part 2 of the book, three authors (two Americans and one Chinese from Taiwan) address the controversial issue of human rights in China from different perspectives. Michael Sullivan analyzes the situation on the mainland, while Shih Chih-yu assesses the perspective of Taiwan, and Linda Butenhoff examines human rights in Hong Kong during the final days of British rule, just before the colony was returned to China. Later in the book, in Part 4, Zhu Feng, a professor at Peking University, criticizes the American emphasis on human rights in US policy toward China.

A pragmatic commitment underlies our contribution to the debate. This is a collective effort to find common ground. Although each author might make a quite different argument about why common ground in the international human rights debate is important, I think that all would agree that achieving a rough consensus on how to protect our common humanity is a vital precondition for mutually beneficial international cooperation to advance human rights. The papers on women's rights in Part 3 of the book (by Radhika Coomaraswamy and Manisha Desai) perhaps represent better than any of the others the opportunity to achieve a working consensus among diverse perspectives.

Inevitably the human rights debate focuses on the performance of the state: the state as protector or abuser of civil and political rights; and the state as the expected provider of social, economic, and cultural rights. In Part 4, for example, Hoshino Eiichi, Zhu Feng, and Daniel Wessner examine the relationship between human rights and interstate relations. Within the debate about the role of the state, governments will obviously try to put their performance in the best light. One important task for independent scholars and activists is to penetrate the propaganda and investigate carefully what governments are actually doing, and to insist on governmental accountability, both to their own citizens, and to the global community with respect to the human rights treaties which they have ratified. Human rights NGOs like Amnesty International play a critically important role in monitoring the human rights performance of all governments and in publicizing cases of abuse.[4]

I have purposefully excluded papers representing official policy in the hope of avoiding self-serving propaganda by governments. Only one author, Kishore Mahbubani, is a governmental official; he is Permanent Secretary of the Singapore Ministry of Foreign Affairs. Mahbubani was invited to participate, like the other authors, for his intellectual contribution, eloquently represented in his earlier essay, "The West and the Rest."[5]

In this Introduction, I want to discuss briefly four topics: (1) the role of the United States in the post-Cold War world as it relates to Washington's claim to be a "champion" of human rights; (2) the international human rights regime and the debate about the standards that have been adopted under United Nations auspices; (3) some of the ways that history and power impinge on the human rights debate; and, finally, (4) how we might proceed in trying our best to protect international human rights.

THE UNITED STATES IN A POST-COLD WAR WORLD

How should we understand our world after the collapse of the Soviet empire in 1989–91? Analysts disagree. Francis Fukuyama expects a rather benign if boring common-marketization of international relations to emerge among those liberal democratic states that have been fortunate enough to find themselves at the "end of history."[6] Others describe a very different, dangerous world: for Robert Kaplan the fear is chaos and anarchy,[7] while Samuel Huntington forecasts a "clash of civilizations."[8] One thing they all agree on, however, is that, at the end of the Cold War, the United States has emerged preeminent as the sole remaining superpower. More recently, the financial crisis in East Asia, which began with a run on the Thai baht in July 1997 and led to stock market crashes and currency devaluations throughout the region, has humbled the "economic miracles" of East Asia and reaffirmed American predominance, as successive Asian governments have turned to the United States and the International Monetary Fund for help to support their collapsing financial systems.

How will the United States use this unprecedented power? No longer constrained by a need to include repressive governments in its anti-Communist alliance against the Soviet Union, Washington has increased its pressure on non-Western regimes, attempting to reshape them to fit an American image of democracy.[9] Identifying itself as a model and champion of human rights, the US, the world's leading military power, has placed conditions on its foreign assistance and has often imposed sanctions on countries that fail to meet its standards. As a permanent member of the United Nations Security Council, the US has also used its influence to press the UN to support American foreign policy objectives, as in the case of the Gulf War in 1991 and the intervention in Haiti in 1994. When the United Nations has been unwilling to endorse its actions, the United States has remained willing to take military action unilaterally, as demonstrated by the US attack on Iraq in September 1996.[10]

There is a profound contradiction between how Americans typically understand their own country and how the US is perceived in much of the rest of the world. President Bill Clinton has described the US, for example, as "the world's indispensable nation, the one the world looks to for leadership because of our strength and our values."[11] Americans like to think of their country as a champion of human rights and a model of democracy, as Daniel Wessner describes in Chapter 12. But American foreign policy on the receiving end is often perceived quite differently. Even Francis Fukuyama has concluded that "virtually no one in Asia today believes it likely that Asian societies will ultimately converge with the particular model of liberal democracy represented by the contemporary United States, or, indeed, that such a state of affairs is remotely desirable."[12]

On the one hand, the American revolutionary experience, the Declaration of Independence and the Bill of Rights, and the American contribution to authoring the Universal Declaration of Human Rights and related UN treaties all have advanced global human rights immeasurably – as has US diplomatic pressure on foreign governments to improve their human rights practices. Moreover, the United States has an admirable history of providing a haven for political dissidents, exiles from persecution in other countries (like the leaders of the student demonstrations in China in 1989); and America is admired by many people in the world as a land of economic opportunity and political freedom.

At the same time, however, the historical realities of genocide against the American Indian population, black slavery, American imperial interventions in the Third World, and the continuing covert and illegal activities of the CIA paint a very different picture of America for the rest of the world, a world which as the target of US foreign policy understands it very differently than Americans do. How, for example, do the objectives of the US Army School of the Americas, where "foreign military officers were taught to torture and murder to achieve their political objectives,"[13] fit into the Department of State's characterization of the US as "the one country in the world that is the absolute champion of human rights"?[14]

Americans pride themselves on being self-critical, but that criticism typically takes place within a set of assumptions about the United States that not much of the rest of the world would accept. For example, Americans show a callous acceptance of the contradiction between, on the one hand, US rhetoric about "we are the best" and a shining example to the world and, on the other hand, the existence in the US of some of the most serious social problems of any of the industrialized countries: including drug addiction, crime, breakdown of the family unit, homelessness, and growing income inequality.[15]

Inevitably, many people in Asia see the United States quite differently than the way Americans see themselves. While Americans describe more of a sharing, caring US role, a generous America benevolent in its international intentions and democratic in its dealings with other governments, the picture painted by foreign critics is often one of an arrogant and self-righteous bully, naive in its understanding of how the world really works.

Two examples illustrate this point. On November 19, 1996, when the UN Security Council voted fourteen to one in favor of offering Dr Boutros Boutros-Ghali a second term as Secretary-General of the United Nations, the US vetoed the proposal supported by an overwhelming majority of the other members, and threatened to default on its $1.4 billion debt to the UN if it did not get its way. As one UN official remarked: "This is not democracy."[16] A second example is Washington's threat to ignore any ruling by the World Trade Organization against the US Helms–Burton law which seeks to punish countries that trade with Cuba. Opposing the US position, 137 UN member-countries, including Britain, called for an end to the thirty-year US trade embargo against Cuba.[17]

The Commission For a New Asia, a panel of prominent leaders from fourteen Asian countries, commenting in their report on the conditions conducive to democratic development in Asia, concluded that "for a democracy to be self-sustaining, it must not only be a do-it-yourself process. It must be the result of the will of the people themselves." Without mentioning the US by name, they noted that:

> the process of dramatic democratisation can not be imposed and bulldozed by external forces, whose understanding of, and whose desire to understand specific situations are all too often extremely limited. In many situations, external interference will prove counter-productive. A fast democratising Asia can not be expected to tolerate myopic arrogance and self-righteous hectoring from governments whose democratic systems are in urgent need of repair and reform.[18]

The tensions in the American role in the post-Cold War world, illustrated in these examples, tend to undermine the positive influence of Washington's support for international human rights.

THE INTERNATIONAL HUMAN RIGHTS REGIME

One of the significant achievements of the United Nations during the first fifty years of its history has been the negotiation and promulgation of a comprehensive set of standards for international human rights. Often called the International Bill of Human Rights, the key documents are the Universal Declaration of Human Rights, adopted by the UN General Assembly in December 1948, and two comprehensive specifications of those rights, both of which were adopted in 1966 and entered into force in 1976: the International Covenant on Civil and Political Rights and the International Covenant on Economic, Social, and Cultural Rights. In addition, some twenty other human rights agreements have been negotiated under United Nations auspices.[19]

Unlike the Universal Declaration, which does not require a formal acknow-ledgement, both covenants and the rest of the treaties call upon all indepen-dent states to sign and ratify these documents in order for their provisions to be binding in international law on the individual governments. The vast majority of independent states have become a party to the two covenants. By July 1, 1995, 127 states had ratified the civil and political rights covenant, and 129 states had ratified the covenant on economic, social, and cultural rights.[20] The United States, however, did not ratify the civil and political rights covenant until 1992; and it still has not ratified the other covenant. China and Singapore, two other exceptional cases, have ratified neither – although Beijing has signed the covenant on economic, social, and cultural rights, and has announced that it will sign the covenant on civil and political rights.

The World Conference on Human Rights held in Vienna in June 1993 (and the regional, preparatory conferences convened before the Conference) made it quite clear that there were important differences between the West and at least some non-Western governments in their ideas about human rights, especially between Asia and the United States. If, after the current financial crisis, the relative economic power of countries in East Asia continues to increase, it is likely that Western human rights positions will become even more contested by critics in Asia. For example, the Chinese government has published a series of white papers on its own human rights situation, and it now regularly publishes a critique of the annual US Department of State human rights report.[21] Beijing places highest priority on economic rights and a country's right to self-determination.[22] President Jiang Zemin reiterated the official PRC view during his official visit to the US in the fall of 1997 when he said: "Concepts on democracy, on human rights, and on freedom are rela-tive and specific, and they are to be determined by the specific national situation of different countries."[23]

Obviously, there is no single "Asian" or "non-Western" view, just as there are various "Western" understandings of human rights. However, there are several main issues that have been central to East vs West differences over human rights. They include the following:

1   the question of universality versus cultural or developmental relativism: whether human rights should be understood as universal principles applying to all humanity, or as values shaped essentially by the particu-larities of each nation;

2   the so-called right to intervene versus the state sovereignty defense against international intervention and the imposition of sanctions[24] to prevent human rights abuse (the non-Western position here also tends to empha-size the right to self-determination and the need to achieve a demo-cratization of relations among states as a basis for protecting global human rights);

3   competing priorities among different categories of human rights, especially: (a) civil and political rights versus economic, social, and cultural rights; and (b) individual rights versus collective or group rights; and

4   concepts of individual rights versus citizen duties.

There are strong arguments to be made on both sides (or the many sides) of each of these issues. The concept of universality, for example, is challenged by relativist arguments from both East and West. PRC official policy asserts that "because history, culture, and social conditions are unique, human rights concepts are different in various countries";[25] while Samuel Huntington at Harvard puts forward an analogous argument: that Western civilization is unique, not universal, and the US should adopt a pull-up-the-drawbridge, protectionist foreign policy to defend the West against civilizational challenges from the non-Western world.[26]

Nonetheless, the human rights standards that have been negotiated under UN auspices are principles that the vast majority of states have voluntarily accepted as at least roughly appropriate. Moreover, by their endorsement of the UN Charter when accepting membership in the United Nations, and by ratifying any of the various human rights treaties, member-states become accountable to the international community in ways that inevitably compromise an absolutist interpretation of state sovereignty. It is also important to note that the United Nations human rights standards are not only Western standards, as critics often assert. Certainly, the idea of rule of law, the concept of nation, and the vision of binding all nations into a global community based on international law have their roots in Western cultural traditions; but the UN human rights treaties themselves have been co-authored by and represent the priorities of the entire international community.

The international human rights regime, as Linda Butenhoff describes it in Chapter 5, is generally considered to incorporate three "generations" of rights. Each generation has emphasized the priorities of a particular grouping of countries. The *first generation* is comprised of civil and political rights, which seek to protect the individual from the state. Amnesty International's focus on murder, torture, and incarceration without due process is a good example of this set of concerns. This generation is indeed deeply rooted in the individualistic Western cultural tradition. The *second generation*, however, which specifies economic, social, and cultural rights, reflects the priorities of the socialist countries and the Marxist philosophical tradition. Here, the focus is on problems of starvation and malnutrition, illiteracy, and disease; and the objective is to increase material standards of living. Finally, people's rights or group rights constitute a *third generation* of rights, and respond to the special concerns of the Third World and the history of colonialism, particularly in their emphasis on the right to self-determination and the right to development.

Taken together, the global human rights regime, built of treaties establishing these three generations of rights in international law, is a set of standards co-authored jointly by the West, the socialist countries, and the Third World – in effect, the entire world. As perhaps a next step, Radhika Coomaraswamy argues in Chapter 8 that the particular problems of protecting women's rights warrant considering women's rights as yet a fourth generation of human rights.

The negotiation and ratification of these various standards reflect an evolving global consciousness with respect to human rights.[27] Inevitably, this is a dynamic process, which assumes that the standards of today will and should continue to evolve and change. In some respects, the different generations of rights are in contradiction with one another, and debates rage about which should have priority. To my mind, this is a good thing. The debates are a lively, creative process, stimulated by a widening circle of concern about how best to protect human rights.[28]

In the debate about "Asian values" among scholars who seek common ground, there are at least two different arguments put forward. Proponents of the first (for example, Chandra Muzaffar in Chapter 1 and, from a different perspective, Edward Friedman in Chapter 3) argue for an acknowledgment of moral equivalence between and among the various religious and philosophical traditions represented in different countries East and West. The second argument differs, however, by first observing fundamental differences between Western and non-Western cultures, and then suggesting strategies for accommodation and cooperation across those differences.

Amartya Sen, the economist and philosopher, made a good case for the first argument in a lecture he presented on "Human Rights and Asian Values." In his lecture, Sen refuted three commonly heard views: the defense of authoritarianism in Asia based on a purported special character of Asian values; the argument that economic development in Asia requires authoritarian rule; and the championing of Asian values as part of a strategy to resist Western cultural hegemony. Sen rejected all three of these views, demonstrating "the presence of conscious theorizing about tolerance and freedom in substantial and important parts of Asian tradition." Sen concluded: "The view that the basic ideas underlying freedom and rights in a tolerant society are 'Western' notions, and somehow alien to Asia, is hard to make sense of, even though that view has been championed by both Asian authoritarians and Western chauvinists."[29]

Onuma Yasuaki, a professor of law at Tokyo University, takes up the second position, identifying cultural differences but seeking accommodation. Onuma points to the individualistic and legalistic aspects of the "Westcentric" concept of human rights, noting the resistance of many non-Western societies to legalism and individualism, both because of civilizational differences and because of hegemonic role enjoyed by the Western position. Nonetheless, Onuma accepts the global human rights mechanism "because we have not yet found a better alternative." His answer to the debate between universalism and relativity is to call for an "intercivilizational" concept of human rights, which, among other things, would give equal priority to both civil and political rights, on the one hand, and economic, cultural, and social rights, on the other.[30]

Most of the contributors to this volume embrace a concept of universality, not because they endorse some homogenizing, hegemonic definition of human rights, but because they realize that consensus is vital to international cooperation. The concept that most would endorse, I think, is a notion of universalism as a continually changing, negotiated, and tentative definition of international human rights. "It is precisely because of the cultural diversity of the world that it is necessary for different nations and peoples to agree on those basic human values which will act as a unifying factor," Aung San Suu Kyi, the Nobel Peace Prize winner, has observed. "The challenge we now face is for the different nations and peoples of the world to agree on a basic set of human values, which will serve as a force in the development of a genuine global community."[31]

For example, when in July 1997, Malaysian Prime Minister Mahathir proposed that the Universal Declaration on Human Rights of 1948, which serves as the foundation stone of the legal edifice of the international human rights regime, should be reviewed and possibly revised, he was rebuffed by US Secretary of State Madeleine Albright, who happened to be visiting Malaysia at the time. But, to my mind, Mahathir should instead have been encouraged to make a concrete proposal, because one of the basic require- ments for achieving and sustaining consensus is to be prepared to reshape global standards whenever better principles are discovered.[32] As Onuma has argued: "we must constantly reconceptualize human rights and adjust them to more universal settings."[33]

HISTORY, POWER, AND HUMAN RIGHTS

As the contributors to this volume debated and discussed human rights at panels we organized for international conferences in Hong Kong and at the University of Denver, and for the Association for Asian Studies in the US, it soon became clear that many of our differences were about history. We found that one of the first questions that we should ask of any author was: histori- cally, when does the author's story begin? For example, when doing research in Japan in 1995 on the fiftieth anniversary of the end of World War II and the atomic bombings of Hiroshima and Nagasaki, I found that Americans typically began their story on December 7, 1941, with the Japanese attack on Pearl Harbor. But, for Japanese, the story began much earlier, with Matthew Perry's "black ships" in the middle of the nineteenth century which forced Japan to open up to the West.

How can contemporary governments come to terms with major human rights atrocities of their past? What might be called "redressing history" has become a principal intellectual concern for several of the authors. For example, both government officials and activists in China and Korea continue to press the Japanese government to atone for its World War II atrocities in their countries. Similarly, anti-nuclear activists, especially in Japan, insist that the United States should apologize for the horrors that the US inflicted on the civilian populations of Hiroshima and Nagasaki and accept responsibility for leading humanity into the Nuclear Age.

With regard to the role of human rights in foreign policy, no government has proven to be a model of consistency. Even among the most consistent, there always seems to be a double standard – or sometimes no standard at all – in the way that governments engage in human rights diplomacy. Human rights abuses committed by friendly governments are typically ignored, while abuses by one's opponents are forcefully condemned. Moreover, when human rights issues are addressed in a systematic way by governments, it is always someone else's human rights abuses that are to be investigated, and almost never one's own.

There is also a problem about governments not practicing what they preach when it comes to formal ratification of the major international agreements negotiated under UN auspices. Some governments, like Australia and the Scandinavian countries, have a good record with regard to ratifying the two covenants and other human rights agreements. Other countries, like China and the US, do not.[34]

To what extent, then, does this debate about values actually mask a competition for power? China, for example, claims that US human rights diplomacy is in reality an effort, by means of so-called "peaceful evolution," to overthrow Communist rule in China. On the other hand, analysts in the West often dismiss any criticism of the Western position as self-serving propaganda put forward by defenders of non-Western governments that persistently abuse human rights. Underlying the Sino-US human rights debate there is an undeniable strategic competition for power,[35] and the struggle about power and principle is reflected in the United Nations deliberations about human rights. China and the US use their power, especially as permanent members of the UN Security Council, to try to shape both human rights standards and how they are implemented by UN institutions.[36]

However, all governments realize that membership in the UN, and becoming a party to international treaties on human rights, inevitably involves making compromises with respect to sovereignty in that member-states agree to be bound, despite their independent status, to certain principles and to act in certain ways. Therefore, the tension between sovereignty and accountability in terms of international law is also a central problem in the human rights debate. All member-states of course understand this, but often their rhetoric conveys the impression that certain activities of the organizations of which they have voluntarily become members are somehow illegally infringing on their sovereign rights.[37]

Fortunately, systematic monitoring and detailed reporting by NGOs of abuse of civil and political rights (e.g. the work of Amnesty International and Human

Rights Watch), and the comparative analysis of economic and social rights performance published by international organizations (e.g. the annual *Human Development Report* put out by the United Nations Development Program) have produced a growing database to support independent analysis and a sustained policy debate about the implementation of UN human rights standards.

Meanwhile, many analysts have been surprised at how the human rights debate has remained high on the agenda of international politics in the post-Cold War world. Realists expected that soon after the Western indignation at the Beijing massacre of 1989 subsided, and certainly once the 1993 World Conference on Human Rights had been concluded, the human rights issue would gradually disappear, inevitably to be superseded by the "real" concerns of international affairs about power. Instead, human rights issues have continued to capture center stage in many post-Cold War confrontations: in Bosnia, Rwanda, East Timor, and Burma. Note, for example, the prominence of human rights issues in President Bill Clinton's joint press conference in Beijing with President Jiang Zemin, during their summit meeting in June–July 1998.[38]

One reason for the prominence of the human rights debate is that it addresses questions about how to establish the moral foundations for a global community after the end of the Cold War. Following forty years of ideological confrontation between the United States and the Soviet Union, there now seems to be general agreement that "democracy" and "human rights" should be fundamental principles of that moral community, but there is substantial disagreement about what those concepts mean and even more disagreement about how they might best be achieved.[39]

Asia takes a central role in the debate not just because of its emerging economic and military power (especially in Japan, China, and India) but also because of the cultural significance of the various Asian historical traditions: including Confucianism, Islam, and the different streams of Buddhism. Most in the non-Western world are determined not to let the United States impose its particular definitions of democracy and human rights upon them, especially if that imposition tends to violate central moral principles of their own cultural communities.

The emerging structure of the post-Cold War world makes working for universal cooperation particularly urgent. Like it or not, we live in an era of globalization, and humanity increasingly shares a common fate. When the United States and the Soviet Union achieved the capacity to destroy human civilization by means of a single, massive exchange of nuclear warheads, the world entered a new era. Subsequently, environmental damage resulting from industrialization and economic modernization has forced similar conclusions. Contemporary strategies for attaining economic growth are not "sustainable" in the sense that, if continued over the long term, they would destroy the ecology of the planet. For example, the environmental crisis in Southeast Asia during 1997 caused by forest fires in Indonesia mixing with industrial pollution, which created a choking smog that spread across the region and produced immediate threats to public health and the region's tourist industry, demonstrated how the rush to achieve economic growth has ignored ecological priorities.[40] Meanwhile, day by day, the peoples of the world are linked more closely through a greater participation by virtually all states in the global market, and because of the evolution of modern information technology. By the end of the century, there will be no place to hide.

Scholars are just beginning to analyze the implications of the combined influence of these separate trends in military technological development, environmental degradation, market participation, and communications. Each trend in a different way links the nations of the world more closely together in patterns of what are usually called "globalization." But what does globalization mean for international human rights?

Nikhil Aziz, in Chapter 2 of the book, discusses Richard Falk's distinction between two kinds of globalization: globalization-from-above, involving the expansion of an international division of labor, the growing power of multinational corporations, and the influence of Western-dominated financial institutions like the World Trade Organization and the International Monetary Fund;[41] as contrasted with globalization-from-below, energized by new democratic social movements (e.g. often focused on human rights, feminism, and the environment), efforts to build transnational solidarity, and the objective of creating a global civil society.[42] Other scholars are not as convinced as Aziz that the movements from below are likely to be democratic, fearing a more fundamentalist and intolerant bent; but the distinction between globalization-from-above and globalization-from-below is obviously an important one.

James Richardson, a professor at Australian National University, interprets the two diverse political movements as both having their philosophical roots in liberalism, but with profoundly different political implications.[43] Globalization-from-above draws on what Richardson calls "the liberalism of privilege," a deterministic notion of the victory of democracy and capitalism in an "end of history" sense,[44] and implying a *rapprochement* in international relations theory in the classic debate between liberalism and realism. Globalization-from-below, however, draws on a different, more radical liberal tradition, which denounces the first as an attempt to establish a homogenizing universalism and an ideological hegemony to serve the interests of the established, capitalist world order. As Aung San Suu Kyi has put it: "The value systems of those with access to power and of those far removed from such access cannot be the same. The viewpoint of the privileged is unlike that of the underprivileged."[45]

From the perspective of globalization-from-below, support for the protection of human rights is based on an assumption that a truly cooperative global society must be founded on a shared commitment to common principles – in effect, a global civil society. Enforced homogenization of values by means of an imposed New World Order will only meet with angry opposition. The answer is to find philosophical common ground.[46]

As the world shrinks, the opportunities for both conflict and cooperation increase, and technologies capable of inflicting massive human and environmental destruction proliferate. Greater participation in the global capitalist market is not necessarily going to make the world's peoples happier with each other.[47] At the end of the Cold War, we have a greater opportunity to make peace and to inflict harm that at any previous time in world history.

THE EAST ASIAN FINANCIAL CRISIS

As late as the July 1997 meeting of ASEAN foreign ministers, ASEAN officials were describing their scheduled, unprecedented summit conference of ASEAN leaders with counterparts from China, South Korea, and Japan in December as a meeting to reshape the strategic order of East Asia. This was Prime Minister Mahathir's much-promoted idea of an East Asian Economic Caucus (EAEC) – the leaders of the region convening and collaborating *without the participation of the West.* In August, an ASEAN official was quoted as saying that "People haven't woken up to the fact that the summit in December will be a momentous event." He continued: "Neither North America nor Europe has paid enough attention to this part of the world. This summit will be a wake-up call for them to do so."[48]

By the time they met in December, however, three of their members (Thailand, Indonesia, and South Korea), devastated by a combination of collapsing currency values and crashing stock markets, had already requested bailouts from the International Monetary Fund. Instead of an assertive, in-your-face challenge to the US and the West from a proud and powerful new EAEC, the summit concluded with a loud call for help![49] By year's end, the stock markets of four summit members in dollar terms had declined for the year by more than 69 percent: Indonesia 73.3 percent; Malaysia 69.1 percent; South Korea 70.2 percent and Thailand 75.9 percent.[50] From economic miracle to economic maelstrom in only six months!

Taking stock at New Year, Robert Manning wrote that "1998 will reveal whether the Asian contagion is a harbinger of a looming global economic disaster akin to that of the 1920s, or more like the less severe 'oil shocks' of the 1970s," concluding that "Now their only certainty is that the old, state-directed, 'catch-up' capitalism is a formula that no longer works."[51] Analysts differ in their assessments of the financial crisis to date: some predicting an end to exceptional East Asian economic performance, and others forecasting the emergence of stronger, more realistic in their expectations, and more competitive East Asian economies over the longer term.[52]

In the short run, the financial crisis in East Asia will damp down the human rights debate as Asian leaders struggle to restabilize their economies and rebuild investor confidence. The abrupt collapse of Asian financial power has shattered the image of the "East Asian miracle" and the self-confidence of some proponents of "Asian values." Over the longer term, however, assuming that the economies of the region can reform and reconstruct a solid foundation for continued economic modernization, I expect that the debate will be renewed, pursuing many of the themes already described.

PROTECTING HUMAN RIGHTS

Cooperation across the immense national differences of culture, history, politics, and standard of living requires some kind of agreement on fundamentals. For example, Charles Taylor has called for an unforced, overlapping consensus on global norms for human behavior "in which convergent norms would be justified in very different underlying spiritual and philosophical outlooks." Thus, he argues, common ground might be achieved on norms for behavior, assuming meanwhile that different groups will justify those same norms in terms of quite different religious and philosophical traditions.[53] Other writers, East and West, have made similar proposals. Václav Havel speaks of "one civilization, many cultures" and calls for "a renaissance of spirituality"[54] in a way that parallels Chandra Muzaffar's arguments in Chapter 1 of this volume about the limits of secular concepts of human rights and his own call for a multifaith dialogue on life and living as a possible road from Western human rights to universal human dignity.

The world's peoples are bound more and more closely together each day by forces, especially the market and technological change, that no one of us can control – as the East Asian financial crisis has dramatically illustrated. To my mind, it is as important to protect people from starvation, disease, and illiteracy as it is to protect them from torture, being "disappeared," or jailed without due process. The principles of the two main human rights covenants are equally important and, as the 1993 Vienna Conference concluded, *indivisible*. Both are vital to establishing the minimum conditions for achieving human rights.

A major problem for authoritarian regimes which make the claim that civil and political rights must wait while they give first priority to economic, social, and cultural rights is that rulers who are not politically accountable can undertake economic and social policies, even with the best of intentions, that result in tragic losses for the citizenry. China provides the most horrific example. As a direct result of the Maoist Great Leap Forward, 1958–61, over 30 million people died in the ensuing man-made famine. Moreover, even when the tragic results became known, Mao continued with the Leap and purged leaders who had the courage to inform him of the devastation.[55] Amartya Sen's research on famines shows that when rulers are politically accountable, famines can be avoided (even in a country like India with a long history of famines), but without political accountability, things can go terribly wrong.[56]

In this shrinking world, institutions like the United Nations encourage us to take responsibility for each other in order to achieve a basis for global cooperation; but we need mutually acceptable ground rules for doing that.[57] The global human rights regime, negotiated and implemented under United Nations auspices, provides both a set of principles and a forum for attempting this. But it is by no means perfect. At its best, the regime might be seen as a set of continually changing, negotiated understandings about that which is most essential to protecting and to enhancing our common humanity.

The Universal Declaration on Human Rights, the two main covenants, and the twenty-odd other human rights treaties, to my mind, represent an exercise of the sort that Charles Taylor recommends: coming to a negotiated agreement on norms from very different ethical and cultural perspectives. Both the UN human rights standards and the ways in which they are enforced are, and should be, subject to continuous scrutiny and review by the world community. The standards are not perfect: they are simply the best that have been identified and agreed upon so far. Nothing more. If Prime Minister Mahathir or anyone else can suggest preferable standards, so much the better.

Implementation of those standards is even more problematic. The United Nations has been notoriously poor in putting into practice the human rights principles that it has proclaimed. Moreover, when UN institutions, like the Commission on Human Rights, do attempt to take action, affected member-states often work to sabotage any real progress.[58] The UN human rights regime at its best is only marginally functional, as the failure of the world community with respect to Bosnia and Rwanda attests.

Yet the UN regime is an important beginning and a useful model for building cooperation. Deliberations about human rights standards in effect ask: what do we share that is most fundamental to our common humanity? This is the right question. And debating about it, competing to see who can come up with better answers, is a constructive exercise.

Moreover, if the international human rights regime comes to mean a joint exercise in helping to construct those institutions in all countries that provide the best protection for human rights, then the world will have taken a major step toward establishing the necessary conditions for pursuing the diversity of human agendas with a much better chance for international cooperation and a considerably lower probability of doing each other serious harm. Protecting human rights in that sense might be both a means to achieving closer cooperation among nations as well as an end in itself.

Part 1 of the book opens with four provocative essays that define many of the general parameters of the human rights debate. The essays in Part 2 then address one of the most contentious subjects, human rights in China, from different perspectives. Next, in contrast, Part 3 demonstrates a growing consensus on at least one important dimension of the debate, women's rights. And, finally, in Part 4, three scholars examine the role of human rights in the international relations of Japan, China, and the United States.

NOTES

1 Anne Gunn, "'Tell the World About Us': The Student Movement in Shenyang," in Jonathan Unger, ed., *The Pro-Democracy Protests in China: Reports from the Provinces* (Armonk, NY: M.E. Sharpe, 1991).

2 Iris Chang, *The Rape of Nanking: The Forgotten Holocaust of World War II* (New York: Basic Books, 1997); Ian Buruma, *The Wages of Guilt: Memories of War in Germany and Japan* (New York: Farrar, Straus, & Giroux, 1994); and "Textbook Nationalism, Citizenship, and War: Comparative Perspectives," a special issue of the *Bulletin of Concerned Asian Scholars,* edited by Laura Hein and Mark Selden, 30, no. 2 (April–June 1998).

3 See, for example, *Towards a New Asia: A Report of the Commission for a New Asia* (1994) (no publisher or place given), convened by Noordin Sopiee, Director General, Institute of Strategic and International Studies (ISIS), Malaysia.

4 Dianne Otto, "Nongovernmental Organizations in the United Nations System: The Emerging Role of International Civil Society," *Human Rights Quarterly* 18, no. 1 (February 1996), pp. 107–41. For a critique of Western NGO monitoring of global human rights and specific proposals for improvement, see Onuma Yasuaki, "The Need for an Intercivilizational Approach to Evaluating Human Rights," *Human Rights Dialogue* (published by the Carnegie Council on Ethics and International Affairs) 10 (September 1997), pp. 4–6.

5 Kishore Mahbubani, "The West and the Rest," *The National Interest* no. 28 (Summer 1992), pp. 3–13.

6 Francis Fukuyama, "End of History?" *The National Interest* no. 16 (Summer 1989), pp. 3–18. See also his *End of History and the Last Man* (New York: Free Press, 1992).

7 Robert Kaplan, *The Ends of the Earth* (New York: Random House, 1996).

8 Samuel P. Huntington *et al.*, *The Clash of Civilization? The Debate* (New York: Council on Foreign Relations, 1993).

9 For the Clinton administration's interpretation of how promoting democracy worldwide serves the US national interest, see Deputy Secretary of State Strobe Talbott's "Democracy and the National Interest," *Foreign Affairs* 75, no. 6 (November/December 1996), pp. 47–63; and The White House, "A National Security Strategy of Engagement and Enlargement," February 1996, in Michael E. Brown *et al.* (eds), *America's Strategic Choices* (Cambridge, MA: MIT Press, 1997), pp. 283–332.

10 *The Economist* (September 7, 1996), pp. 41–2.

11 Quoted in *Canberra Times* (November 18, 1996), p. 8.

12 Francis Fukuyama, "Confucianism and Democracy," *Journal of Democracy* 6, no. 2 (April 1995), pp. 30–3.

13 Quotation from the findings of Representative Joseph P. Kennedy II (Democrat of Massachusetts) in his investigation of the US Army School of the Americas in Panama, where thousands of Latin American military officers have been trained since the 1960s. Lisa Haugaard, "Torture 101," *In These Times* (October 14, 1996), pp. 14–16.

14 The US Department of State response to Human Rights Watch censure for human rights failures in 1995, quoted in *Daily Yomiuri* (December 9, 1995), p. 5.

15 For comparisons of the United States with the other industrialized countries of the world, see the annual *Human Development Report,* published by the United Nations Development Program, particularly their tables on "Profile of Human Distress," "Weakening Social Fabric," and "Violence and Crime." For example, the United States has the highest incarceration rate in the world, seven times higher than the European average. "Violent and Irrational – and That's Just the Policy," *The Economist* (June 8, 1996), pp. 21–3. Drug use by American teenagers increased

78 percent between 1992 and 1995, according to a report by the US Department of Health and Human Services (*Canberra Times*, August 22, 1996, p. 9). And, although the rate of violent crime in the US in 1995 dropped 4 percent on the previous year, the conditions in America's crowded prisons are often horrific: one California judge spoke of "grossly excessive force" and "a rampant pattern of improper or inadequate health care that nearly defies belief" in his report on a relatively new maximum security prison in Pelican Bay, California (*Guardian Weekly*, February 5, 1995, p. 4). More recently, US crime rates have begun to drop markedly (the FBI reported rates for murder and robbery for the country as a whole down by 9 percent (National Public Radio news, November 23, 1997), but income inequality continues to grow (Blaine Harden, "New York's Richest Get Richer, Poorest Poorer," *Washington Post*, December 19, 1997, p. A3).

16 SBS TV World News, Canberra, November 20, 1996.

17 *The Guardian*, reprinted in *Canberra Times* (November 22, 1996), p. 7.

18 *Towards a New Asia*, pp. 35–6.

19 For texts of these documents and a brief history of their adoption, see Department of Public Information, United Nations, *The United Nations and Human Rights, 1945–1995* (New York: United Nations Blue Books Series VII, 1995).

20 For the record of ratifications, see ibid., Document 99, pp. 503–9.

21 Information Office of the State Council of the People's Republic of China, "A Report Which Distorts Facts and Confuses Right and Wrong," *Beijing Review* (March 13–19, 1995), pp. 17–22; "US Human Rights Accusations Refuted," *Beijing Review* (April 15–21, 1996), pp. 7–8; and Ren Yanshi, "A Look at the US Human Rights Record," *Beijing Review* (March 17–23, 1997), pp. 12–19.

22 The market reforms begun in China in 1978 have very substantially improved both the average material standard of living of the Chinese people and their freedom of choice. Carl Riskin notes that, during the period 1978–95, per capita GDP increased by an average of 6.8 percent per year, and that "China is unquestionably a much freer place today than it was two decades ago. There is immeasurably more space for people to pursue their lives, livelihoods and interests unimpeded by ubiquitous state interference" (Carl Riskin, "Behind the Silk Curtain: We Need Summitry Beyond Sanctimony," *The Nation*, November 10, 1997, pp. 11–17).

23 Quoted in the *New York Times* (November 2, 1997), p. 10.

24 As an introduction to the vast literature on sanctions and whether or not they work, see: Edward D. Mansfield, "International Institutions and Economic Sanctions," *World Politics* 47 (July 1995), pp. 575–605; Hans Kochler, *The United Nations Sanctions Policy and International Law* (Penang: Just World Trust, 1995); David A. Baldwin, *Economic Statecraft* (Princeton: Princeton University Press, 1985); and Gary Clyde Hufbauer *et al.*, *Economic Sanctions Reconsidered: History and Current Policy*, second edition (Washington, DC: Institute for International Economics, 1990). For critiques, see Robert A. Pape, "Why Economic Sanctions Do Not Work," *International Security* 22, no. 2 (Fall 1997), pp. 90–136; Richard N. Haass, "Sanctioning Madness," *Foreign Affairs* 76, no. 6 (November/December 1997), pp. 74–85; and George A. Lopez and David Cortright, "Economic Sanctions and Human Rights: Part of the Problem or Part of the Solution?" *International Journal of Human Rights* 1, no. 2 (Summer 1997), pp. 1–25.

25 Cui Tiankai at a PRC Foreign Ministry press briefing in *Beijing Review* (November 25–December 1, 1996), p. 9.

26 Samuel P. Huntington, "The West: Unique, Not Universal," *Foreign Affairs* 75, no. 6 (November/December 1996), pp. 28–46.

27 An observation by Jacinta O'Hagan. Personal conversation in Canberra, November 18, 1996.

28 It may be useful to contrast the position being put forward here with the more orthodox, natural rights argument. See, for example, Jack Donnelly, "Human Rights and Asian Values," a paper presented to a workshop on "The Growth of East Asia and Its Impact on Human Rights," sponsored by the Carnegie Council on Ethics and International Affairs, in Hakone, Japan, in June 1995.

29 Amartya Sen, *Human Rights and Asian Values: Sixteenth Morgenthau Memorial Lecture* (New York: Carnegie Council on Ethics and International Affairs, 1997).

30 Onuma Yasuaki, *In Quest of Intercivilizational Human Rights: "Universal" vs. "Relative" Human Rights Viewed from an Asian Perspective* (San Francisco: The Asia Foundation's Center for Asian Pacific Affairs Occasional Paper no. 2, March 1996), especially pp. 1 and 9.

31 Aung San Suu Kyi, "Freedom, Development, and Human Worth," *Journal of Democracy* 6, no. 2 (April 1995), pp. 15 and 18.

32 Frank Ching, "Is UN Declaration Universal?" *Far Eastern Economic Review* (August 28, 1997), p. 32; and Hishammuddin Hussein, "Calm Approach to Rights," *Far Eastern Economic Review* (October 9, 1997), p. 39.

33 Onuma, *In Quest*, p. 9.

34 For an analysis of how human rights issues might be handled in the bilateral Sino-American relationship, see Peter Van Ness, "Addressing the Issue of Human Rights in Sino-American Relations," *Journal of International Affairs* 49, no. 2 (Winter 1996), pp. 309–31.

35 Peter Van Ness, "The Impasse in US Policy toward China," *China Journal* no. 38 (July 1997), pp. 139–50.

36 Ann Kent, "China and the International Human Rights Regime: A Case Study of Multilateral Monitoring, 1989–1994," *Human Rights Quarterly* 17, no. 1 (February 1995), pp. 1–47; and Beatrice Laroche, "Dodging Scrutiny: China and the UN Commission on Human Rights," *China Rights Forum* (Summer 1997), pp. 28–33.

37 For one prominent example, see Jesse Helms, "Saving the U.N.: A Challenge to the Next Secretary-General," *Foreign Affairs* 75, no. 5 (September/October 1996), pp. 2–7.

38 "Clinton and Jiang Debate Views Live on Chinese TV," *New York Times* (June 28, 1998), pp. 1 and 6–8.

39 See, for example, Fareed Zakaria, "The Rise of Illiberal Democracy," *Foreign Affairs* 76, no. 6 (November/December 1997), pp. 22–43.

40 Seth Mydans, "Its Mood Dark as the Haze, Southeast Asia Aches," *New York Times* (October 26, 1997), p. 3. For an effort to begin to include calculations of the value of the services of ecological systems and natural capital stocks in economic analysis, see Robert Costanza *et al.*, "The Value of the World's Ecosystem Services and Natural Capital," *Nature* 387 (May 15, 1997), pp. 253–60.

41 For an example, see the editorial on the theme "we have seen the future and it looks a lot like Nike," in *Far Eastern Economic Review* (September 5, 1996), p. 5.

42 Richard Falk, "The Making of Global Citizenship," in Jeremy Brecher *et al.*, eds, *Global Visions: Beyond the New World Order* (Boston: South End Press, 1993).

43 James L. Richardson, *Contending Liberalisms: Past and Present* (Canberra: Department of International Relations, Australian National University, Working Paper no. 1995/10).

44 Fukuyama, "End of History?"

45 Aung San Suu Kyi, "Freedom, Development, and Human Worth," p. 13.

46 This argument, which is only very briefly summarized here, has its roots in the cosmopolitanism tradition of international relations theory. See, for example, Paul Keal, "Can Foreign Policy Be Ethical?" in Paul Keal ed., *Ethics and Foreign Policy*, (St Leonards, NSW: Allen and Unwin, 1992).

47 An International Labour Office (ILO) report describes deteriorating employment conditions throughout the world. ILO estimates that nearly one billion people, some 30 percent of the global workforce, are either unemployed or underemployed (reported in *Canberra Times*, November 27, 1996, p. 8). Global market forces produce mixed results: higher standards of living for some; and catastrophe for others.

48 Michael Richardson, "ASEAN Aims to Test Balances of Power," *International Herald Tribune* (August 2–3, 1997), p. 4.

49 Keith B. Richburg, "SE Asians Call for Help as Currencies Plunge," *Washington Post* (December 16, 1997), pp. A1 and A4.

50 In contrast, China's stock markets were up 30.7 percent on the year (*The Economist*, January 3, 1998, p. 98).

51 Robert A. Manning, "Asia Crisis: Now for the Hard Part," *Los Angeles Times* (Washington edition) (January 7, 1998), pp. A2 and A3. See, also, George Soros, "Avoiding a Breakdown," *Financial Times* (December 31, 1997); and Robert B. Zoellick, "A Larger Plan for Asia," *Washington Post* (January 6, 1998), p. A13.

52 For two differing views put forward by prominent American economists, see: Paul Krugman, "The Myth of Asia's Miracle," *Foreign Affairs* 73, no. 6 (November/ December 1994), pp. 62–78; and Steven Radelet and Jeffrey Sachs, "Asia's Reemergence," *Foreign Affairs* 76, no. 6 (November/December 1997), pp. 44–59.

53 Charles Taylor, "Conditions for an Unforced Consensus on Human Rights," paper presented to the project on "The Growth of East Asia and Its Impact on Human Rights" at the Carnegie Council on Ethics and International Affairs.

54 Václav Havel, "Transcending the Clash of Cultures: Democracy's Forgotten Dimension," *Journal of Democracy* 6, no. 2 (April 1995), p. 10.

55 Basil Ashton *et al.*, "Famine in China, 1958–61," *Population and Development Review* 10, no. 4 (December 1984), pp. 613–45; and Jasper Becker, *Hungry Ghosts: Mao's Secret Famine* (New York: Free Press, 1996).

56 For his discussion of positive and negative freedom in this context, see Amartya Sen, "Individual Freedom as a Social Commitment," *New York Review of Books* (June 14, 1990), pp. 49–54. Recent biographical studies of leaders in China and the United States have, to my mind, made important scholarly contributions with respect to establishing political accountability: for example, Seymour Hersh on John F. Kennedy and Li Zhisui on Mao Zedong. Both books have been dismissed by some reviewers as nothing more than salacious gossip from the bedrooms of the famous, but the authors had more serious objectives, most importantly to recount for the record abuses of power by leaders whose decisions shaped the fate of millions. Seymour M. Hersh, *The Dark Side of Camelot* (Boston: Little, Brown & Company, 1997); and Li Zhisui, *The Private Life of Chairman Mao: The Memoirs of Mao's Personal Physician* (New York: Random House, 1994).

57 Richard Falk speaks of an "overriding challenge to create a political community that doesn't yet exist, premised upon global or species solidarity, co-evolution and co-responsibility, a matter of perceiving a common destiny, yet simultaneously celebrating diverse and plural entrypoints expressive of specific history, tradition, values, dreams". Falk, "The Making of Global Citizenship," p. 49.

58 For example, Amnesty International has cited China as one member-state which used procedural tactics for four years in the Commission on Human Rights to block a vote on a resolution which was critical of the PRC's human rights performance (*Amnesty International Report 1996*, pp. 61 and 118).

Part I

ISSUES IN DISPUTE

1

FROM HUMAN RIGHTS TO HUMAN DIGNITY

Chandra Muzaffar

Chandra Muzaffar *sets the stage for this debate, placing it firmly within the historical context of Western imperialism and focusing on how power relates to a debate about values. He concludes that a concept of human rights is insufficient, and that what is needed is a larger spiritual and moral worldview constructed from universals drawn from the world's great religions. Chandra Muzaffar, a founder of ALIRAN, Malaysia's most active NGO, was jailed under the International Security Act by Prime Minister Mahathir Mohamad in 1987 for his political activism, and subsequently identified as a "prisoner of conscience" by Amnesty International. Later, after his release, Muzaffar organized a conference on "Rethinking Human Rights" and invited Mahathir to give the keynote address. This essay is a somewhat revised version of Chandra's own opening address to that 1994 conference.*

It is important, at the very outset, to explain what has come to be accepted as the conventional meaning of human rights. Though the human rights contained in the multitude of UN human rights declarations, covenants, and conventions cover a whole range of rights, including an economic right such as the right to food, and a collective right such as the people's right to self-determination, the term "human rights" as used by most human rights activists today carries a more restricted meaning. Human rights are often equated with individual rights – specifically individual civil and political rights. This equation has a genealogy, a history behind it.

The equation of human rights with individual civil and political rights is a product of the European Enlightenment and the secularization of thought and society of the last 150 years. Whatever the weaknesses of this conception of human rights, there is no doubt at all that it has contributed significantly to human civilization.

First, it has helped to empower the individual. By endowing the individual with rights, such as the right of expression, the right of association, the right of assembly, the right to vote, the right to a fair trial, and so on, it has strengthened the position of the individual as never before in history. These are rights

25

that inhere in the individual as a human being. They are his/her rights: he/she does not owe these rights to a benevolent government or a magnanimous monarch.

Second, by empowering the individual, this particular human rights tradition has contributed towards the transformation of what were once authoritarian political systems into democratic political structures. For the empowerment of the individual – as demonstrated by the history of European democracies – helped to create the political space which resulted in the entrenchment of civil society. It was the growth of civil society in the West which strengthened the sinews of democratic political culture.

Third, the empowerment of the individual and the evolution of civil society played a big part in checking the arbitrary exercise of power of those in authority. In Europe, as in other parts of the world, right through human history, the arbitrariness of the wielders of power and authority has been one of the greatest banes upon the well-being of both individual and community. Human rights ideas born out of the Enlightenment and the secularization of society – more than perhaps any other set of ideas from any other epoch – challenged this blight upon humanity.

Fourth, by curbing their arbitrariness, by regulating their activities, the wielders of power in Europe were compelled to become more accountable to the people. Public accountability developed into a norm of democratic governance. The empowerment and the enhancement of the individual have, in other words, brought governments within the control of the governed through institutions established to ensure public accountability.

But what is sad is that while Europe built the edifice of the individual within its own borders, it destroyed the human person on other shores. As human rights expanded among white people, European empires inflicted horrendous human wrongs upon the coloured inhabitants of the planet. The elimination of the native populations of the Americas and Australasia and the enslavement of millions of Africans during the European slave trade were two of the greatest human rights tragedies of the colonial epoch. Of course, the suppression of millions of Asians in almost every part of the continent during the long centuries of colonial domination was also another colossal human rights calamity. Western colonialism in Asia, Australasia, Africa, and Latin America represents the most massive, systematic violation of human rights ever known in history.

Though formal colonial rule has ended, Western domination and control continues to impact upon the human rights of the vast majority of the people of the non-Western world in ways which are more subtle and sophisticated but no less destructive and devastating. The dominant West, for instance, controls global politics through the United Nations Security Council (UNSC). If certain Western powers so desire, they can get the UNSC to impose sanctions, however unjust they may be, upon any state which, in their view, needs to be coerced to submit to their will. This ability to force others to submit to their will is backed by the West's – particularly the United States'

– global military dominance. It is a dominance which bestows upon the West effective control over high-grade weapons technology and most weapons of mass destruction. The dominant West also controls global economics through the IMF, the World Bank, the World Trade Organization (WTO), and the G7. The self-serving economic policies of powerful states have cost the poor in the non-Western world billions of dollars in terms of revenue – money which, translated into basic needs, could have saved some 15 million lives in the non-Western world every year. The dominant West controls global news and information through Reuters, AP, UPI, AFP, and most of all CNN. Likewise, Western music, Western films, Western fashions, and Western foods are creating a global culture which is not only Western in character and content but also incapable of accommodating non-Western cultures on a just and equitable basis. Underlying this Western-dominated global culture and information system is an array of ideas, values, and even worldviews pertaining to the position of the individual, inter-gender relations, inter-generational ties, the family, the community, the environment, and the cosmos which have evolved from a particular tradition – namely the Western secular tradition. These ideas, values, and worldviews are marginalizing other ideas about the human being, about human relations and about societal ties embodied in older and richer civilizations. It is a process of marginalization which could, in the long run, result in the moral degradation and spiritual impoverishment of the human being.

Though the consequences of domination are enormous for the dominated, the major centres of power in the West – the US, Britain, and France, the Western military establishment, Western multinational corporations (MNCs), the mainstream Western media, a segment of Western academia, some Western NGOs – are determined to perpetuate their global power. They are determined to do this even if it leads to the violation of the very principles of democracy and human rights which they espouse. This is why a super-power like the US has, since 1945, in spite of its professed commitment to human rights and democracy, aided and abetted many more dictatorships than democracies in the non-Western world.

Even today, after the end of the Cold War, the US and its allies continue to suppress genuine human rights and pro-democracy movements in various parts of the world. The US's continued support for Israel against the Palestinian struggle for nationhood is one such example. The US and its Western allies, notably France, have also failed to support the Algerian movement for human rights and social justice expressed through Islam. There are similar move-ments for freedom and justice in Egypt and Saudi Arabia which Western governments see as a threat to their interests in the region. Long-standing movements for self-determination in East Timor, Tibet, and Kashmir also have little support from major Western governments. Perhaps, more than anything else, it is the West's lack of commitment to the human rights of the people of Bosnia and Herzegovina in the initial phases which reveals that in the ultimate analysis it is not human rights which count but the preservation of self-interest and the perpetuation of dominant power.

It is because many people in the non-Western world now know that dominance and control is the real motive and goal of the West that they have become skeptical and critical of the West's posturing on human rights. This skepticism has increased as a result of the deterioration and degeneration in human rights standards within Western society itself, which is occurring in at least five areas:

1   White racism in Europe and North America is making a mockery of the Western claim that it is a champion of human rights. The rights and dignity of non-White minorities are challenged almost every day in the West by the arrogance of racist sentiments among segments of the white population.
2   The economic malaise in the West is eroding fundamental economic rights such as the right to work. Can the West protect the economic rights of its people in the midst of rising unemployment and continuing economic stagnation?
3   As violence, and the fear it generates, increases in Western societies, one wonders whether Western societies are capable any longer of protecting the basic right of the people to live without fear. After all, isn't freedom from fear a fundamental human right?
4   Since the right to found a family is a fundamental human right in the Universal Declaration of Human Rights, isn't the disintegration of the family as the basic unit of society in many Western countries today a negation of a fundamental human right?
5   Confronted by the reality of family disintegration, violence, economic stagnation, and racism, one senses that the Western political system – emphasis upon human rights and democracy notwithstanding – no longer possesses the will and the wherewithal to bring about fundamental changes to society. What is the meaning of individual rights and liberties if they are utterly incapable of affecting meaningful transformations in values, attitudes, and structures which are imperative if the West is to lift itself out of its spiritual and psychological morass?

The dominant West's violations of human rights in the non-Western world, coupled with its inability to uphold some of the fundamental rights of its own citizens, has raised some important questions about the very nature and character of Western human rights:

1   Has the creative individuality of an earlier phase in Western history given way to gross, vulgar individualism which today threatens the very fabric of Western society? Isn't individualism of this sort a negation of the community?

2   Has the glorification and adulation of individual freedom as an end in itself reached a point where individual freedom has become the be-all and end-all of human existence? Isn't freedom in the ultimate analysis a means towards a greater good rather than an end in itself?

3   Isn't this notion of freedom in the West linked to an idea of rights which is often divorced from responsibilities? Can rights be separated from responsibilities in real life?

4   Isn't the dominant Western concept of rights itself particularistic and sectional since it emphasizes only civil and political rights and downplays economic, social, and cultural rights?

5   How can a concept of rights confined to the nation-state respond to the challenges posed by an increasingly global economic, political, and cultural system? Isn't it true that the dominant Western approach to human rights fails to recognize the role of global actors – like the UNSC, IMF and MNCs – in the violation of human rights?

6   Whether one articulates rights or upholds responsibilities, shouldn't they be guided by universal moral and spiritual values which would determine the sort of rights we pursue and the type of responsibilities we fulfill? Without a larger spiritual and moral framework, which endows human endeavor with meaning and purpose, with coherence and unity, wouldn't the emphasis on rights *per se* lead to moral chaos and confusion?

7   What are human rights if they are not related to more fundamental questions about the human being. Who is the human being? Why is the human being here? Where does the human being go from here? How can one talk of the rights of the human being without a more profound understanding of the human being him- or herself?

It is because of these and other flaws in the very character of the Western approach to human rights that there is an urgent need to try to evolve a vision of human dignity which is more just, more holistic, and more universal. In Islam, Hinduism, Sikhism, Taoism, Christianity, Judaism and even in the theistic strains within Confucianism and Buddhism there are elements of such a vision of the human being, of human rights and of human dignity. The idea that the human being is vice-regent or trustee of God whose primary role is to fulfill God's trust is lucidly articulated in various religions. As God's trustee, the human being lives life according to clearly established spiritual and moral values and principles. The rights one possesses, like the responsibilities one undertakes, must be guided by these values and principles. What this means is that human rights and human freedoms are part of a larger spiritual and moral worldview. This also means that individual freedom is not the be-all and end-all of human existence. Neither is the individual the ultimate arbiter of right and wrong, of good and evil. The individual and community must both submit to spiritual and moral values which transcend both individual and community. It is the supremacy of these values and, in the end, of the Divine which distinguishes our God-guided concept of human dignity from the present individual-centred notion of human rights.

The great challenge before us is to develop this vision of human dignity culled from our religious and spiritual philosophies into a comprehensive charter of values and principles, responsibilities and rights, roles and relationships acceptable to human beings everywhere. To do this we should first distinguish what is universal and eternal within our respective traditions from what is particularistic and contextual. On that basis we should conduct a dialogue with people of all religions on the question of human dignity. Even those of secular persuasion should be invited to dialogue with people of faith. Indeed, as we have indicated, there is a great deal in the secular human rights tradition that we should absorb and imbibe in the process of developing our vision of human dignity.

To develop our vision into a vision which has relevance to the realities which human beings have to grapple with, our dialogue should focus upon concrete contemporary issues that challenge human dignity everywhere – issues of global domination and global control of poverty and disease, of political oppression and cultural chauvinism, of moneyism and materialism, of corruption and greed, of the disintegration of the community and the alienation of the individual. It would, in other words, be a dialogue on life and living. This is perhaps the best time to initiate such a dialogue since Asian societies are now beginning to ask some searching questions about the nexus between moral values and human rights.

Of course, not all sections of Asian societies are asking the same questions about the link between morality and rights. Some Asian governments, for instance, have chosen to focus solely upon the adverse consequences of crass individualism upon the moral fabric of Western societies. As an antidote, they emphasize the importance of strengthening existing family and community ties in Asian cultures. For us who seek inspiration and guidance from our spiritual and moral philosophies in a non-selective manner, it is not just family and community that are important. We know that the individual expressing himself or herself through the community also has a crucial place in most of our philosophies. After all, in all religions, the Divine message is, in the ultimate analysis, addressed to the individual. For it is the individual, and the individual alone, who is capable of moral and spiritual transformation. Similarly, it is not just the moral crisis of Western society that we lament; we are no less sensitive to the moral decadence within our own societies – especially within our elite strata. If we adhere to a universal spiritual and moral ethic that applies to all human beings, we should not hesitate to condemn the suppression of human rights and the oppression of dissident groups that occur from time to time in a number of our countries. Our commitment to spiritual and moral values, drawn from our religions, should never serve as a camouflage for authoritarian elites who seek to shield their sins from scrutiny. Indeed, any attempt to do so would be tantamount to a travesty of the eternal truth embodied in all our religions. And what is that truth? That religion's primary concern is the dignity of all human beings.

This, then, is the road that we must travel; the journey we must undertake. From Western human rights, which has been so selective and sectarian, to a genuinely universal human dignity – which remains the human being's yet unfulfilled promise to God.

2

THE HUMAN RIGHTS
DEBATE IN AN ERA OF
GLOBALIZATION
Hegemony of Discourse

Nikhil Aziz

Nikhil Aziz, *born and raised in Bombay, India, is in the final stages of writing his PhD dissertation at the University of Denver on globalization and social movements, based on more than a year's participatory action-research with the National Alliance of People's Movements in India. Beginning with Richard Falk's distinction between globalization-from-above and globalization-from-below, Aziz attacks the Western hegemonic universalism associated with the first, arguing for a truly global universalism encompassing the various world traditions which he sees to be emerging from the second. Turning an argument often made by Western human rights advocates on its head, he criticizes the cultural relativism of Western notions of universalism and the fundamentalist way in which its secularism is propagated.*

INTRODUCTION

We have for over a century been dragged by the prosperous West behind its chariot, choked by the dust, deafened by the noise, humbled by our own helplessness, and overwhelmed by the speed. We agreed to acknowledge that this chariot-drive was progress, and that progress was civilization. If we ever ventured to ask, "progress towards what, and progress for whom," it was considered to be peculiarly and ridiculously oriental to entertain such ideas about the absoluteness of progress. Of late, a voice has come to us bidding us to take count not only of the scientific perfection of the chariot but of the depth of ditches lying across its path.

Rabindranath Tagore[1]

The hegemony of discourse is not a red herring by any means. Certainly not for many non-Western[2] (and non-White) scholars and activists. Whether in neo-colonial settings or Western academe,[3] they have to struggle daily with this aspect of domination in their scholarly and activist lives.[4] This hegemonic discourse is acutely played out in the universal versus relativist debates and the secular versus religious/"fundamentalist" arguments. Although these charges and defenses have long been part of the general social science discourse, they have assumed renewed urgency in recent times with world globalization, in which the human rights debate has assumed a central position.

It is important to note at the outset that this occurs within the context of a larger debate raging in the Third World on the realities of external (Western) versus internal (local ruling elite) domination. I will illustrate this debate using the case of India. The historic question asked in India of "Gandhi or Ambedkar?" is once again being asked. This alludes to the notion held by some that while Gandhi concentrated on liberation from external domination, Dr Bhimrao Ambedkar was concerned with internal domination of the oppressed castes by the dominant castes. The question that therefore arises is which revolutionary struggle the Indian masses should engage in. While dichotomizing this in such simplistic terms would be doing both those great and complex thinkers a disservice, the larger question of which is more important – external or internal oppression – still remains unanswered. The answer is not an either/or solution but is epitomized in Gandhi, Ambedkar, and a host of others. Hegemony and domination have to be addressed simultaneously on all planes or else liberation will be illusory. In addressing the question of hegemony in the human rights discourse, this essay makes the case that many of the Third World scholars/activists/movements seeking to provide an alternative discourse are addressing these issues.[5]

GLOBALIZATION

Nicaraguan scholar Xabier Gorostiaga argues that in this era of globalization humanity is being perceived as fundamentally one, with a common destiny that is the result of a technological revolution in information and communication and the awareness of the unsustainability of the current way of life.[6] But there is more to globalization than this apparent benignity. Further, it must be emphasized that globalization is not a simple but a very complex set of processes that operate at multiple levels – political, economic, and cultural. It is useful, in this context, to analyze it from the basis of Richard Falk's argument that there are two kinds of globalization: "globalization-from-above" (hereafter GA) and "globalization-from-below" (hereafter GB).[7]

I argue that these two kinds of globalization are in a dialectical relationship and that from a left democratic progressive perspective the latter is not only preferable but desirable. The dialectical relationship between GA and GB is demonstrated in the interaction between the different manifestations of globalization – political, economic, and cultural. Although GA and GB are fundamentally opposed, at one level GA creates the space (and the issues) for GB; and ultimately, GB works against GA. For instance, political GA creates the space for political GB through allowing grassroots social movements some political space for operation as a result of "democratization." These movements whose collective actions – the formation of transnational linkages and, especially, the articulation of alternative political visions – are essentially political GB, work against political GA and provide its antithesis. Further, as elaborated below, I concur with Falk that GA is essentially homogenizing[8] and hegemonic in its tendencies whereas GB is inherently pluralistic.

Globalization-from-above

Political GA is reflected in Western countries (particularly the United States) and global financial institutions pressuring countries in the South and the former Eastern Bloc to democratize.[9] This translates as the adoption of a Western-style liberal-democratic system of governance, multi-party elections at regular intervals, respect for individualistic civil and political rights, and so on. As well, it involves doing everything in their (Western) power to crush the resistance of "pariah" nations that dare to be different, like Vietnam, Tanzania, Nicaragua, Cuba, and Iran. On the surface, democratization itself would appear not to be a problematic issue. However, the problem lies in that most of this kind of democratization is aimed at formal democracy – or polyarchy as the critical international relations theorists call it – rather than any genuinely mass participatory democracy.

Economic GA is closely tied to the political aspect in that (1) the source of pressure for change is the same, and (2) close links are alleged between the ideologies of free markets and free societies. Economic GA entails countries of the South and the former Eastern bloc having to accept – within the parameters of the dominant world capitalist system – the imposition of the following: structural adjustment programs by the G7-dominated global financial institutions; overwhelming debt burdens; neo-liberal economic policies, including the wholesale liberalization of domestic economies to allow unrestricted entry to transnational capital; and Western diktats via multilateral trade arrangements such as the General Agreement on Tariffs and Trade (GATT), the World Trade Organization (WTO), and the North American Free Trade Agreement (NAFTA).[10] The overall effects of these policies tend toward a further polarization of incomes and living standards within and between countries,[11] and the rigidification of the international division of labor to the detriment of the Third World.

On a cultural level, GA arises from the control of the global information and communication networks by Western media corporations;[12] and the spread, mainly through this control over the means of increasingly modern technologies, of a consumerist culture, and Western cultural expressions, as *the* global culture. Thus GA poses the most serious threat to global cultural diversity and plurality since the genocide in the Americas following Columbus' disorientation (pun intended).

"The Columbus within" the Third World[13]

Viewing this process of GA as self-propelled (some would say "market-driven") or inevitable can only be explained by either hopeless naïveté or vested interests on the part of those who would propound such an opinion. As noted earlier, the proponents of political, economic, and cultural GA are inextricably linked,[14] and the ruling elite in the Third World are partners in this venture to perpetuate elite domination. Nevertheless, in both cases there is a lack of total unanimity within the ranks; and this arises from/leads to various contradictions which can be exploited by progressive forces such as the democratic social movements discussed below. There are those elements within the Third World ruling elite whose vested interests are best served by such things as the imposition of a highly centralized, Western-style, polyarchic system which falls far short of any meaningful participation by the masses;[15] neo-liberal economic reforms which give them (the elites) room to expand both domestically and internationally; and a continuing cultural enslavement and unrootedness that (1) fosters a neo-colonial mentality with notions of elites = experts = enlightened, and (2) promotes an unrooted, vague definition of "national" culture which is alien to almost everyone.

There are also those elements – the fascistic forces – who propound extreme nativistic positions and argue for returning to some mythical "golden" age in the dim past. One could argue, of course, that such an approach does not fit into the globalization paradigm. Yet, at one level it does, for it has astonishing parallels and is not restricted to any one part of the globe. For instance, they seek to impose particularistic and narrow notions of culture as "national" culture on what are very heterogeneous populations; they support hierarchical and uniform systems of governance and social order which are essentially just as non-participatory and undemocratic; and in the economic sphere they basically support the dominant system and do not (in practice at least)[16] address fundamental questions of egalitarian internal redistribution. In India the Hindu right-wing (the term "fundamentalist" is even more problematic in the Hindu context than in the Islamic one!) concept of "Hindu" culture – which they seek to impose on all and sundry – is narrowly north-Indian-centric, elitist, casteist, misogynist, intolerant, Sanskritic, and Brahminic in its vision. Further, as Indian scholar Aijaz Ahmad and others in the Indian context have argued, there are often but degrees of difference beween the right-wing and the centrists on such issues. Ahmad labels this as "varieties of saffron" (saffron being the color of symbolic significance to Hindus), "hard" in the first instance and "soft" in the latter.[17]

Globalization-from-below

On the other hand, GB is represented in the form of a variety of transnational social movements which have wide-ranging concerns grounded in a notion of human community that is itself based on unity in diversity. Growing economic disparities between and within countries, the failure of societies of various ideological inclinations both in the North and South to redress long-standing social inequalities, and the absence of political power beyond periodic voting have given rise to these movements throughout the world. Their concerns include the environment, human rights, women's issues, sustainable development, peace and justice, universal literacy, and liberation from oppression.[18] Coming under the category of "new" social movements in sociological literature, these movements are distinguished from earlier movements in the socialist/communist mode; although in more ways than less, there are continuities not breaks with the earlier movements. While the object of their critique is much the same, their methods are different. Broadly speaking, of course, their concerns of eliminating political, economic, and social inequalities are the same. However, such movements seek non-violent as opposed to violent revolution; and generally abjure power in the sense of control of the state, seeking instead political alternatives to the state itself. Further, they do not subscribe to the vanguardist notions intrinsic to the historical movements.

Political globalization-from-below

At the political level, GB is reflected in the rise and spread of these human rights movements and, particularly, through the horizontal transnational solidarity linkages they are forming.[19] For instance, negotiations between the Zapatista Front and the Mexican government in Chiapas witnessed the presence of numerous observer groups from around the world who stood in solidarity with the representatives of Mexico's peasants and indigenous peoples. Similarly, a broad-ranging group of people from India and Pakistan have come together to form the Pakistan–India People's Forum for Peace and Democracy (PIPFPD) to initiate and promote a sustained dialogue at the nongovernmental level between the two countries. Such linkages are also being formed and strengthened at the global level by the massive participation in the alternative NGO forums at all of the recent UN world conferences. Political GB is also more than domestic pressure on authoritarian governments to convert to liberal democracy; although this is happening, it is so more as a means of creating political space than as an end in itself. As Japanese scholar Sakamoto Yoshikazu argues:

> The globalization of democracy [from below] is not a mere geographical expansion of the scope of democracy; nor is it the universalization of the Western, let alone the US, type of democracy. It refers rather

to the creation of a global perspective and values in the depths of people's hearts and minds, establishing the idea of a global civil society. It is the global dimension of a deepening of democracy to the level of civil society. . . . In a word, democracy can be deepened only if it is globalized, and it can be globalized only if it is deepened.[20]

Needless to say, this deepening of democracy along with globalization can ultimately be achieved only with the universal eradication of illiteracy. And this is possible when literacy programs are based not simply on formally teaching people to read and write but are grounded in, and encourage them to reflect on, their lived struggles.[21]

In fact, grassroots movements are spearheading the search for alternative forms of governance that are rooted in local tradition and allow for enhanced participation, democratic decentralization, and accountability.[22] Indian[23] scholar/activist Smitu Kothari argues that these movements do not simply empower dominated and oppressed communities but proactively articulate different political visions, and that this diversity of thinking and action is transforming the "traditional" notions of development, democracy, power, and governance.[24] Such societal-level transformations cannot be time-bound, or constrained by short-term success or failure. For instance, the People's Plan 21 for the Asian-Pacific region, which was initiated in Minamata, Japan, in 1989, put forward the notion of "transborder participatory democracy" entailing people's movements simultaneously "criticizing, confronting, intervening in, and changing the power formation" within a country, and "form[ing] themselves into transborder coalitions, eventually leading to the formation of a transborder 'people'."[25] Similarly, there has been some discussion of creating at the global level a forum for people, as opposed to the current United Nations system, which is essentially a club of states.[26]

Economic globalization-from-below

While it is generally the case that macroeconomic relations are not a function of social movements at the grassroots level, they are very much a focus of their critiques; and economic GB is very much an ongoing process. This is manifested through: (1) the fundamental critique of modernization and the patterns of development and progress that are encased in that paradigm;[27] (2) the active offering of transnational resistance to neo-liberal economic reforms, trade relations, structural adjustment programs, rise in prices and general cost of living, job retrenchment in the blue-collar sector, and growing income disparities, all of which have adversely and unevenly affected the underprivileged majority in these countries;[28] (3) the conscious moves led by many farmers' movements to delink from the dominant agro-capitalist system in favor of local-level sustainable modes of cultivation in rural areas; and

(4) the rapid growth of the informal economy,[29] which, although a part of the cash economy, is not accounted for in traditional economic calculations to significant proportions. This does not mean, as is often portrayed by critics, that these movements are arguing for a return to pre-modern modes of existence devoid of any material considerations. Rather, it is a philosophy based in a rejection of the excessive consumerism and consumption that is the hallmark of modernity and capitalism, and a resistance that disproves the Fukuyamaesque inevitability of current trends toward political, economic, and cultural GA. Linking the economic and ecological crises, Malaysian scholar/activist Martin Khor Kok Peng argues that economic GB entails the questioning of the dominant model of development in the South, struggling for a just world economic order, *and* structurally adjusting Northern economies.[30] Ecologically and economically sustainable development in this context does not just mean that Southern economies cannot afford to follow the Northern model, but, more importantly, that Northern economies cannot continue their current unsustainable lifestyles. The "American way of life," in the commonly used economic sense, is simply unsustainable!

Cultural globalization-from-below

Cultural GB is, perhaps, in some ways the most fundamental of all. This is reflected in the virtual explosion, in all quarters of the Third World, of tenacious resistance against the onslaught of Western culture: the struggles for cultural survival of indigenous peoples; the critique and, often, rejection of Western-based notions of modernity and secularism; and the deconstruction of "given universals" that are a function of historical colonialism and imperialism. This can take, and has taken, very ugly nationalistic forms exemplified in the growth of the fascist right-wing across cultures; but, as I argue, these have to be primarily challenged from within using rationalist, universalist, tolerant notions extant within the various non-Western traditions. Such problems are not limited to political movements on the ground either. In the realm of academic discourse too, one finds a growing body of literature (loosely grouped under the label "indigenist") which in its critique of imperialism and hegemony often ends in staking positions which are dangerously close to obscurantism and extreme nativism; and, in fact, these have been coopted by the resurgent fascist forces. Aijaz Ahmad warns against what he calls the "inverted logic" of such arguments which in critiquing the dichotomous categorizations and othering by the dominant discourse themselves fall prey to a similar binary logic.[31]

HEGEMONY OF DISCOURSE IN HUMAN RIGHTS

Human rights have been an integral part of the processes of globalization. In the case of GA, human rights have become another weapon in the arsenal of Western countries in their efforts to bring recalcitrant Third World nations to heel in *their* "'New' World Order." Western nations are increasingly using their very narrow interpretation of human rights as a yardstick with which to judge Third World governments, and in conducting political and economic relations with the latter. US–China relations and the G7-led war against Iraq for the "liberation" of Kuwait are prime examples.[32] The dominant discourse in human rights, which is an integral aspect of GA, emphasizes individual-istic political and civil rights to the exclusion of group/collectivistic economic, social, and cultural rights, and third-generation rights. Malaysian scholar/activist Chandra Muzaffar argues that Western governments, which are economically, technologically, culturally, and politically powerful, have led the way in emphasizing the incorrect notion that human rights are simply polit-ical and civil liberties.[33]

The hegemonic discourse in human rights, at the level of both Western governments and most scholars,[34] refuses to consider the validity of alterna-tive conceptions of rights from the Third World because it addresses the fundamental inequalities of the current world system in which the West has a privileged position of dominance. Moreover, such alternative understanding represents GB and challenges the logic and assumptions underlying the domi-nant GA.[35] Many Western scholars argue spuriously that the concept of rights is somehow devalued by including economic, social, and cultural rights. Human rights are dynamic, not static, or else they would not be able to claim universality. And if they are universal, as the West rightly argues, then the debate should be open to critique and the discourse open to expansion from other sources and traditions.

FOUNDATIONAL PROBLEMS

It is important to note that the hegemonic human rights discourse is girded in the concepts of universalism and secularism.[36] Human rights scholars and advocates in the West generally tend to insist upon the universalism of human rights based on the notion that rights are inherent in our common humanity,[37] and the legality of international human rights documents.[38] With regard to the first argument, it is hardly the case that the notion of the oneness of humanity is limited to the West, or is of Western origin. Various religio-philosophical traditions among non-Western societies have propounded this concept long before the European Enlightenment. Nor is it the case that notions of universalism are not found in other traditions. When governments

39

in different countries – particularly in Asia – insist upon the particularity of "Asian culture" and their sovereignty with respect to human rights, Western governments and scholars alike are quick to react in labeling them as relativist and/or "fundamentalist."[39] There ends the discussion!

It is ironic that there are human rights scholars and activists in Asia, most of whom are victims of their own governments' human rights abuses, who would also espouse – although on a more nuanced and complex level – what are labeled by Westerners as relativist and/or fundamentalist views on the human rights debate![40] It is no secret that many Asian, and other, governments revert to what are indeed relativistic defenses to cover up or justify horrific human rights violations. However, it is not insignificant when scholars and activists who have themselves been victims of human rights abuses adopt positions different from Western standards. What these scholars and activists are arguing for is a genuine universalism, which by definition (1) is inherently inclusive, in that it encompasses various traditions and worldviews, and (2) is not an approximation of the Western notion alone – an ideal that is yet to be attained.

There are at least two problems that arise with regard to the second argument posed by mainstream Western scholars. First, a large number of the declarations, covenants, conventions, and other documents are not signed or ratified by many governments, including Western ones.[41] Many of the instruments and organs of international law, such as the International Court of Justice, are ineffective as their decisions are non-binding. The UN system is representative of states not peoples, and, even within these limits, is unequal and hierarchical in terms of the five "great" powers having veto control through the Security Council. Second, and more fundamentally, most of the Third World governments can hardly speak for the people they purport to represent. This, of course, brings into question the very validity of the current world system; which is what many of the human rights movements and scholars in the South are addressing.

If we ask the question, and we must, *vis-à-vis* collective rights, as to who determines the collective, then we must also raise the issue, when we talk about internationally accepted human rights, of who is doing the accepting and how. This in no way dilutes the significance of these conventions, or what they have achieved so far. They provide, and will continue to, the foundations and inspirations for many GB struggles. The point is, however, that ratification by illegitimate governments and ruling elites, or ratification without implementation, is hardly the way to go in terms of conferring legitimacy on these documents. What is essential is that these norms have to be accepted by peoples everywhere through discussion and reflection, and active engagement.[42] This can only be sustained in a democratic environment that goes far beyond formal electoral democracy.

At this stage we should elaborate a little on the contradictions in the dominant ideologies of universalism and secularism. It is ironic because the hegemonic aspects of these ideas are contrary to their genesis – after all, these concepts were instrumental in the liberating experience of the West in its evolutionary history. First, and foremost, it must be acknowledged that there are very real historical reasons for the domination in general discourse of certain ideas that originated in the West. The Columbus, Da Gama, Albuquerque, and Magellan misadventures resulting in conquest, colonialism, imperialism, and the continuing neo-colonialism were, obviously, not restricted to the realms of politics and economics. Cultures and ideas were enormously affected as well, with Western ideas assuming the status of the "superior" colonizers and non-Western values that of the "inferior" colonized. Indian scholar Ashis Nandy calls this an "imperialism of categories," wherein a theoretical domain is completely hegemonized by a Western concept to the point where the original domain itself is obscured.[43]

This has continued well into present times. As Tagore's chariot analogy reflects (see opening epigraph), an example is the base equation of modernization with Westernization, and both automatically with good. Therefore one must ask the questions of why and how a "universal" is universal. This undoubtedly means walking a tightrope. And this is probably inescapable because, as is argued below, it is clear how easily something which is particular can become universal in a hegemonic discourse; and conversely what is deemed to be universal can easily slip into the realm of relativism. Obviously one has to have certain criteria, but that cannot be done in isolation and needs to be done collectively through dialogue.

THE PARTICULARITY OF HEGEMONIC UNIVERSALISM

The dominant strand of universalism, as distinct from simply the abstract notion of Universalism, was the result of a series of events in Europe's evolutionary history and is, in fact, particular. According to Nandy, the dominant strand of universalism is grounded in a European worldview which accepts as absolute the superiority of the human, the masculine, the adult, the historical, and the modern/progressive over the nonhuman/subhuman, the feminine, the child, the ahistorical and the traditional/savage.[44] In his concept of the error of misplaced absoluteness,[45] Nagarjuna, the Indian Buddhist philosopher who lived in the first century of the Christian era, criticized this kind of absolutism. He reasoned that a specific view, being specific, is not unlimited and therefore one would be erring in conferring absoluteness on what is actually relative. Nandy further writes that in present times the dream of one world has become a nightmare, and a threat to the survival of non-modern/Western cultures. It portends a homogenized, hierarchized world which is sharply categorized into "the modern and the primitive, the secular and the non-secular, the scientific and the unscientific, the expert and the layman, the normal and the abnormal, the developed and the underdeveloped, the vanguard and the led, the liberated and the salvable."[46]

The particularity of the dominant strand of universalism with respect to the human rights question is explicit in the hierarchized dichotomies that Nandy refers to, such as the idea of absolute human superiority over the non-human, and the notion that humans alone have rights simply because they are human. This is very alienating to Buddhists, whose notion of universal rights would never be able to accept such an anthropocentric concept. Rights – along with duties, of course – are not just for humans but all sentient and, even, nonsentient beings. Humans may certainly be the most advanced in the evolutionary chain, but that certainly does not give rights to us alone. In fact, on the contrary, it gives us responsibilities. Humans alone are capable of reaching nirvana and therefore it is incumbent upon us to pave the way for others, through our actions, to be able to realize it as well. This is exemplified in the Buddhist ideal of the Bodhisattva as elaborated by the eighth-century Indian Buddhist sage Shantideva.[47] A Bodhisattva is one who has attained enlightenment and is free to break the cycle of samsara – birth, death, and rebirth – but consciously chooses not to in order to help others reach the Truth.

In the epoch after the European Enlightenment, and continuing into the present, we see a rejection of the hegemonic strand of universalism, a rejection well exemplified in Gandhi but certainly not restricted to either him or his movement. Gandhi categorically rejected many of what he called the evils associated with the modernist project, and the hegemony of the Western dichotomized categories that Nandy refers to above. Gandhi was no less a universalist, but his universalism was not grounded in the hegemony of one particular.[48] Western universalists – that is, those who propound a particular Western universalism – would easily label Gandhi a relativist. That would be nowhere near the truth, for although he argued for the validity of different opinions and celebrated plurality, he grounded it in the concepts of Truth, non-violence, love, compassion, brother/sisterhood, duty, and tolerance which he found in all the religious traditions. Obviously the universalism extant in Gandhi's discourse was not enough, as Asma Barlas reminded me, to persuade a significant section of pre-Partition India's Muslims that they would occupy an equal space in the new Indian nation. Such concerns also seized the Dalits and Dr Ambedkar. Independent India's social, political, and economic trajectory, obviously removed from the Gandhian vision, yet linked to it in part, has tragically proved those fears correct.

THE INTOLERANCE OF POLITICAL SECULARISM

The origins of secularism were in the particular Western experience of the Reformation and, later, the separation of church and state. It is significant to note that secularism began as a dissenting voice against religious orthodoxy, arguing for the validity of alternative forms of belief – the freedom of belief for religious minorities and heterodoxical dissenters. Yet, it is the very same secularism that now disallows dissent and is narrowly intolerant of pluralism. Whether in Algeria or Thailand, freedom of belief has today come to signify the struggle of religious elements against the "secular" state. Equality is certainly not the preserve of a secular ideology – the continuing indignities of racism, sexism, homophobia, and classism/casteism, institutional and individual, in secular, modern societies are testimony to that fact. Even less so are tolerance and a genuine respect for diversity and pluralism.[49] In fact, Nandy argues that tolerance and mutual respect for plurality were pre-secular traditions of non-modern societies.[50] This is of course contentious. His point, however, is not that discord and disharmony did not exist, but that there existed traditional values of tolerance which served as checks.[51] Tolerance, however, is itself a limited concept as it does not necessarily imply anything beyond sufferance or acceptance, even if it is mutual. Equality of necessity has to be worked into this framework, as much as it does in the secular.

Pakistani scholar Ziauddin Sardar and his Welsh co-author, Merryl Wyn Davies, argue that secularism is intrinsically dominating, and that it can be just as fundamentalist and fanatical as the religious worldviews it opposes.[52] This intolerance arises out of the fact that it universalizes as the only universal its particular experience, subsuming all others, and defines what is correct, defensible, and tolerable in beliefs that it opposes.[53] In responding to antisecular reasoning, Indian scholar Rajeev Bhargava makes a well-reasoned argument on the various possible (or not) relationships between politics and religion.[54] He marks a clear difference between, what he calls, political secularism and ethical secularism. The first is the kind that is dominant today and is increasingly under attack by the right as well as secularists having communitarian concerns. Bhargava argues that this version of secularism "has little or no conception of community."[55] The pluralist version of ethical secularism, on the other hand, is a stronger interpretation of secularism "which is both secular and communitarian [and] is worth exploring and enriching."[56]

Gandhi also rejected the anti-religion credo of secularism. His philosophy and his movement were immersed in religion. More so than anyone else in the last hundred years, he injected religion into politics and argued for their inseparability. For him a politics devoid of spirituality was a politics devoid of morality. At the same time, he did not advocate a theocracy. His philosophy of religion was based not on the infallibility of religion but on the imperfectness of it.[57] Humans are less than divine and therefore imperfect, though striving for, and capable of, perfection. The Jain view that all religions are true in that they have part of the truth but not the whole Truth of necessity engenders a certain humility and openness, and this was crucial to Gandhi's thinking. It would be well to remember how much, despite its secular evolution, Western political thought is influenced by and indebted to Christian and pre-Christian "Western" and non-Western religious and moral thought.[58] In any case, as Ahmad has argued, the concept of an Athens-to-Albion and Aeschylus-to-Kissinger Europe is a fabrication of recent derivation.[59] Thus, one cannot but think it suspect when Westerners question the influence of Hindu, Buddhist, Islamic, Confucian, and so on, religious and moral thought in those societies.

Obviously, there are exclusivist and dogmatic interpretations within religious traditions; and, as referred to earlier, not all the religious elements fighting states are pluralistically and democratically oriented. As Indian scholar/activist Gabriele Dietrich has rightly pointed out with reference to Nandy's contention, the ambiguity of much of the debate on cultural decolonization can lead, and has led, to the co-optation of such arguments by nonprogressive, anti-women, fascist, communal, and cultural forces.[60] However, there is the scope – and I would argue that it is imperative – to emphasize and empower the tolerant and pluralistic aspects of these traditions. To do otherwise would be catastrophic to any hope of success for a progressive, pluralistic, participatorily democratic GB.

It is quite evident that the two concepts that are essential pillars of the hegemonic discourse in human rights are problematic. The relativism of the dominant strand of universalism and the fundamentalism (in the sense as it is commonly applied to religious extremism) of the prevalent version of secularism have serious implications for the hegemonic discourse because they strike at the very root of what is claimed and accepted as an unquestioned given. It might be contended that "anti-foundationalist" arguments eventually become an approximation of cultural relativism.[61] While this is no doubt plausible, it is evident that not questioning "given" foundations – thus committing the error of misplaced absoluteness – results in the same thing. The answer lies, therefore, not in succumbing to cultural relativism of either kind but in aggressively pushing for a genuine universalism.

THE SEARCH FOR GENUINELY UNIVERSALIST-PLURALIST ALTERNATIVES

Human rights are the very essence of GB! The diverse social movements – environmental, peasant, indigenous peoples', women's, and so on – all over the Third World may be struggling on a whole range of issues but essentially they are working for human rights and dignity. Many of them even describe themselves as human rights movements,[62] and it is significant to note that their vision of what constitutes human rights is far broader and more inclusive than those rights emphasized by Western governments and scholars. Moreover, their emphasis on collective rights in the economic, social, and cultural spheres by no means excludes civil and political rights. What they are arguing, and struggling, for is a more holistic and integrated vision of rights.

Scholars and activists in the Third World have been actively engaged in attempting to provide genuinely universalist and pluralist alternatives, thus contributing to the general discourse. This occurs through the work of politically engaged intellectuals who are active members of the movements representing GB and are directly responding to the contradictions inherent in the dominant strands of universalism and secularism. In the human rights discourse this has occurred at two levels, both of which, related though separate, are equally significant. One trend is that of delving into our own cultures to try to come up with either notions of rights, or concepts similar to rights, that were/are extant in our multiple traditions.[63] Here it is important to bear in mind the arguments put forward by many Asian scholars/activists, among others, of the need to view rights as inseparable from duties and responsibilities. Gandhi opined, about the Universal Declaration of Human Rights, that rights arose from duties well done. Even the right to live, he argued, came from doing the duty of world citizenship, although this was not in the legalistic/constitutionalist sense of the term.[64] This idea of rights coterminous with duties and responsibilities is common to all the religious traditions. It is only secularism which separates the two, leading to what Muzaffar calls a "rights culture."

The other trend focuses on human rights theory and action based on present realities and needs in the Third World.[65] Muzaffar, for instance, makes a powerful argument for basing human rights, international relations, and, ultimately, universalism on the notion of human dignity;[66] and the oneness of humanity arising from the oneness of a supreme divinity.[67]

The first trend, searching for concepts of rights in a multitude of traditions, is equally concerned with the current situation and needs, on which, in fact, the whole exercise is predicated. The second trend, focusing on present realities and needs, is similarly concerned with cultural relevance and the recognition that cultural plurality is both desirable and vital; and that it alone can lead to a collective and true universalism. Ashis Nandy, Ziauddin Sardar, and Indian scholar/activist Claude Alvares all emphasize the sheer totalitarianism of Western hegemony in arguing that our concepts, our categories, our axioms, our paradigms, and even our very dissent and alternatives largely stem from the dominant discourse, and that any genuine alternatives have to be intrinsically rooted in our own heritages.[68] At the same time, this does not, and cannot, as I stress throughout this essay, preclude a multi-directional flow and exchange of ideas and influences on a mutual basis.

CRITIQUES FROM WITHIN

Such labors do not amount to relativism! It is hardly the case that most of the scholars/activists engaged in human rights struggles are apologists for their various governments. Rather, they are engaged in radical internal critique, a concept that is ingrained in their traditions. The much abused (not just in the West) notion of jihad in Islam, for example, is a concept of internal critique which warrants the acceptance of different ideas that will influence and engineer a revolution based on the interplay of such ideas.[69] The Hindu and Buddhist traditions also abound in similar concepts enjoining the people "*Ánô bhadrá ritávô yantú vishwatáh*" – to let good thoughts come to us from all over the world; to enable the attainment of the universal ideal and not the domination of any one particular. As Indian scholar Amartya Sen and his American co-author, Martha Nussbaum, argue in an article on internal criticism and Indian rationalist tradition that has direct implications for the human rights debate: (1) criticism must be internal, using resources internal to the culture; (2) the norm of objectivity must be one of immersion rather than detachment as objectivity can be maintained through immersion; and (3) internal criticism must be genuinely critical.[70]

In an essay written a few years ago, Singaporean scholar Beng-Huat Chua addressed the question of the hegemonic discourse in human rights by analyzing the role of liberalism, both as an ideology and as a system of liberal-democratic government.[71] Even more importantly, he critically questioned the ideological constructions of "Asianness" and "Asian values," which, as noted earlier, have been used by many Asian governments in defense of pathetic human rights records. Filipina scholar/activist Indai Lourdes Sajor and Egyptian scholar/author/activist Nawal El-Saadawi underscore the need for internal critique on another front – gender – in arguing that the struggle against Western domination by Third World peoples has to go hand-in-hand with the struggle of Third World women against patriarchy and male domination within their cultures.[72] One cannot overemphasize the critical importance of addressing gender, racial, caste, and other such inequalities within our societies and our struggles because for too long, and too readily (on the part of men and "upper" castes), they have been subsumed within a larger class discourse.[73]

Yet another example of internal critique is the publication of essays in defense of free speech for Salman Rushdie by a large number of Arab and Muslim scholars, activists, artists, and so on. Many of these people did not support the content of Rushdie's book. They supported the principle of free speech. Many others criticized the nature of the response – the fatwa pronouncing death – arguing instead for a response by the pen and not the sword. Not all the writers were secular either. In fact, the argument of the non-secular writers, including an Iranian dissident ayátollah, was precisely that the fatwa and the notion of censorship were un-Islamic, and that inquiry and dissent were part of the Islamic tradition.[74] This kind of internal critique, I believe, more than all the fulminations of the West against "fanatical, fundamentalist" Islam, will have a serious and meaningful impact on the Islamic orthodoxy. This jihad – and not Western tantrums – is the real challenge to that establishment.

Further, in line with the point made above on acceptance of different ideas and influences, which is critical for a genuine universalism, Sen and Nussbaum argue that a specific culture is part of a larger plurality. Therefore ideas and concepts from other traditions may, and can, be known and incorporated without imposition from outside; and that an internal critique is (or has to be) by no means exclusively parochial. In fact, as they point out, this widens the scope of internal critique significantly.[75]

Within the framework of internal critique one must also turn to Gandhi, Ambedkar, Phule, and others in the Indian context. Gandhi was certainly not an apologist for religion, particularly Hinduism. While the comprehensiveness of his critique of the caste system may, and should, be questioned, he did attack this evil within Brahmin-dominated Hindu society. And while he carried out his own internal critique of Hinduism, he also sought values and concepts from other traditions, both to strengthen his own judgment and, in his perspective, to enrich Hinduism.[76] Phule and Ambedkar launched more fundamental attacks on the caste system. Phule sought to establish an alternative to caste-ridden Brahminic Hinduism through his *Satyashôdhak Samáj*, which argued for the religion of the oppressed majority from below. Ambedkar, after trying unsuccessfully to resolve the caste contradiction within Hinduism, led his followers out of Brahminic Hinduism into Buddhism, which itself was a rejection of casteist Brahminism over two thousand years earlier. *Panditá* Ramabai focused her battles on improving the social, economic, and political conditions of women (especially widows), and other oppressed castes/classes. And these are but a few examples.

CONCLUSIONS

The two related efforts by Third World scholars and activists in the human rights discourse are advancing the creation and expansion of the terms of debate for an alternative nonhegemonic discourse and simultaneously enlarging the space for action. In this, they are also a vital element of GB, providing a pluralistic counter to the hegemonic discourse.

Both in the Third World and in the West, efforts are underway to initiate dialogue. For instance, Chandra Muzaffar convened a human rights conference in December 1994 in Malaysia bringing together scholars/activists from various Third World and Western countries. Similarly, Peter Van Ness has engaged in a long-term research project on human rights involving Asian and Western scholars and furthering dialogue.

The widening of the terms of the debate is a fundamental necessity. After all, as Ofelia Schutte points out in the context of Leopoldo Zea's attempts at universalism through the concepts of *Mestizáje* (the Mexican "national" ideology) and *Mexicanidad* (Mexicanness), "as long as the notion of humanity on which he [Zea] relies is basically a European construct, the mere addition of color or nationality as a qualifying circumstance to this 'universal man' will not be sufficient to legitimate indigenous and marginalized ethnic cultures *on their own terms*."[77] This being the case, the marginalized groups can only define their freedom and self-determination within what are essentially a little more inclusive European philosophical paradigms.[78]

It is obvious that Western hegemony is not restricted to the human rights discourse. Although central, the latter is but one aspect of the overall processes of globalization. The larger question of hegemony is indicative of the whole process of political, economic, and cultural GA. Ultimately, therefore, the hegemonic human rights discourse has to be seen within that context and addressed as such. The challenge has to come, and, indeed, is coming, from political, economic, and cultural GB. Reflecting on the quincentenary of the Columbus disorientation, Claude Alvares concludes his work on decolonizing history by arguing that:

> Maybe in a distant future, after we have found ourselves, and Europe [the West as a whole] for its part has come to terms with the inevitability of accepting the rest of humankind as equals, we may dream of a new voyage of discovery of mutual attractions that will allow a more harmonious relationship than has existed in the past 500 years. Till that comes to pass, we who refuse the invitation to be Europeans must reject [Western constructs of] the unity of man as well.[79]

Not collectively dreaming of such a voyage is, at the least, shirking responsibility; at worst, it is consigning ourselves and our sisters and brothers in struggle to autogenocide.[80] The social movements that are increasingly globalized from below and see themselves as representative of diverse concerns, as opposed to the traditional Western view of them as localized, single-issue movements, and the scholars engaged with them in these alternative efforts are the twin aspects of GB, integrating theory and praxis in their struggle for a nonhegemonic globalization, and an alternative to (auto)genocide.

NOTES

I would like to thank Asma Barlas, Lori Hartmann-Mahmud, Sakah Mahmud, John McCamant, Ved Nanda, George Shepherd, Peter Van Ness, and some anonymous reviewers for their comments and suggestions. As always, the usual caveats apply. I would further like to acknowledge my deepest appreciation of George Shepherd, who first inspired and enabled me to think and write on human rights through a doctoral fellowship at the Center on Rights Development at the Graduate School of International Studies, University of Denver.

1 Rabindranath Tagore, cited in Smitu Kothari, "Social Movements and the Redefinition of Democracy," in Philip Oldenburg, ed., *India Briefing, 1993*, (Boulder, CO: Westview Press, 1993), p. 131.

2 Some readers may have qualms about the use of certain categories as employed in this essay. For instance, some might have definitional problems with the use of "Western," or may ideologically object to the use of "Third World." In the first case, it is obvious that the West is not a monolithic entity, historically and currently *vis-à-vis* the "other," i.e. the non-West, and reifying it is problematic, but at the same time it is largely coalesced in the other's perception; moreover, the hegemonic discourse in human rights is largely situated in the areas we know as the West, particularly the United States. In the second case, some people object to the use of the term because of its demeaning nature, or because it also involves a certain mythification. I use it here to signify solidarity between the oppressed majority in Asia, Africa, and South/Central America, and more to describe those areas of the globe that directly suffer(ed) the ravages of colonialism and imperialism. As regards a suitable term for the oppressed majority across the globe, the term "global South" is preferable; and I use it elsewhere.

3 See Ward Churchill, "White Studies: The Intellectual Imperialism of Contemporary US Education," *Integrateducation* 19, nos 1–2 (1992), pp. 51–7.

4 I realize, of course, and accept as well, Aijaz Ahmad's point on the non-oppressed origins of most Third World intellectuals in the West and that they are situated therein, or aim to situate themselves, in the dominant classes; and that, for the vast majority, their "diasporic" condition is a result of personal preference and in no way an exile from their countries of origin. See Ahmad, *In Theory: Nations, Classes, Literatures* (London: Verso, 1992).

5 On this see also the Indian scholar Poonam Pillai, "Feminism and the Problem of Epistemic Displacement: Reconstructing Indigenous Theories," *Genders* 24 (1996), pp. 206–47.

6 Xabier Gorostiga, "Latin America in the New World Order," in Jeremy Brecher, *et al.*, eds, *Global Visions: Beyond the New World Order* (Boston: South End Press, 1993), p. 67.

7 Richard Falk, "The Making of Global Citizenship," in ibid., p. 39. See also the introduction to the same book, pp. ix–xxvi.

8 Immanuel Wallerstein establishes a very concrete link between the dominant universalist ideology and the universalizing (globalizing) tendencies of capitalism towards an endlessly homogeneous commodification of all things. See his article "Ideological Tensions of Capitalism: Universalism versus Racism and Sexism," in Etienne Balibar and Immanuel Wallerstein, eds, *Race, Nation, Class: Ambiguous Identities* (London: Verso, 1991), pp. 29–36.

9 For a brilliant analysis of US foreign policy in this regard see William Robinson, "Globalization, the World System, and 'Democracy Promotion' in US Foreign Policy," *Theory and Society: Renewal and Critique in Social Theory* 25, no. 5 (October 1996), pp. 615–65.

10 This is also addressed by Indian scholar Chakravarthi Raghavan and Martin Khor Kok Peng. See Raghavan, *Recolonization: GATT, the Uruguay Round and the Third World* (Mapusa: The Other India Book Press, 1992); and Martin Khor Kok Peng, "Economic Dimensions of Western Global Domination and its Consequences for the Human Rights of Five-Sixths of Humanity," Kuala Lumpur, International Conference on Rethinking Human Rights, December 6–7, 1994. Both emphasize the totalitarian nature of the WTO in that not only current but even future Third World governments, even if formed by those elements or parties that consistently opposed GATT and the WTO, would be virtually powerless to make the rules and regulations conform to norms of justice and equality!

11 See Anuradha Seth, "Who Gains from Economic Liberalization? Working Class Households and the New Economic Policy," *SAMAR: South Asian Magazine for Action & Reflection*, no. 4 (Winter 1994), pp. 4–9.

12 Some estimates put this at almost 90 percent of foreign news and information in the global print media alone being controlled by four Northern news agencies! See Chandra Muzaffar, "Double Standards in the West," *World Press Review* (September 1993), pp. 17–18.

13 See Ziauddin Sardar *et al.*, *The Blinded Eye: 500 Years of Christopher Columbus* (Mapusa: The Other India Book Press, 1993).

14 Noam Chomsky and Edward Herman have extensively shown the links between the media and the political and economic establishments in the West, primarily in the United States. See Chomsky, *Necessary Illusions: Thought Control in Democratic Societies* (Boston: South End Press, 1989); and Herman and Chomsky, *Manufacturing Consent: The Politics of the Mass Media* (New York: Pantheon Books, 1988).

15 India is a perfect example of this style of "democratic" politics; although regular multi-party elections with high voter turn-outs are an established feature of the system, the masses do not really rule, and the system itself is increasingly delegitimized.

16 This point has to be emphasized in light of the Hindu right's misappropriation in India of Gandhi's concept of *swadéshi* (self-reliance) in the economic sphere. However, while the Swadéshi Jágran Manch (Platform for the Awakening [of the Concept] of Self-Reliance) has been vociferously campaigning against multinationals, the states ruled by the Bharatiya Janata Party (BJP–Indian People's Party) have been as active in canvassing multinational investments as those with centrist or even left governments.

17 See Aijaz Ahmad, "In the Eye of the Storm: The Left Chooses," *Economic and Political Weekly* (Bombay, June 1, 1996), pp. 1329–43.

18 Falk, "Global Citizenship," p. 39.

19 It is imperative, I think, to note that these linkages and a general internationalist philosophy have pervaded such movements historically.

20 See Sakamoto Yoshikazu, "The Global Context of Democratization," *Alternatives* 16, no. 2 (Spring 1991), pp. 119–28. He further develops this concept by outlining four dimensions to deepening democracy.

21 For instance, such left democratic literacy movements in various parts of India as the People's Science Movement organized by the Jan Vignyán Védiká in Andhra Pradesh and the Kerala Sástra Sáhítya Paríshad in Kerala; or Freirean pedagogy in South America.

22 It must be ensured, however, that this does not lead to reactionary and undemocratic results. For instance, simply devolving power to the villages in the Indian context without addressing existing unequal social, economic, and political structures would achieve the opposite of what the democratic movements are seeking. Many of the mass democratic movements, for instance reflected in the positions of the Bhárat Jan Ándôlan (Indian People's Movement), have been calling for radical decentralization in which the *grám sabhá* (village community) as opposed to the *grám pancháyat* (village council) will be the primary decision-making unit. See Indian scholar/activist Brahma Dev Sharma, *Whither Tribal Areas? Constitutional Amendments and After* (Delhi: Sahyog Pustak Kutir, 1995).

23 In this essay "Indian" refers to people from India, not Native Americans.

24 Kothari, "Social Movements," p. 162.

25 Muto Ichiyo, "For an Alliance of Hope," in Brecher *et al.*, eds, *Global Visions*, p. 156. See also his "Alliance of Hope and Challenges of Global Democracy," *Lokayan Bulletin* 11, no. 1 (July–August 1994), pp. 33–47.

26 Smitu Kothari, conversation with the author, and others at the Center on Human Rights Development, University of Denver and the Iliff School of Theology, November 1992.

27 See the works of Smitu Kothari, Ashis Nandy, and Claude Alvares cited elsewhere in this essay. See also Vandana Shiva, *Staying Alive: Women, Ecology, and Development*

(London: Zed Books, 1989); Rajni Kothari, *Rethinking Development: In Search of Humane Alternatives* (Delhi: Ajanta Publications, 1988); Dhirubhai L. Sheth, "Grass-Roots Stirrings and the Future of Politics," *Alternatives* 9 (1983), pp. 1–24.

28 The magazine *Third World Resurgence* is an excellent source of information on such resistance struggles. See, for example, "The Struggle for the Seed: Third World Farmers against GATT and the MNCs," *Third World Resurgence* no. 39 (November 1993), pp. 20–40, which covers the Seed Satyagraha led by farmers in Karnataka state in southwest India against the agro-multinational company, Cargill; "TNCs Rule OK?" *Third World Resurgence* no. 40 (December 1993), pp. 18–36; "GATT At Last!" *Third World Resurgence* no. 41 (January 1994), pp. 10–24; and "New 'Trade-Related' Threats to South after the Uruguay Round," *Third World Resurgence* no. 45 (May 1994), pp. 18–41.

29 For instance, in India, 64 percent of the urban female labor force is in the informal sector. See National Institute of Urban Affairs (NIUA), *Gender Bias in Employment of Women in the Urban Informal Sector*, Research Study Series no. 20 (Delhi: NIUA, 1987) cited in Jana Everett and Mira Savara, "Organizations and Informal Sector Women Workers in Bombay," in Alice W. Clarke, ed., *Gender and Political Economy: Explorations of South Asian Systems* (Delhi: Oxford University Press, 1993), pp. 273–321.

30 Martin Khor Kok Peng, "Reforming North Economy, South Development, and World Economic Order," in Brecher *et al.*, (eds), *Global Visions*, pp. 163–70.

31 See Ahmad, *In Theory*.

32 I enter a caveat here. My criticism of the use of human rights as an ideological tool in diplomacy is based primarily on the "consistency of inconsistencies," that is, the flagrant double standards that are part of this diplomacy; and the perpetuation of Western domination that is the basis of much of this type of politics. The right to self-determination of the Tibetans and other oppressed peoples elsewhere is not in question by any means. The right to self-determination itself, generally, has been narrowly construed to mean the right of political secession for minorities and colonized groups. The movements that are the focus of this essay see self-determination more broadly as people being able to have control over their everyday lives and livelihoods.

33 Chandra Muzaffar, *Human Rights and the New World Order* (Penang: Just World Trust, 1993), p. 12.

34 This of course does not include the seminal contributions to widening the human rights discourse by Western scholars such as George Shepherd, Philip Alston, Richard Falk, James Crawford, Henry Shue and others. More recently, scholars like Sigrun Skogly, Alison Dundes Renteln, and William Felice have been doing interesting work that accounts for a more holistic approach to human rights.

35 See Sardar *et al.*, *Blinded Eye*.

36 The critique of universalism, secularism, and modernity in this essay does not arise from a basic unacceptance, on my part, of these creeds. Rather, it is grounded in a rejection of their dogmatic aspects and misplaced absoluteness which are anti-pluralist and anti-religion. In a pluralistic world where the vast majority of people are religious, I believe that it is incumbent upon us to emphasize the tolerant, egalitarian, "fraternal," progressive elements within religion(s), and not let the particularistic, exclusivist, theocratic elements that I associate with GA, whether the *maulvi*s (Muslim teachers) in Iran, the *mahánt*s (Hindu religious sectarian leaders) in India, or the televangelicals in the US, hegemonize the socio-political space. In fact, this is being addressed by many of the democratic social movements being discussed here.

37 See Burns H. Weston, "Human Rights," in Richard Pierre Claude and Burns H. Weston, eds, *Human Rights in the World Community: Issues and Action* (Philadelphia:

University of Pennsylvania Press, 1989), pp. 12–29. Immanuel Wallerstein points out that the notion of human rights being derived from human nature and, therefore, being characteristically human entitlements not privileges (which are usually linked to responsibilities) is a result of modern, European Enlightenment thinking. See Wallerstein, "Ideological Tensions."

38 See for example, Jack Donnelly, "Humanitarian Intervention and American Foreign Policy: Law, Morality, and Politics," in Claude and Weston, eds, *Human Rights in the World Community*, pp. 251–64; and *Universal Human Rights in Theory and Practice* (Ithaca, NY: Cornell University Press, 1989).

39 Not all Asian leaders are unanimous in their perspective on human rights either. For instance, the Tibetan leader HH the Dalai Lama and Aung San Suu Kyi, the leader of the democracy movement in Burma, have both vociferously expressed their belief that human rights are not an alien concept *vis-à-vis* Asian cultures. See HH the Dalai Lama, "Need for Global Thinking: Human Rights in a Shrinking World," *The Times of India* (Bombay, July 24, 1993); Aung San Suu Kyi, "In Quest of Democracy," in *Freedom From Fear and Other Writings* (New York: Penguin Books, 1991), pp. 167–79.

40 This is evident in the reaction of many in the West to what they see as a sell-out when scholars/activists like Chandra Muzaffar share the platform with political elites like Mahathir Mohamad. People only recently eulogized are suddenly now considered to be in the enemy camp. The ironic and hegemonic nature of such categorizing is manifest in that: (1) many of the accusers would not hesitate to share platforms with Western political elites, and it is not readily obvious why that should be any different; and (2) the validity and integrity of the Third World scholar/activist, and her or his position, is intact only to the extent that it falls within Western norms.

41 While aware of the limited nature of this international consensus, Donnelly uses it as part of the foundation for his thesis. And while Freeman raises this question in his critique of Donnelly, he does not question the levels (elitist/ruling class) at which this consensus is arrived at, or issues of power and domination, either. See Freeman, "The Philosophical Foundations of Human Rights," *Human Rights Quarterly* 16, no. 3 (August 1994), pp. 491–514.

42 What really needs to happen – and is happening – is a dialogue at the grassroots. Julian Saurin has similarly critiqued dialogues that exclude the powerless, and are what he calls "self-representations," within the discipline of international relations such as James N. Rosenau, ed., *Global Voices: Dialogues in International Relations* (Boulder, CO: Westview Press, 1993). See Saurin, "Globalisation, Poverty, and the Promises of Modernity," *Millennium: Journal of International Studies* 25, no. 3 (1996), pp. 657–80.

43 See Ashis Nandy, "The Politics of Secularism and the Recovery of Religious Tolerance," *Alternatives* 13, no. 2 (April 1988), pp. 177–94.

44 Ashis Nandy, *The Intimate Enemy: Loss and Recovery of Self Under Colonialism* (Delhi: Oxford University Press, 1983), p. x.

45 See K. Venkata Ramanan, *Nágárjuna's Philosophy as presented in the Mahá-Prajñápáramitá-ástra* (Rutland, VT; Tokyo: Charles E. Tuttle Company, 1966).

46 Nandy, *Intimate Enemy*, p. x.

47 See the translation of Shantideva's *Bôdhícáryavtárá* by Stephen Batchelor, *A Guide to the Bodhisattva's Way of Life by Shantideva* (Dharamsala: Library of Tibetan Works and Archives, 1979).

48 For an excellent discussion of the universal principles underlying Gandhi's discourse, see Bhikhu Parekh, *Colonialism, Tradition and Reform: An Analysis of Gandhi's Political Discourse* (Delhi: Sage Publications, 1989).

49 Iranian scholar Reza Afshari is skeptical of the scope of pluralism and diversity

within an Islamic context. See Afshari, "An Essay on Islamic Cultural Relativism in the Discourse of Human Rights," *Human Rights Quarterly* 16, no. 2 (May 1994), pp. 235–76. This skepticism, however, has to be seen within the context of the dominant Islamic orthodoxies and theocracies. What Chandra Muzaffar, Sudanese scholar/activist Abdullahi Ahmed An-Na'im, and Nawal El-Saadawi are calling for is a genuine revolution within Islam based on the principles of jihad and ijtihad. Although ijtihad has been non-existent for centuries and the concept of jihad is often narrowly interpreted to mean "holy war," dissent within Islam has historical (and continuing) precedents in the heterodoxical Sufis and the even more radical (in terms of a progressive and egalitarian ideology) Qarmathians, who have been continuously suppressed by the dominant Islamic elites.

50 Nandy, "Politics of Secularism," p. 188.
51 See Sardar *et al.*, *Blinded Eye*, pp. 79–80.
52 Ziauddin Sardar and Merryl Wyn Davies, *Distorted Imagination: Lessons from the Rushdie Affair* (Kuala Lumpur: Berita; London: Grey Seal, 1990), pp. 277–8.
53 Ibid., pp. 31–2.
54 See Rajeev Bhargava, "How Not To Defend Secularism," *South Asia Bulletin: Comparative Studies of South Asia, Africa and the Middle East* 14, no. 1 (1994), pp. 33–41. The version of this chapter that appeared as an article in the *Bulletin of Concerned Asian Scholars* 27, no. 4 (1995) was critical of aspects of Bhargava's article based on my misreading of it, and so I make amends in this revised version.
55 Bhargava, "How Not To Defend," p. 40.
56 Ibid.
57 See Mohandas Gandhi, *All Religions Are True*, ed. Anand T. Hingorani (Bombay: Bharatiya Vidya Bhavan, 1962).
58 Martin Bernal, *Black Athena: The Afroasiatic Roots of Classical Civilization, Volume 1: The Fabrication of Ancient Greece 1785–1985* (New Brunswick, NJ: Rutgers University Press, 1987).
59 Ahmad, *In Theory*, p. 183.
60 Gabriele Dietrich, *Reflections on the Women's Movement in India: Religion, Ecology, Development* (Delhi: Horizon, 1992), p. 95.
61 Freeman, "Philosophical Foundations," p. 501.
62 See Smitu Kothari and Harsh Sethi, eds, *Rethinking Human Rights: Challenges for Theory and Action* (Delhi: Lokayan; New York: New Horizons Press, 1989).
63 See, for example, the Indian scholar Purushottama Bilimoria, "Rights and Duties the (Modern) Indian Dilemma," in M. Smart and Shivesh Thakur, eds, *Political and Ethical Dilemmas of Modern India* (New York: St Martin's Press, 1993); Bilimoria, "Is *Adhikāra* Good Enough for 'Rights'?" *Asian Philosophy* 3, no. 1 (1993), pp. 3–13; Thai scholar/activist Roongraung Boonyoros, "Buddhist Ethics in Everyday Life in Thailand: A Village Experiment," in Charles Wei-hsun Fu and Sandra A. Wawrytko, eds, *Buddhist Ethics and Modern Society: An International Symposium* (Westport, CT: Greenwood Press, 1991), pp. 215–28; Nepali scholar the Rev. Sunanda Putuwar, *The Buddhist Sangha: Paradigm of the Ideal Human Society* (Lanham, MD: University Press of America, 1991); Claude E. Welch, Jr, and Virginia A. Leary, eds, *Asian Perspectives on Human Rights* (Boulder, CO: Westview Press, 1990); Abdullahi Ahmed An-Na'im and Francis Madeng Deng, eds, *Human Rights in Africa: Cross-Cultural Perspectives* (Washington, DC: The Brookings Institution, 1990).
64 Mohandas Gandhi, cited in Robert Traer, *Faith in Human Rights: Support in Religious Traditions for a Global Struggle* (Washington, DC: Georgetown University Press, 1991), pp. 131–2.
65 This is a major concern for many of the Third World human rights scholars/ activists. See, for example, Kothari and Sethi, eds, *Rethinking Rights*, particularly the chapters by D.L. Sheth and Upendra Baxi; Muzaffar, *Human Rights and the*

New World Order, Asian Coalition of Human Rights Organizations (ACHRO), *Human Rights Activism in Asia: Some Perspectives, Problems and Approaches* (New York: Council on International & Public Affairs and International Center for Law in Development, 1984). In this context see also Tanzanian scholar Issa G. Shivji, ed., *The Concept of Human Rights in Africa* (Dakar and London: CODESRIA, 1989). Shivji critiques the dominant discourse in human rights dominated by non-Africans as emphasizing the history of ideas and not social history. Here one must also make reference to Western scholars like Shepherd and Falk who have consciously adopted a human needs-based approach to human rights theory and practice. See George W. Shepherd, "The African Right to Development: World Policy and the Debt Crisis," *Africa Today* 37, no. 4 (1990), pp. 5–14; and Richard Falk, "The Quest for Human Rights in an Era of Globalization," San José, Costa Rica, Symposium on Multilateralism and the UN System, December 18–19, 1995.

66 See Chapter 1.

67 This is the Islamic concept of *tawhíd*, the unity of the supreme being and therefore of all creation. Similarly, within the Judeo-Christian traditions the notion of God as the Father of all creation provides the basis for universality. In Hinduism, notions of universalism are found in the Vedanta and other philosophical traditions which locate the fundamental unity of diverse humankind in the oneness of the diverse universe. Buddhism's emphasis on the interrelatedness of everything in the universe in "dependent co-origination" provides the ground for universalism.

68 See Ashis Nandy, "The Impact of Western Hegemonic Policies upon the Human Rights of People in South Asia"; Ziauddin Sardar, "The Quest for Human Rights in Asia"; Claude Alvares, "Intellectual Dimension of Western Global Domination and its Consequences for the Human Rights of Five-Sixths of Humanity"; all in Kuala Lumpur, International Conference on Rethinking Human Rights, December 6–7, 1994. See also Sardar *et al.*, *Blinded Eye*.

69 As noted earlier, Abdullahi Ahmed An-Na'im forcefully argues for the reinvigoration of the concept of *ijtihad* – interpretation and legal reasoning leading to reform, associated with the Qur'anic scholars of yore. See An-Na'im, *Toward an Islamic Reformation: Civil Liberties, Human Rights, and International Law* (Syracuse, NY: Syracuse University Press, 1990).

70 Martha C. Nussbaum and Amartya Sen, "Internal Criticism and Indian Rationalist Tradition," in Michael Krausz ed., *Relativism: Interpretation and Confrontation* (Notre Dame, IN: University of Notre Dame Press, 1989), p. 308.

71 See Beng-Huat Chua, "Australian and Asian Perceptions of Human Rights," in Ian Russell *et al.*, *Australia's Human Rights Diplomacy* (Canberra: Australian National University, Research School for Pacific Studies, Australian Foreign Policy Papers, 1993), pp. 87–97.

72 See Indai Lourdes Sajor, "The Impact of Western Hegemonic Policies upon the Human Rights of People in South-East Asia," Kuala Lumpur, International Conference on Rethinking Human Rights, December 6–7, 1994; Nawal El-Saadawi, *The Hidden Face of Eve: Women in the Arab World* (Boston: Beacon Press, 1982).

73 For instance, it was ironic and, sadly, typical that at the Kuala Lumpur conference it was even controversial to raise the issue of gender and women's rights. This was manifested in the mainly male negative reaction to Indai Lourdes Sajor's paper ("The Impact of Western Hegemonic Policies"). See Rose Ismail, "Hiccup in Conference," *New Straits Times* (Kuala Lumpur, December 11, 1994), p. 15.

74 See Anouar Abdallah, *et al.*, *For Rushdie: Essays by Arab and Muslim Writers in Defense of Free Speech* (New York: George Braziller, 1994). Originally published in French

as *Pour Rushdie: Cent intellectuels arabes et musulmans pour la liberté d'expression* (Paris: Éditions la Découverte, 1993).

75 Nussbaum and Sen, "Internal Criticism," p. 319.

76 Parekh, *Colonialism*, p. 23.

77 Ofelia Schutte, *Cultural Identity and Social Liberation in Latin American Thought* (Albany: SUNY Press, 1993), p. 127 (emphasis in the original).

78 Ibid.

79 Claude Alvares, *Decolonizing History: Technology and Culture in India, China and the West, 1492 to the Present Day* (Mapusa: The Other India Book Press, 1991), p. 248.

80 M. Annette Jaimes reinvented this concept (first used to describe the Khmer Rouge massacre in Kampuchea) to refer to a collective entity – an ethnic minority for instance – disappearing through either forced or "voluntary" assimilation. See Jaimes, "La Raza and Indigenism: Alternatives to Autogenocide in North America," *Global Justice* 3, nos 2 and 3 (July–August/September–October 1992), pp. 4–19.

3

ASIA AS A FOUNT OF UNIVERSAL HUMAN RIGHTS

Edward Friedman

Edward Friedman *is an American political scientist and a China specialist. His current research focuses on the processes of democratization in Asia. Arguing that the notion of East versus West misleads, Friedman identifies commonalities across what other analysts see to be an immense cultural divide. Friedman challenges the "Asian values" defense of authoritarian rule, affirming that all cultures contain democratic elements, and that each nation must institutionalize democracy in its own way. "East" and "West" are not coherent cultural categories, he argues; every culture cares about the dignity of its peoples.*

MISCONCEIVING EAST AND WEST

Asia, to spokespeople for Asian Authoritarianism, stands for the geographical region of East and Southeast Asia in a positive way, a world of humane values and world-renowned economic success. In contrast, in Europe, Asia is regularly perceived as incompatible with civilized progress or as the enemy of humanity.[1] The conventional wisdom from Russia west is that Communist Party dictatorships were a continuation of Asian despotisms, the impositions of Mongols or Ottomans, imagined as heirs of the ancient Persians who had threatened freedom in Greece in the classical age. When Communist tyrannies crumbled in Eastern Europe, people understood democratization as leaving the despotism of the East for the freedom of the West.[2]

The imposition of singular values on large diverse places such as Asia and Europe, of course, distorts. A vice-minister of Japan's Ministry of International Trade and Industry commented, "Asia is only a geographical word. Asian nations share nothing in common."[3] In historical fact, both Europe and Asia contain a spectrum of polities from the best to the worst. Twentieth-century Europe has been home to Nazi genocide and Stalinist savagery as well as to the glories of democracy in Western Europe and a burgeoning human rights movement. Twentieth-century Asia has been home to Khmer Rouge genocide and the savageries of Mao Zedong and Kim Il Sung as well as to the glories of two of the three most populous democracies on the planet, India and Japan. In the second half of the twentieth century, in contrast to the image of democracy as the venue of a European bourgeoisie, actually far more rural Asians have enjoyed the ordered liberty of constitutional governance than have urban Europeans.

HUMANISTIC ASIA

Asia and Europe should be rethought to overcome misleading stereotypes. Problematizing Asia and Europe to understand the societal strengths that undergird late twentieth-century Asia's equitable economic dynamism makes manifest why Asia could well become a world leader in human rights in the twenty-first century, and why the conventional European comprehension of Asia as a despotic negative opposite is so dangerously misleading.

The leaders and spokespeople of Singapore and Malaysia have long defended their governments as embodiments of Asian values, which are claimed to be superior to an imagined West conceived of as too individualistic to bring social order and economic growth. Both nations actually are would-be democracies whose elites – much as France in 1794 or Britain in 1832 or the South in the United States before 1965 or Afrikaaners in South Africa before the 1990s – resist fuller democratization.

There is no good reason to believe that such nations cannot democratize. Even Harvard University Professor Samuel Huntington, for decades the proponent of the claim that Confucian societies cannot democratize, took it all back in 1996 and acknowledged that even the government in Beijing could do so.

AUTHORITARIAN ASIA?

While spokespeople for the government of Singapore have argued that Asian culture and the world of democracy are incompatible, in contrast, the leaders of Asia's many democracies, of Japan, India, the Republic of Korea, Mongolia, and Taiwan, do not comprehend their rich Asian cultures as singularly antidemocratic. The many Asian voices promoting democracy as at one with Asian humanisms have significance for all who care about the future of human freedom because, given Asia's ever larger weight in the world, Asian actions and ideals will impact on all humanity. In fact, Asia can be decisive for the future of human rights.

Ironically, the notion that Asia did well economically because of "soft authoritarianism" is an American idea concocted in the 1960s as the US economy seemed to run into trouble and Japan's economy soared. The idea resonated with American neo-conservative views that the 1960s produced too much freedom and disorder in the United States. It was not until the 1970s that rulers in Singapore welcomed this perspective that Asian enlightened authoritarianism was superior to Western liberal democracy. They did so upon reconsidering the dominant power of the ruling party in Malaysia, which had limited its democracy in order to contain potential communalist strife.[4] They did so, moreover, to confront threats to Singapore's survival after the United States had been forced out of Vietnam in 1975.

Malaysia committed itself to authoritarianism following murderous communalist conflict in 1969, after Chinese Malaysians did far better in an election than Muslim Malaysians, who had expected to win easily. That outcome seemed to subvert the promise of democracy dominated by Muslim Malaysians, people who had forced Chinese-dominated Singapore into a separate existence in 1965 and had incorporated Muslim-dominated Sabah and Sarawak on the island of Borneo, and who, therefore, through their newly crafted larger percentage of Muslim Malays, would electorally control politics and leverage that power to narrow the economic gap with Chinese Malaysians. When democratic elections did not deliver what the Muslim Malaysian political elite sought, an alliance was forged to guarantee the equitable raising of Muslim Malaysians. Similar affirmative discriminations had been integral to India's democracy from its inception.

Public discussion of "sensitive issues (citizenship rights of non-Malays, position of the Sultans, status of the Malay language, and Malay special rights)" was prohibited.[5] The notion of shared Asian values is meant to deal with the experienced conflict in Malaysia between two communities, one associated with Muslim values and one with the amalgam of values tied to Confucianism, Buddhism, and Taoism. The political project legitimated as Asian values is both an ideological obfuscation of and a Malaysian strategy for equitable nation-building that will, hopefully, avoid divisive communalist clashes and preserve a fragile and ultimately valuable national entity.[6]

In actuality, neither the Malaysian state nor the one in Singapore was constructed on a model of Asian values. Both were legatees of the British colonial state. "Those who glibly laud the success of East Asian Confucianist societies should perhaps consider rediscovering the roots of this highly authoritarian brand of state-centered capitalism in anticommunist Western imperialism."[7] But India's democracy also continues British colonial institutions yet, as in Malaysia, tackles the communalist issue in ways dissimilar to how the English treated the Irish.

Singapore's patriarch Lee Kuan Yew, only late in life, long after Singapore had already risen economically in an earlier era, when English was promoted in Singapore as an international language of science and business, turned to the notion of Asian values to try to build a common Singapore national identity that would include people who identified with Islam and Hinduism as well as Chinese Confucians. Yet the Chinese element dominated. A speak-Mandarin campaign was launched in 1979 although less than one percent of Singaporeans considered Mandarin a native language. Communalist equity is never easy, anywhere, ever.

Singapore has abandoned its synthetic project for a multicultural one.[8] Although seldom noted in America, Singapore's leaders, wooing America to stay in Asia for Singapore's security, spoke in the mid-1990s of combining the best of the East with the best of the West. Communalist distinctions did not readily give way to propaganda about common Asian or Confucian values. Likewise, in Malaysia, "racial polarization has increased."[9] In short, in Malaysia and Singapore, what is wrongly dubbed Asian Authoritarianism is a difficult project originally legitimated as building an equitable nation with a common identity.

The governments of Singapore and Malaysia are neither blood-thirsty nor parasitic. Many analysts would classify Malaysia, which has held numerous contested elections, as a flawed democracy rather than an authoritarian state. Democratization anywhere and everywhere is a prolonged and flawed process. Surely the leaders of Malaysia's government, which outlaws street demonstrations and tries to monopolize the media to promote the views of the ruling national front, can easily conclude that the flaws in nineteenth- and twentieth-century American democracy, including legal slavery and institutionalized racism, were far, far worse.

What's worrisome are the rationales for this Asian innovation proposed by influential people in the West who have lost faith in democracy. Concerned over problems at home, many analysts in the West have accepted the notion that there is a correlation between authoritarian Asian cultural values and Asian economic success. Actually the claim that hard work, diligence, and politeness are authoritarian or uniquely Asian or Confucian is absurd. Nineteenth-century Victorian European values were similarly defined. Counterparts exist in virtually all cultures. Propagandists for Asian Authoritarianism ignore what lies pulsating beneath the façade of a nostalgic desire for repressive normality – strong Asian individuals.

Chinese see their male children as rambunctious, almost uncontrollable. Confucius declared that he could not control his self-regarding passions until he was 70. Most Chinese so worry about the narrow, materialist greed of their brethren that they often find Chinese the world's least public-regarding people.[10] Victor Chung, one of the richest Southeast Asians of Chinese descent, proclaims, "Money is the only measure of value; nothing else is real."[11] Familism is said by many Chinese analysts to preclude concern for the common weal. In short, Chinese do not invariably surrender local concerns to some proclaimed national good. Likewise in Japan, "Voters will prefer a candidate who works for local benefits over one who works for more universal benefits."[12]

UNIQUE ASIAN VALUES?

Roger Ames has shown that Confucians have a very strong sense of self. Indeed, feeling themselves overly selfish and factionalized, early twentieth-century Chinese democrats envied European democracies their national cooperation, harmony, and solidaristic energies.[13] The proclamation of unique Asian values as an actualized harmonious community base of so-called Asian Authoritarianism is pure propaganda.

The project is appealing, nonetheless, to many hardliners in China who experience chauvinistic pleasure in claiming moral superiority over former oppressors. It also appeals to Chinese who fear that rapid democratization could destabilize a fragile status quo so as to make former Yugoslavia and the former Soviet Union seem peaceful and united by comparison.[14]

In Singapore too, Asian values seemed a political imperative of national survival meant to inculcate "new values" in people "with little shared sense of national identity."[15] In addition, Singapore's Lee Kuan Yew was betting that xenophobic-militaristic tendencies in China would win out in China's post-Deng succession. Lee would persuade an emerging Chinese Leviathan whose ships and troops might soon be heading south that Singapore was not its enemy.[16]

Singapore has serious survival problems. It is surrounded by Malay Muslim nations and can be seen as a Chinese fifth column. It is mocked as "a Chinese shrimp in a Malay sea." It may have seemed to draw too close to China after Lee Kuan Yew supported the crushing in spring 1989 of China's burgeoning democracy movement. In the 1990s Singapore has had to side with ASEAN efforts to deter Chinese expansion in possibly oil-rich waters just off their coasts that a distant China with a bigger navy claims and seizes. Singapore must prove to neighbors it is not a Chinese fifth column.

> Adopting a policy of national harmony, the Singapore government no longer maintains Chinese . . . as the only official language. Instead, Malay has been stipulated as an official language. Along with Chinese, Tamil and English, they make up four equally official languages.[17]

Thus Singapore's boasts about the unique superiority of Asian values actually thinly mask ordinary and threatening tensions. The popular acceptance in Singapore of a survivalist need to resist palpable dangers permits repression to be largely self-repression. The ideology of Asian values obscures painful political problems.

Similarly the popular basis of support for Malaysia's ruling front is hidden by the misleading language of Asian values. The rise of Dr Mahathir's Bumiputra Investment Foundation, including its National Equity Corporation, caused apprehension among Malaysians of Chinese ancestry because its activities seemed overly biased in favor of Malaysians who were Muslim. Also, the government tried to reduce foreign corporate involvement, thereby slowing economic growth, which hurt business interests. Only after the global depression and international debt crisis of 1982 made capital scarce did Malaysia open up to joining East Asian economic dynamism. When the 1985 Plaza Accord on foreign exchange rates suddenly gave Japan, Taiwan, and South Korean light industry workers higher wages that made their exports uncompetitive in American import markets and also gave the East Asian economies a bonanza in foreign exchange, Malaysia, because of its 1982 shift, was ready to welcome their capital, technology, and market know-how to manufacture products to be exported to the United States. Wealth expansion zoomed up as Malaysia welcomed foreign investors.

Still, the ruling front was challenged by growing Islamic fundamentalist sentiment,[18] which the front tried to co-opt, and by open partisanship by Chinese Malaysians, who felt increasingly ill-treated by the ruling front. In short, not only was Malaysia's growth not caused by Asian values, but, in addition, the communalist split has not healed. Some richer Malaysians of Chinese descent have emigrated to the Perth area of West Australia, while some poorer ones have gone to Hong Kong, both "disaffected by their country's discriminatory policies."[19] Attaining communalist equity is not easy.

A national agenda of economic openness, shared cultural values, communalist equity, and national growth promoted by strong states with energetic leaders may make great sense. But, in fact, there is "increasing ethnic polarization."[20] The sources of Malaysia's impressive growth lie in particular economic policies unrelated to Asian values. Nonetheless, Malaysia's project of communalist equity is most meritorious.

Any person aware of Catholic–Protestant communalist struggles in Ireland or the long history of racial and ethnic strife in the United States or similar divisive issues almost everywhere should not conclude that the rulers of Malaysia and Singapore have taken a uniquely erroneous path. There is no known wisdom on tamping down communalist tensions that guarantees civic peace, openness, and empathetic identification. Surely Americans should remember how long its ruling groups kept one community enchained in slavery. Legal emancipation was no easy thing to achieve while maintaining national union and political democracy.

Even after an amended Constitution ended slavery in the USA, racists rolled back the gains of the Civil War and reimposed a reign of terror on the African-American community for almost another century. At the outset of the twenty-first century, racism still pervades the United States such that communalist bloc voting is pervasive and the liberal-democratic norm of "one person, one vote" remains an unrealized ideal, indeed, an experienced threat to many in the numerically dominant group, such that communalist politics cripples and misshapes the attempt to make democracy inclusive in the United States.[21] While critics insist that Asian values in Malaysia are merely a unique cover for

Muslim hegemony and in Singapore for Chinese hegemony, actually, as shown by the treatment of Irish Catholics by the English and of African-Americans by European Americans in the USA, all fledgling democracies have problems with true inclusiveness. All are flawed democracies. East/West polar binaries can misleadingly elide Western flaws and emphasize Eastern ones.

The construction of a political identity to hold a nation together is not easy. Even when England first rose, it experienced itself as on the defensive, threatened by powerful and ubiquitous Catholic enemies which could even subvert the nation's cultural essence. "Under Elizabeth, England was 'the beleaguered isle,' holding on against fearful odds in face of a hostile Europe." The view spread that only "divine favour" led England to be able to defeat the Spanish Armada and to escape the Gunpowder Plot.[22] Eliding London's cruel mistreatment of Irish Catholics, England's cause was presented as religious human dignity, the birthright of a free people, God's chosen. In reality, division and suspicion were papered over with a peculiar notion of English values, very much as Asian values are used in Singapore and Kuala Lumpur. Asian values are but a myth and a project, an experiential imperative of national survival.

But rulers in Singapore and Malaysia have not sought understanding for efforts to deal with explosive problems. Rather, they insist they are a model of success. In fact, communalist division and mistrust simmer. Consequently there is no basis for the claim embraced by many neo-conservatives in China and the West that Asia's great economic achievements along with political stability have been premised on proven policies of Asian Authoritarianism. The discourse on Asian values obscures the actual sources of Asian growth as well as the indigenous roots of democracy.

As with post-World War II Austria, Italy, and Germany, Japan's constitutional democracy built on its democratic heritage, including the unique Taisho era (1912–26) electoral system of multiple seats but one vote. Japanese re-institutionalized their democracy after World War II.[23] Every nation's democracy is crafted to suit that nation's particularities.[24] Humanistic concern for human rights in Japan has a long and deep history.[25] But contingent events such as the Great Depression and the militarist policies of the Showa emperor prematurely but temporarily ended a prior, truly Japanese effort to craft a suitable democracy.

Apologists for Asian Authoritarianism treat the Japanese as mere putty and insist that the United States "imposed" democracy on an essentially authoritarian Japan which inherently resists human rights activism.[26] In contrast, Japanese Nobel Laureate Kenzaburo Oe finds that Japan's constitution, which Americans helped craft, reflected the aspirations of most Japanese, while the constitutions drafted by Japanese reactionaries did not.[27] Since all civilizations are full of diverse possibilities, including democratic ones, only a nasty and narrow view of Japanese culture will not see that Japan too enjoys democratic potentials.

Proponents of Asian Authoritarianism, however, reproduce the self-blinding imperialist argument for Enlightened Despotism. In the English colonial discourse, traditional Asians lack the capacity for democratic self-government. Respect for the indigenous culture therefore meant providing authoritarian rule that brought political tranquility, economic prosperity, and cultural continuity. This Orientalist colonial discourse is regurgitated in finding that China's great 1989 democracy movement sought "better living conditions, not democracy."[28]

From Korea, the world's most Confucian society, President Kim Dae Jung wrote "A Response to Lee Kuan Yew" on "The Myth of Asia's Anti-Democratic Values." Mr Kim found that "Asia has a rich heritage of democracy-oriented philosophies and traditions." In fact, "Asians developed these [democratic] ideas long before the Europeans did."[29] One finds democratic elements in Mengzi's (Mencius) people-based philosophy.[30]

> Such an understanding [of our Asian cultures as democratic] can also be derived from Gautama Buddha's teaching that all creatures and things possess a Buddha-like quality ... In fact, Asia has achieved the most remarkable record of democratization of any region since 1974. By 1990 a majority of Asian countries were democratic, compared to a 45 percent democratization rate worldwide.

Mr Kim concluded that "The biggest obstacle [to democratization] is not ... cultural heritage but the resistance of authoritarian rulers and their apologists."[31] The dictators in "Beijing and Rangoon are most opposed" to democracy and human rights.[32]

Tyrants the world over rationalize despotic evil as patriotic good. Nobel Peace Prize Winner Aung San Suu Kyi, whose political party in Burma overwhelmingly won the May 1990 democratic election, only to be placed under house arrest by a cruel military junta, noted that "There is nothing new in ... governments seeking to justify ... authoritarian rule by denouncing liberal democratic principles as alien. ... [T]hey claim for themselves the ... sole right to decide what ... conform[s] to indigenous cultural norms."[33] As a scholar of Buddhism, Aung San Suu Kyi found the religion supportive of democracy.[34]

THE JAPANESE PARADIGM

All cultures contain democratic elements. Each nation must institutionalize democracy in its own way. Consequently, the democratic institutions of the federalist United States might have much in common with those of federalist India, while a more nationally centralized France might be more like a nationally centralized Japan. Likewise, Taiwan and Italy have a lot in common.

The opposition of West and East misleads. There is no such thing as Western democracy, which, in fact, is a rhetorical category, not an analytical one.

The usual contrast between a so-called "West" and a so-called "East" such that the West allegedly privileges the individual over the group while the East privileges the group over the individual forgets that all nation-states put the national whole first. One cannot choose not to pay taxes for policies of which one disapproves. One is required to risk one's life in war when called on to do so. In business, sports, or any other endeavor, citizens are told in the supposedly individualistic United States to get on the team and subordinate themselves to the group's purpose. "There is no 'I' in team" is the repeated refrain of the leader. The group comes before the individual in "the West" too. In fact, when England's John Stuart Mill argued against stifling the opinion of the one, it was mainly because to suppress the one could injure the many.

Legitimators of Asian Authoritarianism who dismiss human rights concerns as mere selfishness do not see how much of that concern is religiously rooted. To dismiss human rights commitments reveals an extraordinary religious intolerance, an inability to hear the moral worth of ultimate human values.

Every culture cares about the dignity of its people. Asia nourishes magnificent and distinctive people as a high priority. In fact

> throughout Asian history there has been a broad awareness of the individual as a morally self-directed and responsible entity – in the Brahmin's lonely working out of his individual karma, in the Buddhist's progress toward enlightenment, and in the . . . humanistic self-cultivation of the . . . Confucian.[35]

Asia also includes brilliant charismatic leaders in places such as Malaysia and Singapore.

Defenders of Asian Authoritarianism appeal to prejudices when they dismiss democracy, claiming it as the cause of "slow economic growth in democracies like India and the Philippines, as well as the desperate . . . conditions in Russia."[36] Actually, statistical studies show there is nothing to the assertion that democracy hurts development.[37] No sensible economist finds that India's rate of growth is caused by its constitutional political system. Conversely, Singapore was doing well economically long before it decided to promote Confucianism. Likewise, Malaysia remains a land not of shared Asian values, but of two major communities. The notion that Asian Authoritarianism is the unique source of economic success and communalist harmony is untrue.

President Ramos of the Philippines, when informed that Singapore's leading patriarch Lee Kuan Yew had suggested that the Philippines could solve its problems through authoritarianism, acidly responded that the Philippine people had just liberated themselves from two decades of authoritarian rule under Ferdinand Marcos, who had plunged the Philippines from being the richest country in Southeast Asia to the poorest. Ramos said that the authoritarian "prescription fails to consider our ill-fated flirtation with authoritarianism not so long ago." The Philippines economy is doing far better with democracy than with Marcos's crony kleptocracy. China's dictators will not find solutions in Asian Authoritarianism.

Most people take Japan's success as defining the Asian way. Singapore's rulers contend that a political economy that combines "a dominant party system, a centralized bureaucracy and a strong interventionist government" is "a final form"[38] pioneered in Japan, emulated in South Korea and Taiwan, successfully institutionalized in Singapore and now being copied by China and Southeast Asian governments. "Authoritarian" Japan supposedly is humankind's better future.

Japan has in fact been a democracy since the end of the Asian-Pacific War.[39] The dominant party system is not in power in Japan, Taiwan, or Korea. It never was a reality in South Korea. In Japan, where it was a fact for a period of time, it emerged from a democratic process of building a broad national consensus.[40] Japan is democratic.

Still, the era of hegemony for the Liberal Democratic Party in Japan was just that, a moment. In Taiwan, where an opposition party controls the capital region, a dominant party system never was institutionalized. The prior ruling party split in the 1990s. The supposedly final and general Asian authoritarian polity, the dominant party system, survives only in Malaysia and Singapore. If ruling groups choose to emulate Asian Authoritarianism, they, in fact, will be emulating two unproven attempts to resolve difficult communalist dilemmas masked as a secret of economic success.

Yet, the plaint that liberal democracy, understood as a continuing clash of individuals and interests, is in conflict with Confucian or Muslim values is a real experience. The conventional Anglo-American self-understanding of democracy in which a free people emerged from a democratic culture of Protestant individualism is dangerously misleading. The description of democracy as a clash of interests where "ins" and "outs" regularly replace each other in a democratic culture which thrives on individualism slights how difficult it was to get beyond a narrow, elite conservative consensus even in Britain.[41]

To put it anachronistically, the West long ago followed today's Asian route to democracy of building on a grand conservative coalition.[42] Many pro-democratic people misunderstand the long and tortuous struggle to broaden and deepen democracy when they do not see that even in England, France, and America the original successful democratic consensus was made possible by a broad and moderate alliance that did not immediately welcome a transfer of political power to militant challengers. Grand conservative coalitions help institutionalize fledgling democracies. This general truth is now increasingly apparent to democrats involved in political transitions defined in terms of reconciliation in Latin America, South Africa, and Southern Europe.[43]

Thus, the standard Anglo-American description of democracy as premised on individualism and clashing interests is a mystification which misunderstands democracy's own early history, even in England and America. The actual history of how non-conforming Protestants had to flee England to find religious freedom for their communities or how English Protestants long oppressed and suppressed the community of Irish Catholics should be a reminder of how long and difficult is the struggle for inclusiveness, equity, and democracy among communities the world over.

A memory of John Stuart Mill as a champion of English culture's individualism gets Mill all wrong. His classic essay "On Liberty" is, in large part, a description of how English Protestant culture, far from being a culture of individualism and tolerance that facilitated robust democratic clashes, was, in fact, still an enemy of liberty more than two hundred years after Protestant pilgrims fled to America and Irish Catholics were slaughtered. Mill pointed to an "infirmity of English minds" that led regularly to a "revival of bigotry" because of the nature of the religion. "The ravings of fanatics or charlatans from the pulpit" provide "no security of the public mind." Consequently, "this country [is] not a place of mental freedom." Instead, "every one lives as under the eye of a hostile and dreaded censorship." Far from welcoming assertive individuals, Calvinism insists on docile surrender to God's way. The result is a tyranny that will "maim by compression, like a Chinese lady's foot, every part of human nature which stands out." English Protestantism, Mill found, supports a fanatic moral intolerance that wars against individual joy and dignity. It has provided a "sanction to slavery"; "it inculcates submission to all authority."

In contrast, non-Christians have produced "a large portion of the noblest and most valuable moral teachings." "It is in the Koran, not the New Testament, that we read the maxim – 'A ruler who appoints any man to office when there is in his dominions another man better qualified for it, sins against God and against the State.'"[44] In fact, English Protestant culture, as Asian cultures, holds strong hierarchical and authoritarian tendencies.[45]

OPPOSING ASIAN AUTHORITARIANISM

The continuing challenge to democracy from Anglo-Protestants who would preserve human dignity by ferreting out homosexuals, criminalizing abortion, censoring all that is called obscene and by having the state promote Christianity is real even today. To understand what actually makes for the flourishing of democracy and human rights that can nourish people with differing moral ultimates, it is most important not to imagine Anglo-American Christian culture as some utopian idyll that, in fact, it never was, and certainly is not yet today.

The real West was not a singularly open culture that happily adopted all that was new and progressive, as imagined by Asian Authoritarians who read

Western culture as uniquely democratic. The polar binary of East versus West, Asia versus Europe obscures similar struggles in all societies.

As the great German novelist Thomas Mann put it in 1914,

> Whoever would aspire to transform Germany into a middle-class democracy in the Western-Roman sense and spirit would wish to take away from her all that is best and complex, to take away the problematic character that really makes up her nationality; he would make her dull, shallow, stupid, and un-German, and he would therefore be antinationalist who insisted that Germany became a nation in a foreign sense and spirit.[46]

A similar cultural divide expressed as pitting patriots against aliens murderously split England in the sixteenth and seventeenth centuries. Heartfelt cultural nationalists the world over, including America and Europe today, still fear full democratization. Thus, purifying cultural, religious, nationalistic, and communalist passions can always be mobilized against the tolerant heterogeneity of democracy, taken as an immoral relativism.

All nations, even England, built the new nation-state in a context of national defensiveness and great anxieties. The Asian values discourse obscures the divisions in both East and West. Malaysia's Prime Minister Mahathir contrasts a Christian West, the executioner, with an East of Muslim and other civilizations of profound wisdom made into victims. Any policy disagreement with "the West" can then be interpreted as resistance to the executioner's attempt to keep the victim vulnerable, weak, and poor. This is the worldview of Confucian authoritarians in China and their factional Islamic counterparts in Iran or Malaysia. For people who see through such eye-glasses, the United States opposes an East Asian Economic Conference only because the US wants to stop East Asia from developing "into the world's most dynamic economic powerhouse," because the US wants to maintain "its dominant power in the region."[47] Stigmatizing any other explanation in advance as a lie does not understand policy in the United States.

Actually, East Asia already is the world's most dynamic economic powerhouse. What inspired a monstrous new vision of America was the victory of America's microelectronic weaponry in the Gulf War and the implosion of Soviet Communism to be replaced by governments seeking, politically, a liberal democracy and, economically, a world market orientation, both conceived of as inherently Western. These events engendered a fear among anti-imperialist cultural purists that America was all-powerful and that all others were nakedly vulnerable.

Members of the privileged party-state apparatus in China were similarly anxious after the implosions in East Europe, Central Europe, Mongolia, and the former Soviet Union made ruling groups in Beijing experience themselves as lone survivors of dictatorial Leninist socialism in great states. Fearing that human rights, liberty, and democratization would win the hearts of the young, China's despots, feeling extremely vulnerable, energized a campaign to persuade their people that Confucian authoritarianism, true Chinese culture, was the secret of economic success throughout the region and that alien values such as liberal democracy were part of a plot by imperialists who were out to run the world, and who therefore wanted to destroy authoritarian Chinese cultural values which supposedly gave China the wherewithal to rise in dignity as one of the great and prospering world powers. China's dictators reached out to the governments of Malaysia and Singapore which felt similar anxieties about a purportedly crusading America.

MISUNDERSTANDING THE WEST

Muslims, as Chinese, can feel under the gun. They often imagine the United States and the West as out to get all the rising peoples of Asia. Human rights and democracy are then imagined "as a mandate to intervene."[48] Asian authoritarians see little but hypocrisy in America's human rights diplomacy.

Are children starving in Iraq? It is not because a predatory Iraqi government has policy priorities that determine this outcome but because of a US-willed United Nations embargo. Are Palestinian rights still denied? The United States must be the real cause. Do children die of starvation in the Third World? It cannot be because of anything their own governments have done but because Northern bankers (Jews?) manipulate interest rates.[49]

Because these Muslim friends of the downtrodden imagine themselves as the champions of human rights, they seek proof that "the West" actually is a major violator of human rights. They ask the UN to investigate the causes of the huge prison population and the large number of executions in the United States. They urge an examination of the "new citizenship and immigration laws in Europe" for evidence of systematic discrimination against Muslims.[50]

At the same time that the United States is seen as a powerful threat, America and/or the West is/are, contrariwise, imagined in the Asianist discourse as (a) pitiful failure(s) "buffeted by unemployment and recession."[51] Crime and violence are seen as spreading in the West such that "the very fabric of Western society" unravels. Western exports "are no longer competitive." People drown in a "spiritual and psychological morass," all supposedly caused by unbridled individualism, materialism, hedonism, and greed, that is, caused by putting human freedom above God's moral plan.[52] Drugs, family disintegration, and increasing poverty are the destiny of the West. Anything and everything, to "Eastern" cultural purifiers, must be done to keep out an antireligious "West."

This language of keeping satanic strangers outside the gates appeals to chauvinists in China who imagine their Great Wall as protecting them by keeping foreigners out. For nativistic purists, people should not be so concerned about material prosperity. They should curb their appetites and integrate into society harmoniously.[53] True liberation, after all, is an inner liberation in which one becomes a vehicle for God's way.[54] The West's "Capitalist democracy . . . is a betrayal of God's ultimate truth."[55] The "question is whether Westerners . . . are capable of believing . . . in God."[56] The religious intolerance in this comprehension of the West is manifest. Another community's notion of human dignity is treated as a devilish conspiracy.

Such discourse defends communalist cleansing. It is a poisonous threat to humanity from Christian Serbia to Islamic Iran. The purifiers would end openness and interchange, derail peace and prosperity, crush freedom and democracy. Their perspective does not permit understanding and healing among the major human communities.

Yet the Asian Authoritarian attack on allegedly Western-style human rights, understood as merely secular individual freedoms, is a two-edged sword. It contains, besides the possibility of a tyrannical reaction, also the possibility of a broadened human rights dialogue that could advance the cause of freedom and dignity. The genuine concern for democracy and human rights in this Asian perspective should not be gainsaid.

Malaysia's prestigious advocate of anti-imperialist culturalism, Chandra Muzaffar, after all, in considering the question of "whether development should precede democracy," answers "no."[57] The source of East Asia's economic success is not dictatorship and the repression of labor. "Effective human resource development . . . rather than political regimentation, is the secret of their success."[58] He denies that the political restrictions on freedom in Malaysia imposed "through the Internal Security Act (ISA), which allows for detention without trial, and other similar laws" are the sources of Malaysia's economic development.[59] He instead credits "parliamentary democracy."

> It is this system of governance which legitimates both multi-party competition and political dissent that is partly responsible for social stability – which in turn has facilitated continuous economic growth and progress. The ability of the national leadership to balance the diverse, sometimes conflicting interests of the different communities . . . should also be given due weight.[60]

The defense of Asian Authoritarianism obscures continuing struggle, East and West, between democrats and their enemies. Yet the Asian message of communalist equity is worth heeding at a time when anti-democratic and culturally chauvinistic communalist forces have been gaining strength worldwide. To the extent that East Asia has built insulating statist institutions to buffer its people a bit from the pains of polarizing global finance and has also imagined the issue of equitable growth as a priority matter, it is difficult to resist the contention of Malaysia's Prime Minister Mahathir that it is worth learning from Asia. Chandra Muzaffar believes "the West" is too greedy to learn. The inequality of the neo-liberal world that became ideologically hegemonic in the West in the 1980s is immoral to those within the Asian value discourse who marvel that no Western government will "introduce legislation which seeks to close the income gap . . . Most of all, no government would have the courage to formulate . . . policies which would result perhaps in a lower standard of living for the upper class and sections of the middle class in order to enhance the quality of life of the majority of the people."[61]

Since stable democracy is difficult to maintain without growth plus equity, it is just possible that democratic institutionalization in a rapidly growing and more equitable Asia may, in the long run, prove far more stable than in a neo-liberal West. One can imagine a future where neo-liberal and polarizing nations in "the West" find their democracies economically buffeted and socially weakened such that revivalist communalisms or fascist forces rise, while equitable and growing Asian nations become the homeland of stable and dynamic democracies.

Since a fledgling democracy seldom includes all the people after the initial breakthrough to democracy, if the economic pie does not expand, then the only way the previously excluded can get their fair share of the pie is to take a big bite out of what established elites already have. Fear of this economic attack will usually lead to political resistance by elites. Political polarization and a democratic failure can result. A polarizing democracy in neo-liberal guise can eventually seem the enemy of most of the people. This danger challenges numerous new democracies. Thus it is more than imaginable that the twenty-first century will find a growing and equitable Asia to be the world center of democracy and human rights, should Asia's culturally purist and fascist-prone forces be defeated.

State intervention on behalf of equity – as with the way Singapore tries to make housing available to all, as with Malaysia's success with state aid to rural dwellers – can help sustain democratic institutionalization. Because neo-liberal orthodoxy wrongly conflates a free market (not just a market orientation) with political democracy, the defenders of Asian values may well be right in their prognosis that the momentarily hegemonic neo-liberal prescription is a formula for political disintegration and economic failure, a counterproductive project that is making more likely a world where democracy is far less stably rooted.

There then is truth in the contention "that the West has a lot to learn from the East."[62] But this is because any human can learn from any other who does well, not because East and West are coherent cultural categories. They are not. They are symbols mobilized and manipulated for political purposes. In the European socialist version of the nativistic stigmatization of the great civilizations of Asia and their contemporary economic achievements, Greece's Andreas Papandreou blamed "low wage workers in places like East Asia" for Europe's unemployment, economic stagnation, and "frenetic competition" at the cost of social welfare so that Europe can keep up with Asians.[63] Europeans generally tend to experience the new globalization as threats to their social welfare states from unfair Asian competition. In this manic portrayal of an Asia of miserable prison, slave, and sweatshop labor, one would never guess that Hong Kong's domestic product per capita actually is already higher than Britain's, that South Korea outproduces France or Italy. Automobile workers in Japan earn far more than their counterparts in the United States. Perhaps conventional Western notions about rising Asia are more out of touch than are Asian notions of the declining West.

In an era of economic globalization and penetrable borders, many workers in industrial democracies are anxious that free trade with nations whose authoritarian governments smash unions and permit child labor puts at risk the jobs of workers in democracies with legal unions and protected rights. That is not how the issue looks from Asia. Aware that early industrialization in Europe included similar or worse labor abuses, the Asians speak for all developing nations in denouncing a supposed human rights concern for the conditions of labor among developing nations as, in fact, a hypocritical attempt by rich nations to keep poor nations poor.

The governments in France and the United States, which have been trying to negotiate minimum labor standards as a condition of market access, are not impressed by an argument similar to saying that because Westerners legitimated torture in the middle ages, they should not try to stop torture in the twenty-first century. Asians seem hypocritical in claiming to put economic rights before political ones but then refusing to recognize the legitimacy of economic rights. The claim that Asian values put group rights and economic rights first is not true. Perhaps the Asian culturalists would be better off focusing more on basic human rights and insisting that economic policy was a matter of sovereign choice, of strategic economic policy.

Most startling, given the Asian culturalist approach to human rights, many Asian public figures embrace the universality of human rights concerns. The government of Malaysia has been publicly angry at Burma for its ill-treatment of Muslims (the Rohinggas), who were forced to flee into Bangladesh.[64] Yet they do not practice at home what they preach abroad, even as their economies boom. Growth does not automatically turn into democracy. The Asian Authoritarian tendency at the end of the twentieth century is more growth, but less democracy: "the political systems in Malaysia and Singapore have progressively become more authoritarian."[65] It was courageous people who struggled politically and risked their lives who ended torture and tyranny in South Korea and Taiwan. Free markets did not evolve into democratic polities.

Even the government of China, which grew more authoritarian after 1989, did not denounce human rights as such. Instead, it chose to defend its human rights record and attack that of its detractors. In response to charges made to the United Nation Human Rights Commission in 1995 that China systematically violated human rights, the Chinese representative boasted of the achievements of China in this field. Beyond hypocrisy's bow to virtue, there is a possibility that Asian self-confidence and growth are facilitating a feeling of superiority that makes Asian governments willing to challenge the West even on human rights.

A Chinese scholar explains that in the view of the Chinese government, "human rights is no longer seen as a 'slogan of the bourgeois.'" People should be "promoting human rights and the rule of law today." "Deprivation of human rights is illegal at all times." As in Western traditions, "Confucianism, Taoism and Buddhism are also full of the idea of freedom." Chinese culture too respects personal dignity. Proud of the many Chinese who "gave their lives for righteousness and for a just cause, assailed dark and corrupt politics and even laid claims to the right of wiping out tyrants," this Chinese analyst declared, "The Chinese people are advocating and promoting human rights together with the people all over the world."[66]

Another Chinese analyst pointed to the hypocrisy of Americans who forget that the California constitution of 1879 did not include people from China as humans with rights,[67] and who ignorantly criticize China's heritage, not knowing that China is the home of Huang Zongxi, a Ming Dynasty philosopher who, two centuries before the European Enlightenment, developed a legitimation for legal rights for all the people.[68] Human dignity is a living tradition.

> For instance, when the Manchus . . . enforced on the Han the brutal decree that "those who keep their hair cannot keep their heads," the customary right of the Hans of wearing their hair long was infringed. . . . During the "cultural revolution" . . . [there] were unbridled insults to the right of human dignity. Reflections upon the latter prompted the Chinese legislature to include the phrase "human dignity of citizens shall not be infringed upon" as a legal right of citizens in the Constitution of 1982.[69]

Proud of the April 5, 1976 struggle against the group who would have continued to assault the human rights and human dignity of China's people,[70] this analyst welcomed "struggle waged by the people" so that "those in power are compelled to legalize human rights."[71]

The project of democracy and human rights has attained such legitimacy that neither Singapore nor Malaysia nor China boasts that its way is superior because it negates human rights. The Asian value discourse insists that the Asian human rights record is superior to that of their accusers.

Democratic Japan has yet to have a civil rights revolution and has yet to face up to its long mistreatment of Asians in Japan. That is, in Japan, as in racist America, formal democratic institutions are not a self-enforcing guarantee that human rights abuses cannot occur. On this too, the Asian value critique is again correct. It is worth listening when Chinese or Malaysians or Singaporeans address continued human rights violations elsewhere.

ASIA ADVANCES HUMAN RIGHTS

It is also worth remembering how recent is the rise of human rights as a legitimate international relations issue. Until the United States civil rights revolution of the 1960s, until America ended its bombing of Vietnamese in Asia, the US had too much blood on its hands to seem sincere in a human rights posture. Of course, Malaysia, Indonesia, and Singapore in that era worried about their own Communist "subversives" tied to Mao's China and fully supported the American war in Vietnam. The world following the US withdrawal from Vietnam from 1973 to 1975 changed as the plight of over a million Vietnamese boat-people, publicity for the crimes of the Mao era, and the genocidal acts of Pol Pot's Khmer Rouge helped legitimate a global human rights agenda with striking swiftness.

Once the Helsinki accords put human rights high on the political agenda, it would have been difficult for the United States not to side with the forces of democracy and human rights. Aided by the new electronic media and nongovernmental organizations committed to human rights, the issue of human rights was globalized. Some specialists find Asian NGOs the world's most vigorous. Consequently, the US government at the end of the 1970s no longer was silent about repression in Seoul and Taipei and Manila. Consequently, the factors that permitted Mao's China to escape scrutiny on systematic violations of most basic human rights disappeared in the post-Mao era. This cannot help but seem unfair to Asian Authoritarians who formerly had the support of the United States in a prior era of repression.

In short, global political change has put human rights much higher on the political agenda at the end of the twentieth century. Muthiah Alagappa concedes that indigenous Asian forces favoring democracy and human rights are spreading and growing stronger in Malaysia, Singapore, Indonesia and China. He acknowledges that the discourse of democracy has become virtually hegemonic.[72] In fact, given how slowly Europe progressed on human rights after Magna Carta in 1215, the extraordinary rise of human rights sentiment in Asia in the last quarter of the twentieth century could betoken a great future potential for democracy and human rights. Given an opportunity, Burmese would again opt for democracy. I believe Chinese would embrace democracy if they but had the opportunity. In sum, Asia could become a world leader in democratization and human rights.

Malaysian Prime Minister Mahathir Mohamad found in 1995:

> When Malaya became independent in 1957, our per capita income was lower than that of Haiti. Haiti did not take the path of

democracy. We did. Haiti today is the poorest country in all of the Americas. We now have a standard of living higher than any major economy in the Americas, save only the United States and Canada.

We could not have achieved what we have achieved without democracy.[73]

In like manner, Malaysian Deputy Prime Minister Anwar Ibrahim declared on December 7, 1994 that "human rights are enshrined in the Quran. . . . The Prophet said, 'Your lives, your possessions and your dignity are as sacred as this day (of the Great Pilgrimage).'" He noted "that more nations have been impoverished by authoritarianism than enriched by it. Authoritarian rule has been used as a masquerade for kleptocracies, bureaucratic incompetence, and . . . unbridled nepotism and corruption."[74]

Should successful and self-confident Asian democratic forces continue to grow, then the recent material defending Asian Authoritarianism will seem to be precisely what Kim Dae Jung and Aung San Suu Kyi said – a standard apologia by dictatorships. The Asia of authoritarian legitimations could give way to an almost fully democratic Asia. After all, even Samuel Huntington, who had invented legitimations for authoritarianism for a quarter of a century, in 1991 refused to rule out an Asia in which "A Chinese proponent of *glasnost* could come to power in Beijing. . . . Japan could use its growing economic clout to encourage human rights and democracy in the poor countries to which it makes loans and grants."[75] That could be the basis of a politics where Asia leads the world in promoting human rights and considers conditioning loans to the United States or European countries on ending Western racism and stopping the coddling of neo-fascist groups.

Are threats to democracy in "the West" building? Economic polarization defended as neo-liberal wisdom is a disaster for democracy. The chief officer of Barclays found in 1995 that "British capitalism's rejection of social values and reaction against earlier collectivist excesses has gone too far. Too much individualism is bad for too many individuals."[76] World pressures based on this ultra-individualism legitimated as pure market rationality are fostering political forces that facilitate proto-fascist communalist forces experienced as a minimal response to pressing problems of foreign pollution in a penetrated and polarizing world system.

As the earlier quote from Thomas Mann suggests, the emotions and experiences that produce anti-liberal chauvinist tendencies are not confined to one part of the world. Purist parochialism endangers all. In France and Germany, there is growing support among rightists for the view that Europe's economic problems are caused by an invasion of Muslims, from Turkey into Germany, from North Africa into France – a mirror image of the Asian authoritarian nightmare of invasion by "the West."

European fascism in the earlier twentieth century built on cultural purism, with tough Germanic forest dwellers ridding themselves of softening ideas of

Christianity, understood as an Asian import, and the Gauls trying to purify France of foreign influence. Blood-based anti-foreign hatred can grow in an economically anxious Europe that feels it cannot compete with exploitative Asians.[77]

The European proto-fascist argument is "that Arab Islamic immigrants cannot be assimilated." As Le Pen put it, "I love the North Africans. But their place is in North Africa." Nations, for European racial purists, are biologically distinct. Cultures are different. The enemies of national survival, which suffocate the vital energy of a unique people, are multiculturalism and homogenization. These universal humanitarian ideals, to European purists, are imports from Asia. European identities have "been attacked, colonized and corrupted by a 'foreign mentality' Judeo-Christianity. . . . Totalitarianism was born 4,000 years ago somewhere between Mesopotamia and the Jordan valley. It was born on the day when the idea of monotheism appeared." European states are enervated by Asian culture. These Asian cultures based on "oriental religion" which is "foreign to" Europeans must be expelled so that Europeans again can be free and strong and not subverted by state-imposed, Asian-style equality and multiculturalism.[78]

Christ, indeed all that is dangerously egalitarian and universalistic in the Judeo-Christian tradition, came from West Asia. These Asian values purportedly have been undermining the vital martial energies of the tribes of Europe. To save itself from millennia of Asian invasions by egalitarians, universalists, and democrats, by Christians, Jews, and Muslims, Europe must defend its unique and sacred culture from Asia, understood as the historical fount of democracy and human rights. The "other" of the "fascist" mind is the open, liberal, and human rights-oriented democrat, imagined by proto-fascist Europe as Asia, by proto-fascist Asia as Europe. An imaginatively divided geography hides a shared political problematique.

Continuing economic decline and polarization could strengthen fascism, permitting, in Europe, a greater welcome for an anti-Asian scapegoating of Muslims and Confucians. How could the East which scapegoats the West complain about policies which are a mirror image? I devoutly hope that Asians who embrace purist culturalism will instead build on their commitments to human rights and to equitable alliances among communities and peoples, that they will join the burgeoning forces of democracy and human rights that are spreading in Asia and could yet encompass almost all Asia's peoples. Should fascists again win power in Europe, the more government-guided, stable, and equitable development of Asia may have strengthened the Asian forces of human rights and democracy so as to be in a position to condemn and sanction the undemocratic Europeans. Victims of human rights violations in the West may someday need today's Asian opponents of Western human rights hypocrisy who by then would, perhaps, take pride in understanding Asian cultures as a fount of inspiration for human rights and dignity for all humankind.

NOTES

1 Edward Friedman, *The Politics of Democratization* (Boulder, CO: Westview Press, 1994), p. 1; Friedman, *National Identity and Democratic Prospects in Socialist China* (Armonk, NY: M.E. Sharpe, 1995), Chap. 12.

2 Since East and West are accordion-like terms, different viewers see the supposed opposition differently, ranging from a little West (Protestant England and Holland) against a huge East (all the rest of the world), to a big Europe, understood to include every place its cultures had a major influence (e.g. Australia, Argentina, Armenia, Alaska), against a smaller Asia, which for some would not even include Russia or the Ukraine. And, of course, some Europeans idealize Asia, rather than demonize it. But the dominant contrast pits a purportedly liberal and individualist West against an authoritarian and collectivistic East, understood by supporters of Asian Authoritarianism as an orderly and just world opposed to a narrowly selfish and self-destructive West.

3 T.J. Pempel, "Between Two Worlds," paper presented at a Conference on Asian Regionalism, Ithaca, March 1995, p. 31.

4 Haji Ahmad Zakaria, "Evolution and Development of the Political System in Malaysia," in Robert Scalapino *et al.*, eds, *Asian Political Institutionalization* (Berkeley: Institute of East Asian Studies, 1986), pp. 221–40.

5 Ibid., p. 229.

6 Negative stereotypes held by Muslim Malaysians of Chinese Malaysians mark Chinese as alien by their dietary habits, clothing, dogs at home, relatives, etc. Even converts to Islam are treated in terms of the negative stereotype such that they are deemed insincere, proof that Chinese are merely wily materialists.

7 H.A. Yum (pseud.), "The Political Process of Singapore's New Industrialization," *Social Justice* 21, no. 2 (Summer 1994), p. 87.

8 Kenneth Whiting, "Singapore Officials Abandon Efforts for National Identity," *Wisconsin State Journal* (January 30, 1995), from the Associated Press.

9 Zakaria, "Evolution and Development," p. 238.

10 Roger Ames, "The Focus-Field Self in Classical Confucianism," in Roger Ames, ed., *Self As Person in Asian Theory and Practice* (Albany: SUNY Press, 1994), pp. 187–212.

11 Lynn Pan, *Sons of the Yellow Emperor* (Tokyo: Kodansha, 1991), p. 368.

12 Toshio Nagahisa, "The Electoral Reform That Can Mobilize Japan for Security Cooperation," paper presented at a conference on Cooperation in East and Southeast Asia, Milwaukee, April 28–9, 1995, p. 3.

13 Edward Friedman, *Backward Toward Revolution* (Berkeley: University of California Press, 1974).

14 Liu Qing, "Human Rights and Democracy in China," in *Political Activism and the Prospects for Democracy in China* (Stockholm: Stockholm University Center for Pacific Asian Studies, 1995), pp. 14–27. Liu Binyan, "China: A Country Politically Rich But Also Poor," in ibid., pp. 28–31.

15 Boon Hiok Lee, "Political Institutionalization in Singapore," in Scalapino, *et al.*, eds, *Asian Political Institutionalization*, p. 203.

16 Andrew Nathan, "Beijing Blues," *New Republic* (January 23, 1995), pp. 39–40.

17 Lien-te Hung, "China's Relations with Southeast Asia," *World Outlook* (Taiwan) 3, no. 5 (September–October 1994), pp. 36–7.

18 Long Litt Woon, "Zero As Communication: The Chinese Muslim Dilemma in Malaysia," in Mikael Gravers *et al.*, eds, *Southeast Asia Between Autocracy and Democracy* (Aarhus, Denmark: Aarhus University Press, 1989), p. 125.

19 Pan, *Sons of the Yellow Emperor*, pp. 362, 367.

20 Woon, "Zero As Communication," p. 132.
21 Chandler Davidson and Bernard Grofman, eds, *Quiet Revolution in the South* (Princeton, NJ: Princeton University Press, 1994).
22 Christopher Hill, *The English Bible and the Seventeenth Century Revolution* (London: Penguin, 1995 [1994]), p. 265.
23 Masanori Nakamura, "Democratization, Peace, and Economic Development in Occupied Japan, 1945–1952," in Friedman, ed., *The Politics of Democratization*, pp. 61–80.
24 Giuseppe DiPalma, *To Craft Democracies* (Berkeley: University of California Press, 1990).
25 Richard Kagan, "Japan's International Human Rights Policy," unpublished paper.
26 Muthiah Alagappa, "Democratic Transition in Asia," East–West Center Special Reports, No. 3 (October 1994), p. 6.
27 Kenzaburo Oe, "The Day the Emperor Spoke in a Human Voice," *The New York Times Magazine* (May 7, 1995), p. 105.
28 Alagappa, "Democratic Transition," p. 13.
29 Kim Dae Jung, "A Response to Leo Kuan Yew," *Foreign Affairs* (November–December 1994), pp. 191, 192.
30 Defenders of Asian Authoritarianism respond that Mencius's people-based political philosophy never transcended paternalist patriarchy. Immanuel Kant argues that paternalism is the worst despotism. Such an approach errs in not seeing that Mencius's people-based political philosophy can be interpreted in more than one way. A people's heritage is a repertoire of possibilities. As a matter of fact Chinese despots did indeed see Mencian philosophy as too democratic in its insistence not only on putting the people first but also in legitimating the overthrow of a tyrannical ruler.

> Emperor Ming Taizu . . . was most critical of Mencius . . . The emperor even said, "If that old guy were alive today, he would be severely punished." He extirpated offensive passages, such as . . . "The people are the most elevated, next comes the state, the sovereign comes last"; "Emperor Jie and Zhou had lost the world because they lost the hearts of their people"; "I have only heard that a loner Zhou was executed, but I have not heard a sovereign was assassinated." . . . 85 chapters were deleted from the 260 chapters of Mencius. (Fu Zhengyuan, *Autocratic Tradition and Chinese Politics*, New York: Cambridge University Press, 1993, p. 60)

31 Kim, "A Response," pp. 192, 194.
32 Alagappa, "Democratic Transition," p. 8.
33 Aung San Suu Kyi, *Freedom From Fear and Other Writings* (New York: Penguin, 1991), p. 167.
34 "The tenth deity of kings, non-opposition to the will of the people (*avirodha*), tends to be singled out as a Buddhist endorsement of democracy, supported by well-known stories from the *Jakatas*. Pawridasa, a monarch who acquired an unfortunate taste for human flesh, was forced to leave his kingdom because he would not heed the people's demand that he should abandon the cannibalistic habits. A very different kind of ruler was the Buddha's penultimate incarnation on earth, the pious King Vessantara. But he too was sent into exile when in the course of his strivings for the perfections of liberality [compassion? generosity?] he gave away the white elephant of the state without the consent of the people. The real duty of non-opposition is a reminder that the legitimacy of government is founded on the consent of the people, who may withdraw their mandate at any time if they lose confidence in the ability of the ruler to serve their best interests. In invoking

the Ten Duties of Kings, the Burmese are . . . drawing on time-honored values to reinforce the validity of the political reforms they consider necessary. It is a strong argument for democracy that governments regulated by principles of accountability, respect for public opinion and the supremacy of just laws are more likely than an all-powerful ruler . . . uninhibited by the need to honor the will of the people, to observe the traditional duties of Buddhist kingship. Traditional values serve both to justify and to decipher popular expectations of democratic government" (ibid., pp. 172–3).

35 Ivan Hall, "Japan's Asia Card," *The National Interest* no. 88 (Winter 1994–5), p. 23.

36 Alagappa, "Democratic Transition," p. 9.

37 Stephen Haggard and Robert Kaufman, *The Political Economy of Democratic Transitions* (Princeton, NJ: Princeton University Press, 1995).

38 Alagappa, "Democratic Transition," p. 11.

39 There surely is no reason to doubt that an economically superior Japan can be a global leader in cultural matters, with innovations such as karaoke, toys such as Bandai's Mighty Morphin Power Rangers, electronic video games such as Nintendo's Donkey Kong and Super Mario, and Sony Walkmen harbingers of much more Japanese cultural leadership to come from lowbrow to highbrow, where Japanese architects have already won the international competition three times in the last twenty years.

40 See Nakamura, "Democratization, Peace, and Economic Development."

41 Dietrich Reuschemeyer *et al.*, *Capitalist Development and Democracy* (Chicago: University of Chicago Press, 1992).

42 Friedman, *The Politics of Democratization.*

43 Lawrence Weschler, *A Miracle, A Universe: Settling Accounts With Torturers* (New York: Pantheon Books, 1991).

44 John Stuart Mill, *On Liberty and Other Writings* (New York: Cambridge University Press, 1989 [1859]), pp. 33, 37, 61, 69, 50, 52, 51.

45 Since Mill was employed on behalf of Britain's colonial project in India, not surprisingly his work, even "On Liberty," is replete with apologias for British imperialism (ibid., pp. 12, 71–2, 96).

46 Thomas Mann, *Reflections of a Non-Political Man* (New York: Praeger, 1983 [1914]), p. 26.

47 Chandra Muzaffar, "The Clash of Civilizations or Camouflaging Dominance?" *Just Commentary* (Penang) no. 5 (September 2, 1993), p. 3.

48 Chandra Muzaffar, "High Commission for Human Rights," *Just Commentary* (Penang) no. 7 (January 3, 1994).

49 Ibid., pp. 3–4.

50 Ibid., p. 4.

51 Muzaffar, "The Clash of Civilizations," p. 4.

52 Chandra Muzaffar, "From Human Rights to Human Dignity," address to the International Conference on Rethinking Human Rights, December 6–7, 1994, p. 3.

53 Ibid., pp. 18–19.

54 Ibid., p. 20.

55 Ibid., p. 21.

56 Ibid., p. 23.

57 Ibid., p. 1.

58 Ibid., p. 3.

59 Ibid., p. 4.

60 Ibid.

61 Ibid., p. 15.

62 Alagappa, "Democratic Transition," p. 28.
63 Andreas Papandreou, "Europe Turns Left," *New Perspectives Quarterly* (Winter 1994), p. 51.
64 Alagappa, "Democratic Transition," p. 20.
65 Ibid., p. 26.
66 Xia Yong, "Three Topics on the Philosophy of Human Rights: A Chinese Perspective," *Chinese Social Science Yearbook 1994*, pp. 268, 276, 266, 269, 275, 278–9.
67 Gao Daohui, "Human Rights, Social Rights and Legal Rights," *Chinese Social Science Yearbook 1994*, p. 248.
68 Ibid., p. 257.
69 Ibid., p. 249.
70 Ibid., p. 258.
71 Ibid., p. 248.
72 Alagappa, "Democratic Transition."
73 Mahathir Mohamad, "Let's Have Mutual Cultural Enrichment," *New Straits Times* (March 16, 1995), p. 11.
74 Anwar Ibrahim, address to the Conference on Rethinking Human Rights, Kuala Lumpur, December 7, 1994.
75 Samuel Huntington, *The Third Wave: Democratization in the Late Twentieth Century* (Norman: University of Oklahoma Press, 1991), p. 8.
76 Marten Taylor, "Search for a New Economic Orthodoxy," *Financial Times* (March 16, 1965), p. 14.
77 Paul Hockenos, "Right Cultural Revolutionaries: Making Hate Safe Again in Europe," *The Nation* (September 19, 1994), pp. 271–4.
78 Pierre André Taguieff, "From Race to Culture: The New Right's View of European Identity," *Telos* nos 98–99 (Winter 1993/Spring 1994), pp. 124, 113, 117, 100, and 105.

4

AN ASIAN PERSPECTIVE ON HUMAN RIGHTS AND FREEDOM OF THE PRESS

Kishore Mahbubani

Kishore Mahbubani *is both an official in the Ministry of Foreign Affairs in Singapore and a prominent intellectual. His provocative essay, "The West and the Rest," published in 1992 set the stage for much of the subsequent East versus West debate. Here, he takes issue with one of the best defended principles in Western democracy: freedom of the press. Noting that the value of freedom of the press is virtually absolute and unchallengeable in the West, Mahbubani puts forward ten "heresies" in his critique of Western concepts of press freedom. Describing an irresponsible Western press, he asks why, especially in a democratic society, the media shouldn't also be held accountable. Although he first presented this paper in 1993, Mahbubani feels strongly that his criticisms are still valid today.*

INTRODUCTION

I would like to begin with an analogy:

> ... from the viewpoint of many Third World citizens, human rights campaigns often have a bizarre quality. For many of them it looks something like this: They are like hungry and diseased passengers on a leaky, overcrowded boat that is about to drift into treacherous waters, in which many of them will perish. The captain of the boat is often harsh, sometimes fairly and sometimes not. On the river banks stand a group of affluent, well-fed and well intentioned onlookers. As soon as these onlookers witness a passenger being flogged or imprisoned or even deprived of the right to speak, they board the ship to intervene, protecting the passengers from the captain. But those passengers remain hungry and diseased. As soon as they try to swim to the banks

80

into the arms of their benefactors, they are firmly returned to the boat, their primary sufferings unabated. This is no abstract analogy. It is exactly how the Haitians feel.[1]

This is just one of the many absurd aspects of the aggressive Western promotion of human rights at the end of the Cold War. There are many others. Yet when I tried in seminars at Harvard University to challenge the universal applicability of democracy, human rights, or freedom of the press, I discovered that these values have become virtual "sacred cows." No one could challenge their intrinsic worth. Worse still, when I persisted, I was greeted with sniggers, smug looks, and general derision. The general assumption there was that any Asian, especially a Singaporean, who challenges these concepts was only doing so in an attempt to cover up the sins of his government.

I am as convinced now as I was then that the aggressive Western promotion of democracy, human rights, and freedom of the press to the Third World at the end of the Cold War was and is a colossal mistake. This campaign is unlikely to benefit the 4.3 billion people who live outside the developed world, and perhaps not even the 700 million people who live inside. This campaign could aggravate, instead of ameliorate, the difficult conditions under which the vast majority of the world's population live.

But to get this central point into Western minds, one must first remove the barriers that have made these topics into untouchable sacred cows in Western discourse. A Westerner must first acknowledge that when he discusses these topics with a non-Westerner, he is, consciously or unconsciously, standing behind a pulpit. If it is any consolation, let me hasten to add that this attitude is not new. As the following passage from the *Dictionary of the History of Ideas* indicates, it goes back centuries:

> The concept of despotism began as a distinctively European perception of Asian governments and practices: Europeans as such were considered to be free by nature, in contrast to the servile nature of the Orientals. Concepts of despotism have frequently been linked to justifications, explanations, or arraignments of slavery, conquest, and colonial or imperial domination. The attribution of despotism to an enemy may be employed to mobilize the members of a political unit, or those of a regional area. Thus the Greeks stigmatized the Persians as despotic in much the same way that Christian writers were to treat the Turks. By an irony not always perceived either by the purported champions of liberty against despotism, or by their historians, such arguments often became the rationale, as in Aristotle, for the domination by those with a tradition of liberty over others who had never enjoyed that happy condition."[2]

On the eve of the twenty-first century, this European attitude to Asians has to come to an end. The assumption of moral superiority must be abandoned. A level playing field needs to be created for meaningful discussions between Asians and Americans. That will be my first goal in this essay. In the second half, I will put across the view of one Asian on human rights and freedom of the press.

A LEVEL PLAYING FIELD

It is never a pleasant experience to be lowered from a pedestal. I apologize for any psychological discomfort that my remarks may cause. Yet to achieve this objective in one essay, I will have to be ruthless if I am to be brief. To remove the "sacred cow" dimension surrounding the subjects of human rights and freedom of the press, I propose to list ten heresies which the West, including the US, has either ignored, suppressed, or pretended to be irrelevant or inconsequential in their discussions on these subjects. If these heresies have any validity at all, I hope that this will lead Western writers to accept that they do not have a monopoly of wisdom or virtue on these subjects and that they should try to exercise a little more humility when they discourse on these subjects to a non-Western audience.

Heresy no. I: American journalists do not believe in the Christian rule: "Do unto others as you would have others do unto you"

From Gary Hart to Bill Clinton, there has developed an honorable journalistic tradition that the infidelities of a politician are public property, to be exposed in every detail. But those who participate in this tradition do not feel themselves bound by Jesus Christ's statement: "Let he who has not sinned cast the first stone."

To the best of my limited knowledge, based on my limited stay in Washington, DC, the average level of infidelities seemed about the same in all sectors of the society: whether it be in Congress or in the press corps. Power proves to be a great aphrodisiac. Both politicians and journalists have equal difficulty resisting the temptations that flow their way. Yet the actions of one group are deemed immoral and subject to public scrutiny, while those of the other are deemed private matters. But in the informal pecking order worked out in Washington, DC (as in any other tribal society), many a senior journalist enjoys far more effective power than a Congressman. But they are subject to different levels of scrutiny.

The same disparity applies to personal finances. Any aspiring politician, even the few unfortunate ones who may have entered politics to do a service to the nation, has to declare every penny of his or her financial worth. Yet none of the Washington, DC, journalists, many of whom enjoy far greater incomes, feel any moral obligation to declare all their financial worth; nor do they feel any need to declare how their own financial worth would be enhanced by discussing the financial worth of an aspiring politician. A full disclosure of income and wealth on the part of those who make and those who influence public policy decisions (including lobbyists and journalists) will probably indicate the great mismatch in financial muscle between the actual policymakers and those who seek to influence them. It may also help to illustrate why despite so many rational discussions so many irrational public policy choices are made.

Heresy no. II: Power corrupts: the absolute power of the Western journalist in the Third World corrupts absolutely

The greatest myth that a journalist cherishes is that he is an underdog; the lone ranger who works against monstrous bureaucracies to uncover the real truth, often at great personal risk. I never understood this myth when I was in Washington, DC. Cabinet Secretaries, Senators, and Congressmen, Ambassadors and Generals promptly returned the phone calls of and assiduously cultivated the journalists in Washington, DC. Not all these powerful office-holders were as good as Kissinger or Jim Baker in seducing American journalists, but none would dare tell an American journalist of a major paper to go to hell. It was as inconceivable as trying to exercise dissent in the court of Attila the Hun.

The cruellest results of this myth are experienced in the developing world. On arriving in a Third World capital, no American journalist would shake out from his unconsciousness the deeply embedded myth that he was once again arriving as a lone ranger battling an evil and corrupt Third World government. Never would he admit that he had arrived in a Third World capital with as much power as a colonial proconsul in the nineteenth century. In both cases the host government ignored these emissaries at their peril. The average correspondent from an influential Western journal, who arrives in a Third World capital, would of course ask to see the President, Prime Minister, and perhaps Foreign Minister. If, heaven forbid, any of these leaders should refuse, this is a typical response:

> Given that Kings and Presidents throughout the world regularly grant interviews to *The Guardian* (please note our recent exclusive interview with the King of Jordan) and, indeed, sometimes write in *The Guardian* (as with former President Gorbachev), I do wonder by what token *The Guardian* is not considered worthy of such a request. We are, after all, the second highest selling quality national daily in the UK.

(Note: this is an extract from an actual letter.)

A Western journalist would be thoroughly puzzled by a request for reciprocity from, say, a journalist from the *Times of India* in Washington, DC. Pressed for a justification for this imbalance, he would dismiss the case for reciprocity on the grounds that the *New York Times* (*NYT*), for example, is a better paper than the *Times of India*. Never would he admit to himself that the Prime Minister, even of India, would hesitate turning down a *NYT* request knowing that the *NYT* controlled the gateways to key minds in Washington, DC. What was sweet about this exercise of power by a *NYT* correspondent is that he would never have to admit that he was savouring the delicious fruits of power, since it came with no obvious trappings of office.

Heresy no. III: A free press can serve as the opium of society

This statement is not quite as outrageous as Marx's dictum that religion can serve as the opium of society, but it will probably be dismissed as quickly as Marx's statement was when he first uttered it. The American media pride themselves on the ability of their investigative journalism to uncover the real truth behind the stories put out by government, big business, and other major institutions. They could never stomach the proposition that they could serve as the opium of American society. But they have.

In the last twenty years, there have been two developments which have taken parallel trends. First, American journalism has become much more aggressive than it has ever been. Kennedy was the last US President to be treated with kid gloves; his sexual excesses were well known but not publicized. Since then no US President (e.g. Bill Clinton today) has been considered off-limits for total coverage, giving the impression that the US government is under total and close scrutiny.

The parallel trend is this. The last thirty years have also seen increasingly bad government. LBJ felt that he could fight a war and create a good society without raising taxes. This began the process of fiscal indiscipline. Richard Nixon's flaws are well known, as are Jimmy Carter's. Then, under two Republican Administrations, America went from being the world's largest creditor country to the world's largest debtor country. A Swiss investment consultant, Jean Antoine Cramer, noted,

> [I]t took 150 years for the US government to create a debt of $1000bn, and only 10 years to quadruple this debt. With a GNP of $5600bn, the situation is beyond repair. American consumers owe $7000bn, corporations $5000bn and the government $5000bn.[3]

No American politician, in the land of the free press, dares to utter any hard truths on the sacrifices needed to stop this rot. The consequence has been irresponsible government on a mind-boggling and historically unparalleled scale. Equally striking are the parallel troubles of some of America's largest corporations, including previous blue-chip names, like Citicorp, GM, and IBM, all of whom have also been under close scrutiny by the press.

It would be impossible for me, even if I had unlimited space, to prove that there is a causal connection between a more aggressive free press and increasingly bad government. It may have been purely a coincidence. After all, the American press has been second to none in exposing the follies of the American government. But have all their exposures served as opiates, creating the illusion that something is being done when nothing is really being done?

There may be an even more cruel example of the free press serving as an opiate. One of the post-World War II achievements that America is very proud of is the political emancipation of the Blacks. The press played a key role in this. But did this emancipation in turn foster the illusion that the fundamental problems of the Blacks had been solved? The impression given was that equality had finally been given to the Blacks. The doors had been opened. All they had to do was to walk through.

Thirty years after the famous Civil Rights marches, if one were to ask an average Black family: "Are you better off than you were thirty years ago?", how many would say yes and how many would say no? What did the large-scale rioting after the Rodney King episode demonstrate? That perhaps thirty years of discussion of Blacks' problems have served as a substitute for thirty years of action, creating an illusion of movement when there had been little or none. Is it enough for the American media to say, we did the best we can. Or should they begin to ask: Did we contribute to this failure in any way?

Can the minds generated by the freest press in the world conceive of such questions?

Heresy no. IV: A free press need not lead to a well-ordered society

A key assumption in the West is that a good society needs a free press to keep abuse of power in check. Freedom of information checks bad government. Its absence leads to greater abuses and bad government.

This may well be true. A free press can lead to good government. But this is not necessarily a true proposition. A free press can also lead to bad government.

In Southeast Asia, we have seen an unfortunate demonstration of this. By far, the one country in Southeast Asia that has enjoyed the freest press for the longest period of time (except for the Marcos Martial Law interregnum) was the Philippines. But the Philippines is also the ASEAN society that is having the greatest difficulty in modernization and economic progress, suggesting that a free press is neither a necessary nor a sufficient condition for development and progress.

India and China provide two massive social laboratories to judge what prescriptions would help a society develop and prosper. Between them, they hold about two-fifths of the world's population, two out of every five human beings on the planet. Each has taken a very different political road. The West approves the freedom of the press in India, frowns on the lack of it in China. Yet which society is developing faster today and which society is likely to modernize first?

The Ayodhya incident in December 1992 demonstrated one important new dimension for societies all around the globe. The Indian media tried to control emotional reactions by restricting the broadcasting and distribution of video scenes of the destruction of the mosque. But many Indian homes could see video clips (transmitted through satellites and tapes) from foreign news agencies which felt no reason to exercise social, political or moral restraint. Those who happily transmitted the video clips never had to bear the consequences themselves. They were sitting comfortably in Atlanta, Georgia, or in Hong Kong, while the riots that followed in India as a result of their TV transmissions never reached their homes. Unfortunately, these media personnel did not stop to consider whether they could have saved other human lives, not their own, by exercising restraint.

Heresy no. V: That Western journalists, in covering non-Western events are conditioned by both Western prejudices and Western interests; the claim of "objective" reporting is a major falsehood

Let me cite three major examples. First, the coverage of Islam. Edward W. Said, in his book *Covering Islam*, states,

> The hardest thing to get most academic experts on Islam to admit is that what they say and do as scholars is set in a profoundly and in some ways an offensively political context. Everything about the study of Islam in the contemporary West is saturated with political importance, but hardly any writers on Islam, whether expert or general, admit the fact in what they say. Objectivity is assumed to inhere in learned discourse about other societies, despite the long history of political, moral, and religious concern felt in all societies, Western or Islamic, about the alien, the strange and different. In Europe, for example, the Orientalist has traditionally been affiliated directly with colonial offices: what we have just begun to learn about the extent of close cooperation between scholarship and direct military colonial conquest (as in the case of revered Dutch Orientalist C. Snouck Hurgronje, who used the confidence he had won from Muslims to plan and execute the brutal Dutch war against the

86

Atjehnese people of Sumatra) is both edifying and depressing. Yet books and articles continue to put forth extolling the nonpolitical nature of Western scholarship, the fruits of Orientalist learning, and the value of "objective" expertise. At the very same time there is scarcely an expert on "Islam" who has not been a consultant or even an employee of the government, the various corporations, the media. My point is that the cooperation must be admitted and taken into account, not just for moral reasons, but for intellectual reasons as well.[4]

Second, the American media coverage of the Vietnam War, a major event, some say a glorious chapter, in the history of American journalism. By the late sixties and early seventies, as American bodies were brought back from Vietnam, American public sentiment turned against the war. The US had to get out. The American media helped to manufacture a justification: that the US was supporting the "bad guys" (the crooked and wicked Saigon and Phnom Penh regimes) against the "good guys" (the dedicated incorruptible revolutionaries in North Vietnam or the Cambodian jungles). Books like *Fire in the Lake*, a glorification of the Vietnamese revolution, became the bible of American reporters. When the last American soldier left Vietnam, most American journalists felt satisfied and vindicated.

The subsequent Communist victories in Cambodia and Vietnam exposed the true nature of the revolutionaries. The story of the Cambodian genocide is well known, as is the story of the thousands of boat people who perished in the South China Sea. The level of human misery increased, not decreased, after the revolution. Yet virtually no American journalist came forth to admit that perhaps he was wrong in quoting from *Fire in the Lake* or in calling for the abandonment of the Saigon and Phnom Penh regimes. As long as American journalists had fulfilled vital American interest by saving American lives, there was no need for American journalists to weigh the moral consequences of their actions on non-Americans, the Vietnamese or the Cambodians.

Third, the coverage of Tiananmen, a Chinese event that became a global media event. The essential Western media story is that it was a revolution by Chinese democrats against Chinese autocrats. The constant portrayal of the students' Goddess of Democracy, vaguely modeled on the American Statue of Liberty, provided the pictorial image for this. Yet for all its massive coverage of Tiananmen, the Western media failed to explain how this event was seen through *Chinese* eyes. Few Chinese intellectuals believe that China is ready for democracy. Most are as afraid of chaos and anarchy (a persistent Chinese disease) as they are of a return to Maoist totalitarianism. It was a battle between soft authoritarians and hard authoritarians. The Western media vividly reported the apparent victory of the "hard-liners" but it has failed to tell the world the true aftermath: the soft authoritarians have come back to power.

During Tiananmen, several Western journalists were blatantly dishonest. They would lunch with a student on a "hunger-strike" before reporting on his "hunger." They were not all bystanders reporting on an event; several advised the students how to behave. None stayed to face the consequences that the students had to face.

The biggest indication of how American journalists are affected by American interests in their portrayal of China is to compare their reporting of China in the early 1970s and the 1990s. When Nixon landed in China in 1972, the American media had a virtual love-fest with a regime that had just killed millions in the cultural revolution. Yet in the 1990s, a much more benign regime that has liberated millions from poverty and indignity and promises to launch them on the road to development is treated as a pariah regime.

Heresy no. VI: That Western governments work with genocidal rulers when it serves their interest to do so

It was August 1942, a dark moment in World War II. Churchill had flown secretly to Moscow to bring some bad news personally to Stalin: the allies were not ready for a second front in Europe. Stalin reacted angrily. Nancy Caldwell Sorel, who described that meeting, said:

> Discord continued, but on the last evening, when Churchill went to say goodbye, Stalin softened. . . . the hour that Churchill had planned for extended to seven. Talk and wine flowed freely, and in a moment of rare intimacy, Stalin admitted that even the stresses of war did not compare to the terrible struggle to force the collective farm policy on the peasantry. Millions of Kulaks had been, well, eliminated. The historian Churchill thought of Burke's dictum "If I cannot have reform without injustice, I will not have reform," but the politician Churchill concluded that with the war requiring unity, it was best not to moralize aloud.[5]

The story elicits a chuckle. What a shrewd old devil Churchill was. How cunning of him not to displease Stalin with mere moralizing. Neither then nor now has Churchill's reputation been sullied by his association with a genocidal ruler. Now change the cast of characters to an identical set: Mrs Thatcher and Pol Pot. Historically they could have met but of course they never did. Now try to describe a possible meeting and try to get a chuckle out of it. Impossible? Why so?

Think about it. Think hard for in doing so you will discover to your surprise that it is possible for thoughtful and well-informed people to have double standards. If the rule that prevents any possible meeting between Mrs Thatcher and Pol Pot is that "Thou should not have any discourse with a genocidal ruler," then the same rule also forbids any meeting between Stalin and Churchill. Moral rules, as the English philosopher R.M. Hare has stressed, are inherently universalizable. If we do want to allow a meeting between Churchill and Stalin (since, until recently, no historian has ever condemned Churchill, that must be the prevailing sentiment), then the rule has to be modified to "Thou should not have any discourse with a genocidal ruler, unless there are mitigating circumstances."

This is not a mere change of nuance. We have made a fundamental leap, a leap best understood with an analogy contained in the following tale: a man meets a woman and asks her whether she would spend the night with him for a million dollars. She replies "For a million dollars, sure." He says, "How about five dollars." She replies indignantly, "What do you think I am?" He replies, "We have already established what you are. We are only negotiating the price." All those who condone Churchill's meeting with Stalin but would readily condemn any meeting with Pol Pot belong in the woman's shoes (logically speaking).

In Stalin's case, as England's survival was at stake, all was excused. In Pol Pot's case, as no conceivable vital Western interest could be met in any meeting with him, no mitigating excuse could possibly exist. Hence the total and absolute Western condemnation of any contact with Pol Pot or his minions in the Khmer Rouge. The tragedy for the Cambodian people is that the West, in applying this absolute moral rule only because its own vital interests were not involved, did not stop to ask whether the sufferings *of the Cambodians* could have been mitigated if the West had been as flexible in their dealings with the Khmer Rouge as Churchill had been with Stalin.

Throughout the 1980s, when several Asian governments were trying to achieve a viable Cambodian peace settlement (which would invariably have to include the Khmer Rouge), they were vilified for their direct contacts with the Khmer Rouge. American diplomats were instructed never to shake hands with Khmer Rouge representatives.

In the former Yugoslavia, the atrocities committed by Radovan Karadžić and his Serbian followers (in full view of the American media) should be sufficient justification to put them in the same league as Pol Pot or Idi Amin. Yet no Western diplomat has hesitated to shake the hands of these Serbian representatives. Is there one standard for Westerners and another for Asians?

Heresy no. VII: That Western governments will happily sacrifice the human rights of Third World societies when it suits Western interests to do so

The current regime in Myanmar (Burma) overturned the results of the demo-cratic elections in 1990 and brutally suppressed the popular demonstrations that followed. Myanmar was punished with Western sanctions. Asian governments were criticized for not enthusiastically following suit.

The current regime in Algeria overturned the results of the democratic elections in 1992 and brutally suppressed the popular demonstrations that followed. Algeria was *not* punished with Western sanctions. The Asian governments have never been provided with an explanation for this obvious double standard.

But the reasons are obvious. The fear of Western sanctions triggering off greater political instability, leading to thousands of boat-people crossing the tiny Mediterranean Sea into Europe, made Western governments prudent and cautious. Despite this, they have no hesitation in criticizing Asian governments for exercising the same prudence for the same reasons when it came to applying sanctions against Myanmar or China. Double standards, by any moral criteria, are obviously immoral. How many Western papers have highlighted this?

Heresy no. VIII: That the West has used the pretext of human rights abuses to abandon Third World allies that no longer serve Western interests

The sins of Mohamed Siad Barre (Somalia), Mobutu (Zaïre), and Daniel Arap Moi (Kenya) were as well known during the Cold War as they are now. They did not convert from virtue to vice the day the Cold War ended. Yet behavior which was deemed worthy of Western support during the Cold War was deemed unacceptable when the Cold War ended.

It is remarkable how much satisfaction the Western governments, media, and public have taken over their ability finally to pursue "moral" policies after the end of the Cold War. Yet this has not come with any admission that the West was (logically speaking) pursuing "immoral" policies during the Cold War. Nor has anyone addressed the question whether it is "honorable" to use and abandon allies.

Heresy no. IX: That the West cannot acknowledge that the pursuit of "moral" human rights policies can have immoral consequences

At the end of the Paris International Conference on Cambodia (ICC) in August 1989, the then Vietnamese Foreign Minister, Mr Nguyen Co Thach, insisted that the conference declaration should call for a nonreturn of the genocidal policies and practices of the Khmer Rouge. All present there knew that Nguyen Co Thach was not really that concerned about Pol Pot's record. (Indeed, Thach once made the mistake of privately confessing to Congressman Stephen Solarz that Vietnam did *not* invade Cambodia to save the Cambodian people from Pol Pot, even though this was the official Vietnamese propaganda line.) However, Thach knew that the Khmer Rouge, a party to the Paris conference, would not accept such a reference. Hence the conference would fail, a failure which the Vietnamese wanted because they were not ready then to relinquish control of Cambodia. Western officials did not dare to challenge him for fear that Nguyen Co Thach would expose them to their own media. At the same time, despite having scuttled a conference that could have brought peace to Cambodia, Nguyen Co Thach came out smelling good in the eyes of the Western media because he had taken a strong stand against the Khmer Rouge. Yet in practical terms, from the viewpoint of the ordinary Cambodian, the strong Western consensus against the Khmer Rouge had backfired against the Cambodians because it prevented the Western delegations from exposing Nguyen Co Thach's blatant scuttling of the peace conference. Out of good (the Western media condemnation of Pol Pot) came evil (the destruction of a peace conference). This was not the first time it had happened in history. As Max Weber said in his famous essay *Politics as a Vocation*, "it is *not* true that good can only follow from good and evil only from evil, but that often the opposite is true. Anyone who says this is, indeed, a political infant."[6]

The morally courageous thing for a Western delegate to have done at that Paris conference would have been to stand up in front of the Western media and explain why the inclusion of the Khmer Rouge was necessary *if one wanted a peace agreement to end the Cambodians' sufferings*. No Western leader even dreamt of doing so, so strong was the sentiment against the Khmer Rouge. This produced a curious contradiction for moral philosophers: the ostensible morally correct position (i.e. of excluding the Khmer Rouge) produced immoral consequences – prolonging the Cambodian agony.

This was not by any means the first of such moral dilemmas confronted by Western officials. Max Weber asserts that "No ethics in the world can dodge the fact that in numerous instances the attainment of 'good' ends is bound to the fact that one must be willing to pay the price of using morally dubious means or at least dangerous ones."[7] Unfortunately, there is no living Western statesman who has the courage to make such a statement for in the era of "political correctness" in which we live Western media would excoriate any such brave soul. Out of moral correctness, we have produced moral cowardice.

Heresy no. X: That an imperfect government that commits some human rights violations is better than no government in many societies

At least two nation-states have broken apart since the end of the Cold War, Somalia and Yugoslavia. Both shared a common characteristic of being useful to the West in the Cold War. The sins of their governments were forgiven them. When these ruling regimes were abandoned (each in a different way), the net result has been an increase in human misery. A utilitarian moral philosopher would have no difficulty arguing that the previous situation of imperfect government was a better moral choice because it caused less misery.

The inability of the West to accept this can lead to a repetition of Yugoslavia's and Somalia's experiences. Take Peru, for example. It was drifting towards chaos and anarchy. President Fujimori imposed emergency rule to halt the slide. He should have been praised for his courage in taking decisive action to prevent anarchy. However, because the *form* of his action, a temporary retreat from parliamentary rule, was deemed unacceptable by the West, the beneficial consequences of his action *for the Peruvian people* were ignored by the West. In trying to maintain its form of ideological purity, the West was prepared to sacrifice the interests of the Peruvian people.

If current Western policies of punishing authoritarian governments had been in force in the sixties and seventies, the spectacular economic growth of Taiwan and South Korea would have been cut off at its very inception by Western demands that the governments then in power be replaced by less authoritarian regimes. Instead, by allowing the authoritarian governments, which were fully committed to economic development, to run the full course, the West has brought about the very economic and social changes that have paved the way for the more open and participative societies that Taiwan and South Korea have become. The lessons from East Asia are clear. There are no short-cuts. It is necessary for a developing society to succeed *first* in economic development before it can attain the social and political freedoms found in the developed societies.

HUMAN RIGHTS AND FREEDOM OF THE PRESS

There is no unified Asian view on human rights and the freedom of the press. These are Western concepts. Asians are obliged to react to them. Predictably, there is a whole range of reactions ranging from those who subscribe to these concepts *in toto* to those who reject them completely. An understanding of the Asian reactions is clouded by the fact that many Asians feel an obligation to pay at least lip service to their values. For example, many Japanese intellectuals, who remain children of the Meiji restoration in their belief that Japan should become more Western than Asian, proclaim their strong adherence to Western values on human rights, although they have a curious inability to discuss Japan's record in World War II in the same breath. From New Delhi to Manila, to name just two cities, there are many strong and sincere believers in these values. But in most Asian societies there is little awareness, let alone understanding, of these concepts. The essential truth is that the vast continent of Asia, preoccupied with more immediate challenges, has not had the time or energy to address these issues squarely.

I shall therefore make no pretence of speaking on behalf of Asia, although I am reasonably confident that my views will not be dismissed as eccentric by most Asians. My hope here is to find some credible middle ground where both Asians and Americans can have a dialogue as equals and with equally legitimate points of view. I will be so bold as to venture five principles that should guide such a discourse.

1. Mutual respect

The first principle that I want to stress is all discussions between Asians and Americans on the subject of human rights and freedom of the press should be based on mutual respect. I have visited the offices of four great American newspapers, the *New York Times*, the *Washington Post*, the *Los Angeles Times*, and the *Wall Street Journal*. In any one of the four, if you ventured out of their offices at night and strayed a few hundred yards off course, you would be putting your life in jeopardy. Yet, despite this, none of the editorial desks or writers would argue in favor of the reduction of the civil liberties of habitual criminals. Danger from habitual crime is considered an acceptable price to pay for no reduction in liberty. This is one social choice.

In Singapore, you can wander out at night in any direction from the *Straits Times* and not put your life in jeopardy. One reason for this is that habitual criminals and drug addicts are locked up, often for long spells, until they have clearly reformed. The interests of the majority in having safe city streets are put ahead of considerations of rigorous due process, although safeguards are put in place to ensure that innocent individuals are not locked up. This is another kind of social choice. Let me suggest that none is intrinsically superior. Let those who make the choice live with the consequences of their choice. Similarly, if this statement can be received without the usual Western sniggers, let me add that a city that bans the sale of chewing gum has as much a moral right to do so as a city that effectively allows the sale of crack on its streets. Let us try to avoid the knee-jerk smug response that one choice is more moral than the other.

I do not want to belabor this point, but it will be psychologically difficult for the West to accept the motion that alternative social and political choices can deserve equal respect. For 500 years, the West has been dominant in one form or another. After World War II, most of Asia, like much of the Third World, was politically emancipated. But the process of mental emancipation, on the part of both the colonized and the colonizers, is taking much longer. This explains why Chris Patten could march into Hong Kong, five years before its date of return to China, and suggest a form of government that was completely unacceptable to China. The British would be shocked if a Chinese Governor were to arrive in Northern Ireland and dictate terms for its liberation from the United Kingdom. But they saw nothing absurd in what they did in Hong Kong. The British, like many in the West, feel that they have a right to dictate terms to Asians.

Eventually, as East Asia becomes more affluent, the discussions will take place from a position of equality. But debates like ours in this book can anticipate this by trying to create a form of discourse in which we approach each other with mutual respect.

2. Economic development

Second, the fundamental concern of Western proponents of human rights is to remove egregious abuses and improve the living conditions of the 4.3 billion people who live outside the developed world. Let me suggest that the current Western campaign (even if it is rigorously carried out, which it is unlikely to be) will make barely a dent on the lives of the 4.3 billion people, although there will be symbolic victories like the Aquino revolution and the award of the Nobel Peace Prize to Aung San Suu Kyi.

There is only one force that has the power to "liberate" the Third World. Economic development is probably the most subversive force created in history. It shakes up old social arrangements and paves the way for the participation of a greater percentage of society in social and political decisions. The Chinese Communist Party can no longer regain the tight totalitarian control it enjoyed in Mao Zedong's time. Deng Xiaoping and Jiang Zemin's reforms have killed that possibility. Hence, if the West wants to bury for ever Mao's totalitarian arrangements, it should support the reforms to the hilt, even if China's leaders have to crack down occasionally to retain political control. The fundamental trend is clear. It is therefore not surprising that a decade after Tiananmen, it is the "soft" and not the "hard" authoritarians who are in charge in Beijing. Clearly, if the Clinton administration wants to fulfill its goal of moving China towards greater respect of human rights, it should do all in its power to accelerate China's economic development, not retard it.

Unfortunately, the promotion of economic development (unlike the promotion of democracy and human rights) is difficult. It has significant costs, direct and indirect, for developed societies. What may be good for the Third World (promoting economic development) would prove painful for Western societies in the short run. The EU, US, and Japan, for example, would have to abandon their massive agricultural subsidies. Unfortunately (and paradoxically) the very nature of Western democratic societies (which inhibits politicians from speaking about sacrifices) may well be one of the biggest barriers to the effective spread of democracy and human rights in the Third World, including Asia.

3. Work with existing governments

Third, do not even dream of overthrowing most of the existing governments in Asia. I say this because I was present at a lynching in Harvard, the lynching of the Indonesian government. This was at a forum organized at the Kennedy School of Government to discuss the unfortunate killings in Dili in November 1991. Two of the American journalists, who had a close shave in the incident, were there to present vivid first-hand accounts and whip up the crowd to a frenzy, with the help of a few leftist critics of the Indonesian government. This left a hapless State Department official to explain why the US should continue working with the Suharto government. If the people in that room had the power to depose the Indonesian government, they would have done it instantly, without paying a thought to the horrendous consequences that might follow. This is the attitude of many human rights activists: get rid of the imperfect governments we know – do not worry of the consequences that may follow. On their own, such activists will probably cause little trouble. But when they get into positions of influence, their ability to cause real damage increases by leaps and bounds.

In dealing with Asia, I am calling on America to take the long view. These are societies which have been around hundreds, if not thousands, of years. They cannot be changed overnight, even if, for example, Fang Lizhi is elected President of China. The experience of President Aquino should provide a vivid lesson to those who believe that one change at the top can reform everything.

What Asia needs at its present stage of development are governments who are committed to rapid economic development. Sporadic instances of political crackdowns should be criticized, but these governments should not be penalized as long as their people's lives are improving. Only societies like North Korea and Myanmar, which have let their people stagnate for decades, deserve such disapproval.

4. Establish minimal codes of civilized conduct

To a Western human rights activist, the suggestion that he should be a little moderate in making human rights demands on non-Western societies seems almost as absurd as the notion that a woman can be partially pregnant. In psychological attitudes, such an activist is no different from a religious crusader of a previous era. He demands total conversion and nothing else. Such activists can do a lot of damage with their zealotry. Unfortunately, since they occupy the high moral ground in Western societies, no government nor media representative dares to challenge them openly.

But some of the demands of these human rights activists would be unacceptable under any conditions. Most Asian societies would be shocked by the sight of gay rights activists on their streets. And, in most of them, if popular referendums were held, they would vote overwhelmingly in favor of the death penalty and censorship of pornography.

But both Asians and Americans are human beings. They can agree on minimal standards of civilized behavior that both would like to live under. For example, there should be no torture, no slavery, no arbitrary killings, no disappearances in the middle of the night, no shooting down of innocent demonstrators, no imprisonment without careful review. These rights should be upheld not only for moral reasons. There are sound functional reasons. Any society which is at odds with its best and brightest and shoots them down when they demonstrate peacefully, as Myanmar did, is headed for trouble. Most Asian societies do not want to be in the position that Myanmar is in today, a nation at odds with itself.

5. Let the free press fly on its own wings

Finally, on the difficult issue of the freedom of the press, let me suggest that neither the West nor the USA should set itself the self-appointed role of being the guardian of the free press in societies around the globe. Let each society decide for itself whether it would help or hinder its development if it decides to have a free press.

I have yet to meet an American who has any doubts about the virtues of having a free press. Even those who despise most journalists as the scum of the earth would not have it any other way. The value of the freedom of the press is absolute and unchallengeable. The paradox here is that while they believe the virtues of a free press to be so self-evident, they show no hesitation in ramming this concept down the throats of societies which are not enamored of it.

Over time, a Darwinian process will establish whether societies with a free press will out-perform those without one. So far, the record of the twentieth century shows that societies which have free newspapers like the *New York Times* or the *Washington Post* have outperformed societies with *Pravda* and *Izvestia*. This winning streak may well continue. And if it does, more and more societies will naturally gravitate to social and political systems which can handle a totally free press, in the belief and hope that they will join the league of winners in the Darwinian contest between societies.

But let these decisions be made autonomously by these societies. There need be no fear that they will remain ignorant of the virtues of the American media. The globe is shrinking. With the proliferation of satellite dishes into villages in India and Indonesia, the sky is shrinking too. CNN and the BBC are available worldwide. The *International Herald Tribune* and the *Wall Street Journal* can be obtained practically anywhere around the globe. Let the merits of these papers speak for themselves. The American media should not resort to the strong arm of the American executive branch or the Congress to sell their virtues for them.

In short, live and let live. If the US is convinced that its system of human rights and freedom of the press are the best possible systems for any society around the globe, let the virtues of these systems speak for themselves. As in the world of ideas, if a social system has merits, it will fly on its own wings. If it does not, it will not. Most Asians now know enough of these systems to make their own choices. Let them do so in peace.

NOTES

This essay was originally presented to a conference on "Asian and American Perspectives on Capitalism and Democracy," held in Singapore in January 1993. Mr Mahbubani delivered these remarks in his personal capacity. They should not be read as a reflection of the Singapore government's views.

1   Kishore Mahbubani, "The West and the Rest," in *The National Interest* no. 28 (Summer 1992), p. 10.
2   Essay on "Despotism" by Melvin Richter in Philip P. Wiener, ed., *Dictionary of the History of Ideas* (New York: Charles Scribner's Sons, 1973), p. 1.
3   For data on US debt, see "Deficits and the Debt, 1940–1997," *The New York Times 1998 Almanac* (New York: New York Times, 1997), p. 345.
4   Edward W. Said, *Covering Islam: How the Media and the Experts Determine How We See the Rest of the World* (New York: Pantheon Books, 1981), p. xvii.
5   Nancy Caldwell Sorel, "First Encounters: Josef Stalin and Winston Churchill," *The Atlantic Monthly* (November 1991), p. 141.
6   Max Weber, *Politics as a Vocation* (Philadelphia: Fortress Press, 1965), p. 49.
7   Ibid., p. 47.

Part II

HUMAN RIGHTS
IN GREATER CHINA

5

EAST MEETS WEST
Human Rights in Hong Kong

Linda Butenhoff

Linda Butenhoff *is an American social scientist and activist specializing in human rights. In this essay, which is based on her PhD dissertation research in Hong Kong, Butenhoff describes Hong Kong as an example of the implementation of the full range of human rights as specified in United Nations agreements. She, first, reviews the three generations of rights as specified by the United Nations and, then, shows how each of these three generations of human rights was (and was not) implemented in Hong Kong under British rule, up to the July 1997 transfer of power to the People's Republic of China.*

INTRODUCTION: THE DEBATE

Is it possible to implement or even conceive of human rights in a holistic fashion as laid out in the Universal Declaration of Human Rights and the United Nations' covenants on human rights? Or should human rights be thought of and put into practice as determined by a country's history, culture, and level of development? Further, should certain rights have priority over other rights? Currently human rights research has focused on the debate between what has been called individual versus collective human rights. On one side of the debate are Western nations, which tend to define human rights in terms of individual rights, arguing that civil and political rights are the most important of human rights (even at times referring to them as "universal rights"). Others, primarily from developing countries, argue that human rights should be seen in relation to a country's culture, history, and level of development (often referred to as cultural relativism). At the heart of this debate is the question: which rights have priority when defining and implementing human rights, the individual or the collective? This debate has been especially intense between Asian and Western countries. By examining a case that has a unique history influenced by both Eastern and Western culture, this chapter investigates some of the central questions raised in the debate.

Hong Kong seems to be a case where the individual and the collective notions of human rights have coexisted for over 150 years, in an intermingling of Eastern and Western philosophies and cultures. How have human rights in Hong Kong developed over time? How are they defined and implemented today? What is the government's official position? Does the public envision them differently? Are human rights defined and implemented in a combination of individual and collective rights, as its history may indicate? Much of the scholarship on human rights in Hong Kong has centered on the enhancement of civil and political rights.[1] Nonetheless Hong Kong has recognized the importance of such collective rights as housing (Hong Kong is one of the world's largest public housing providers). Moreover, how did the prospect of the transfer of governance to China affect the development of human rights?

The first section of this chapter is a theoretical discussion of the literature surrounding the debate over individual versus collective rights, such as the opposing perspectives of Jack Donnelly and Chandra Muzaffar. The second section examines the development of human rights in Hong Kong as an illustration of a society that is a mix of both Eastern and Western influences. It would appear that this would be an ideal environment to find a combination of individual and collective rights both conceptually and in practice. Within this discussion this chapter also investigates the role that China, the United States, and Great Britain have played in the development of human rights in Hong Kong, both historically and in the 1997 transition process. In order to examine the extent of the coexistence of first- and second-generation rights, this chapter uses several indicators in its examination of the development of human rights in Hong Kong, such as civil and political rights, elections and voting rights, due process of law, free speech, and freedom of the press. Regarding social and economic rights, the chapter discusses such provisions as housing, health care, and education. Because of the transitional nature of the Hong Kong government, the chapter examines policies that are both enacted and under consideration. Finally, the chapter reviews third-generation rights, including the protection of the environment, the right to self-determination, and the right to development.

THREE GENERATIONS OF HUMAN RIGHTS

The twentieth century has witnessed the emergence of human rights as a central issue in international affairs. Yet beyond that point there is considerable debate over the concept of human rights, even though most would agree that human rights are tools for defending the poor and the powerless. Although the topic of human rights covers a broad spectrum, ranging from freedom of speech to the right to a clean environment, one of the most frequently debated issues is which rights, if any, should be given priority. Central to this is the debate between individual versus collective concepts of human rights and human nature. One side argues that human rights protect and promote the individual. Collective rights are, in this view, too vague and flexible, giving states the opportunity to abuse human rights, whereas individual civil liberties are easier to implement because they merely require the absence of government intervention in people's lives. Moreover, proponents of civil and political rights argue that human rights are inherently independent of civil society, individualistic, and any implementation of collective rights would require a depreciation of an individual's liberty and equality.[2] Jack Donnelly sums up the argument:

> The key conceptual issue is the distinction between acts of omission and acts of commission ... that "negative" civil and political rights deserve priority because their violation involves the direct infliction of injury, whereas the violation of "positive" economic and social rights usually involves only the failure to confer a benefit.[3]

The other side argues that the community or collective needs are above individual needs, and without an emphasis on such basic needs as food, individuals have no need for the luxuries of political freedoms. This clash is most evident between nations of the North (Western industrialized countries) and the developing countries of the South. It raises questions over whether or not human rights may be applied universally and if there is a global basis for a consensus on human rights as appears in the Universal Declaration of Human Rights, written immediately after World War II when most current nations were still colonies.

Nevertheless, in order to build a foundation for human rights that goes beyond rhetoric and political manipulation, the United Nations' Universal Declaration of Human Rights and the international covenants and resolutions on human rights are a place to begin to build common ground. Subsequently a universal or holistic conception of human rights could be based on the Universal Declaration, the International Covenant on Civil and Political Rights (ICCPR), the International Covenant on Economic, Social, and Cultural Rights (ICESCR), and people's or solidarity rights, which are rooted in the United Nations Charter, the 1976 Algiers Declaration (the Universal Declaration of the Rights of Peoples) and the Organization of African Unity's Banjul Charter on Human and Peoples' Rights.

Civil and political rights: the first generation

Although, as indicated above, the conception and priority of human rights continues to be debated, the literature (and UN documents on human rights) has been divided into three generations of rights.[4] The first generation of rights is comprised of civil and political rights, which seek to protect the individual from the state.[5] Civil and political rights also enjoy a sound foundation in the international legal instruments of Western society. Richard Lillich states that these rights are "commonly considered to be the most basic and fundamental of all human rights, [and] will be familiar to readers versed in US constitutional law."[6]

Traditionally the West has glorified the individual, while manifesting a distrust for groups. As a result, first-generation rights, for the most part, have their origins in Western culture and the development of natural law. This concept of rights evolved out of the struggle between the church and the state, and the individual's quest for freedom from both. Natural law doctrine conceives of rights due to all human beings, not just obligations of the state. This evolved in the eighteenth and nineteenth centuries into liberal, laissez-faire notions of the rights of man: freedom and equality, consisting of the right to due process of law, the right to vote, the right to free speech, and the right to a free press.

This conception of rights emphasizes the notion that human beings are inherently granted certain rights that the state cannot take away, a perspective best stated by John Locke: "Certain rights self-evidently pertain to individuals as human beings; chief among them are rights to life, liberty and property; the failure of the state to secure these rights gives rise to a right to responsible revolution."[7] In essence, this is the individual, civil and political rights argument for what is central to the promotion of human rights.

Economic, social, and cultural rights: the second generation

The basis for second-generation rights emerged out of the rise of socialism. Economic and social rights were almost unknown to natural rights thinkers of the eighteenth century because rights originally were thought of historically and philosophically as the ideology of the wealthy, and were associated with the rising middle class.[8] Recognizing the inadequacies of civil and political rights towards meeting the basic needs of the people, socialists thus submit that these rights emanate from a conception of the individual's role in society and the development of the predominant mode of production. This results in an understanding of human rights as relating to the stage of development of a particular society.

More recently, proponents of economic and social rights have emphasized that without meeting a person's subsistence needs there is little human development and progress. Proponents of these rights also stress that human rights have corresponding duties and obligations that firmly connect individuals with their societies.[9] The ICESCR are the second-generation rights and usually are referred to as positive rights because the society needs to provide the rights of adequate food, shelter, health care, employment, and the right to join trade unions. This means that the state provides the necessary resources of survival and development to its citizens.

People's rights: the third generation

Third-generation rights have risen in popularity and support in developing countries and "are a result of the growing consciousness of common humanity that transcends the limitations of the nation-state system."[10] These solidarity or people's rights center on the right to development as referred to by Article 28 of the Universal Declaration, which states that "everyone is entitled to a social and international order in which the rights set forth in the Declaration can be fully realized."[11]

Solidarity rights have two priorities: combating violations of the human rights of peoples, and the realization of a transformed global economic system. This requires a global distribution of power, wealth, and other important values that consist of the right to economic, social, and cultural self-determination; the right to economic and social development; the right to participate in and benefit from our "common heritage"; the right to peace; the right to a healthy and balanced environment; and the right to humanitarian disaster relief.[12] Thus the idea behind these rights is that particular groups in disadvantaged situations (i.e. poverty) have a special claim on the world community for assistance in achieving their development goals.[13] In order to fulfill these goals, people's rights call for a restructuring of the global system because the nation-state system, dominated by the North, has failed to provide either adequate protection or development. Implementation of these rights seeks to level the playing field between states in the international system. Although these rights generally are presented as collective rights, because everyone must have access to the distribution of resources, they also emphasize the relationship and pattern of interaction between the individual and the group.

A holistic framework

Despite the arguments for the universality of individual rights or the need for cultural relativism, few would, as Louis Henkin states, "dare dissent from human rights today."[14] This point alone suggests the need to build a better consensus for understanding and implementing human rights. In addition, it should be recognized that human rights are dynamic – they evolve and change over time, and any attempt to apply human rights universally should be qualified by stating that the concept, no matter how broad its cross-cultural and international acceptance, reflects the understanding of the period.[15] In the post-Cold War era, in particular, a state's human rights situation has taken on a new meaning, and has become the basis for tensions between states. For instance, the United States upholds the first-generation rights as universal, arguing that civil and political rights are the universal definition of rights, and applies them selectively to other countries.

On the other hand, states like China argue that rights are cultural and should be determined by the state, based on development, even if that means using violence to suppress domestic dissent. Developing countries and development agencies struggle over which set of rights should take priority in implementation. While individualist arguments are problematic, any discussion that stresses purely economic, social, and cultural rights at the expense of civil and political rights should be questioned as well. Indeed it may be argued that the debate over individual versus collective rights justifies prioritizing rights which therefore may provide a smoke screen for states to abuse rights. Thus, does this division of rights get us very far in actually promoting the progress of people and communities?

Moreover, the strength of authoritarian governments, the increasing level of poverty, and persistent underdevelopment in the South (comprising five-sixths of the world's population), as well as the violence, increasing poverty, and cynicism in the North, attest to the need to think about human rights holistically. Although there are those who strictly adhere to the dichotomy between individual and collective rights, more and more states and students of human rights are recognizing the need to incorporate both aspects in order to achieve a coherent human rights program of action. Once the notion that there need not be a hierarchy of human rights is recognized, there is a demand for implementing human rights comprehensively. For instance, Henry Shue submits that a holistic notion of basic rights, which consist of physical security, economic subsistence, and political participation, provides the basis for a justified demand that the actual enjoyment of rights be socially guaranteed against standard threats in the society.[16] Recently the demand for change has been illustrated by the increased mobilization of grassroots social movements, seeking a healthy environment, adequate social policies, and popular participation in government. As Chandra Muzaffar states:

> A holistic approach will not only give equal attention to the various aspects of human rights – civil, political, economic, social and cultural – but will also balance individual rights with collective rights. In most non-Western traditions, it must be remembered that the individual does not possess an inherently conflictual relationship with his community. Indeed, very often it is through the community that the individual realizes his self by fulfilling both his rights and responsibilities.[17]

HUMAN RIGHTS IN HONG KONG

The development of human rights

Hong Kong was established in 1842 to provide Great Britain with a trading post in Asia, primarily serving China. Throughout much of Hong Kong's history, the British colonial government took a laissez-faire approach towards domestic affairs, preferring to focus on commercial endeavors. This policy was a result of the attitude that government interference would potentially limit trade and commerce. Moreover, the early political system in Hong Kong was divided between the European and Chinese population, where histori- cally the Europeans were ruled under British common law, while the Chinese population were ruled under Chinese traditions and customs. Thus it was left up to the Chinese community to rule themselves socially and politically.

Nonetheless, in the interwar period the Chinese population began to make demands to be included in the Hong Kong administration, and in the postwar period a system of indirect consultation emerged. However, Hong Kong remained an undemocratic system, and the colonial government made no effort to enfranchise the population or make reforms to include them in the decision-making process. Their control mechanisms included such measures as the Public Order Ordinance, the Societies Ordinance, and the Education Ordinance (which prohibited the provision of civic education in schools). Thus not only did the Hong Kong government avoid involvement in social, economic, and cultural aspects of Hong Kong society, it also limited political participation. Consequently, while the United Nations was formed and human rights were enshrined in the Universal Declaration of Human Rights in 1948, followed by the covenants on civil and political rights and economic, social, and cultural rights (both signed by Great Britain in 1976), the people of Hong Kong were without any mechanisms to implement these basic human rights. Even as Hong Kong industrialized and emerged as a newly industrialized economy in the 1970s, the protection and implementation of human rights continued to be minimal.

Challenges to protect human rights in Hong Kong

Regardless of its unwillingness to implement human rights in Hong Kong, the colonial government began to face greater challenges and increasing demands to reform the system. For instance, in the aftermath of the 1966–7 riots and disturbances (influenced by China's Cultural Revolution), Hong Kong witnessed a movement to reform and broaden representation throughout Hong Kong, although, for many, the subsequent government reforms (i.e. the creation of the rural District Advisory Boards and Mutual Aid Committees) were merely measures to absorb criticisms and citizen complaints, not an effort to include the people in the political system.[18] Despite the colonial government's efforts to absorb complaints and unrest at the grassroots level, the people, especially throughout the 1970s, made demands on it to make substantial changes in its policies and laws related to the rights of the Hong Kong people. For instance, these movements included the students' efforts to institute Chinese as an official language of Hong Kong, and the urban movement which sought greater and better housing for the Hong Kong people, marked by the Yaumatei Typhoon Shelter Resettlement Movement in 1977–9. The activists in this movement not only requested that the government provide housing for these people, they also challenged the legitimacy of the Public Order Ordinance, which limited the people's right to assembly and to demonstrate in public.[19]

Contemporary human rights

Most discussions concerning human rights in Hong Kong center on the establishment of the Special Administrative Region government, and the crisis in confidence that resulted from the 1989 suppression of the nonviolent democracy movement on the mainland. On the one hand it is argued that the British common law system, which is based on such principles as neutrality, rationality, and impartiality, represents a government of laws, not people; British common law was to be the cornerstone for the protection of civil and political rights,[20] and should be the foundation for protecting human rights in the post-handover period. On the other hand, it is argued that the concern over the protection of civil and political rights is a form of Western domination, and it is more important to have a smooth and stable return to Chinese sovereignty that will continue economic development and further human dignity.[21]

There is also a third contention in this debate. This argument, put forward by nongovernmental organizations (NGOs) and activists in Hong Kong, submits that human rights in Hong Kong have always been poorly protected, whether they be individual or collective rights, and that there should be an effort made to comprehensively protect the human rights of the Hong Kong people.[22] This section of the chapter discusses contemporary human rights in Hong Kong and government measures for implementing and protecting human rights in Hong Kong. It also examines international factors, such as pressure from China and Britain as well as the international community to implement human rights measures in Hong Kong.

First-generation rights: civil and political rights

During British rule, Hong Kong was governed by the British common law system, and since Great Britain is a signatory to the ICCPR these rights were extended to Hong Kong. Often during the colonial period, Hong Kong was cited as an Asian society that was free from government repression; however, the British attached several reservations to the ICCPR which prohibited the

Hong Kong people from participating in the political system, including: the right to self-determination; persons deprived of liberty shall be treated with human dignity; the right to leave any country and enter one's own country; children's rights; and the right to take part in the conduct of public affairs.[23] Britain justified the reservations by stating that Hong Kong was not ready for self-rule; there was no real desire on the part of the population for democracy (due to its cultural traditions of Confucianism); and China would never allow it to occur.[24]

In 1984 the Chinese and British governments signed the Sino-British Joint Declaration, which laid out the transfer of sovereignty from Great Britain to the People's Republic of China on July 1, 1997. The Joint Declaration states that Hong Kong would become a Special Administrative Region of the People's Republic of China (SAR) with a high degree of autonomy, and Annex I, Section XIII stipulates that the provisions of the ICCPR as applied to Hong Kong shall remain in force. After signing of the Joint Declaration, the colonial government took steps to expand local representation in the political system as a way of preparing the Hong Kong people for self-rule after 1997 as stipulated in the Joint Declaration. The colonial government began the process by first expanding the elected number of District Board (DB) members to one-third in 1982. In addition, in 1984 the colonial government published the *Green Paper: On the Further Development of Representative Government in Hong Kong*, proposing that the people of Hong Kong directly elect members to the Legislative Council (LegCo) and the Municipal Councils (the UrbCo and RegCo) in the 1988 elections.[25] However, under pressure from the mainland, the colonial government postponed the 1988 direct elections until 1991, stating that there was not enough support by the people for them.[26]

Another measure impacting human rights in the post-1997 era is the Basic Law written by the Basic Law Drafting Committee, which consisted primarily of mainland Chinese and Hong Kong businessmen and elites. The Basic Law, passed by China's National People's Congress in 1990, has been severely criticized by the Hong Kong people for not upholding the promise of the Joint Declaration's "Hong Kong people ruling Hong Kong," thus questioning its ability to ensure or protect any civil and political rights. This disappointment, coupled with the Tiananmen Square massacre, brought on a crisis in confidence. Subsequently the Hong Kong people and the government moved to implement provisions that would protect human rights and local autonomy. As a result, in 1991 the Bill of Rights Ordinance (the domestic application of the ICCPR) was enacted, and Governor Chris Patten announced an electoral reform package to quicken the pace of democracy.

Even though Hong Kong has in place legal provisions to protect civil and political rights, the actual enforcement and implementation of these rights is another story. Civil and political rights of the people continue to be limited by the government's ability to control the people's civil liberties. For instance, the people's right to freedom of expression and information is restricted through the Film Censorship Ordinance which censors films and entertainment materials; the Official Secrets Act, which limits the public's access to information; and the Public Order Ordinance and the Societies Ordinance, which restrict the right to freedom of assembly and association. The Public Order Ordinance, for example, requires that any group that wants to demonstrate or assemble must first apply for a permit with the Commissioner of Police, who is empowered to stipulate the conditions of the license. This ordinance has been severely criticized because it restricts free speech and movement, such as when the police prohibited women from singing, chanting, or using a loud-speaker during International Women's Day in 1988.[27] The Societies Ordinance also limits the people's right to assemble by requiring all groups to register with the government, which has the ability to monitor their activities, their constitution, and their accounts. According to the Hong Kong Human Rights Commission's October 1995 report to the United Nations Human Rights Committee, "the meaning of 'breach of peace' is so broad that it can be abused to suppress the rights of people."[28]

Political rights continue to be restricted as well, even though the government has implemented political reforms and the Bill of Rights Ordinance. In addition, while there has been the evolution of political parties and direct elections to LegCo, the DBs, and the Municipal Councils, the "pre-handover" political reforms introduced did not permit the direct election of all members of the government, and allowed some people to vote more than once through the functional constituency system.

Even though China repeatedly stated that this process did not converge with the Basic Law, and that Hong Kong's three-tiered government would be dismantled by July 1, 1997, electoral politics became an important process in returning some confidence to Hong Kong. And although Beijing disapproved of the process, it came out and supported the pro-China political parties in the September 1994 DB and September 1995 LegCo elections. Moreover, due process and the freedom to run for office was overshadowed by political concerns for appeasing China. For instance, during the summer of 1994, Lau San-ching, a pro-democracy activist who had spent most of the 1980s in a mainland jail for political activities during the Democracy Wall movement, was prohibited from running for a DB seat. The colonial government justified this by stating that he did not fulfill the residency requirement that stipulates that a candidate must be a Hong Kong resident for the last ten years.

While the colonial government offered only minimal and gradual progress for promoting civil and political rights, Hong Kong citizen groups and NGOs are more persistent in demanding that these rights be expanded and protected. For instance, grassroots organizations like the short-lived United Ants, Emily Lau's The Frontier, and the Hong Kong Voice of Democracy work towards the implementation of comprehensive human rights and democracy. These groups seek a Hong Kong government that is fully elected by the Hong Kong people. In addition, the now defunct United Ants monitored the colonial government's respect for civil and political rights. Indeed, one member stated that the Ants saw no reason why Hong Kong could not be independent. The member explained that the Hong Kong people were sold-out by both Beijing and London, which had only their domestic economic interests in mind when they signed the Joint Declaration.[29] Nonetheless, the Ants were critical of both the pro-China and democratic forces in Hong Kong politics. For instance, in 1994 they called for the resignation of four Meeting Point, LegCo members because they went against their pro-democracy election promises when they abstained from voting on LegCo member Emily Lau's Full Democracy bill, which ended up being defeated by a single vote. Two members of the Ants also filed a "first of its kind" lawsuit challenging the constitutionality of the government's functional constituency seat system, which allows people to have more than one vote in elections (the suit has since been over-ruled by a Hong Kong court).

Second-generation rights: economic, social, and cultural rights

While civil and political rights were essentially prohibited throughout most of Hong Kong's history, the institutionalization and implementation of social, economic, and cultural rights have not fared much better. As noted, the colonial government was reluctant to become involved in Hong Kong society, and as a result most of the social welfare responsibilities fell to either the Chinese community or the churches, through such private organizations as the Kaifong Associations, the Tung Wah Group of Hospitals, and the Hong Kong Council of Social Services. So while Hong Kong was not a social welfare state, the most basic provisions for life were met by private institutions.

Although early in Hong Kong's history the colonial government did establish the Labour Department and the Secretary for Chinese Affairs, it was not until Hong Kong industrialized that the government established the Department of Social Welfare to coordinate the welfare activities through its divisions of social security: family services; group and community work; and probation, corrections, and rehabilitation.[30] Probably the most influential impetus for the government to become involved in society was the 1955 Shek Kip Mei fire, which left hundreds, if not thousands, of people without homes and prompted the development of Hong Kong's social welfare system. The fire forced the colonial government into changing its position on involvement in Hong Kong's social development, and from that time on the government became involved in Hong Kong society. Indeed, today half of Hong Kong's population resides in public housing, making it the second largest public housing provider in the world (behind Singapore).[31] During the postwar years the colonial government also improved and expanded its education, health care, and labor policies. However, it should be noted that the government primarily did this by providing funds to NGOs, such as churches and the Kaifong associations. These organizations, then, provided the health care, education, and community programs to the people. In recent years this has been carried out by one of Hong Kong's most active community-based organizations, the Society for Community Organization (SoCO). Founded in the early 1970s to promote grassroots community development by which to empower people to change their lives, SoCO works toward developing the social and economic rights of the Hong Kong people.

Just as with the ICCPR, Britain also signed the ICESCR, applying reservations to such articles as the right to equal pay to men and women for equal work in the private sector and the right of trade unions to establish national federations in Hong Kong.[32] However, the protection and implementation of these rights are inadequate compared to Hong Kong's per capita gross domestic product (at approximately US $19,000 in 1992), which places it in the upper division of the world's development. Hong Kong was ranked by the World Development Report in 1992 as having the greatest disparity in its distribution of wealth among industrialized nations; between 1971 and 1991 Hong Kong's gini coefficient[33] measured from .43 to .48.[34]

Despite the efforts of private organizations, it is apparent that economic, social, and cultural rights need greater protection and enforcement. The absence of any governmental efforts to implement and protect these rights has raised calls from the people to improve the situation, arguing that Hong Kong's level of development can afford a more equitable distribution of wealth. One Hong Kong social activist explained that Hong Kong has become a society for the very wealthy and has left behind the middle class and a struggling low-income population that cannot afford both housing and sending their children to college.[35] An example of the level of inequalities in Hong Kong is the living conditions for many of Hong Kong's elderly, especially those in the "cage homes." These people have no retirement funds, survive on public assistance, and cannot afford their own homes. They therefore share a flat with up to ten people or families, protecting their belongings by surrounding their bed with a cage.[36] Conditions such as these have been responded to by NGOs, such as SoCO, as well as activists, with the demand for the institution of an old-age retirement scheme which would provide all Hong Kong people with a minimum subsistence in their retirement years. In the summer of 1994, the colonial government published a paper on "Taking the Worry out of Growing Old." This paper was received with support from workers, half of the Legislative Council members, and most opinion polls. However, due to pressure from China and the business community, on Chinese New Year, 1995, the government shelved the Old-age Pension Scheme, stating that public opinion was divided.[37]

Another second-generation right, the right to work and to strike, continues to be restricted in Hong Kong. Hong Kong's labor laws state only that workers have the freedom to strike and not the right to strike. This means that if labor negotiations fail and the workers declare a strike, it would be considered a breach of contract and employers could legally replace all the striking workers. Because Hong Kong workers generally are hired on the basis of individual contracts, their ability to negotiate collectively is hampered. Moreover, trade union activity is restricted by the Societies Ordinance, which facilitates police control over strikes and demonstrations. As a result there has been limited development of Hong Kong's labor movement, even though it is an industrialized economy. The labor laws, for instance, allow employers to dismiss workers without requiring any justification.[38] Accordingly, because of the government's failure to protect workers' rights, groups like the Hong Kong Christian Industrial Committee (CIC) and the umbrella trade union organization the Confederation of Trade Unions (CTU) are politically and socially organizing workers to apply pressure on the government to protect their rights. Leung Po Lam of the Asian Monitor Resource Center, a labor monitoring group, maintains that Beijing is unwilling to protect workers' rights. Thus he argues that workers should act collectively, within Hong Kong and across borders, to achieve change.[39]

Third-generation rights: peoples' rights

As already mentioned, third-generation rights, more commonly known as peoples' rights, are made up of the right to development with social justice, the right to a clean and sustainable environment, and the right to preserve a society's culture. In Hong Kong, these rights have not been legally instituted or implemented, and only recently have found any sort of general support. Since the colonial government pursued economic development from its inception, the right to development has not been stressed as in other developing countries. However, at the grassroots level and through NGOs citizens have called for a more equitable and just method of development so that it is not just the few who reap the benefits from a prosperous society. These organizations and groups have stated that the people of Hong Kong have the right to be treated justly and equitably.[40] The development of other third-generation rights, such as the right to a sustainable environment, is also growing. For instance, the colonial government minimally supported the environmental movement with its creation in the late 1980s of a public education and awareness program to help combat waste and water pollution, even though raw sewage continues to be dumped directly into Hong Kong's harbor.[41] Although the green movement is young and both the colonial and SAR governments have taken only limited action to either recognize or implement these rights, there is a strong movement by university students to protect Hong Kong's environment.[42]

Another peoples' right that has not been protected but is a growing concern is the right to self-determination. The collective right of the Hong Kong people to determine their future was violated by the process which led to the signing of the Sino-British Joint Declaration, which did not involve and was not consulted on by the Hong Kong people. This was a bilateral process between the governments of China and Great Britain. Once the negotiations were settled, the agreement was signed and the deal set that would transfer approximately six million people over to a new government. Nowhere in this process were the Hong Kong people allowed to participate or to determine for themselves what should happen with their society. In the absence of the protection and implementation of the right to self-determination, the people of Hong Kong became anxious over the 1997 transition and their future under the Hong Kong SAR administration.[43] This anxiety was exacerbated by the Beijing government's establishment of the Provisional Legislature in 1996 and the announcement in December 1996 that Tung Chee-hwa would be the SARs first chief executive.[44] Stepping in to illustrate their disapproval of these developments, a coalition of Hong Kong NGOs, citizens, and LegCo members staged demonstrations to protest the illegal and undemocratic nature of the selection of the chief executive and the dismantling of the existing government, especially the Legislative Council.[45]

A final growing concern is the right to protect and preserve the cultural heritage of the Hong Kong Cantonese people and its international character. The Hong Kong people are worried that in the post-handover era the Han culture and *putonghua* language (the PRC's official national language) will overshadow the unique Hong Kong way of life. They argue that there has been much disdain of Hong Kong culture. Cultural purists state it has been contaminated by the West and does not follow Confucian *zhengtong*, "the orthodox way," which in contemporary times is linked to nationalism and xenophobia.[46] In response to this concern, along with cultural activities there has been a movement to preserve Cantonese and English in the schools and the government.

Within this perspective of human rights a division has emerged. On the one hand, individuals and NGOs, like the Hong Kong Christian Council (HKCC), submit that the British and Western concern over civil and political rights in Hong Kong is another form of domination. The HKCC's Secretary General Dr Tso Man-king explained to the author in an interview that even the term "human rights" is inappropriate, preferring to use the term "human dignity" instead. Consequently what is important for Hong Kong is to continue its economic prosperity as well as to build a closer relationship with the mainland's population for the good of all of China.[47] On the other hand, Ho Hei Wah, Executive Director of SoCO, submits that civil, political, economic, social, and cultural rights of the Hong Kong people need to be protected and advanced for the overall development of the society.[48] Accordingly, SoCO agrees with the pro-China and conservative forces in Hong Kong that collective rights are important; however, they also argue that Hong Kong society can only prosper if human rights are implemented comprehensively.

International factors and human rights in Hong Kong

From its foundation, both the Beijing and British governments have been influential in the domestic matters of Hong Kong. For instance, as early as 1925–6 the paralyzing labor strikes and boycott could not have been so effective if the workers had not received support from Guangzhou and left the colony for the mainland. The government probably also would never have instituted its public housing program if the British had not been so outraged over the living conditions of the people in postwar Hong Kong. Moreover, without having to worry about Great Britain's image in returning Hong Kong to Chinese sovereignty, the colonial government would never have introduced political reforms in the 1980s. And without the outcry by the international community following the crushing of the nonviolent democracy movement in 1989, the British government would not have appointed Chris Patten as their final governor of Hong Kong. Being a politician, as governor, Patten was not afraid to be controversial. He, for example, introduced greater political reforms in October 1992, even at the risk of upsetting China. Thus the domestic pressure to ensure some sense of autonomy for Hong Kong and to alleviate Britain's guilt brought on by the "selling-out" of the Hong Kong people led to pressure to ensure greater human rights measures leading up to 1997.

On the other hand, all the way up to the transfer of sovereignty China continued to place pressure on Britain and Hong Kong to restrict the institution of human rights and political reforms. Many believe that it is not in China's interest to have a democratic Hong Kong because it may destabilize the mainland, where it may instill an "if they have it why can't we?" expectation. Moreover, the mainland is fearful that an elected legislature will enact greater social welfare reforms in Hong Kong. This, they feel, would ultimately bankrupt the SAR, and Hong Kong would cease to be the source of the "golden egg."

Other countries, like the US, also have played a role in influencing human rights in Hong Kong, in several ways. For instance, immediately after the Tiananmen Square massacre, the United States imposed sanctions on China and began deliberations about whether or not to renew China's Most Favored Nation (MFN) trading status, the denial of which would have an immensely negative economic impact on Hong Kong's economy. The United States also passed domestic legislation which calls for the monitoring and annual submission of reports on Hong Kong's human rights situation. The United States has been supportive of the pro-democracy advocates in general, offering to have several activists tour the US in order to educate Americans about Hong Kong's human rights situation.[49] Finally, in 1995, the European Parliament designated US $1.8 million to establish a human rights center in Hong Kong, in part because of the controversy over whether or not China will continue to submit periodic reports to the UN on the human rights situation in Hong Kong to aid in monitoring the human rights situation there.

CONCLUSION

The implementation and protection of human rights in Hong Kong has faced many obstacles and challenges. It is evident that the debate between Asian and Western conceptions of human rights continues in Hong Kong today. In particular, this debate has emerged between NGOs and activists in Hong Kong, who disagree over the implementation of civil and political rights and the pace of democratization. Organizations like SoCO, the CTU, and the Hong Kong Voice of Democracy argue that civil and political rights are relatively simple to monitor and implement through the rule of law. On the other hand, China and the pro-China forces in Hong Kong would prefer that Hong Kong remain at the status quo. They maintain that changing the system will only upset Hong Kong's continued prosperity. NGOs and grassroots activists, however, argue that human rights need to be implemented holistically as stated in the United Nations Declaration, covenants, and regional documents. They argue that the division between the Asian and Western definitions of human rights is a cloak that governments use for not granting people greater political and social autonomy. For instance, they point to Article 23 of the Basic Law, which places limits on local organizations' contacts with international groups, which in the end will limit their solidarity efforts with other NGOs.

In sum, this chapter has used a holistic framework to review the human rights situation in Hong Kong. It has submitted that a holistic framework does not distinguish between these rights, but that human rights should be implemented simultaneously in order to obtain a comprehensive recognition of these rights. It was found that although Hong Kong is a society that is a blending of cultural influences, ranging from Confucianism to British common law, the actual realization of either set of human rights and values is minimal.

The lack of comprehensive human rights protection places Hong Kong in a precarious position in the post-handover era. The Hong Kong people not only have restricted civil and political liberties, they have minimal protection of subsistence rights and the collective rights of the people to self-determination and cultural preservation are indeed either prohibited or in jeopardy. Without providing comprehensive human rights it is the people in society who suffer. Recognizing this, grassroots organizations and NGOs are actively pursuing the expansion and implementation of human rights. Whether it is the Hong Kong Voice of Democracy, promoting and monitoring civil and political rights; the CIC and CTU, advocating worker rights; or SoCO's work in community development, the pursuit for the actualization of human rights is alive in Hong Kong.

NOTES

The author would like to thank Joy Sobrepeña Wagner, Apo Leung, and the editor of this volume for their comments and suggestions for the revision of this essay.

1 For example, see Raymond Wacks, ed., *Human Rights in Hong Kong* (Hong Kong: Oxford University Press, 1992).
2 See Maurice Cranston, *What are Human Rights?* (London: The Bodley Head, 1973); and Hugo Bedau, "Human Rights and Foreign Assistance Programs," in Peter Brown and Douglas MacLean, eds, *Human Rights and US Foreign Policy* (Lexington, MA: Lexington Books, 1979).
3 Jack Donnelly, *Universal Human Rights in Theory and Practice* (Ithaca, NY: Cornell University Press, 1989), p. 34.
4 See Henry Shue, *Basic Rights: Subsistence, Affluence, and U.S. Foreign Policy* (Princeton, NJ: Princeton University Press, 1980), Chapter 2, for a discussion on the need to apply human rights comprehensively.
5 See Jack Donnelly, *The Concept of Human Rights* (London: Croom Helm, 1985).
6 Richard Lillich, "Civil Rights," in Theodore Meron, ed., *Human Rights in International Law, Legal, and Policy Issues, Volume 1* (Oxford: Clarendon Press, 1984), p. 116.
7 John Locke, *Second Treatise of Government*, in *Two Treatises of Government*, ed. Peter Laslett (Cambridge: Cambridge University Press, 1967 [1690]), sect. 4, pp. 1–8.
8 Saneh Chamarik, "Some Thoughts on Human Rights Promotion and Protection," in Harry Scoble and Laurie Wiesberg, eds, *Access to Justice: Human Rights Struggles in South East Asia* (London: Zed Books, 1985), p. 9.
9 Valadmir Karashkin, "The Socialist Countries and Human Rights," in Karel Vasek and Philip Alston, eds, *The International Dimensions of Human Rights* (Westport, CT: Greenwood Press, 1982), p. 2.
10 George W. Shepherd, Jr and Mark O.C. Anikpo, eds, *Emerging Human Rights: The African Political Economy Context* (Westport, CT: Greenwood Press, 1990), p. 2.
11 Universal Declaration of Human Rights (UN Doc A/811), Dec. 1948, Article 48.
12 Richard Pierre Claude and Burns H. Weston, eds, *Human Rights in the World Community: Issues and Action* (Philadelphia: University of Pennsylvania Press, 1989), p. 18.
13 Shepherd and Anikpo, eds, *Emerging Human Rights*, p. 4.
14 Louis Henkin, *Rights of Man Today* (Boulder, CO: Westview Press, 1978), pp. 27–8.
15 Jack Donnelly, "Cultural Relativism and Universal Human Rights," *Human Rights Quarterly* 6, no. 4 (1984), pp. 400–19.
16 Shue, *Basic Rights*, pp. 13–19.
17 Chandra Muzaffar, *Human Rights and the New World Order* (Penang: Just World Trust, 1993), p. vii.
18 These reforms included the establishment of government offices (the District Advisory Boards) in the rural areas and the establishment of Mutual Aid Committees in urban public housing estates. See Ambrose Y.C. King, "Administrative Absorption of Politics in Hong Kong: Emphasis on the Grass Roots Level," *Asian Survey* 15, no. 5 (May 1975), pp. 422–39.
19 See "The Yaumatei Boat People Case," in Hilda Chan, S.H., *Putting Justice and Human Rights in Focus: A Report on Hong Kong to the Human Rights Committee of the United Nations*, August 1980.
20 See Peter Wesley-Smith, "Protecting Human Rights in Hong Kong," in Wacks, ed., *Human Rights in Hong Kong*, pp. 17–21.
21 Tso Man-king, secretary general, Hong Kong Christian Council, interview with the author, summer 1994.

22 For instance, this is the position of the Hong Kong Human Rights Commission.
23 Nihal Jayawickrama, "Hong Kong and the International Protection of Human Rights," in Wacks, ed., *Human Rights in Hong Kong*, pp. 129–31.
24 This was highly contested by Hong Kong social activists.
25 *Green Paper: The Further Development of Representative Government in Hong Kong* (Hong Kong: Government Printer, 1984).
26 This point has been widely disputed by the public opinion polls published in local newspapers, which showed that there was considerable support for direct elections in 1988.
27 Rev. Kwok Nai Wang, "Human Rights in Hong Kong" (Hong Kong: Church of Sweden Mission Annual Report, 1990).
28 Hong Kong Human Rights Commission, "Report to the United Nations Human Rights Commission on the Fourth Periodic Report by Hong Kong under Article 40 of the International Covenant on Civil and Political Rights" (Hong Kong, 1995), p. 36.
29 The United Ants, interview with the author, summer 1994.
30 See *Social Welfare in Hong Kong* (Hong Kong: Government Printer, 1992).
31 James Lee, "Housing and Social Welfare," in *Indicators of Social Development: Hong Kong, 1990* (Hong Kong: The Chinese University of Hong Kong Press, 1992), p. 55.
32 Jayawickrama, "Hong Kong and the International Protection of Human Rights," pp. 139–41.
33 The gini coefficient varies from 0 (complete equality) to 1 (complete inequality) and is a measure of income inequality derived from the Lorenz Curve, which relates percentages of individuals or households to percentages of personal income received by each.
34 Hong Kong Human Rights Commission, "Human Rights Now and Beyond 1997," p. 9.
35 Rita Kwok, interview with the author, summer 1994.
36 See Society for Community Organization, *Annual Report, 1991–1992* (Hong Kong: SoCO, 1992), pp. 23–5.
37 Hong Kong Christian Institute, *Newsletter* no. 77 (March 2, 1995).
38 Hong Kong Human Rights Commission, "Human Rights Now and Beyond 1997," pp. 10–12.
39 Leung Po Lam, director, Asian Monitor Resource Center, interview with the author, summers 1993, 1994, and 1996.
40 For instance, see the annual and special reports produced by SoCO and the Confederation of Trade Unions.
41 Cecilia Chan and Peter Hill, *Limited Gains: Grassroots Mobilization and the Environment in Hong Kong* (Hong Kong: The Centre of Urban Planning and Environmental Management, 1993), pp. 38–9.
42 For instance, both the Chinese University of Hong Kong and Hong Kong University have active student groups. The students are planting trees and rice paddies in the rural areas and are involved in public awareness campaigns to clean up the harbor and "Keep Hong Kong clean."
43 See Rev. Kwok Nai Wang, "Human Rights in Hong Kong," p. 1.
44 The PRC's National People's Congress established the Preparatory Committee (PC) in preparation for transfer of sovereignty and the dismantling of the current government. It was primarily comprised of Hong Kong businessmen and elites, who were approved by the Beijing government. The selection process for the first chief executive was outlined during a plenary session. It consisted of the following. Those wishing to run for chief executive needed to indicate their intention to the PC presidium by submitting a form before November 1, 1996. (As the Selection

Committee was established after November 1, 1996, this meant that candidates would be announced before the members of the committee had been decided.) The presidium would review the forms to ensure candidates met age and residency criteria. The nominees would then become candidates if they won the nomination from at least fifty people on the Selection Committee. A secret ballot would then be held to select the chief executive, and the winner had to gain more than 200 of the 400 Selection Committee votes (July 1 Link, *Newsletter*, November 1996, p. 5).

45 July 1 Link, *Newsletter* (January 1997), pp. 5–6.
46 See Paul C.K. Kwong, "Internationalization of Population and Globalization of Families," in Choi Po-king and Ho Lok-sang, eds, *The Other Hong Kong Report, 1993* (Hong Kong: The Chinese University of Hong Kong Press, 1993).
47 Tso Man-king, secretary general, Hong Kong Christian Council, interview with the author, summer 1994.
48 Ho Hei Wah, executive director, Society for Community Organization, interview with the author, summer 1994.
49 Ho Hei Wah, interview with the author, summer 1994.

6

DEVELOPMENTALISM AND CHINA'S HUMAN RIGHTS POLICY

Michael J. Sullivan

Michael J. Sullivan *is an American political scientist studying elite Chinese political debates over development and political change as they relate to specific PRC domestic and foreign policies. He is also researching how business and human rights interests in the United States influence US policy toward China. This essay examines how official China engages in the human rights debate, especially Beijing's assessment of foreign and domestic human rights issues from the perspective of developmentalism. Note the differing positions on these issues presented by Sullivan in this chapter and Zhu Feng in Chapter 12.*

> The improvement of human rights is a continuously developing process along with the political, economic and cultural progress. China, as a developing country, is restricted by its historical and realistic conditions and the country's human rights conditions still have room for further improvement.
>
> State Council Information Office (1997)[1]

> [A]s soon as man . . . takes refuge in doctrine, as soon as crime reasons about itself, it multiplies like reason itself and assumes all the aspects of the syllogism. Once crime was as solitary as a cry of protest; now it is as universal as science. Yesterday it was put on trial; today it determines the law.
>
> Existentialist philosopher Albert Camus (1956)[2]

> Human rights have become a popular topic of conversation lately and even the Party line on the issue seems to have softened somewhat. It has declared that it intends to "study human rights theories and questions in order to deal with the peaceful evolution of hostile forces," and so on. . . . One thing I do know for sure, however, is that your Party unyieldingly holds the same view of human rights that the Nazis did, which helps explain why you gnash your teeth

at the mere mention of human rights and are so eager to get rid of them.

Letter to President Jiang Zemin and Premier Li Peng from democratic dissident Wei Jingsheng (1991)[3]

INTRODUCTION

The record of the Chinese Communist Party (CCP) on human rights[4] has been dismal. These violations have included torture, forced prison labor, repression of autonomous worker unions, suppression of ethnic collective rights, religious persecution, forced sterilization, and unethical medical violations of human organ transplants.[5] The CCP's human rights violations before and after 1949 have been concretely documented by China scholars, Chinese dissident organizations, foreign governments, and international human rights NGOs.[6] Besides civil and political liberties, the violation of economic, social, and cultural human rights has also been clearly documented.[7] Such documentation explodes the myth, held by many Chinese and foreign observers alike, that communist rule succeeded with economic and social rights while "lagging" behind in political and civil rights.[8]

The CCP actively employs multifaceted tactics in response to international and domestic criticisms. On the one hand, it relies on repression to quell domestic human rights aspirations. Naked repression primarily occurs in remote areas, far away from the international press corps, overseas Chinese dissident organizations, and international human rights organizations.[9] In major cities, security organizations combine overt political repression with less explicit techniques, such as frivolous criminal charges and secret arbitrary detention, to silence domestic political opposition.[10] The cases of Dai Xuezhong, a member of the Shanghai-based Chinese Human Rights Association, and Zhou Guoqiang, a Beijing dissident, exemplify this trend. Dai, who was detained in May 1994 for his human rights activities, was sentenced to a three-year jail term for allegedly "evading taxes" in December 1994.[11] Zhou was sentenced to three years of reeducation through labor on the charge of "disturbing public order" by printing T-shirts carrying labor rights slogans.[12]

On the other hand, the CCP leadership employs arguments and tactics to justify its human rights violations and to deflect criticisms of its human rights record.[13] International norms on civil and political rights are painted as alien "capitalist" concepts for "socialist" China.[14] Organizations from the Ministry of Foreign Affairs to the "nongovernmental" China Society for Human Rights Studies either falsely extol the CCP's human rights record or wantonly justify its refusal to abide by international norms on human rights.[15] The logic of Chinese officials often appears fatuous. In May 1991, then NPC chairman Wan Li countered Italian criticisms by comparing China's student demonstrators crushed by the military to the Italian mafia.[16]

While the duplicity of such tactics is quite apparent, attention must focus on the strategies employed to justify the CCP's human rights violations. As French theorist Michel Foucault has argued in the context of the former Soviet Union, it is "easy to mock the theoretical contradictions that characterize the Soviet penal system, but these are theories that kill."[17] In a similar vein, while it is relatively easy to criticize the spurious content of the CCP's formal ideologies, those ideologies are often employed to rationalize inhumane acts. Since 1989, official government organizations have increasingly been sophisticated in manipulating information, international norms, and foreign anti-human rights discourses to legitimize the CCP's human rights positions.

This increasing sophistication reveals that the CCP's human rights policies are neither immutable nor monolithic. In fact, it is increasingly difficult to identify a single, and monopolized, voice on human rights that speaks for all Mainland Chinese. Human rights discourses since 1989 can be categorized into four broad types.[18]

1　*Neo-Maoist discourses* emphasize how the promotion of human rights reflects efforts by global "capitalist" powers, led by the United States, and domestic "bourgeois-liberal" groups to overthrow CCP rule through "peaceful evolution" (*heping yanbian*). The Research Institute for Resisting Peaceful Evolution, established in the early 1990s by then-director of the CCP Propaganda Department Wang Renzhi, publishes articles on and submits reports to the central leadership on human rights that reflect this perspective.[19]

2　*Reform-Leninist discourses* accept the distinction between Marxist and capitalist human rights concepts, without the fanatical conspiracy mentality associated with neo-Maoism. Marxist concepts prioritize how human rights constitute a category of social relations related to a certain historical stage of economic development. Capitalist concepts stress how human rights are abstract and naturally innate to the human condition and protect private ownership of dominant economic classes. Capitalist concepts are treated as being incompatible with "socialist" China, even with a developing market economy.

3　*Developmentalist discourses* promote economic growth at the expense of the environment, civil and political liberties, democracy, and human rights. They tend to rely on non-socialist texts. These discourses posit that marketization should proceed without "destabilizing" political-liberalization policies, such as democratization and the enforcement of human rights legislation. This thinking has gained popularity since it promises high economic growth rates under conditions of political stability, as perceived by the development experiences in Taiwan, South Korea, and Singapore.

4　*Universalist discourses* hold that human rights not only are innate to the human condition, but must also be abided by to facilitate the expansion of individual liberties under conditions of rapid economic growth. These discourses are found on elite and local levels, such as in dissidents' political writings, student protests, workers' unionizing efforts, and peasant uprisings.

Many analysts emphasize the political tensions between official party discourses (which have been a combination of neo-Maoist and reform-Leninist discourses since June 1989) and dissidents' universalist discourses on human rights. Less attention has been given to how political discourses on nationalism, development, and culture increasingly characterize the CCP's domestic and foreign policies.

This chapter analyzes the influence of developmentalism on Chinese political discourses on human rights from 1989 to 1995. It develops three inter-related arguments. First, developmentalism represents one powerful attempt to systematize a relativist perspective on human rights within a political logic that universalizes the CCP's development experiences and *guoqing* (national situation). Relativism maintains that a country's "unique" religious–cultural and socio-economic systems exempt it from international standards on human rights. Second, a shift occurred in the CCP's tactics to achieve its human rights policy's objectives during the early 1990s.[20] These new tactics either discriminately appropriate international norms (e.g. the right to self-determination, developmental rights, and collective human rights) or selectively highlight aspects of socialist and non-socialist political discourses (e.g. racial-nationalist sentiments and developmentalism) to counter domestic and international pressures to improve the CCP's human rights record. Third, the use of developmentalism bolsters the CCP's efforts to narrowly define human rights in terms of national sovereignty, subsistence rights, and development rights. These constructions divert attention away from international criticisms and domestic aspirations for civil and political liberties. They are also used to justify the CCP's civil and political human rights violations.

My analysis of developmentalist strains in the CCP's human rights policy should be seen as more than a heuristic exercise. The acceptance of developmentalism by Chinese political elites, foreign governments, and international businesses perpetuates a logic that can legitimize the systematic violation of human rights. When crimes such as human rights violations take refuge in doctrines, human suffering ceases, as Albert Camus warned in 1956, to be a cry of protest. The privileging of development or any other macro-level concerns at the expense of civil and political liberties risks systematizing policies that condone crimes against basic human dignity.[21] Will the increasing attractions of China's "big market" result in human rights violations being ignored? Will a silencing of human rights concerns allow China's human rights violators to determine the course of political change? Or will the solitary cries of protest help to shape a humane reform of Chinese politics?

UNDERSTANDING HUMAN RIGHTS WITHIN THE ASIAN CONTEXT

The popular, academic, and political discourses on human rights in China and Asia tend to be couched in a "West–Asia" binary logic. This logic, pitting a universal "West" against a peripheralized "Asia," produces two broad human rights perspectives.[22] The "universality" perspective posits that norms on human rights, as enshrined in various international documents and regimes, can be applied to all political and social contexts, regardless of cultural and historical traditions. As various scholars have argued, strains in China's cultural, historical, and intellectual traditions are compatible with global norms on human rights.[23] The "relativist" perspective argues that the application of universal notions of human rights in non-"Western" countries either represents "neo-imperialist" intentions by capitalist "core" countries or ignores the particularities of the peripheral countries' political, social, and cultural traditions.[24] The relativist "China is different" perspective has been both manipulated by the CCP for its own political imperatives and assimilated into dominant intellectual discourses in China studies. This perspective emphasizes the uniqueness of China, thus showing greater deference to the CCP's human rights violations than to other governments in the developing world or Asia.

The binary "West–Asia" construction is highly problematic. It de-emphasizes aspirations for human rights and democratic political change indigenous to China and Asia. Human rights aspirations should not be perceived as solely emanating from exogenous European and North American sources. In the PRC, domestic aspirations for political liberties evolved directly out of political terror, personal experiences of persecution, and extreme political acts of inhumanity. The "West–Asia" binary also simplifies the complexity among international political actors involved in human rights debates within Asia. After blocking a draft resolution criticizing the CCP's human rights violations at the 1995 session of the United Nations Human Rights Commission in Geneva, Jin Yongjian, head of the Chinese delegation, argued that human rights are being used as a political weapon since "as the Cold War is over . . ., the United States and other Western countries, after losing their former rivals, have turned their spearhead of attack to the developing countries."[25] While the complex politics behind human rights criticisms of China are beyond the scope of this chapter,[26] such accusations made by Jin and others fail to mention that Japan, an East Asian industrialized country, was one of the initial supporters of the resolution. The "West–Asia" binary essentially ignores the role that Asia's democratic countries (e.g. Japan, South Korea, Taiwan, the Philippines, and Thailand) and indigenous Asian human rights NGOs are playing in promoting human rights and democracy in Asia.[27]

Two analytical strategies can be employed to overcome this binary logic. The "reconciliation" strategy bridges the gap between the "universality" and "relativist" perspectives on human rights. This perspective emphasizes a meeting point in which shared aspirations for human rights are expressed through categories indigenous to an individual or group. Such aspirations often find expression in different moral-philosophical and religious narratives, but are similar in their desire for basic respect for human dignity. A constructivist-instrumentalist strategy emphasizes the important role of the struggle over the meaning of human rights within a country and among countries. This perspective focuses on how human rights discourses (1) have a multiplicity of meanings and (2) are capable of being manufactured as a tool in struggles among domestic and foreign political actors.

My study, receptive to the "reconciliation" school, relies on a constructivist-instrumentalist perspective to analyze China's human rights dilemma within the context of Chinese domestic politics. Chinese political actors are capable of constructing discourses for or against human rights to promote divergent political imperatives.[28] Diverse local political actors from intellectuals to workers promote shared notions of human rights based on ideas from popular culture, ancient Confucian texts, Marxist texts, non-Marxist-Leninist scientific thought, international norms of human rights, or individual personal experiences of persecution. They seek to promote political change that will result in protecting basic individual liberties and human dignity. Some elite political actors construct relativist arguments on China's *guoqing* to reject international norms on human rights and to justify human rights abuses. These tactics should not be perceived to be something unique to China's authoritarian leaders. Brutal authoritarian leaders elsewhere often manipulate cultural and religious relativist arguments to justify human rights abuses and to reject international standards on human rights.[29]

THE CORE ELEMENTS OF THE CCP'S HUMAN RIGHTS POLICY

The two core elements within the CCP's human rights policies are (1) a relativist emphasis on China's *guoqing* and (2) an instrumentalist perspective on the political use of human rights. The relativist-*guoqing* argument holds that China's national characteristics (e.g. development level and large population) prohibit the application of universal standards on civil and political liberties. One tenet holds that the CCP's different human rights standards are a result of unique cultural and historical traditions and distinct economic and political systems. As one report argues,

> [I]t is unrealistic to expect that countries with different social systems and varying economic and cultural development standards . . . will have an identical interpretation of the definition of human rights. . . . [T]he safeguarding . . . of human rights [is] conditional on, and subject to, the influence of different countries' political systems as well as their social, economic, and cultural conditions.[30]

Participants at a 1991 seminar, "The History and Present Situation of the Human Rights Issue," unanimously argued that human rights concepts should be modified "according to certain historical, social and cultural conditions."[31] The "nongovernmental" China Society for Human Rights Studies issued a report refuting the US State Department's 1994 human rights report on China. This report argued that the CCP's human rights record should not be assessed from "individual events or a few persons." Instead, assessments should be "an overall assessment from an objective, historical and developmental perspective."[32]

Another tenet emphasizes that the CCP's acceptance of civil and political liberties should be based on its developmental stage.[33] One commentator has argued that the role of human rights in a country's "development strategies should be based on its own national conditions."[34] He argued elsewhere against applying standards of civil and political liberties since the PRC, in order to "effectively promote national economic and social development ... has, in light of China's specific conditions, pursued a fundamental state policy to control the population growth and improve the quality of the population."[35]

Chinese political elites utilize relativist-*guoqing* arguments to achieve domestic and foreign policy objectives.[36] During a 1991 meeting with former US President Jimmy Carter in Beijing, Premier Li Peng argued that the PRC's yearly population increases and limited arable farmland made the right to subsistence the most important human rights concern. Carter responded that homelessness and other social ills are major problems in the United States.[37] Domestic propaganda organs manipulated Carter's statement to criticize the so-called "hypocrisy" of US foreign policy on human rights that Carter helped formulate during the late 1970s.[38] While attending the 1993 APEC meeting in Seattle, Party General Secretary Jiang Zemin argued that the PRC adheres to different human rights standards since "developed and developing countries have different concepts of human rights due to varying cultural traditions, ways of life, and stages of development."[39] Jiang's statement has also had domestic implications. It was widely propagated by propaganda organs to counter domestic aspirations for civil and political liberties.

Relativist-*guoqing* arguments do not exist in isolation. Powerful nationalist sentiments often shore them up. One commentator argues that human rights have been

> obtained by the Chinese people through hard struggle and sacrifice with bloodshed. When signboards saying "no admittance to Chinese and dogs" were hung on the gates of Chinese parks, what human rights did the Chinese people have? China is a developing country with a large population, and the right of development is an important right that has a bearing on the destiny and future of the Chinese nation. This is China's national situation [*guoqing*], and the European and American countries have a different kind of national situation.[40]

Emotional anti-foreign nationalist sentiments influence domestic political struggles over human rights. Fence-sitting political actors on human rights are swayed to forgo supporting domestic human rights aspirations. More importantly, such a combination bolsters the relativist-*guoqing* strain in Chinese political thought and popular culture. As twentieth-century Chinese history has sadly demonstrated, the combination of nationalist sentiments with potent racial and anti-foreign popular attitudes often leads to frenzied political movements that eventually undermine a movement's original progressive intent.[41]

The second predominant element in the CCP's human rights policies concerns the view that human rights issues are inherently politicized. The PRC has used human rights as one strategic weapon to promote broad foreign policy objectives. Maoist China joined other countries in supporting Third World liberation struggles. They protested the violation of self-determination and national sovereignty in places ranging from South Africa to Vietnam and from Palestine to Cuba. After gaining a seat in 1971, the PRC used the United Nations as a forum to criticize human rights violations of its opponent (e.g. the 1979 Soviet invasion of Afghanistan). Human rights issues, such as securing development as a right, have also been promoted to achieve the goal set out by Mao Zedong for the PRC to become the leader of the developing world. In the 1990s, the PRC officially adheres to the view that

> the UN should give priority to the massive and brutal violations of human rights resulting from colonialism, racism, foreign aggression and occupation, and should put an end to such acts through international cooperation. China is opposed to any interference in the internal affairs of UN member states under the pretence of safeguarding human rights.[42]

The PRC has forged alliances with other authoritarian governments to promote a "Third World" position on human rights, such as in the 1993 Bangkok Declaration, to counter the global trend toward accepting basic human rights standards.

The CCP's behavior at recent international conferences on human rights and women exemplifies the continuing politicization of its human rights position. Foreign human rights critics are perceived to be involved in a sinister plot to harm the PRC's national dignity and to topple the CCP. These critics are accused of harboring an "anti-Chinese" agenda. During the rigid ideological period between 1989 and 1992, neo-Maoist propaganda attacked the United States' and other countries' human rights policies as "human rights imperialism" (*renquan diguozhuyi*).[43] These policies seek to destroy the CCP through peaceful evolution strategies.[44] Neo-Maoists emphasize that a propaganda war must be waged to defend "the Chinese nation's sovereignty, the motherland's unity, and this country's territorial integrity."[45] One internal report argues for coordinated action in the area of propaganda "in order that no handle will be seized by the opposite side against us. ... [T]he issue of exporting products made by prison labor was also seized by them as a way to attack us. Therefore, we must be very careful in our propaganda."[46]

Despite the relative demise of neo-Maoists after Deng Xiaoping's 1992 Southern Tours, Chinese human rights statements still include disparaging criticisms of international human rights diplomacy. The United States and some European countries are portrayed as maliciously using human rights as a political tool against the PRC.[47] Zhu Muzhi, Director of the China Society for Human Rights Study, argues that the aim of US criticisms of the CCP's human rights record is "not to protect human rights, but to force China to be 'westernized' and 'decentralized.'"[48] "Westernization" pressures refer to how US delegates at international meetings promote the view "that democracy and individual freedom . . . [are] the preconditions for development and stress . . . free elections and the establishment of democratic mechanisms."[49] Criticisms of the CCP's human rights record at international conferences are perceived as obstructing "China's economic development, thus forcing Chinese people to change the path of development which they have chosen according to their national conditions."[50] The actions by the United States are particularly feared since the United States regards the PRC as "a major obstacle to their [i.e. the US] practice of hegemonism and power politics."[51] International human rights NGOs are also vilified in Chinese propaganda, and the PRC strives to prevent NGOs from participating in and raising human rights concerns at international meetings.[52]

The PRC takes a similar tack on domestic aspirations for human rights. Human rights dissidents are constructed as political enemies of the state. They support bourgeois liberalization (*zichanjieji ziyouhua*), which, it is claimed, undermines the CCP's so-called "socialist spiritual civilization." These activists are vilified for "making a big fuss over the human rights issue . . ., slandering China's socialist system and the people's democratic dictatorship." They are also accused of acting in collusion with foreign critics, who maliciously "interfere in China's internal affairs under the pretext of 'safeguarding human rights.'"[53] A 1991 Party-sponsored theoretical conference on human rights concluded that "bourgeois liberals" use "'human rights' as a slogan to stir up trouble and [to] create turmoil."[54] Domestic aspirations for human rights are criticized for falsely relying on ideas incongruous with the PRC's national situation. "[T]he abstract ideas of freedom, democracy, and human rights are basically the same as Sartre's, Nietzche's, and Freud's which became popular in the universities after the 'Cultural Revolution.'" The popularity of these ideas, a 1992 internal report concludes, reflects the blind acceptance of the "abstract theory of human nature and modern Western humanism."[55] Basic human dignities are constructed to be alien and harmful to the PRC's national objectives and its people.

THE 1990s CHALLENGE

The dual nature of the CCP's human rights policy – a relativist-*guoqing* perspective and the inherent politicization of human rights – remains central to the

CCP's human rights policies. Nonetheless, the economic reforms initiated by Deng Xiaoping have created new tensions and dilemmas for the CCP's human rights policies. In the early 1980s, the CCP's human rights position consisted of an inconsistent mix, arguing, on the one hand, against how hegemonism, colonialism, and imperialism violated the human rights of the developing world, and, on the other hand, against those assailing the CCP's domestic human rights record as interfering in China's internal affairs.[56] This mix waned during the late 1980s, especially since post-Mao elites gradually moved their foreign policy away from ideological commitments to Third World liberation struggles. Also, reformist leaders Hu Yaobang and Zhao Ziyang allowed increased domestic political liberalization. The 1989 crackdown on peaceful student demonstrators drastically altered China. Repression intensified. Foreign policy became rigid in some areas (e.g. human rights) and relaxed in others (e.g. normalization of ties with former enemies Vietnam and South Korea). Incessant international criticisms threatened the PRC's international political standing and its domestic economic development. The CCP, under the guidance of Deng Xiaoping, strove to prevent its demise and China's disintegration.

The CCP implemented propaganda campaigns to reverse the domestic appeal of human rights and democracy. Jiang Zemin set out the broad parameters of this propaganda war at a July 1989 national conference on propaganda. He argued that domestic propaganda should address two questions for the younger generation that have not been fully resolved: one is why China absolutely had to take the path of socialism; and the other is how to approach the questions of democracy, freedom, and human rights from a Marxist viewpoint.[57] In 1991, the leadership ordered the writing of a human rights position paper. The fall 1991 "White Paper on Human Rights" was designed to serve as a weapon "to fight with [hostile] foreign forces and . . . to educate our cadres, masses, and, in particular, our young people at home."[58] The CCP formally established research centers, such as the Chinese Society for Human Rights Studies in 1994 and the Ministry of Justice's Human Rights Center, to assist this propaganda war.[59]

The CCP similarly exploited patriotic sentiments to reverse the appeal of human rights and political democracy. Propaganda appropriated the anger, and tears, associated with the PRC's failed 1993 bid for the Olympics. The US-led "Western" bloc trampled on the PRC's national dignity. As outspoken literary theorist and dissident Liu Xiaobo argued,

> It may be that the fear of blood and prison have silenced our consciences. . . . It may be that the tangible benefits of money have exposed the hollowness of freedom and democracy. Or it may be that China's unsuccessful bid to host the Olympic Games triggered off an outburst of national pride. . . . [M]ainland China has suddenly been engulfed in a wave of nationalism and patriotism which reaches

every corner of the land and involves everybody, from the government
to the ordinary people.[60]

Some intellectuals have increasingly turned away from universal notions of
human rights and democracy, embracing ideas indigenous to China.
Intellectuals debate both Harvard political scientist Samuel Huntington's 1991
Foreign Affairs article "The Clash of Civilizations" and theorist Edward Said's
Orientalism in order to extol the "essence of being Chinese." They hope to
rejuvenate the withering national spirit. Chen Kaige and Zhang Yimou's internationally award-winning movies are criticized for exploiting homespun
material in order to ingratiate themselves with foreigners. Such sentiments
intersect with, and bolster, the CCP's propaganda against universalist notions
of human rights as being incompatible with China's national situation.

These efforts should not imply that the CCP has won China's domestic
human rights battle. A major tension has been how socialist narratives (e.g.
the tenet that private ownership leads to human exploitation) conflict with
China's expanding market economy.[61] Acknowledging this problem, one
commentator argues that "the study of human rights theory has fallen far
behind and thus failed to meet . . . objective needs"[62] Market reforms have
provided space for individualism and empowerment that were severely
constrained in Maoist China. Compensating for these developments, the CCP
increasingly relies on other arguments, traditions, and texts to promote its
human rights position. The CCP increasingly uses developmentalism, which
holds that successful socio-economic development produces civil and political
liberties and that collective rights are more important than individual rights.

NON-SOCIALIST DEVELOPMENTALIST
THINKING IN CHINA[63]

The post-Mao Party elites have relied upon a host of political strategies to
bolster the CCP's domestic political rule. One important development
since the mid-1980s concerns the reliance on non-socialist texts, such as
developmentalism. Developmentalist discourses, which first emerged in private
political circles in mid-1980s and later entered the political realm after 1988,
stress an authoritarian-development model that would establish a market-
oriented economy at the expense of political liberties. After reaching an
unspecified high level of development and creating a middle class, an enlightened political elite would then liberalize the political system, allowing greater
political liberties, such as political democracy and human rights protections.
These discourses have been unique in that they (1) legitimize a pervasive
market-oriented economy at the expense of conventional socialist-development
models, (2) promote a modified democratic project by conceptualizing political liberalization as the product of economic and social liberalization,

(3) believe that the immediate implementation of democratic political reforms would lead to societal instability, causing a conservative anti-reform backlash, (4) rely on non-socialist texts to legitimize this authoritarian-development model, and (5) recast the relativist-*guoqing* argument within a perspective that promotes the PRC's development interests as an East Asian country rather than as a socialist leader of the so-called "Third World."

Developmentalism has been popularized in the PRC by neo-authoritarianism (1986–9) and neo-conservatism (1990–present). Neo-authoritarians argue for the implementation of destabilizing market-oriented economic reforms under an authoritarian government. A transitional period of authoritarianism would ideally create a market economy by forcing through painful reforms while retaining political and societal stability. Some neo-authoritarians promote the use of state power to make a quick and stable transition to a market-oriented economy. Others propose to combine state power with elements within China's traditional culture to gradually implement economic reforms. State power is seen less as a means to create a market economy and more as a necessary tool to retain a unified and stable political order to handle the disruptive forces caused by the implementation of reforms. Neo-conservatives, building on the more gradual approach to neo-authoritarianism, advocate a gradual approach to modernizing China. It seeks to control the import of foreign technology and ideas, use elements in traditional culture to legitimize CCP rule, and rely upon modernizing elites. Neo-conservatives are not as hostile as neo-Maoists, but they advocate gradual change and resistance to the import of foreign ideas in order to prevent political instability.

Neo-authoritarianism and neo-conservativism have had three broad political implications since the mid-1980s. First, they both have been manipulated by various elite political actors, such as former-Party General Secretary Zhao Ziyang, current Party General Secretary Jiang Zemin, and several groups within the "Princes' Party" (*taizidang*), the well-connected sons and daughters of high-level cadres, to promote different methods of implementing economic reforms. Second, they have been constructed by certain ruling political groups to promote liberal economic and social development at the expense of political liberties in order to counter potential hardline reactions to economic reforms. Finally, while neither has been accepted as a formal development ideology, they both have had an impact on formal and informal political discourses. Literary theorist and dissident Liu Xiaobo, as quoted above, exposes the growing influence that the appeal of China's "big market" has on elite, intellectual, and popular discourses. As I have argued elsewhere, the increasing appeal of developmentalism, especially among young and middle-aged intellectuals and policy advisors, deserves attention and critical reflection since a post-Deng political elite may rely on such thought to legitimize military-authoritarian rule.[64]

THE DEVELOPMENTALIST STRAIN IN THE
CCP'S HUMAN RIGHTS POLICIES

Developmentalism increasingly characterizes the CCP's human rights policies. These arguments reinforce the relativist-*guoqing* and instrumentalist-political strains within the CCP's human rights policies. What makes developmentalism more potent is that it appropriates and reformulates the strain on development rights within the international human rights regime. The right to development is used not only as a political tool to deflect international criticisms, but also as a construction to legitimize the CCP's human rights violations.

Several arguments are subsumed within developmentalist human rights discourses. Arguments on the right to development are based on a selective reading of the 1986 UN General Assembly's declaration on the right to economic, social, and cultural development. The PRC interprets the right to development as only implying the right of a nation's development rather than the right of individuals to control their own destiny.[65] By the early 1990s, Chinese political elites and human rights scholars considered development rights to be composed of three tenets: (1) the incorporation of individual, collective, and national rights; (2) the development of a nation's self-autonomy; and (3) the right to implement development policies that match a country's *guoqing*.[66]

Another key argument emphasizes that human rights are not immutable and abstract. Rather they are relative to the development of society. A 1991 article argued that the PRC has

> a population of 1.1 billion ... [and has] very little arable land. As far as China is concerned, feeding and clothing its people, ensuring medical and health care, and providing education are more important than empty talk about human rights.[67]

Chinese political elites often rely on these arguments to publicly reject norms on civil and political rights. Jiang Zemin has argued that

> without social stability it will be impossible to achieve economic development, without economic development there will be no social progress, and without progress for the whole society it will be impossible for human beings to take their destiny in their own hands.

He concludes that aspirations for democracy, liberty, and human rights are but "empty talk."[68] Paradoxically, this relativist perspective is often construed as "an inalienable human right" for developing countries.[69] The 1991 "White Paper on Human Rights" concludes that the PRC's unspecified "low" development levels necessitate that the right to subsistence supersedes all other rights.[70]

132

Developmentalist discourses are increasingly intermixed with arguments on development rights.[71] A 1991 article combines both facets, arguing that guaranteeing a country's national sovereignty and right of development will serve as a requisite for domestic social and political order.[72] Order and stability are central objectives of developmentalist discourses. These arguments have been appropriated to promote the CCP's human rights objectives. A commentator for the domestic edition of *Renmin ribao* argued that:

> Those who are in favorable circumstances do not know the bitterness and anxiety of those who are in trouble. To developing countries, "one man, one vote," cannot fully embody "human rights." To them, the most important is political and social stability, economic development, and basic insurance of people's livelihood.[73]

This statement exemplifies how the developmentalist concerns of economic growth under political stability increasingly have entered official propaganda on human rights. They are used as political weapons in the CCP's attack against the norm that political democracy is conducive to economic growth. Developing countries that adopt such mechanisms, one human rights commentator argues, mistakenly adopt "Western" models of political and economic development.[74]

Some developmentalist discourses make less polarized arguments. These discourses argue the inseparability between the development of the nation and all forms of human rights. National development must precede the fulfillment of human rights standards, such as civil (*gongmin*), political, economic, social, and cultural rights. One commentator develops this perspective, arguing that:

> If there is no development of the nation . . ., then one can't even begin to talk about the development of the individual. Only with the development of the country and its people can [there be] beneficial political, economic, and societal conditions for the development of the individual. When the individual is developed on this basis, then one can facilitate and protect the development of a country and society. It is a mistake to perceive the development of the nation and the individual as opposites.[75]

He concludes that "only with successful long-term development of a nation's economy and with the improvement and raising of people's living standards can people be insured to fully benefit from every type of human right and basic freedoms." Another human rights commentator uses the PRC's developing nation status to argue that:

> the human rights issue in China has not been perfectly resolved. As all of China is currently striving to achieve modernization, the first thing is to develop the economy in order to provide the perfect

conditions for the realization of freedom, democracy, and all kinds of human rights, [and to] allow the people fuller enjoyment of kinds of democratic rights.[76]

These discourses argue that individual human rights concerns should not be fully addressed until the CCP raises "the economic, social, and cultural development of the people, so as to eliminate poverty and hunger and raise the nation's cultural level."[77]

Developmentalist human rights discourses also claim to promote human rights from a more realistic perspective. In a direct criticism of Maoist fundamentalism, one commentator argues that peasant revolutions raise utopian slogans of equality and leveling socio-economic wealth. These promises were but "beautiful dreams ... [that] could not be turned into reality primarily because of the lack of the necessary economic and social foundations."[78] This utopianism has also been attacked by China's developmentalist thinkers. Neoconservative thinker Xiao Gongqin argues that the PRC does not possess the historical conditions for Western-style democracy and liberalism and that "radicalism" has inhibited the PRC's modernization efforts. Xiao, who publicly supported the military crackdown in 1989, argues that those seeking democratization adhere to an "institutional determinism." They promote the view that old economic and political institutions inhibit reform and that China needs to adopt Western-style economic and political institutions to facilitate modernization.[79]

Some developmentalist discourses make universal arguments on the sequential development of human rights. One commentator posits that the European Industrial Revolution achieved social progress and human emancipation through liberating productive forces. Ideas on natural rights and the equality of human beings, he postulates, are not the "patent" of Western countries.[80] Instead, they are the natural product of a universal economic and social development model. Chinese developmentalist discourses resemble the perspective once popular in North American and European intellectual discourses on both the modernization paradigm and the sequential development process based on industrialization in Great Britain. Despite claiming a universal way to achieve civil and political liberties, developmentalist discourses do not argue that human rights are inalienable to the human condition. Rather, China's development level determines the extent to which human rights should be guaranteed.

THE FATE OF HUMAN RIGHTS SINCE DELINKING MFN

When President Bill Clinton formally announced in May 1994 the end of the United States' efforts to link human rights to China's Most Favored Nation

(MFN) status, the human rights issue declined rather precipitously within the context of Sino-US relations. The US joined many foreign governments in prioritizing economic and security concerns over human rights concerns in their relationships with China.[81] The Chinese government has not sat back gloating in victory. Domestic and international human rights challenges still confront them. The CCP has continued its active political war against foreign and domestic political actors who criticize China's human rights situation and who promote universal human rights norms. China strategically uses its growing economic might to undermine the will of Western governments to exert pressure to improve China's human rights situation. In this context, developmentalist human rights discourses continue to be promoted, but with a slight and important modification.

The core elements of China's human rights policies continue to be promoted. A PRC commentator on China's 1995 White Paper made an argument representative of these two elements. He argued that

> the people's rights to subsistence and development are the primary human rights; [the White Paper] stresses that China resolutely opposes any practices of hegemonism and power politics pursued by certain countries which impose a double standard on human rights against other countries.[82]

Premier Li Peng reconfirmed the relativist position of China's human rights policies in April 1996, arguing that human rights standards depend on China's specific cultural and historical traditions and on its current stage of economic development.[83] The second core element on the political motivations behind human rights policies has intensified to counter the remaining international efforts to promote human rights in China (e.g. the US Department of State's "Human Rights Reports").[84] One commentator titled his attack on the United States "To Hell with U.S. 'Human Rights Diplomacy.'"[85]

PRC human rights commentators attempt to justify China's human rights violations and policies with developmentalist tenets. Some commentators promote abstract concepts on the relativistic nature of human rights *vis-à-vis* a country's development level. One commentator argued that

> as human society develops, the content of human rights continues to be substantial, enriched, and developed. Hence, there is no definition of human rights that is acceptable to everyone in this world.[86]

Human rights are instead achieved according to different interpretations of the concept of human rights. This argument received official sanction at the 1996 annual UN Human Rights Forum in Geneva. The official PRC delegate Zhang Yishan asserted that

> Western democracy is by no means the only model, not least the best one. Nations at various stages of development are entitled to choose their own systems in the light of their own national condition.[87]

The relativist developmentalism intersects with the oft-promoted PRC perspective that democracy is solely a "Western" concept. As experiences from around the world have clearly demonstrated, binary constructions posing the "West" versus the "East" are highly problematic. They de-emphasize aspirations for human rights and democratic political change indigenous to China and Asia.[88]

Another developmentalist tenet highlighted by PRC commentators concerns how civil and political liberties are a by-product of social and economic developments. This tenet appears increasingly with glowing references to the "successes" of the Dengist era. A report published by the Information Office of the State Council argued that the

> four years since 1991 constituted a critical historic period in China during which it fully implemented the 8th 5-year plan of National Economic and Social Development. . . . Today, China is politically stable, its economy is developing, its society is advancing, and there is national unity. The people live and work in contentment, the living standard is rising steadily, and the state of human rights is good as improvement is being made across the board.[89]

Economic development under political stability is constructed as the formula for the improvement of human rights in China. In another report by the Information Office of the State Council, "China's human rights situation is marked by comprehensive improvement, while the country enjoys political stability, sound economic growth, and social progress."[90]

One important development in the post-MFN delinking period concerns the rationalizations for this so-called formula of achieving "improved" human rights standards. By spring 1995, PRC commentators began extolling how the Dengist policies of reform and openness produced the improvements in human rights. In a representative article published in March 1995, a PRC commentator argues that in the

> years since the commencement of reform and opening up, China's political, economic, and social conditions have seen tremendous and positive changes, and steady improvements have been made in living standards. The human rights of the Chinese people have received greater respect and protection.[91]

According to the Chinese government, the accelerated pace of reform from 1992 onwards is considered to have brought "about a comprehensive improvement to the country's human rights situation under conditions of reform, development, and stability."[92] China's formula is not entirely unique. Many advocates of developmentalism place their vision of China in the context of the East Asian and Southeast Asian newly industrializing countries. These countries "achieved the quickest economic development in the world today [due] to their political stability." They achieved political stability because they did "not interfere in each other's internal affairs."[93] Many PRC scholars and political officials believe that China's destiny increasingly mirrors Singapore's. The development of human rights becomes delegated as a "long-term task of the Chinese people and the Chinese government."[94]

CHINA'S FUTURE: THE DANGER OF DEVELOPMENTALISM?

My analysis of developmentalist strains in the CCP's human rights policy should be seen as more than a heuristic exercise.[95] The promotion of developmentalism by PRC political elites legitimizes the systematic violation of human rights. This trend has several important consequences for future political developments in Chinese domestic politics. First, developmentalist discourses promote an enlightened, modernizing elite to develop a market economy. This faith in modernizing political elites can be easily accepted in Chinese politics given the predominant role of elitism in Chinese political thought, especially the CCP's adherence to a Leninist vanguard leadership. One *Qiushi* commentator argued in 1991 that

> in certain stages of history and some spheres of life, states, nations, political parties, groups and so on are the carriers of various collective rights. Simply understanding the collective and its representation as "autocracy" and expropriation of human rights is, at least, a shallow understanding of human rights.[96]

This elitist mentality undermines local aspirations for human rights and political change. As twentieth-century Chinese political history has demonstrated, local pressures for change, such as student movements, worker protests, and peasant rebellions, are either suppressed or manipulated by political elites to promote specific political agendas.

Second, the increasing influence of developmentalism opens up powerful possibilities for blinding nationalist sentiments to prevail over human rights aspirations. The 1991 White Paper on Human Rights argues that only with strengthening "national might and [enhancing] the level of economic development and people's living standards, can the right to subsistence of the people be reliably guaranteed."[97] National political, military, and economic strength are seen as requisites for even basic socio-economic rights. Virulent anti-foreign nationalism often creeps into Chinese human rights discourses.

Foreigners concerned about China's human rights record are treated as condescendingly "instructing" Chinese. One commentator argues that the people concerned about China's human rights conditions

> miscalculate this point. China is a sovereign state with national dignity, and will never yield to any external pressure. China will never follow foreigners' instructions to do anything within the jurisdiction of its own sovereignty.[98]

The efforts of foreign governments and international NGOs represent, as another commentator argues, "a new form of racial discrimination in the current world affairs."[99] Twentieth-century Chinese history demonstrates that such racial-nationalist sentiments, often embodied in the Chinese modern political dream of national "wealth and power," have resulted in political elites from Jiang Jieshi to Mao Zedong and from Yuan Shikai to Deng Xiaoping trampling on human aspirations for democracy and human rights. These domestic political consequences make it imperative that human rights violations in the PRC should never be forgotten.

NOTES

This essay was originally presented at the 47th Annual Meeting of the Association of Asian Studies Washington, DC, April 6–9, 1995. I appreciate the assistance and comments provided by Edward Friedman, Tatsuo Yamada, Andrew Nathan, Ann Kent, and the editor of this volume. I claim responsibility for the views expressed in this essay.

1 State Council Information Office, "Progress in China's Human Rights Course in 1996," *Beijing Review* 40, no. 16 (April 21–7, 1997), p. 19.
2 Albert Camus, *The Rebel: An Essay on Man in Revolt* (New York: Vintage Books, 1991 [1956]), p. 3.
3 Wei Jingsheng, *The Courage to Stand Alone* (New York: Penguin, 1997), p. 164.
4 In this essay, human rights refers not only to civil, political, social, and cultural rights, but also, and more importantly, to institutional protection for the individual against the state.
5 See the Human Rights Watch/Asia reports "Organ Procurement and Judicial Execution in China" (August 1994) and "China: Persecution of a Protestant Sect" (June 1994); *Detained in China and Tibet: A Directory of Political and Religious Prisoners* (New York: Human Rights Watch, 1994); and Bernard Levin, "Behind Chinese Walls: In Tibet, Buddhist Monks and Nuns are Being Horrifically Persecuted – But Why?" *The Times* (October 18, 1994).
6 For documentation prior to 1949, see Dai Qing, *Wang Shiwei and "Wild Lilies": Rectification and Purges in the Chinese Communist Party, 1942–1944* (Armonk, NY: M.E. Sharpe, 1994). For conditions in post-1949 China, see Samuel S. Kim, "Human Rights in China's International Relations," paper presented at "What If China Does Not Democratize" Marquette University, July 11–12, 1997; Michael J. Sullivan, "Development and Political Repression: China's Human Rights Policy

Since 1989," *The Bulletin of Concerned Asian Scholars* 27, no. 4 (1995), pp. 24–39; James D. Seymour, "Human Rights in Chinese Foreign Relations," in Samuel S. Kim, ed. *China and the World*, (Boulder, CO: Westview Press, 1994), pp. 202–25; Ann Kent, *Between Freedom and Subsistence: China and Human Rights* (Hong Kong: Oxford University Press, 1993); and R. Randel Edwards, *et al.*, eds, *Human Rights in Contemporary China* (New York: Columbia University Press, 1986).

7 See Wei Jingsheng, *Courage to Stand Alone*; and Kent, *Between Freedom and Subsistence*.

8 For examples of this perspective, see Information Council of the State Council, "Human Rights in China," *Beijing Review* (November 4–10, 1991), pp. 8–45; and Stephen C. Thomas, "Chinese Economic Development and Human Rights in the Post-Mao Era," in George W. Shepherd and Ved P. Nanda, eds, *Human Rights and Third World Development* (Westport, CT: Greenwood Press, 1985), pp. 149–64.

9 See *Anthems of Defeat: Crackdown in Hunan Province, 1989–92* (New York: Human Rights Watch, 1992).

10 See Human Rights in China, "China: Use of Criminal Charges Against Political Dissidents" (October 3, 1994).

11 Hong Kong AFP (January 6, 1995), in Foreign Broadcast Information Service (hereafter FBIS) (January 6, 1995), p. 7.

12 See Bruce Gilley, "Judge Denounces Dissident for 'Anti-Social' Behavior," *Eastern Express* (March 14, 1995), p. 8, in FBIS (March 14, 1995), p. 26.

13 See China Freedom and Democratic Party, "A Statement on Human Rights Issue in China" (November 12, 1991), *Ming pao* (November 16, 1991), p. 6, translated in FBIS (November 18, 1991), p. 22; Wei-chun Lee, "With Open Arms? China and Human Rights in the United Nations," *Pacifica: A Journal of Pacific and Asian Studies* 2, no. 1 (January 1990), p. 31; and Roberta Cohen, "People's Republic of China: The Human Rights Exception," *Human Rights Quarterly* 9 (1987), p. 491.

14 See Guo Qing, "Zhongguo zai renquanshang de qiben lichang he qiben shijian" [The Basic Positions and Practices of Human Rights in China], *Qiushi* 23 (1991), pp. 14–19; and Nan Feng, "Distinguish Two Different Concepts of Human Rights," *Shaanxi ribao* (August 7, 1991), p. 3, in FBIS (August 29, 1991), pp. 32–4.

15 See Information Office of the State Council, "Human Rights in China"; and China Society for Human Rights Studies, "Comments on US State Department Human Rights Report on China," *Beijing Review* (June 13–19, 1994), pp. 8–13.

16 "Italian Group Finds Wan Li Remarks 'Shocking,'" FBIS (May 10, 1991), p. 24.

17 Michel Foucault, *Foucault Live (Interviews, 1966–1984)* (New York: Semiotext(e), 1989), p. 129.

18 In this essay, "discourse" refers to all that is written, spoken, and acted upon. More broadly, it refers to the political and intellectual processes associated with the interconnected human struggles over power and meanings.

19 See this institute's report on the "Main Viewpoints and Methods Used by Western Countries to Attack Socialist Countries on the Human Rights Issue and the Countermeasures We Should Adopt," as printed in "Confidential Document on Study of Human Rights Issue (Part One)," *Dangdai* No. 15 (June 15, 1992), in FBIS (June 23, 1992), pp. 32–6.

20 See Zhou Wei, "The Study of Human Rights in the People's Republic of China," in James T. H. Tang, ed., *Human Rights and International Relations in the Asia-Pacific Region* (New York: Pinter, 1995), pp. 83–96.

21 Harvard Sinologist Stuart Schram exemplifies this tendency, recently arguing that "Without endorsing Mao's own joyful enthusiasm for destruction, it can be acknowledged that . . . [b]y shaking up the ancient, patriarchal, stratified world of China, Mao opened the way for the emergence of new ideas and institutions" (see Stuart Schram, "Mao Zedong a Hundred Years on: The Legacy of a Ruler," *China*

Quarterly no. 137, March 1994, p. 143). For alternative perspectives on the human costs of Mao's "joyful enthusiasm," see Edward Friedman, *National Identity and Democratic Prospects in Socialist China* (Armonk, NY: M.E. Sharpe, 1995); and Orville Schell, "Dragons and Dungeons," *China Quarterly* no. 139 (September 1994), pp. 783–93.

22 I owe this distinction to John Kelsay and Sumner B. Twiss, eds, "Universality vs. Relativism in Human Rights," in *Religion and Human Rights* (New York: The Project on Religion and Human Rights, 1994).

23 See Baogang He, *The Democratization of China* (New York: Routledge, 1996); Edward Friedman, ed., *The Politics of Democratization: Generalizing East Asian Experiences* (Boulder, CO: Westview Press, 1995); Wei-chin Lee, "Heaven Can Wait? Rethinking the Chinese Notion of Human Rights," *Asian Thought and Society* 16, no. 46 (January–April 1991), pp. 28–39; and W. Theodore de Bary, "Neo-Confucianism and Human Rights," in Leroy S. Rouner, ed., *Human Rights and the World's Religions* (South Bend, IN: University of Notre Dame Press, 1988), pp. 183–98.

24 See James C. Hsiung, ed., *Human Rights in East Asia: A Cultural Perspective* (New York: Paragon House Publishers, 1985). For Marxist perspectives, see Leszek Kolakowski, "Marxism and Human Rights," *Daedalus* 112, no. 4 (1983), pp. 81–92; and Xu Zhongdao and He Deliang, "Drawing a Clear Line Between Two Different Concepts of Human Rights," *Sichuan ribao* (May 24, 1991), p. 4, in FBIS (June 26, 1991), pp. 30–1.

25 Xinhua (March 9, 1995), in FBIS (March 10, 1995), p. 3.

26 For balanced studies on the politics associated with the Clinton administration's China policy, see Peter Van Ness, "The Impasse in US Policy Toward China," *The China Journal* no. 38 (July 1997), pp. 139–52; and Edward Friedman, "The Challenge of a Rising China: Another Germany?" in Robert Lieber, ed., *Eagle Adrift* (New York: Norton, 1996).

27 See David Arase, "Japanese Policy Toward Democracy and Human Rights in Asia," *Asian Survey* 33 (1993), pp. 935–52; Yasunobu Sato, "New Directions in Japanese Foreign Policy: Promoting Human Rights and Democracy in Asia – ODA Perspective," in Friedman, *The Politics of Democratization*, pp. 102–24; and "Showing Disapproval," *South China Morning Post* (March 10, 1995), p. 22, in FBIS (March 10, 1995), p. 4.

For the important role of Asian NGOs, see James V. Riker, "Redefining Civil Society in the Global Political Economy," paper presented at the 36th Annual Meeting of the International Studies Association, Chicago, February 21–5, 1995; Nobleen Heyzer, *et al.*, eds, *Government–NGO Relations in Asia* (New York: St Martin's Press, 1995); and Lawrence T. Woods, *Asian-Pacific Diplomacy: Nongovernmental Organizations and International Relations* (Vancouver: UBC Press, 1993).

28 See James D. Seymour, "The Crux of the Struggle: Human Rights in Chinese Foreign Relations," paper presented at the "University Seminar on Modern China," Columbia University, December 9, 1993, and He Baogang, "Chinese Dissidents' Ideas of Human Rights: A Constructivist Critique," *Thesis Eleven* 30 (1991), pp. 56–74.

29 See Jill Crystal, "Authoritarianism and Its Adversaries in the Arab World," *World Politics* 46 (January 1994), pp. 262–89.

30 "Modified, Supplemented Version of Thesis by Gu Chende, Submitted to 1990 Beijing World Law Conference: 'China Safeguards, Protects Human Rights,'" FBIS (May 30, 1991), p. 19.

31 "Scholars Discuss Concepts of Human Rights," *Zhongguo tongxun she* (June 20, 1991), in FBIS (June 25, 1991), p. 35.

32 China Society for Human Rights Studies, "Comments on US State Department Human Rights Report on China," p. 12.

33 See Yi Ding, "Fandui liyong renquan ganshe bieguoneizheng: bo suowei 'renquan-wuguojie'" [Oppose the Use of Human Rights to Violate Domestic Sovereignty: A Refutation of "Human Rights Knows No Boundaries"], *Qiushi* 20 (1989), pp. 16–19.

34 Guo Jisi, "Fazhanquan shi yixian buke boduo de renquan" [Development is an Inalienable Right], *Qiushi* 14 (1991), p. 20.

35 Guo Jisi, "China Promotes Human Rights," *Beijing Review* (January 28 – February 3, 1991), p. 17.

36 On China's use of relativist-*guoqing* arguments in UN forums, see Xinhua (March 2, 1994), in FBIS (March 3, 1994), p. 2, and "Qian Qichen's Two Speeches in the United States," *Hsin wan pao* (September 28, 1991), p. 1, in FBIS (September 30, 1991), pp. 1–2.

37 "Top Leaders on Human Rights Issues," *Beijing Review* (April 22–8, 1991), p. 8.

38 One should note that the history of US human rights foreign policy has been inconsistent and, at times, hypocritical. The irony of this propaganda attack is that Carter introduced a less inconsistent and hypocritical notion of human rights into American foreign policy. There are organizations (e.g. Human Rights Watch and Amnesty International) and individuals within government (e.g. John Shattuck and Morton Halpern) struggling to develop more consistent standards within US foreign policy and defense establishments.

39 Quoted in Shi Qian, "Cultural Traditions and the Concept of Human Rights," *Renmin ribao* (February 14, 1994), p. 6, in FBIS (February 15, 1994), p. 9.

40 Ibid.

41 See Michael J. Sullivan, "The 1988–1989 Nanjing Anti-African Protests: Racial Nationalism or Nationalist Racism?" *China Quarterly* 138 (June 1994), pp. 438–57.

42 Guo Jisi, "China Promotes Human Rights," p. 21.

43 Lu Fan-chih, "United States' So-Called Human Rights Diplomacy Is Violation of Others' Sovereignty," *Wen wei po* (May 19, 1991), p. 7, in FBIS (May 20, 1991), pp. 9–10.

44 Huang Meilai and Du Feijin, "A Meeting of Theoretical Workers in Beijing Proposes Strengthening the Theoretical Study of the Human Rights Issue," *Renmin ribao* (March 22, 1991), in FBIS (March 28, 1991), p. 27.

45 "CPC Takes Offensive on Human Rights Issue," *Dangdai* 16 (July 15, 1992), in FBIS (July 22, 1992), p. 17. Also see comments made by Nie Dajiang, deputy head of the Central Propaganda Department, in Dou Guangsheng, "CPC Official Views Rights Question, Theories," Xinhua (November 8, 1991), in FBIS (November 12, 1991), pp. 25–6.

46 "Confidential Document on Study of Human Rights Issue (Part One)," p. 36.

47 See "Another Talk on Human Rights," *Ban Yue Tan*, (July 10, 1991), in FBIS (August 29, 1991), pp. 1–4; Wei Ming, "Performance of US Human Rights Diplomacy in Latin America," *Wen wei po* (November 26, 1994), p. A7, in FBIS (December 13, 1994), pp. 6–9; Xinhua (March 2, 1995), in FBIS (March 2, 1995), pp. 3–4; "It is Unpopular to Interfere with Other Countries' Internal Affairs Under the Pretext of Human Rights," *Renmin ribao* (March 12, 1993), p. 1, in FBIS (March 15, 1993), pp. 3–4; and Ku Lu-chieh, "Brief Discussion of Human Rights," *Tzu ching* 8, no. 5 (May 1991), in FBIS (May 14, 1991), pp. 38–9.

48 Zhongguo Xinwen She (March 3, 1995), in FBIS (March 6, 1995). Also see Yi Ding, *Qiushi*, p. 16, and Guo Jisi, "On Human Rights and Development Right," *Beijing Review* (February 11–17, 1991), p. 18.

49 Gu Chunde, "Right to Development: A Basic Human Right," *Beijing Review* (May 10–16, 1991), pp. 10–11.

50 "Western Anti-China Draft Rejected," *Beijing Review* (March 21–7, 1994), p. 37.

51 Xinhua (March 2, 1995), in FBIS (March 2, 1995), p. 4. Also see Ma Jun, "Human Rights: China's Perspective," *Beijing Review* (April 28 – December 4, 1988), pp. 21–2.

52 See Linda Gail Arrigo, "A View of the United Nations Conference on Human Rights, June 1993," *Bulletin of Concerned Asian Scholars* 25, no. 3 (July–September 1993), pp. 69–72.

53 "Modified, Supplemented Version of Thesis by Gu Chunde," p. 19.

54 Huang and Du, "A Meeting of Theoretical Workers," p. 27.

55 "CPC Takes Offensive on Human Rights Issue (Continued)," p. 28.

56 Andrew J. Nathan, "Human Rights in Chinese Foreign Policy," *The China Quarterly* no. 139 (September 1994), p. 630. Also see Lang Yihuai, "The Practice of Human Rights in Socialist Society and the International Human Rights Struggle," *Qiushi* 1 (January 1, 1992), pp. 10–15, in FBIS (February 27, 1992), pp. 33–4.

57 Quoted in ibid.

58 "CPC Takes Offensive on Human Rights Issue," p. 15. For the official public explanation, see "Why China Publishes the White Paper on Human Rights," *Beijing Review* (November 11–17, 1991), pp. 23–5.

59 See Xiao Bian, "US Report on Rights Just 'Distort' Facts," *China Daily* (March 7, 1995), p. 4, in FBIS (March 8, 1995), p. 5; and "Justice Ministry to Set Up Human Rights Center," FBIS (February 17, 1995), p. 16.

60 Liu Xiaobo, "Chinese Patriotism Driven By Inferiority Complex," *Kaifang* 11, no. 1 (November 1, 1994), in FBIS (March 2, 1995), p. 18.

61 See Shen Baoxiang, "A Review of the Theories on the Human Rights Issue," *Jiefang ribao* (November 27, 1991), p. 6, in FBIS (December 3, 1991), p. 27; Guo Qing, "Zhongguo zai renquanshang de qiben lichang he qiben shijian"; "It is Unpopular to Interfere With Other Countries' Internal Affairs Under the Pretext of Human Rights," pp. 3–4; Wu Xiongcheng, "Several Questions on Human Rights," *Renmin ribao* (November 8, 1991), p. 5, in FBIS (November 12, 1991), pp. 23–5; and Sun Qimeng, "Socialism Has Thoroughly Changed Human Rights Situation in China," *Renmin ribao* (December 2, 1991), p. 5, in FBIS (December 11, 1991), pp. 24–5.

62 See Shen Baoxiang, "A Review of the Theories on the Human Rights Issue."

63 For a more detailed analysis, see Michael J. Sullivan, "Democracy and Developmentalism: Contending Political Struggles over Political Change in Dengist China, 1978–1995" (PhD dissertation, University of Wisconsin-Madison, 1995).

64 See Michael J. Sullivan, "The Impact of Western Political Thought on Chinese Political Discourse on Transitions from Leninism, 1986–1992," *World Affairs* 157, no. 2 (Fall 1994), pp. 79–91.

65 See Seymour, "The Crux of the Struggle," p. 3; and "Confidential Document on Study of Human Rights Issue (Part One)," p. 34.

66 Guo Jisi, "Fazhanquan shi yixian buke boduo de renquan," pp. 19–20.

67 "Another Talk on Human Rights," p. 3.

68 Quoted in Xinhua (November 1, 1991), in FBIS (November 1, 1991), p. 37.

69 Guo Shan, "China's Role in the Human Rights Field," *Beijing Review* (February 9, 1987), p. 23.

70 See "Why China Publishes the White Paper on Human Rights," p. 24; Dong Yunhu, "The Right to Subsist Remains the Most Important Human Right for China and the Developing Countries at Present," *Renmin ribao* (January 15, 1993), p. 5, in FBIS (February 10, 1993), pp. 19–20; and Cheng Xiaoxia and Zhang Junli, "Defend State Sovereignty, Oppose Interference in Internal Affairs," *Fazhi ribao* (June 17, 1992), p. 4, in FBIS (July 22, 1992), pp. 17–18.

71 See Guo Shan, "China's Role in the Human Rights Field," pp. 23–4.
72 Guo Jisi, "On Human Rights and Development Right," pp. 16–18.
73 Dong Yunhu, "The Right to Subsist," p. 20.
74 See Guo Jisi, "On Human Rights and Development Right," p. 16.
75 Guo Jisi, "Fazhanquan shi yixian buke boduo de renquan," p. 19.
76 Ku Lu-chieh, "Brief Discussion of Human Rights."
77 Guo Jisi, "On Human Rights and Development Right," p. 17.
78 Ibid., p. 16.
79 See Xiao Gongqin, "Reform and the Open Policy Under the 'Four Basic Principles,'" *Beijing qingnian bao* (September 4, 1990), p. 4; and Ma Fan, "History Opposes Romanticism: Associate Professor Xiao Gongqin Discusses the Radical Mode of Thinking," *Beijing qingnian bao* (January 19, 1992), p. 6.
80 Guo Jisi, "On Human Rights and Development Right," p. 16.
81 Peter Van Ness, "Addressing the Human Rights Issue in Sino-American Relations," *Journal of International Affairs* 49, no. 2 (Winter 1996), pp. 302–31; and Sidney Jones, "Asian Human Rights, Economic Growth, and United States Policy," *Current History* 95, no. 605 (December 1996), pp. 419–27.
82 Gu Chunde, "A True Record of Human Rights in China," *Renmin ribao* (March 4, 1996), p. 11, in FBIS (March 20, 1996), pp. 22–3.
83 See "PRC: Li Peng Comments on Human Rights Issue, Taiwan," FBIS (April 15, 1996), p. 17.
84 See "PRC: Army Paper Criticizes US Foreign Policy," FBIS (July 5, 1996), pp. 6–9; Information Office of the State Council, "A Report Which Distorts Facts and Confuses Right and Wrong – On the Part about China in the 1994 'Human Rights Report' Issued by the US State Department," FBIS (March 24, 1995), pp. 3–8; and Information Office of the State Council, "PRC: 'Full Text' of State Council Human Rights Commentary," FBIS (March 29, 1996), pp. 5–10.
85 Zhang Heshi, "To Hell with U.S. 'Human Rights Diplomacy,'" *Renmin ribao* (April 1, 1996), p. 6, in FBIS (April 6, 1996).
86 Shi Zhi, "Questions and Answers on Human Rights (Part One)," *Shijie zhishi* (Beijing) 5, no. 1 (March 1995), p. 1, in FBIS (May 3, 1995), pp. 44–8.
87 "PRC: Beijing Underscore 'Diversity of Human Rights,'" FBIS (April 22, 1996), pp. 1–2.
88 See Sullivan, "Development and Political Repression," pp. 24–39.
89 Information Office of the Chinese State Council, "Human Rights Progress in China," FBIS (June 10, 1996), p. 23.
90 Information Office of the Chinese State Council, "PRC: 'Full Text' of State Council Human Rights Commentary," p. 10.
91 Shi Zhi, "Questions and Answers on Human Rights," p. 45.
92 See commentary on the Information Office of the State Council, "Progress of Human Rights in China," (December 27, 1995) in FBIS (March 4, 1996), p. 11.
93 Yu Quanyu and Liu Zhengrong, "Human Rights and Government," *Renmin luntan* 3, no. 8 (March 1995), pp. 36–7, in FBIS (March 22, 1995), pp. 35–7.
94 Shi Zhi, " Questions and Answers on Human Rights," p. 45.
95 For a description of the domestic challenges to developmentalism, see Sullivan, "Development and Political Repression," pp. 35–8.
96 Lang Yihuai, "The Practice of Human Rights," p. 33.
97 "Why China Publishes the White Paper on Human Rights," p. 24.
98 Bao Xin, "Letter from Beijing: Further on Human Rights," *Liaowang Overseas Edition* 39 (September 30, 1991), p. 2, in FBIS (October 4, 1991), p. 18.
99 "Say No to Politicization of Human Rights," in FBIS (November 9, 1995) p. 14.

7

HUMAN RIGHTS AS
IDENTITIES

Difference and Discrimination in Taiwan's
China Policy

Shih Chih-yu

Shih Chih-yu, *a professor at National Taiwan University, is one of the most productive young political scientists anywhere, having published five books in English and nineteen books in Chinese so far. In this third chapter on Greater China, he addresses the human rights situation in China as seen from Taiwan. Shih investigates changing attitudes toward human rights in Taiwan from the perspective of changing and competing definitions of national identity on the island. He challenges the idea of universality, arguing that human rights ideals are historically constructed concepts that mean different things in different contexts to different people. Shih suggests that this may be a generic problem in human rights policies around the world.*

INTRODUCTION

For most people, the concept of human rights is about political ideals, policy guidelines, and/or life practices. As such, they have often become a pretext for one state to intervene in the internal affairs of other sovereign states or become a bargaining chip to exchange for other desired values. Human rights advocates today condemn the use of human rights for purely political purposes, and suggest that such use undermines the credibility of human rights arguments in the long run.[1] Their critical perspective presumes, indirectly perhaps, a *status quo ante* where human rights are both natural and universally guaranteed. That is exactly what this chapter will dispute. I will argue not whether human rights are good or bad, right or wrong, but that, in practice, human rights are not part of an original state of nature, and are, rather, psycho-cultural derivatives of wo/men's quest for collective identities. In other words, human rights are historically constructed notions that without question mean different things in different contexts for different people.

The idea of universal human rights assumes that men and women all over the world have identical needs, at least in certain realms.[2] This idea paradoxically allows most human rights advocates to discover how different people really are.[3] Nonetheless, in discovering the difference, human rights advocates have defined a mission for themselves: to spread the human rights gospel to those areas that have failed to meet so-called universal human rights standards. Here, the ideal of universal human needs is preserved through a vision of transformation, from a condition lacking universal human rights into one offering them. These advocates' self-identity as "humane individuals" is put forth as a model for those living under different conceptions of human rights and it is the difference between them that provides their sense of mission. The mission, in turn, animates the ideal, and the ideal helps to clearly reinforce (henceforth reproduce) the difference. Human rights advocates thus gain a sense of historical progress by trying to contribute to those areas where they find longing for human rights.

This is not to say, however, that these advocates' understandings of human rights are completely meaningless. They are, and indeed have to be, very real. Any thought otherwise would deny the life experiences and identities of those universal human rights advocates, and would not do justice to their genuine beliefs. In fact, each group of people has at least some culturally based understanding of the natural rights that are associated with individual human existence, the most important of which usually involves the right to life. However, this does not, for example, mean that regardless of one's perspective killing is always wrong. What is often in question is what type of killing can or cannot be justified. If justifications are matters of political practice and derivatives of historical experiences, they are different for every group. Certainly one would feel deeply threatened if a type of killing that is entirely at odds with one's own understanding of life were to be justified.[4] Thus it is only natural that people would seek to demonstrate that their own justification for killing is the universal model.

Controversies have often arisen when human rights advocates in the United States try to persuade the world that their understanding should be the universal standard. The kinds of criticism they typically face are threefold. First, Western notions of individualist human rights are not necessarily applicable in collectivist cultural areas like Singapore or Korea.[5] Second, Western notions of human rights are products of economic development and as such are not applicable to developing countries, like Malaysia or Iran.[6] Third, the human rights advocates' government often adopts a double standard when applied to strategically allied countries like El Salvador and South Africa, strategically contestant countries like Cuba and Iraq; or between independent countries like China and Russia and dependent countries like Taiwan and Panama.[7]

Though these critiques are at the same time valid, politically motivated, and somewhat self-centered (through expressing who they think they are and who they do not want to be), they are not the focus of this chapter. Instead, we will look into cases where a concept of universal human rights has guided political action and examine how in those cases human rights are in fact a function of identity. Ensuing discussion will examine how the Republic of China (or Taiwan) has attempted to change its human rights practices from those sympathetic with national security arguments to those in line with so-called "universal" understandings of human rights. I will then interpret these changes not as convergence toward universal standards but as a reflection of identity politics in Taiwan, one that used to present itself in affective terms but does so now in intellectual and cognitive terms. Two case studies will illustrate how the "universal" understandings of human rights which guide Taipei's official norms today serve as a mechanism to differentiate Taiwan from China, with the ironic effect of discriminating against many Chinese.

IDENTITY POLITICS AND HUMAN RIGHTS IMPLICATIONS

The anti-Communist identity

To understand Taiwan's position on human rights, one must first review the changing national identity on the island. Taiwan's national identity is usually defined in terms of its relationship with China. When the regime in Taiwan regarded Mainland China and Taiwan as one country, there was no need to make a distinction between Chinese and Taiwanese human rights. One could legitimately sacrifice Taiwanese human rights in order to promote Chinese human rights in the long run. However, as the regime in Taiwan gradually redefined itself as an independent actor outside of the China sphere, there has also developed a need to differentiate Chinese human rights from Taiwanese human rights. Indeed, one could now legitimately set aside concerns for Chinese human rights in order to suggest that Taiwan and China are two separate polities.

For decades, anti-Communism has made the Kuomintang (KMT) more sympathetic with national security arguments against human rights concerns. The KMT–Chinese Communist Party (CCP) conflict has shaped the China–Taiwan conflict and human rights concern in Taiwan since the end of the Chinese civil war in 1949. In order to appreciate the meaning of Taiwan's human rights policy after 1949, one should therefore trace the China–Taiwan conflict back to 1927 China, when Jiang Jieshi (Chiang Kai-shek), the former leader of the still-ruling KMT, cracked down for the first time on China's Communist Party organization. The Communists, upon advice from Stalin, had at that time joined the KMT. This crackdown, however, started what has been six decades of confrontation between the two and was followed by a series of annihilation campaigns, which sent the CCP off to a ten-thousand-mile march (what is now known as the Long March) through China's countryside. Thousands of Communist comrades died during the March, ensuring that the conflict between Jiang Jieshi's KMT and Mao Zedong's CCP would be intensely personal as well as political and ideological.

Indeed, the story thereafter only reinforced the hatred between them – in 1936, the Communist Party participated in a coup attempt against Jiang, known as the Xi'an incident which compelled Jiang to engage in a premature and unwanted war with Japan. The eight-year Sino-Japanese war not only saved the CCP from the KMT's attack but actually enabled the CCP to enlarge its sphere of influence, ultimately gaining the support of one-fourth of the Chinese population. The subsequent four-year civil war resulted in a thorough defeat of the KMT and its ultimate flight to Taiwan in 1949. Military collisions have continued between the two sides of the Taiwan Straits since that time up until 1979 with the CCP determined to reunite China and the KMT to recover the Mainland.[8]

In short, the war mentality between two Chinas is a unique product of their history, and is completely different from those that have existed between other nations, for example the United States and the former Soviet Union. In the first place, it was not a cold war. Indeed, despite the fact that the American leaders distrusted the Soviets, they did not really hate them. The American people learned consciously to distrust Russia – because it was Communist, totalitarian, expansionist, and so on. However, there was no learning required for the KMT to maintain their hatred – it was in some respects a part of them.[9] Conceptually, it was a fight between two Chinese entities over the right to rule China, thus they had little choice but to despise each other. The KMT's propaganda concentrated not on why the CCP was evil, but how it was evil; for example, its suppression of the freedom of the Chinese people, elimination of the Chinese cultural tradition, and exhaustion of the social resources for people's livelihood.[10] The superpowers' cold war was an intellectual war, while the Taiwan–China conflict was both physical and emotional, a contest to decide which was the real "representative" of China.

Human rights issues seemed trivial in comparison with the seemingly grand mission of China's reunification. The KMT's long-term struggle to maintain its goal of recovering China gave people in Taiwan a clear sense of direction, which in turn encouraged, and was promoted by, a determination to self-sacrifice. Human rights concerns were not germane to political legitimacy before the 1980s. Whenever its violation of human rights met overseas criticism, especially from the United States, the KMT appealed to national security pragmatism. For the KMT, the Communist enemy was evil, threatening, and ever-present. Sacrifice on the human rights front actually dramatized the KMT-led collective quest for a just return to China, and the impact of human rights concerns and the American desire to provide continued support to Taiwan could not offset the anti-Communist spirit which the sacrifice strengthened.

Indeed, if human rights had been of the utmost importance, the fight against Communism would have lost importance. Therefore, not only would the KMT's personal war with the CCP have lost justification, the immigrant KMT's rule in Taiwan would have also forfeited its guiding point of reference.[11]

What has therefore determined human rights policy (or the lack thereof) on Taiwan has been, first, an affective need to express institutionally the KMT's hatred toward the CCP; second, an anti-Communist national identity to explicate the difference between the KMT and the CCP; and, third, a sense of being threatened in order to maintain the negative image of the Communists over time. Political psychologists have found in cases elsewhere that on an affective level, contestants in a conflict tend to perceive their own culture as superior to the adversaries'; by contrast, on the cognitive level they care less about the status of the adversaries than about why they are adversaries and therefore treat them more as an equal rather than an inferior.[12] Clearly, after its personal experiences with Mao's Communist Party, the KMT under Jiang Jieshi and his successor Jiang Jingguo (Chiang Ching-kuo) was operating on an affective level and never intended to treat the Communists as its equal. In fact, they consistently predicted the eventual fall of the CCP regime. The psychological need for a positive image of themselves compelled the Jiangs to demonstrate self-confidence, which explains, to a large extent, why Taipei appeared unreasonably adamant in severing diplomatic relationships with any country attempting a policy of dual recognition of both Taipei and Beijing.

The KMT–CCP relationship has obviously been emotionally driven with the KMT attempting to prove its superiority by acting as if it were more Chinese than the CCP. This, in turn, has pushed it toward a further institutionalization of Confucian ethics wherein leaders' duties are not responses to people's rights, but products of their role as social benefactors. Rights conceptions were anathema, and carried with them a message that leaders were not trustworthy. As a corollary, exposing the evil nature of the CCP relied primarily upon signs of political instability on the Mainland, and thus clearly suggested that the CCP did not have the Chinese people's respect. Human rights violations in China in the Western sense were rarely condemned by the KMT as such. The KMT attended to these violations in order to calculate how much support the CCP could still mobilize, rather than what relief the people might need as human beings.[13] The only remedy that the KMT could envision was only the familiar prescription to substitute the KMT for the CCP.

Sovereignty outside of China

One might expect that human rights concerns in Taiwan would shift focus if Taiwan's identity began to change, and indeed this change actually occurred. When anti-Communism lost momentum, so did national security arguments against human rights concerns. Identity politics in both China and Taiwan drifted indecisively at the end of the 1970s; however, several developments challenged the established anti-Communist identity to which the KMT subscribed for over fifty years. First of all, the post-Cultural Revolution regime in China looked away from moral purity and toward productive power as the answer to socialism's ills. The CCP opened up China to overseas Chinese who were seeking investment opportunities, tourist entertainment, and lost kinship in the Mainland. Chinese in Taiwan were among the most eager participants. Communism was under reform, and the CCP was in a way more critical than the KMT of its own practice of political economy in the Mainland. The simple image of an evil Communist China was not only difficult to maintain, but at the same time, the reforms in China challenged the relevance of the KMT's anti-Communist identity.[14]

No less serious was the loss of a meaningful identity for the Taiwanese. As most countries in the world began to recognize the People's Republic of China as the sole representative of China, which included Taiwan, the KMT's claim to recover the Mainland became increasingly untenable. When the Republic of China lost its seat in the UN to the PRC in 1971, the KMT decided that it would have to win popular support in Taiwan in order to maintain legitimacy. This awareness prompted the KMT to institute the electoral mechanism after 1971. Subsequently, people in Taiwan received their legal and political rights to elect legislative representatives at all levels, and in the process, the KMT has been forced to demonstrate how a regime dedicated to the recovery of the Mainland could also be a government for the people in Taiwan. Thus, the KMT's Taiwanization of the party structure was initiated. In hindsight, this process unavoidably created friction within the party between those more locally oriented and those who still saw themselves as contenders for Greater China.[15] When people in Taiwan are no longer considered the same as people in China, the way their human rights get treated is necessarily different.

The locally oriented KMT was structurally ready to prevail over the China-oriented wing of the KMT because of the sheer numbers it could mobilize in an election. However, the senior Mainland-oriented party officials continued to act in the moral (i.e. committed to China reunification) and ideological (i.e. anti-Communist) realms. In order to establish their own legitimacy, the emerging indigenous forces throughout the late seventies and early eighties began to redefine Taiwan's identity *vis-à-vis* China. After a series of maneuvers by both the indigenous forces within the KMT and by the local Democratic Progressive Party (DPP), which maintained close ties with this indigenous wing of the KMT, China was successfully depicted as an oppressor of Taiwan and Taiwan as a colony of the immigrant (i.e. Chinese) KMT regime. In fact, this reinterpretation of history culminated in President Li Denghui's (Lee Teng-hui's) widely quoted depiction in 1994 of the KMT as a "foreign regime." Ironically, Li claimed that it was he, as the leader of the KMT, who led the transformation of the KMT into an indigenous regime.[16] The implication is that the rights of people living in a foreign area are different from those of domestic citizens.

Identity politics on both sides of the Taiwan Straits has rendered anti-Communism a trivial matter. Indeed, from the perspective of Taiwan's new identity, Communism is no longer a substantive threat to Taiwan. The birth of a "new KMT" (President Li's term) asserts itself by publicly jettisoning the KMT's previous mission of recovering China.[17] This demonstrates that the regime is now genuinely indigenous, and effectively demolishes the legitimacy of any policy that continues to see the KMT as a contender in Chinese politics. The problems such a situation engenders are twofold. First of all, the KMT had successfully educated most of its people with regard to their mission in China. People still maintain strong emotional and affective ties with developments in China. Second, a good number of people in Taiwan have rejected this indigenous campaign, most of whom are the men and women who fled to Taiwan in 1949 and their children. These people simply cannot make sense of the new indigenous direction that the KMT has taken wherein Communism in China is acceptable and the CCP is no longer a deadly enemy.

Indeed, these counter-indigenous forces still possess power sufficient to compel the indigenous wing of the KMT to keep intact at least one element of its former agenda: the claim that its ultimate goal in China is to reunite Taiwan and China. This outcast wing has to date retained this pledge from the new KMT leadership because, as a crucial minority in local elections, they still determine whether or not the KMT will win in each election.

The task of the KMT is now extremely subtle and difficult. It must overthrow its old identity in order to compete with the DPP as a genuine indigenous force, but it must preserve some part of the old identity in order to win the critical support of the pro-unification minority within its own party. There has been a sophisticated shift in the KMT's self-portrayal to accommodate those seemingly contradictory identities – it is the ruling party of the Republic of China on Taiwan, a term that could be interpreted as its continued attachment to the name "China" (to satisfy the minority and the senior leadership), or as its intended limitation of the term "China" to the geographical sphere of Taiwan (to meet the requirement of the indigenous identity).

The code word associated with this formulation is "sovereignty," which defines China as belonging to the outside (the anarchical world in which human rights concerns no longer apply). The KMT says that it would still strive to reunite Taiwan and China if Mainland China were to demonstrate its respect for Taiwan by granting sovereignty to the Republic of China on Taiwan.[18] The CCP understandably declines this invitation, worrying that once the Republic of China on Taiwan becomes an independent country, repossession would be extremely unlikely. This anticipated rejection allows the KMT to depict the problem as one of Taiwan–China relations, not one of the KMT–CCP contention within China. The quest for sovereign status promotes the image of a China outside of Taiwan; through a perception of

continued oppression, China's rejection of sovereignty further assists the indigenous wing of the KMT in constructing the impression that Taiwanese are
not Chinese. Differentiating between Taiwan and China on the sovereignty
issue also persuasively silences the counter-indigenous forces, for they too
would like to see the name Republic of China accepted globally and thus feel
frustrated by the CCP's continued antagonism.[19]

Taiwan's official position on human rights issues has witnessed concomitant
changes. In order to further differentiate Taiwan from China, the KMT has
used its struggle against the senior, anti-indigenous wing of the party as proof
that it has followed universal democratic and human rights standards. National
security concerns have disappeared and those who were previously against
reunification with China have become national heroes, celebrating the triumph
of an indigenous democracy. Indeed there cannot be a better show of human
rights practices than released political criminals of Jiang Jieshi's regime winning
legislative elections and the return of expatriated politicians to Taiwan as the
President's guests of honor.

But whose human rights have been promoted by this seemingly laudable
change of policy toward "universal" standards? Definitely not those of the
pro-democracy advocates in China. The KMT's lukewarm response to the
Tiananmen massacre of 1989 surprised, if not shocked, many anti-Communist
supporters; the government continues to cut the budget allocated to support
the pro-democracy movement in as well as outside of China. This is, however,
in line with Taiwan's new indigenous identity – China is a sovereign state
and Taiwan, as an equal sovereign state, has no right to intervene in Chinese
affairs.

The meaning of the Taiwan–China confrontation dramatically changed
within the framework of Taiwan's new identity. Although the KMT still needs
a different, antagonistic China to consolidate its indigenous identity, it is no
longer a personal, affective kind of conflict. The indigenous wing of the KMT
does not hate the CCP as its predecessor did. Indeed at present, this threat
is considered to come from China, not from the CCP, and the task is to
explain why China, now as an external actor, instead of the CCP, which used
to be an internal enemy, is the problem. The answer is simply that China is
not democratic; it violates human rights and refuses to recognize the Republic
of China on Taiwan. In other words, for the KMT, the Taiwan–China
confrontation is now an intellectual one, and if the KMT and the CCP are
not enemies, the people on Taiwan therefore have to learn why Taiwan and
China cannot be friends.

Yet at the same time, the indigenous wing of the KMT does need to distance
Taiwan from China lest its emerging indigenous identity be obscured if Taiwan
and China should develop a good relationship. An improved relationship
between Taiwan and China would likely renew the call for reunification and
consequently undermine the appeal of the nascent indigenous identity. Thus
the new KMT now must look for signs of anti-democratic incidents in China

in order to firmly establish the differences between China and Taiwan. This sense of difference serves as a new source of danger, and so, for the KMT, sovereignty is necessary to protect Taiwan from intrusion.[20]

Under these circumstances, the KMT often finds human rights violations in the Mainland a reason to feel elated, for it demonstrates the difference between the democratic Taiwan and the undemocratic China. Not only is it unnecessary to rescue those who are suffering in China (since they are outside of Taiwan), it is also psychologically necessary to ignore them (so as to show that their affairs are their own business). As a result, human rights thus conceived refer to rights of the Taiwanese people, not of the Chinese people. The KMT has recently begun to treat human rights issues involving Taiwanese and Chinese differently. This discrimination consolidates the indigenous identity, for human rights violations in the Mainland are not a reason to recover the Mainland; on the contrary, it is a show of difference and a reason to refuse reunification.

The following case studies actually illustrate the intellectual need on the part of the KMT to construct images of human rights violation in China and overlook actual violations in Taiwan. If the rectification of past human rights violations is a show of indigenous identity, then current human rights violations that are overlooked are also a similar demonstration. The two cases we will examine reveal the identity at the root of the human rights practices in Taiwan in the 1990s: the KMT's need for China to violate the human rights of the Taiwanese people and need to prevent Taiwanese from caring about the human rights of the Chinese people.

THE THOUSAND ISLAND LAKE INCIDENT

In order to remind those on Taiwan, who have gone to the Mainland with an incredible frequency in the 1990s, of Taiwan's unique identity, it has become a psychological necessity for the KMT regime to constantly construct reference points that can bring into focus the differences between the two. Differentiating Chinese human rights and Taiwanese human rights in practice would reproduce the sense of difference between China and Taiwan, which can help consolidate the identity of a unique Taiwan. One key message that has been communicated is that while Taiwan is civilized, China is not. The KMT points to the fact that Taiwan allows for opposition parties, runs elections at local as well as central levels, and has broad economic freedom. In contrast, China appears in Taiwan's media as an authoritarian system rife with corruption and crime. Evidence otherwise has rarely attracted attention and politicians revealing an inclination toward this more positive image would be committing political suicide by inviting a "pro-China" (hence anti-Taiwan) label.[21] Indeed, this environment has not been at all conducive to genuine scholarly comparison between Taiwan and China regarding electoral practices or the type and volume of corruption and crime, and as a result, it has been difficult to ascertain the real scope of the differences between the two. Such was the background of the Thousand Island Lake incident.

Thousand Island Lake, Zhejiang Province, is a large national park in China, covering approximately 80 acres of water and another 80 of forest. The lake has the best quality water in China, and the crystalline lake allows one to see 25 feet below the surface. To date, the lake has been one of the most visited spots for tourists from Taiwan. On April 1, 1994, a group of twenty-four Taiwanese and eight Chinese guides and staff were murdered on Thousand Island Lake. In the beginning, the Zhejiang authority denied all clues indicating foul play and refused reporters' requests to visit the yacht on which the victims had been burned to death. This aroused great suspicion on the Taiwan side, and encouraged the belief that government officials must have been involved in the killing. Family members eventually arrived in the prefecture of Chuenan, to whose administrative district Thousand Island Lake belonged. However, there was virtually no official channel to assist the Taiwanese families in locating responsible officials in Zhejiang.

In 1991, Taiwan and China had in fact agreed on a formula for dealing with the rapidly increasing interactions between people from both sides of the Taiwan Straits. The KMT, originally out of the concern for its decades-old anti-Communist identity, designed a quasi-official organ, the Straits Exchange Foundation (SEF), to deal with the cross-Straits affairs. The Foundation is largely funded by the government, but acts as a private organization to avoid the embarrassing implication of formal ties with Beijing. (In 1991, when the SEF was set up, Taipei officially still claimed its sovereignty over the Mainland.)

The indigenous faction of the KMT, having decisively defeated the anti-Communist wing, was now ready to confront Beijing as an equal, sovereign state. Beijing could not accept this for the obvious reason that it was not prepared to give up the nationalist goal of reunifying China and Taiwan. However, having anticipated the victory of the indigenous wing in the KMT, Beijing had consented to Taipei's request and set up its own quasi-official organ, the Association for Relations Across the Taiwan Straits (ARATS), back in 1992. Ironically for Taipei, this institutional design later kept the indigenous wing of the KMT from gaining the implied official recognition of Taipei it sought through talks between the two nominally private organizations.

In April 1994, despite these new channels of communication, the SEF failed to get any useful information about the Thousand Island Lake massacre from the ARATS. There were three key reasons. First of all, the ARATS was a newly established organ and was definitely not capable of overcoming bureaucratism in Zhejiang. Second, Beijing agreed to establish the ARATS for the sole purpose of avoiding any hint of official recognition of Taipei, thus the ARATS was not institutionally ready to deal with affairs within the Mainland. Third, and most importantly, the ARATS did not trust the SEF. The two organizations arranged for a meeting between their chairmen in Singapore in April 1993. For China, it was a major breakthrough in the cross-Straits relations because Taipei had continually refused this type of political contact. For Taipei, however, it was an opportunity to show the world that the two sides had met in an international forum – outside of the two Chinas – as two sovereign states (despite the fact that neither SEF nor ARATS was official). Taipei's subsequent, unilateral, and painstaking claim at home that Beijing had tacitly recognized Taiwan's sovereignty in Singapore must have caused great anxiety in Beijing and hindered the ARATS from responding to the SEF positively in April 1994.[22]

In any case, the ARATS's cold reaction and inability to help collect information about the massacre actually served Taipei's purpose better. What Taipei needed at that particular moment was proof of the complete lack of human rights in the Mainland, so that there was no justification on either the Chinese side or the outcast wing of the KMT to request the reunification of China and Taiwan. The Thousand Island Lake incident occurred at a time when the indigenous wing of the KMT was struggling to demonstrate the difference between China and Taiwan and therefore the incident provided the desired proof by highlighting the different nature of politics in China and by depicting Taiwan as a victim of China in this event. The KMT was thus able to clearly point out the differing conceptions of human rights in China and Taiwan.

Premier Lian Zhan (Lien Chan) was the first to launch the attack. He accused the CCP of senselessly ignoring human rights and "disposing of human lives like grass."[23] President Li, also the Chairman of the KMT, then began a series of attacks on the Mainland regime. He denounced the CCP as a bandit (*tufei*) regime which Chinese people had for a period of time jettisoned. He questioned how a group of evil forces could be the ruling party of a government.[24] One top official of the SEF called those behind the ARATS decision not to help the SEF "turtle eggs" (a curse typically uttered among lower classes, meaning one's father is a turtle).[25] In addition the media geared up to accuse the CCP of sabotaging the investigation and blocking the families from knowing the truth. Rumors flew and the lethargic response from the Zhejiang authorities intensified the criticism from Taiwan. President Li's National Security Council reported to the legislature that there was evidence that the People's Liberation Army was involved in the crime; this substantiated Li's earlier claim that it had been the CCP who had brutally slaughtered "our compatriots."[26]

The opposition DPP also could not let go of the opportunity to prove that it, not the indigenous wing of the KMT, was the central force guiding Taiwan's emerging identity and with it a new human rights perspective. General Secretary Su Zhenchang declared that the Thousand Island Lake incident justified the necessity for Taiwan to become an entirely independent country, for the Taiwanese people could not stand China's weak response to Taiwan's human rights concerns as reflected in its lack of empathy for the families. The lesson, according to Su, was that Taiwan and China were two totally different states. For him, reunification, to which the KMT still nominally attached, was in itself a weapon being used to kill Taiwanese.[27]

The most important feature arising from this incident was the tendency to portray all Taiwanese as victims of China's human rights violation. The sense of self-pity revealed itself in the remarks that if there had been foreigners (meaning non-Taiwanese) on the yacht, China would have never dared to block the news or conceal the investigation.[28] The media sounded particularly bitter as they complained about the lack of international exposure, compared with that given to Taiwan's environmental problems at home. It seemed clear to them that the world cared little about Taiwan. Li, in the aforementioned remarks, contended that it was the Taiwanese who were the real victims. A DPP legislator used the opportunity to remind his countrymen of the "evil bully" mentality China maintained when dealing with Taiwan and urged anyone who still embraced the dream of reunification to give it up.[29]

Interestingly, even though no single piece of evidence linked the People's Liberation Army to the crime, when China arrested three suspects, the SEF again raised the possibility of PLA or other official involvement. The SEF argued that three could not have killed thirty-two, and that there must have been someone else involved; moreover, denying that others were involved simply indicated that those others must have had official affiliations. After making a thorough explanation, the ARATS arranged to have the SEF, accompanied by criminal experts from Taiwan, investigate all the evidence at the crime scene. Suspicion continued in Taiwan, but there remained no evidence that the PLA or any fourth person was involved. The Mainland court ordered the quick execution of the three criminals; however, from Taiwan's perspective, this did not demonstrate China's determination to punish or curb crime in China as a whole. On the contrary, such a quick execution only suggested that China was afraid that the three would eventually tell the truth.

The lack of substantive evidence linking the crime to the Chinese government prevented Taipei from exaggerating the CCP regime's involvement and weakened Taipei's own human rights charges. In addition, despite the death of two Taiwanese in an earlier air crash in Russia and another five to six Taiwanese by a criminal group involving policemen in Thailand, there were never any official requests for clarification or accusations against the Russian or Thai governments with regard to human rights. While Taipei's commentators appeared particularly hypocritical critiquing Beijing's human rights stance while remaining officially silent when pro-democracy advocates in China were imprisoned, other reporters complained that news articles taking a noncritical stand toward Beijing never got published in periods following the Thousand Island Lake incident.[30] It is interesting to note that China treated the families of the twenty-four Taiwanese victims dramatically better than it did those of the eight Mainland Chinese victims and adopted an apologetic posture exclusively toward the Taiwanese families. However, no one in Taiwan thought to mention Chinese treatment of the families of those eight Chinese victims.

In short, human rights are not just abstract, idealist standards. Rather, it is essential for us to know who violates whose human rights. In the Thousand Island Lake incident, certain forces in Taiwan wanted (and needed) to see China violating Taiwanese human rights. This specific search for "the oppressor" explained Taipei's lukewarm reaction to the Russian and Thai incidents and its total neglect of the other eight Chinese victims. It was precisely because the indigenous regime was struggling to define the difference between Taiwan and China that the subsequent anti-China media campaign was mobilized. Taipei's China policy was theatrically illuminating in this regard: the government launched a boycott against all China tours;[31] the SEF talked about boycotting the talks coming up with the ARATS on matters concerning cross-Straits exchange generally; the Ministry of Economics also requested boycotting investments in China, factory exports to China, and invitations of Chinese businessmen to Taiwan; and a DPP legislator pushed to cut the entire budget relating to cross-Straits exchanges.[32] Like all these policy gestures, the human rights issue for Taiwan was a matter of establishing differences and creating new boundaries.

THE OFF-SHORE HOTEL ISSUE

If the Li regime was in fact seeking an identity outside the traditional anti-Communist, China-centered complex, then it would become important to construct new boundaries between the Mainland and Taiwan. In this sense, an identity-based human rights treatment toward Mainland people, which would symbolize Taiwan's advanced social status relative to the Mainland, would be useful. This new treatment turned out to be a pattern of comprehensive legal discrimination against Chinese people in the Mainland and Hong Kong. The application of legal discrimination of this sort in the 1990s serves the quest for an indigenous identity. Consequently, the statutes that now govern Taiwan–Mainland relations and Taiwan–Hong Kong relations deny people in these two places the rights normally granted to the Taiwanese or even those enjoyed by aliens in Taiwan.

For example, people legally entering Taiwan from the Mainland and Hong Kong can potentially be expelled without any due process of law and are subject only to administrative discretion on national security grounds. They are not provided any legal channels through which to seek remedy. People in the Mainland are not eligible to receive bequests from a Taiwanese will over US$80,000 because they have clearly not contributed to Taiwan's economic development. The same limit, or even discussions of it, have never applied to non-Chinese aliens. The Hong Kong people are legally divided into overseas Chinese and ordinary Hong Kong people, and depending on their regime loyalty are entitled to different rights. This legal design in many ways resembles a caste system.[33] A relevant government organ in Taiwan can revoke all conditioned political and economic rights granted to the Hong Kong and Mainland people overnight if it judges that their relations with the Mainland (authorities as well as people) are close enough to threaten Taiwan's national interests. There are no provisions with regard to remedy or compensation. While the law treats the Mainland and Hong Kong people like other non-resident aliens in many respects, they cannot in any way expect protection or assistance from their mother government that most countries can provide. In fact, it is exactly their ties with their governments that jeopardize their legal status in Taiwan.[34]

In short, human rights for the Mainland and Hong Kong peoples in Taiwan have no true legal basis. Rights vary according to Taiwan's national interests, the persons' overseas Chinese status, and their connections with the Mainland people or government. These three categories of consideration are the legal pretexts to confine, reverse, or violate human rights of those who come to Taiwan from the Mainland or Hong Kong.

Under these circumstances, Taiwan's economic, social, and cultural needs to develop relations with the Mainland face numerous uncertainties. However, the needs are too great to be completely disrupted by these legal obstacles. In reality, the Taiwan authorities are not capable of controlling fast-developing relations in all areas. Legal bans can at best push underground actual exchanges of investment, tourists, and services. Indeed it is against this background that the issue of an off-shore hotel system has emerged on the political stage.

Taiwan's fishing business first built the off-shore hotels sometime in the mid-1980s to accommodate illegal fishermen from Southeast Asian countries. The government later legalized the employment of alien fishermen. Ironically, however, the business has since looked not to Southeast Asia but to the Mainland for even cheaper employment. Mainland workers are also culturally and linguistically easier to manage for the owners of the fishing industry. Because the Cross-Straits Relations Act (CRA) forbids Taiwanese employers from hiring Mainland labor, the industry has rebuilt a few out-of-date boats into "sea hotels" for the temporary residence of the Mainland workers.[35] As long as police authorities do not physically see the hotels floating miles off-shore, they will not pursue them. Indeed a few sea hotels built by companies with political connections have actually moored inside the harbors, and the one time when police attempted to expel them, the political pressure brought to bear on the police and the fierce demonstrations mobilized by the fishing industry demonstrated the inability of authorities to prevent such behavior.

These floating hotels typically lack adequate food or sanitation, and are vulnerable to epidemics, abuse, and so on. The Mainland fishermen are physically as well as legally marginalized as they belong to neither the Chinese nor the Taiwanese sphere, and this in turn leads to periodic abuse and violence.

Violence has even occurred between Mainlanders from different home towns: infighting once led to over ten fishermen from the town of Pingtan being thrown into the sea by a larger group from the town of Huian. The most dangerous aspect of these "hotels" are typhoons which visit Taiwan frequently during summer and autumn months. It is believed that any typhoon could cause serious casualties on the off-shore hotels. However, since the CRA bans employment of Mainlanders and the National Security Act (NSA) prohibits the illegal immigrants from landing, no government agencies were willing to get involved in these national identity-related matters simply for human rights reasons. Moreover, as noted before, it was psychologically imperative for the indigenous authorities to ignore the human rights of the Chinese fishermen.

Unfortunately, Typhoon Tim struck on July 10, 1994. For fear of the NSA penalties, the owners and the captains of the off-shore hotels first persisted in anchoring off-shore. They also tried to get in touch with local government officials to request an exemption to the NSA prohibitions and permission to come into Taiwan's harbors. As Typhoon Tim approached, hotel captains finally decided to force their way into harbors. Local authorities maintained the position that the owners would be subject to NSA penalties, but gave the boats access to humanitarian shelter in the harbor. The Mainland fishermen, however, were still required to remain on board. This humanitarian concession came too late as one boat, the *Shanghao*, trapped by its own fishing net, ran onto a reef. Most of the fishermen were forced to jump into the soaring waves and swim to the shore. Rumor spread that several men were drowned, but the owner of the boat denied the charge and the authorities all claimed that there was no evidence of drowning.[36] Meanwhile, the government claimed that those who swam to shore would be dispatched back to the Mainland along with smugglers.[37]

In the next few days, bodies floated ashore one after another. However, the owners of the off-shore hotels and their Mainland customers refused to recognize the bodies as their co-workers' for fear of possible criminal prosecution.[38] The government, interestingly, continued to state that there was no evidence of Mainland fishermen killed during the typhoon. News reporters recorded, with disbelief, a dramatic statement made by the Council of Mainland Chinese Affairs (CMCA) that it had nothing to do with the deaths of these obviously Mainland Chinese fishermen, as long as no one could legally prove who they were.[39] A week passed and a total of ten barely identifiable bodies were discovered. The owner of the *Shanghao* finally acknowledged that his books indicated that there were indeed ten Mainland fishermen missing.

This confession started a bureaucratic battle as all the parties involved wanted to evade responsibility for the deaths of the fishermen. The Council of Agricultural Affairs in charge of fishing policy criticized the CMCA for inappropriately maintaining a ban on employing Mainland fishermen and for the subsequent development of illegal off-shore hotels. The CMCA blamed the coastal police for tolerating the existence of illegal off-shore hotels in practice and the Council of Agricultural Affairs for consistently failing to come up with a practical proposal to persuade the CMCA that there was at least some way to regulate the fishing industry after lifting the ban. The local coastal police complained, however, that it was in charge of inland security, not harbor security, and thus could not board the hotel to enforce the NSA regulations.[40] Unlike most cases involving deaths wherein different authorities vied for jurisdiction, no one wanted jurisdiction over the deaths and the related human rights issues stemming from the *Shanghao* incident.

Interestingly, a parallel was drawn in the media between the Thousand Island Lake incident and the *Shanghao* off-shore hotel incident, and CMCA officials were furious about the comparison. They contended that in the Thousand Island Lake incident, Taiwanese tourists who entered the Mainland legally were killed, while in the *Shanghao* incident, the fishermen had entered Taiwan illegally. Besides, the Mainland authorities intended to hide the truth while the Taiwan authorities had after all allowed the illegal entry on humanitarian grounds. Finally, the CMCA agreed that the *Shanghao* incident was an accident but asserted that the Thousand Island Lake incident was a crime. These arguments remain problematic.[41] First of all, Taiwan has yet to legally allow its citizens to tour the Mainland, so the Taiwanese tourists were in fact illegal from the Taiwanese government's perspective. However the Mainland fishermen hired by the Taiwan fishing industry all had permission from the Mainland authorities. Indeed the Taiwanese tourists in the Mainland were no more legal than the Mainland fishermen in Taiwan.

Second, and most importantly, legality should not be the essential element in determining the kind of universal human rights position to which Taiwan pledges. In actuality, Taiwan is using legal terminology to differentiate the value of the thirty-two who were killed on the Thousand Island Lake and the ten who drowned off the coast of Taiwan. By legal definition, all those lucky enough to swim ashore from the *Shanghao* immediately became illegal immigrants and were put into the smuggler category. Those staying on the other boats which sought shelter in the harbor were not placed in that category because they gained legality on humanitarian grounds. Evidently, one's physical position distinguishes the humanitarian entrant from the illegal – in this case landing or not was the criterion for applying the humanitarian argument. The Mainland authorities later refused to receive the *Shanghao* fishermen along with the smugglers precisely for the reason that fishermen were legal workers from the Mainland point of view.[42] They believed that their case must be separate from the smugglers.

Finally, the *Shanghao* incident, like the Thousand Island Lake incident, was not just an accident. Any foreign crafts could have sought shelter in Taiwan's harbor, but the *Shanghao* and other off-shore boats from Taiwan had to wait until the last minute and eventually show determination in order to get permission.[43] This was apparently because the status of the Mainland fishermen on these off-shore hotels was an important symbol of what differentiated Taiwan from the Mainland. In this sense, the so-called "humanitarian" permission granted was by no means humanitarian. Instead, it was a claim of exception, an abnormal state of affairs, and thus was a logic designed to protect the fabricated difference between Taiwan and the Mainland from being destroyed. Moreover, this so-called "humanitarianism" did not exempt the owners from the NSA penalty, and understandably delayed the escape of fishermen from the typhoon. To consider the *Shanghao* incident as an accident means that events outside the national boundary generally have no humanitarian relevance. This means that the boundary-drawing actions (i.e. discrimination against Mainland fishermen) in the *Shanghao* incident define the scope of humanitarianism and are themselves not subject to humanitarian consideration. In other words, humanitarianism presupposes national identity and the consolidation of national identity requires a clear boundary, which is tautologically embodied in the way that one applies humanitarianism.

CONCLUSION

Political acts that objectify certain human beings as the targets of human rights protection and others as irrelevant have come to be identified by the current KMT regime as central dimensions of an emerging indigenous image. The construction of that image is a psychological necessity in an age when the KMT's anti-Communist identity has faded into history. The confrontation between China and Taiwan lost ground on the affective level as the role of the old KMT, who knew and personally hated the CCP, has declined in politics. However, the new regime faces competition from an opposition which declares itself as the genuine representative of people on, and only on, Taiwan. In order to reproduce its own source of legitimacy and move beyond the anachronistic anti-Communist pursuit, the KMT has had to appeal to an indigenous identity whose meaning is rather vague to most people. Moreover, for the sake of preserving the necessary support of the anti-Communist wing while at the same time winning over those who subscribe to the indigenous movement, confrontation between China and Taiwan will have to continue.

The problematic in Taiwan's identity politics has changed. The premise has shifted from a Taiwan led by the anti-Communist KMT seeking to be a contender in Chinese politics to a Taiwan led by the indigenous wing of the KMT seeking to be a sovereign entity outside of China. Since many on Taiwan still regard themselves as Chinese, the identity of a sovereign Taiwan requires conscious construction. Indeed the political problems presented in Taiwan have recently invariably addressed, directly or indirectly (but not less importantly), the problematic of a Taiwan outside of China. In this regard, the human rights concerns, which are always presented as universal values but in fact are not, become a showcase of the new identity. This affective need for identity, when confronted with the political reluctance of the old wing of the KMT, necessitates a politics of difference: defining someone outside as an antagonist, instead of refining one's own self-understanding. The task therefore becomes to draw boundaries, not to clarify what is within the boundaries.[44] This boundary-creating mentality further compels local human rights policies to attend only to the human rights of the in-group, and to conceive of those of the out-group as inconsequential.

The indigenous wing of the KMT, by identifying whose human rights are valid and whose are not, tells the Taiwanese people how to differentiate themselves from the Chinese. Thus, the wedge of difference opens up a new problem of discrimination. The Taiwanese authorities ignored the eight Chinese victims on Thousand Island Lake and thus consolidated their perception of a Chinese violation of Taiwanese human rights. Similarly, they dismissed the deaths of the Mainland fishermen from the off-shore hotels in Typhoon Tim as a matter of natural accident. This chapter has therefore suggested that universal human rights advocates should more carefully examine other cases in the rest of the world to find out if the identity problematic is endemically present in all human rights policies in the world.

NOTES

1 See Jimmy Carter's remarks quoted in the *New York Times* (May 23, 1977), p. 12; Xin Li, "Human Rights Concern or Power Politics?" *Beijing Review* 33, no. 10 (March 5–11, 1990).
2 See, for example, J.I. Dominguez *et al.*, eds, *Enhancing Global Human Rights* (New York: McGraw-Hill, 1979).
3 Peter Van Ness, "China's Human Rights Diplomacy," *Working Paper No. 141*, The Peace Research Centre, Australian National University (1993).
4 Similarly, it would be an enormous threat to those who considered certain crimes deserve capital punishment to learn that there are claims that no death penalty can be justified.
5 For a summary of Chinese perspectives, see Chih-yu Shih, "Contending Theories of 'Human Rights with Chinese Characteristics,'" *Issues and Studies* 29, no. 11 (November 1993), pp. 42–64.
6 See Jack Donnelly, "Recent Trends in the UN Human Rights Activity," *International Organization* 35, no. 4 (Autumn 1981).
7 For a more detailed discussion, see A. James Gregor and Maria Hsia Chang, *The Republic of China and U.S. Policy* (Washington, DC: Ethics and Public Policy Center, 1983).
8 See Warren Kuo, *Zhonggong shi lun* [On the History of the Chinese Communist Party] (Taipei: Institute of International Relations, 1989).
9 Robert Jervis stated in his keynote speech at the 1988 International Society for Political Psychology's annual meeting (Meadowland, NJ) that past American studies of war never mentioned the element of hatred. In contrast, hatred seems to be a crucial factor according to Taiwan's China experts: see Cheng Nian-tse's interview of her father (unpublished term paper, National Taiwan University, 1994). A shorter version appears in *Mainland China Studies Newsletter* 3 (June 1994), p. 17.

10 All these themes were in the KMT's platforms before the 1970s. See Song Hsi, *Zhongguo Guomintang Zhenggang zhengce de yanjin* [The Evolution of Kuomintang's Platforms and Policies] (Taipei: Chengchung, 1976).

11 Some go as far as calling the KMT regime a Chinese colonial set-up in Taiwan. According to them, the KMT's call to recover the Mainland serves to disguise the true nature of their colonialism; people in Taiwan would eventually see themselves as Chinese, leaving in oblivion their Taiwanese origin. On the other hand, if the KMT was no longer interested in competing in China's political arena, thus separating Taiwan from China politically, this would mean that, as a regime that emigrated from China, the KMT would be foreign to Taiwan.

12 Martha Cottam, "Image Change and Problem Presentations after the Cold War," presented at the International Studies Association annual meeting (Washington, DC, March 29–April 1, 1994).

13 For a recent example, see Editorial, "Lofty Ideas Gain Strength," *The Free China Journal* (June 7, 1990), p. 6

14 China studies in Taiwan have been in a state of shock. See Chou Yangshan, "Taiwan daluxue zhi huigu yu zhangwang" [A Backwards and Forwards Look at Taiwan's Sinology], presented at the Conference on the Retrospect and Prospect of the Forty-year Evolution of Cross-Taiwan Straits Relations (Taipei, May 26, 1990).

15 Taiwan experts in China have produced numerous articles in this regard, for an example, see Zhu Tianshun, ed., *Dangdai taiwan zhengzhi yanjiu* [Studies of Politics in Contemporary Taiwan] (Xiamen: Xiamen University Press, 1990).

16 Li Denghui, "Shengwei taiwanren de beiai" [The Sorrow of Being Born a Taiwanese], *Zili wanbao* [*Independence Evening*] (April 30–May 2, 1994).

17 The Constitution was revised in 1992 to end the Mobilization Period, during which the CCP was a subversive and outlawed regime.

18 See Huang Kun-hui, *Guo tong gangling yu liangan guanxi* [Guidelines for National Reunification and Cross-Straits Relations] (Taipei: Council for Mainland Chinese Affairs, 1992).

19 Other code words include "Taiwan life community," "Taiwan residents," "21 million people," etc., all signaling that China is foreign to Taiwan.

20 This need for an external threat is dictated by the sense of difference and the sense of belonging. For a discussion of the influence of emotion and affection on cognition, see Vernon Hamilton *et al.*, eds, *Cognitive Perspectives on Emotion and Motivation* (Boston: Kluwer Academic Publishers, 1988).

21 The KMT's research institute once informed its contract authors that studies of China's competitive elections and their evolution were not welcome topics, for they would influence and contradict the impressions of those who read the reports. The spokesman of the Presidential Office once claimed on TV that China never had any elections, and the CCP was ignorant of the conduct of elections. The point here is not just that the spokesman was wrong, but that there existed a collective psychological system underneath, which needed, sought, and allowed this type of misinformation. Though this was probably not consciously intended, the misinformation reflected a matter-of-course kind of mentality.

22 For a good analysis, see Hua Cheng-shao, "Taibei mishi zai qian dao hu chuan nan shijian zhong" [Taipei Loses its Way in the Incident of the Thousand Island Lake Boat Disaster], *Guancha* [Observation Bi-weekly] 5 (April 25, 1994), pp. 10–11.

23 Lian Zhan's remarks quoted in *Zhongyang ribao* [Central Daily] (April 8, 1994), p. 1.

24 Li Denghui's remarks quoted in *Zhongyang ribao* (April 10, 1994), p. 1.

25 Chiao Jen-ho's words, see *Guancha* 5 (April 25, 1994), pp. 12–14; he also accused the SEF of acting like a "fool" (*bendan*), see *Zhongguo shibao* [China Times] (April 11, 1994), p. 2.

26 Li Denghui's words, see *Zhongyang ribao* (April 10, 1994), p. 1.

27 Su Chen-chang's remarks quoted in *Zhongguo shibao* (April 11, 1994), p. 2.

28 See Hua Chengshao, *Guancha* (April 25, 1994), p. 11.

29 Hung Chi-chang's remarks quoted in *Guancha* (April 25, 1994), pp. 12–14.

30 Both the Central News Agency, run by the government, and the *China Times* [Zhongguo shibao], one of the two largest newspaper networks in Taiwan, have reporters who complained to me that they were not allowed to write versions deviant from the official tone.

31 Interestingly, Taipei has never officially allowed tours to Mainland China, but tours have continued anyway. This embarrassing situation effectively impeded the government from really regulating tourist activities. So, the boycott had to depend on the cooperation of the private sectors, which only lasted for a few weeks. However, the government still threatened to suspend the licenses of those who continued to arrange Mainland tours (as if the illegal tour arrangements before the Thousand Island incident had been acceptable).

32 Chang Chun-hsiung, a leading DPP legislator, made this statement in a policy debate broadcast on a widely subscribed cable TV channel. For transcripts, see *Guancha* 5 (April 25, 1994), pp. 36–41.

33 In order to protect their interests, those with overseas Chinese status develop a tendency of exaggerating the difference between themselves and other non-overseas Chinese Hong Kong people. They especially like to claim loyalty to the Taipei government and alienate themselves from the rest of Hong Kong society. This was in fact anticipated by the drafters of the Taiwan–Hong Kong Relations Act. A split among the Hong Kong people could reinforce the image that there is a pro-Taiwan and a pro-China group, thus reinforcing the impression that Taiwan and China are two completely separate entities.

34 See the discussion in Chih-yu Shih and Nigel Li, *Shijian liang-an guanxi* [Practicing Cross-Straits Relations] (Taipei: Chengchung, 1994), pp. 108–36.

35 A fishing boat has to drop the Mainland fishermen at sea hotels before delivering the fish to their respective destinations. Sea hotels are where the fishermen stay while they wait for the boat to pick them up for another fishing job.

36 The first official claim that all were rescued appeared on July 12, see *Zhongguo shibao* (July 13, 1994), p. 7.

37 Large numbers of Mainland-Chinese smugglers have searched for illegal job opportunities on the Taiwanese labor market. When caught, they are put under house-arrest and then sent to a prison camp to await the next ship heading for China.

38 See *Zhongguo shibao* (July 20, 1994), p. 6.

39 See ibid.

40 This bureaucratic farce was recorded in *Zhongguo shibao* (July 19, 1994), p. 6. The only aggressive branch of government was the Agency of Sanitation, which spoke on behalf of the environment, worrying that excrement discharged from the hotels polluted the sea, thus further alienating Taiwan's inhabitants from the Mainland fishermen (see *Zhongguo shibao*, July 22, 1994, p. 4).

41 See *United Daily* (July 19, 1994), p. 3.

42 In fact, even the smugglers' camp in Taiwan refused to receive the *Shanghao* fishermen for a similar reason (see *Zhongyang ribao*, July 21, 1994, p. 3).

43 Columnists all agreed on this point. For example, see *Zhongguo shibao* (July 18, 1994), p. 11.

44 A useful text in this regard is David Campbell, *Writing Security* (Minneapolis: University of Minnesota Press, 1992).

Part III

WOMEN'S RIGHTS

8

REINVENTING INTERNATIONAL LAW

Women's Rights as Human Rights in the International Community

Radhika Coomaraswamy

Radhika Coomaraswamy, *a lawyer from Sri Lanka, first presented this essay as an Edward A. Smith Lecture to Harvard Law School in March 1996. The analysis is drawn from her work as Special Rapporteur on Violence Against Women for the United Nations Human Rights Commission.* Opening with a discussion of the importance of the principle of universality while acknowledging its origins in the Enlightenment, Coomaraswamy describes herself as a critic of the negative aspects of the Enlightenment and at the same time a fervent believer in universal human rights. She describes the victories achieved for the principle of women's rights as human rights at the World Conference on Human Rights in Vienna in 1993 and the 1995 World Conference on Women in Beijing, and analyzes some of the implications for international law. Coomaraswamy discusses the special responsibilities of the state with respect to women's rights, and some of the questions now being raised about the issue of gender difference and "the special quality of being female." Reviewing the understanding of UN agreements to date as constituting three "generations" of human rights, as earlier described by Linda Butenhoff in Chapter 5, Coomaraswamy suggests that the problems of protecting women's rights may be sufficiently distinctive to merit their being considered a fourth generation of human rights, indivisible and equally as important as the other three.*

INTRODUCTION

In some ways women's rights are the most popular of international initiatives, but they are also the area with the most profound disagreements. As of January 1996, 121 nations had ratified the Convention on the Elimination of All Forms of Discrimination Against Women (CEDAW, or the Women's Convention). Although it enjoys the privilege of having this exceptionally large membership, CEDAW is also the human rights convention with the largest number of state reservations. This says much about the international community and the question of women. Relative to other fields, women's rights are more fragile, have weaker implementation procedures, and suffer from inadequate financial support from the United Nations.

Both in Vienna at the UN World Conference on Human Rights in 1993 and in Beijing at the UN World Conference on Women in 1995 women's rights were recognized as human rights. For the first time their articulation was accepted as an aspect of international human rights law. The underpinning of women's rights with human rights would give women's rights discourse a special trajectory, emerging as a major innovation of human rights policy within the framework of international law. But before we analyze the discussion of women's rights as human rights, we must meet the argument challenging the very premise of the debate.

Many scholars from the Third World argue that human rights discourse is a product of the Enlightenment and therefore not universal. This type of limitation is often introduced and underscored in the area of women's rights. Women are seen as the symbol of a particular cultural order. To grant universality to their rights is to undermine the cultural framework of a particular society. When it comes to issues such as female genital mutilation, *sati* (Hindu widow immolation on a husband's pyre), punishment according to Shariah (Muslim personal) law, and other practices that are particular to cultural communities, this argument is made even more forcefully by those who believe that many values are culturally relative. It is therefore necessary to underscore the universality of human rights as an essential first step in the recognition of human rights as women's rights.

In many ways the privileged personality of international human rights law is the so-called "Enlightenment personality" – a man, endowed with reason, unfettered and equal to other men. This construction of the world underpins most of the instruments on international human rights law. What is essentially called liberal feminism is now keen on extending these postulates to women, who should also be recognized as endowed with reason and unfettered in spirit. This project to extend the Enlightenment ideal to women received widespread support from all sectors of the women's movement as an important starting point for the discussion of women's rights, especially at the international level. However, to accept such postulates in many parts of the world is to acknowledge the cultural victory of Enlightenment Europe, a truth that is often unpalatable in the non-Western world. I would like to deal with this issue – the question of the universal legitimacy of women's rights as human rights. If human rights doctrine has its origins in Enlightenment Europe and in North America, should we work toward its universalization? This dilemma is a real one for all academics who are concerned with the development of political values in the non-Western world.

On the one hand there is the intellectual quest that is a result of colonialism and the experience of the Enlightenment as a colonial subject. Throughout my academic career I have agreed with thinkers like Foucault that there was a need to demystify the Enlightenment project. In addition, writers such as Parha Chatterjee and Ronald Inden have shown the negative aspect of this project in the colonial world. The colonial venture, imbued by the philosophy of the Enlightenment, has led to morbid structures and developments in these postcolonial societies. Many scholars, including Sri Lanka's Gananath Obeyesekere, have described this morbidity and contradiction in very clear and unambiguous terms.[1] I myself have strong reservations about Enlightenment ideas in their defining, classifying, and excluding large segments of the world's population. I have objections to the notions of order and discipline couched in terms of a paternalistic enterprise that perhaps was the greatest contribution of Enlightenment ideas in the field of law. Nonetheless, I am today an active instrument of the Enlightenment, promoting international standards, urging people to discipline and punish the violators of those standards, especially those who are the perpetrators of violence against women.

How does one confront this philosophical dilemma – to remain a critic of the negative aspects of the Enlightenment while being a fervent believer in human rights? Even though human rights may be a product of the Enlightenment, they are universal in scope and application. In certain contexts and social experiences the Enlightenment project of human rights provides us with a framework to deal not only with brutality and violence but also with arbitrariness and injustice that must necessarily shock the conscience. Second, human rights and their postulates such as the equal dignity of human beings resonate in all the cultural traditions of the world. In that sense there is enough analysis in every cultural tradition that fosters and promotes the value of human rights. Though its exact articulation in terms of rights and duties of the state *vis-à-vis* individuals is an Enlightenment formulation, the spirit of human rights may be said to have universal appeal.

Many political thinkers in the Third World have shown how indigenous concepts and processes are animated by a commitment to the ideals of human rights. I refer here to the writings of Ashis Nandy, Veena Das, and Chandra Muzaffar, among others.[2] The discourse of human rights allows us to deal with issues of violence and injustice not only within many different indigenous traditions but also with some measure of universality and a common humanity. The discourse has resonance in the everyday experiences of individuals. Otherwise it would not have developed so dynamically and have become used by such different groups throughout the world. In other words – yes, perhaps human rights in its present-day incarnation is a product of the Enlightenment, but its general thrust has resonance in diverse spiritual and cultural experiences. In terms of political values, like the concept of democracy, it is an important civilizational step forward for all human beings and all cultures. If one accepts the proposition that human rights are universal, then the acceptance of women's rights as human rights is a major landmark in the international struggle for women's rights.

There are historical reasons why the claim that women's rights are human rights has gained ascendancy in the world today. "Rights offer a recognised vocabulary to frame political and social wrongs."[3] Women are increasingly using this vocabulary to articulate their grievances. The availability of human rights discourse for the translation of women's rights into internationally acceptable norms allows for a greater visibility for the issues of women's rights. In addition, the diverse machinery set up at the international level for the promotion of human rights now remains available for women's rights activists. This access to international machinery of implementation is also an important development in the search for women's equality.

In earlier times the relationship between international human rights law and women's issues was not a happy one. International human rights law has also been subjected to a feminist critique. Such law was, after all, state-centered and individualistic in content. Its structure and appeal was basically toward male subjects, with only passing reference to women's inequality. Most importantly, international human rights law reinforced the division between the public world and private life. By insulating the internal practices of states from scrutiny, it ensured that community and private life continued without any reference to international standards. There was considered to be a public sphere where the state and the international system may intervene and a private sphere where state intervention and international scrutiny were prohibited. It is assumed that privacy was a neutral, powerless realm of human experience, and that there was no power hierarchy within the private space of the family. As critics have argued, the absence of legal intervention to protect women in the community and in the home devalued women's roles and kept the traditional male-dominated hierarchy of the family intact.

The founding theorists of international law were all male and did not recognize the political nature of private life.[4] In international law as in political life generally, much depends on who controls the influential discourses.[5] Men formulated and to date actually control international mechanisms of implementation. This corresponds to the privileging of public life over the personal. In addition the state was the primary, sovereign actor in international law. Intervention in the activities of the nation-state was absolutely unacceptable until a few years ago. This sovereignty ensured that community and private life located within the jurisdiction of the nation-state were secluded from scrutiny.

The roots of this state-centeredness in international law and international human rights law lie in liberal theories of social contract that privilege the negative minimalist state rather than the interventionist one. In addition, the rise of totalitarianism in Europe in the forms of Fascism and Communism led many to stress the protection of private life by insulating it from activity in the public sphere. By carving out a special area for private expression, there were necessary safeguards aimed at preventing the totalitarian state from destroying the dignity of human beings. Liberal theory of the minimalist state and fear of state monopoly of private life contributed to the rigid dichotomy between the public and the private, a dichotomy that until recently was the unshakable foundation of international law in general and international human rights in particular.

A revolution has taken place in the last decade. Women's rights have been catapulted onto the human rights agenda with a speed and determination that has rarely been matched in international law. There are two aspects to this process: first, the attempt to make mainstream human rights responsive to women's concerns; and, second, the conceptualization of certain gender-specific violations as human rights violations. These developments may have far-reaching implications for the theory and practice of human rights in the United Nations system.

Let us begin to consider these implications by taking the issue of violence against women as a case study of women's rights emerging as a major concern at the international level. How and why did this recently emerge as an international issue? What have been the implications of its emergence for the theory and practice of international law?

INTERNATIONAL RESPONSE TO VIOLENCE AGAINST WOMEN

In the 1970s the most prominent women's issues related to discrimination against women in the public sphere and the need to ensure equitable participation of women in the development process. In the Convention on the Elimination of All Forms of Discrimination Against Women, which came into force in 1979, explicit prohibition of violence against women is singularly absent. Except for prohibitions against trafficking and prostitution, there is no mention of the subject. Until the 1980s the issue of violence was invisible from the international perspective.

The UN Third World Conference on Women in Nairobi in July 1985, which was called to mark the end of the UN Decade for Women, concentrated on the themes of equality, development, and peace. The forward-looking strategies agreed to by the member-states at that conference do mention violence against women but as a side-issue to discrimination and development. As a result of this formulation there were a number of *ad hoc* initiatives in the UN system. By 1990 violence against women was on the international agenda, but as an issue of women's rights and crime prevention rather than of human rights.

In 1991 both the UN Economic and Social Council and the Commission on the Status of Women decided that the problem of violence against women was important enough to warrant the development of further international measures. Following these decisions a group of experts recommended that violence against women be included in the reporting under the Women's Convention, that a Special Rapporteur on Violence Against Women be appointed, and that a Declaration on Violence Against Women be drafted. As a consequence, in 1992 the CEDAW committee issued General Recommendation No. 19, which states that gender-based violence is an issue of gender discrimination, and that states should comment on this matter in their reports to the CEDAW committee. The Commission on the Status of Women began to formulate a draft Declaration on Violence Against Women, which was ready by the summer of 1993.

The major turning point, however, was the UN Conference on Human Rights in Vienna in 1993. The women's lobby at this conference had an important impact. More importantly, women's groups were determined to make women's rights human rights. Their lobbying effort succeeded. Article 18 of the Vienna Declaration and Program of Action states:

> The human rights of the girl child are an inalienable, integral and indivisible part of universal human rights. The full and equal partic-ipation of women in political, civil, economic, social and cultural life, at the national, regional and international levels, and the eradication of all forms of discrimination on grounds of sex are priority objectives of the international community. . . . The human rights of women should form an integral part of the United Nations' activities, including the promotion of all human rights instruments relating to women.

The Vienna Declaration and Program of Action also called for the appoint-ment of a Special Rapporteur on Violence Against Women by the UN Human Rights Commission as well as the adoption of the Declaration on the Elimination of Violence Against Women (DEVAW). In December 1993 the UN General Assembly adopted the declaration, and in February 1995 appointed a special rapporteur on violence against women. Within a year the women's lobby had won a major victory: women's rights were recognized as human rights, and two UN mechanisms were in place to deal specifically with violence against women.

The victories achieved in this period were consolidated at Beijing and at the UN Conference on Population and Development in Cairo. In spite of attempts to roll back the clock, the Beijing Declaration contains a special section on violence against women, which draws extensively from the Declaration on the Elimination of Violence Against Women. In fact, as one commentator points out, the provisions were so entrenched that she felt that governments were actu-ally more comfortable with obligations relating to violence than with obligations relating to the human rights of women in general.[6] It was also a major victory in Beijing when rape during time of armed conflict was recognized as a war crime, with victims having a right to compensation.

THE DECLARATION ON THE ELIMINATION OF VIOLENCE AGAINST WOMEN

The Declaration on the Elimination of Violence Against Women provides the normative framework for all international action in the field of violence against women. Article 1 defines violence against women as

> any act of gender-based violence that results in or is likely to result in physical, sexual or psychological harm or suffering to women, including threats of such acts, coercion or arbitrary deprivation of liberty, whether occurring in public or private life.

Violence includes but is not limited to physical, sexual, and psychological violence in the family such as battering, sexual abuse of female children in the household, dowry-related violence, marital rape, female genital mutilation, and other traditional practices harmful to women. The declaration also prohibits violence against women in the general community by rape, sexual abuse, sexual harassment, and intimidation, whether at work, in educational institutions, or elsewhere, as well as through trafficking and forced prostitution. Finally, it recognizes that violence can be perpetrated as well as condoned by the state. The definition of violence is broad and all-inclusive and acquires a certain transformative character. This broadness of scope and vision is reiterated in the mandate of the special rapporteur, where there is a call for the elimination of violence against women in the family, in the community, and by the state.

What are the implications for international law in general and human rights in particular of including such subjects within the purview of international human rights? Traditionalists claim that broadness of scope of the women's rights movement will destroy human rights and its meaning in the world today. As an angry human rights activist told me once, "Now human rights is the kitchen sink." I and others argue that the women's question enriches human rights and is an important part of the flexibility and adaptability of the human rights paradigm to new challenges.

INTERNATIONAL CIVIL SOCIETY

The first topic that interests me in terms of the implications of violence against women in the international arena is the process that made it such an important part of human rights. It is no secret that certain international women's groups have lobbied governments heavily to place this issue on the international agenda. The Global Tribunal on Violence Against Women in Vienna, which was sponsored by a women's nongovernmental organization, made a powerful impact on the international community. Women's groups have also taken part

173

in expert group meetings and helped draft many of the resolutions and declarations that began to take shape at international forums. The women's lobby has put the issue on the agenda, articulated the project in human rights terms, and introduced the mechanisms to help in the implementation of this mandate. This same lobby is now requesting that there be an optional protocol to CEDAW involving the right of individual petition, and that attention be given to an international convention on violence against women that, unlike a General Assembly resolution, will bind its parties.

This striking growth of the women's movement is an important factor in international politics today. It points to the significance of what Richard Falk called "international civil society" as an initiator of programs and mechanisms in the UN system.[7] What is the nature of this lobby, and why has it been so successful?

First, the women's lobby is made up of an international coalition of women's groups that have focused their energies and efforts on violence against women. Distinct lobbies have made up the whole. Initially there was the humanitarian women's lobby – those interested in the problems of violence against women in armed conflict. The events in Bosnia Herzegovina influenced this process, with the mass rapes and killings having an important effect on the work of these women's groups. The lobby has also included East Asian groups working with "comfort women," the victims of the Japanese government's military sexual slavery during World War II.

A second lobby of African and Asian women has been interested in health problems such as female genital mutilation, dowry deaths, and customary practices that were violent toward women. These issues had previously been brought before the UN Human Rights Subcommission in reports and through working groups relating to traditional practices.

The third lobby of North American, European, and Latin American women has been interested in the issues of domestic violence, rape, and sexual harassment. These groups, the most active and best coordinated, have had a measure of influence over their governments. They have relied on alliances with Third World coalitions, although at Beijing, perhaps for the first time, a certain resentment was articulated at the Western dominance of the women's lobby, especially in connection with UN instruments. There were arguments that UN procedures should be relaxed to allow more NGOs from the Third World to be accredited to the Economic and Social Council.

Another lobby that has played a major part in these international initiatives was Women Living under Muslim Laws, which has made a strong case for including the violation of women's rights resulting from religious extremism as a major area of concern. Because of their pressure the mandate of the special rapporteur refers to religious extremism as a cause of violence against women that should be the subject of the rapporteur's scrutiny. Finally, a lobby from Southeast and East Asia has dealt with the problem of trafficking and forced prostitution. It has been very active at both the regional and national level.

174

NGO lobbies have truly assisted UN value formation. Many of the concerns of the Human Rights Commission and Subcommission are animated by the international NGO movement. This activist role for international civil society actors marks a major step forward in the process of creating normative international standards. The victories at Vienna and Beijing are largely attributable to the consistent pressure of these NGOs.

However, the dominance of NGOs in the international process has not been accepted by all parties. Many states have NGO "phobia" and feel that the role of NGOs has to be curtailed. In addition they point out that many of the accredited NGOs are from the developed West and exert disproportionate influence and power. Whatever the sensitivities of certain governments, the NGOs have not only consolidated their presence but are in the process of lobbying for greater representation in UN functions and conferences. They have become an important part of the international process relating to human rights. But curbing violence against women is their special victory.

THE NATION-STATE

What are the implications now that violence against women has been firmly entrenched by the UN Human Rights Commission as an important and fundamental issue of human rights? One important aspect of violence against women becoming an issue of international law is that it is a part of the new assault on the powers and structure of the nation-state. First, according to commentators, governments controlling nation-states are no longer the only focus of women's agitation. Instead, women are taking their issues directly to the international community.[8] Many international activities are becoming transnational, with groups taking normative initiatives without waiting for state authorization.

Women transcending national boundaries in search of international protection is part of parallel developments in other areas of human rights. The dynamic growth of human rights law in the past two decades has challenged the hegemony of the nation-state and the sanctity of sovereign borders. For the first time there is an expansion of principles operating below the level of the nation-state that render its actions and the exercise of its discretion subject to scrutiny. The internal practices of states have become an important concern of the international community. The Montevideo Convention on the Rights and Duties of States contains the old requirements of state recognition, which include a permanent population, a defined territory, a government, and the capacity to enter into relations with other states. However, the European Community guidelines with regard to the recognition of the states of the former Soviet Union and the Yugoslav Republic speak of respect for the UN Charter, the rule of law, democracy, and human rights. They also make reference to guarantees of the rights of ethnic and national groups and minorities. They do not as yet speak specifically of women's rights.

The important development is that human rights have come a long way from involving a soft scrutiny of states to becoming an integral part of what constitutes a state and its ability to conduct international relations. For some commentators the nation-state itself has been radically reconstructed to include the value of human rights, at least at the normative level. The applications of these principles have generated a host of criticism, and the European Community has been accused of applying these principles in an arbitrary manner. But it is still important to realize that human rights have moved from the periphery to the center of international law. By articulating women's rights as human rights, women's issues therefore receive the benefits of the space created by recent developments in the theory and practice of international law.

STATE RESPONSIBILITY FOR THE CONDUCT OF NONSTATE ACTORS

While human rights doctrine in itself has resulted in greater scrutiny of state action, the women's movement has also moved the frontiers of this scrutiny. Specifically, the movement to counter violence against women has taken the further step of taking international scrutiny into the marital home, thus profoundly affecting the existing doctrine on state responsibility. Under traditional international law, states were only responsible for their actions or the acts of their agents. In today's context, and especially in the area of violence against women, states may be held responsible for not preventing, prosecuting, and punishing individuals and communities that violate the rights of women. CEDAW and the women's convention began the process by stating in Article 2(e) that states should take all appropriate measures to eliminate discrimination against women by any person, organization, or enterprise – that is, by persons or organizations that were part of government as well as those in the private sphere. The rather narrow construction of state action that used to dominate international discourse has in fact been changed by the inclusion of violence against women as an important development of human rights law. Since the UN documents declare that violence against women can take place in the family or the community or be carried out by the state, the arena of state action has been expanded. States are responsible for the violation of women's rights that take place in the marital home if they do not use due diligence to prevent, prosecute, and punish offenders.

The forerunners of this unusual theme are the Latin American cases on disappearances, the most important of which is *Velasquez Rodriguez v. Honduras*. In that case the Inter-American Court of Human Rights held that Honduras was responsible for politically motivated disappearances even if they were not carried out by government officials. The state has an affirmative duty to protect human rights against such violations to the extent and with the means suggested by a "due diligence" standard. It has a duty to "organize the government apparatus to ensure the full and free exercise of all rights."[9] States are exhorted to make good-faith efforts to prevent disappearances.

The cases on disappearances in Latin America make states indirectly responsible for violence in the community perpetrated by nonstate actors. But UN documents on violence against women go a step further. States are held responsible for their failure to meet international obligations by protecting women against violence, even when violations grow out of conduct of private individuals in the privacy of their home. When extended to the family this principle means that states may be held responsible for their failure to meet international obligations even when the violence occurs in what was considered a sacred and distinct private space. The Declaration on the Elimination of Violence Against Women in Article 4(c) requires that states should "exercise due diligence to prevent, investigate and in accordance with national legislation, punish acts of violence against women."[10] Such violence includes acts committed in the family or community as well as by the state. Private violence in the home is no longer beyond scrutiny. States may be held responsible for not exercising due diligence in the investigation, prosecution, and punishment of perpetrators of violence against women. This violence may be by the state, but it may also include violence in the community and in the family.

EQUAL PROTECTION

Though the UN documents such as the Declaration on the Elimination of Violence Against Women present a "due diligence" standard, groups active in the field of human rights have articulated other theories to ensure state accountability for the violation of the rights of women. Scholars and human rights groups have argued that in addition to violating the due diligence standard, nonprosecution of individuals who commit violence against women also violates equal protection in the implementation of laws. Research suggests that the investigation, prosecution, and sentencing of crimes of domestic violence[11] occur with much less frequency than for similar crimes. Wife murderers receive greatly reduced sentences, domestic battery is rarely investigated, and rape frequently goes unpunished. This inequality of treatment can be verified by gathering data, as Human Rights Watch did in the case of Brazil, to show the inequality in the administration of justice.

The doctrine of state responsibility is, then, in the throes of a revolution. The family has come to be seen as a political unit that may entertain power hierarchies that use their power arbitrarily and violently. Intimacy and privacy are no longer justifications for the nonintrusion of the state. It is important that the hierarchy within the family be challenged and equalized, and that victims of violence within the home be given access to redress.

The discussion on state responsibility gives us pause to consider the construct of the state envisioned by women's rights activists. On the one hand, there is the view of the state as the perpetrator of violence or in complicity with those who commit violence against women. At the same time, there is the view of the state as having what I have called "a Scandinavian aura," as being an activist interventionist state extending paternalistic protection to the battered, violated woman. These views only prove the ambivalence we have toward the nation-state, and how, despite our many attempts to bypass its tangled web, there is no escape, not only from state-directed violence but also because of our necessary reliance on that very state apparatus to protect the woman victim against nonstate violence. The Janus face of the state poses its own dilemma. The duality is an aspect that runs through many of the writings of women experts on this subject.

REINTERPRETATION OF HUMAN RIGHTS DOCTRINE FROM A GENDER PERSPECTIVE

Not only the basic tenets of international law such as state responsibility but also human rights doctrine itself is being transformed by the discourse on women's rights. It is often said that civil and political rights are the first generation of human rights; economic, social, and cultural rights are the second generation; and group rights and the right to self-determination are considered to be the third generation. It may be argued that women's rights are the fourth generation, radically challenging the private–public distinction in international human rights law and pushing for the rights of sexual autonomy.

One way in which human rights doctrine is transformed is through a radical reinterpretation of the earlier generation of rights to meet the concerns of women. For example, the rights to life and freedom from torture are being invoked as new rights that should be reexamined in light of violence against women.

Rhonda Copelon has put forward the interesting idea that torture should include violence against women in the home.[12] In international legal instruments torture requires severe physical or mental harm and suffering that is intentionally afflicted for a specific purpose by a person with some form of official involvement. Copelon stresses the official involvement as state inaction, and the inability to get redress. Though this is considered a radical formulation, there are many women's groups that have accepted this framework as one way to analyze violence against women as a human rights violation.

Another strand of feminist writing examines the question of equality, a cardinal principle of human rights and the first step in the recognition of women's rights. Recent arguments about universality and difference have been applied to the equality provisions of international human rights. The principle of nondiscrimination against women is firmly entrenched in international law and is the anchor of all women's rights and the core subject of the women's convention. But feminist writings have experimented with the concept to bring in the issue of difference – the special quality of being female as an aspect that should be respected by the principle.[13] In other words they want the human rights concept of equality to be reimagined to include and understand gender difference.

Equality in the past has meant women's access to places and positions that were traditionally male. But how, then, do we treat pregnant women, violence against women, and other gender-specific issues? It is argued that sex-specific violations should gain visibility as an aspect of equality in the world of international human rights. It is argued that programs for affirmative action would be more firmly rooted if difference is also accepted and recognized. In addition, Third World women argue that difference in culture and lifestyle should also be accepted, albeit within the general framework of equality. Finally, there are those like Martha Minow who have argued that masculine and feminine are differences that require analysis and conceptualization without making them hierarchical.[14] Women's experiences are different and women's rights should learn to respect these differences without resorting to male privilege.

In this context it must be recognized that while some feminists are attempting to go "beyond equality" to a deeper analysis of what it means to say that men and women are equal, a few state actors in the international arena such as Sudan have argued that the word "equality" be completely removed and replaced with the word "equity" when it comes to gender-based issues. Equality is seen as not desirable; rather, equity and fairness, as more abstract provisions, should guide state action toward women. I suggest a cautious approach to this suggestion, for as much as women's activists are interested in developing human rights doctrine in one direction, there are others who seek to tamper with the doctrine from a nonfeminist perspective.

Another aspect of human rights doctrine that is challenged by women's rights is the right to self-determination, a founding right and first article in both international covenants on civil and political rights and economic and social rights, and the ultimate basis of pluralism in the world today. We have learned through this right to respect the rights of communities to speak their own language, practice their own religion, and live their own lifestyle. The UN Declaration on the Rights of Minorities has made these norms international standards. But what if these cultures have aspects that violate the rights of women? This is perhaps the most controversial aspect of women's rights. The right to self-determination is pitted against the CEDAW articles, which oblige the state to remove any inconsistency between international and human rights law and the religious and customary laws operating within its territory.

Though this dilemma of the self-determination of groups brings to mind issues such as female genital mutilation and Shariah-type punishment, many states are guilty of violations because they do not want to antagonize their minorities. This is particularly true in the multiethnic states of Asia where a pattern of live and let live has come to guide communal action. As a result, the applicable personal law differs for women depending on which community they belong to. Marriage, divorce, custody of children, inheritance, maintenance, and so on, are decided by which community you belong to and not by your national status. Many of these personal laws violate the basic tenets of the women's convention. India, for example, signed CEDAW with reservations, that is, it refused to agree to the parts of the treaty that would affect the personal law of Muslims and other minorities.

Consider the Shah Bano case of a few years ago in India, where a Muslim woman sued for maintenance under the criminal law of the land, using a provision against destitution. In India, Muslim men do not have to pay maintenance under personal law, but by drawing on the criminal law provision the Supreme Court decided in favor of Shah Bano. This led to a major uproar and to outbursts of rioting in the major cities of India. Rajiv Gandhi, then Prime Minister, had to amend the criminal law to appease an angry Muslim minority. Shah Bano withdrew the case under pressure from her community. The arguments put forward by the Muslim minority concerned the right to self-determination, pluralism, and diversity. Given the political contours of India, women's rights had to give way to the ethics of pluralism.

Pluralism envisions a state that allows a thousand flowers to bloom. But unless there are bottom-line standards, pluralism will be at the expense of women and their bodies. Female genital mutilation, *sati*, punishment by stoning, and inequity in personal law will prevail over universal standards. Women's groups argue that pluralism is necessary but must be built on a firm foundation of human rights.

Women's rights are therefore the main reason why many states are against human rights and fundamental freedoms. In Beijing the universality clause of human rights for women was debated until the eleventh hour. The final formulation read:

> While the significance of national and regional peculiarities and various historical, cultural, and religious backgrounds must be borne in mind, it is the duty of states, regardless of their political, economic, and cultural systems, to promote and protect all human rights and fundamental freedoms.

Many of us in Asia want to promote pluralism and autonomy to ensure ethnic harmony in our region. But pluralism also means that diverse standards for the private lives of women will prevail. This is perhaps the most controversial area of women's rights. If all women are equal, then why do Muslim women have different rights from Hindu women, or Malay women from Chinese women? This dilemma is a very real one in many Third World societies.

Women's groups have come forward with alternative formulations that rely on the notion of women's consent. Women and men should be given the right to choose which law should govern their private lives. If they wish to be governed by Muslim law, that is their prerogative; but if they wish to be guided by general secular law, that should also be a right granted to the individual. This notion of choice is integral to a human rights understanding of the issue of cultural pluralism, and many feel that our attitude toward cultural diversity should be conditioned by this choice. Cultural diversity should be celebrated only if those enjoying their cultural attributes are doing so voluntarily. By protecting choice, voluntariness, and the integrity of female decision-making we may be able to reconcile the dilemma between cultural diversity and the need for the protection of women's human rights.

ARTICULATION OF NEW NORMS – SEXUAL RIGHTS

As I mentioned earlier, there is a case for calling women's rights the fourth generation of human rights. The reason is that the movement is not only generating new interpretations of existing human rights doctrine, whether it is the right to be free from torture, to enjoy equality, or to limit the right to self-determination, but it is also leading to the articulation of new rights, the most controversial of which is the issue of sexual rights. Sexual rights refer generally to woman's control over her sexuality and her access to primary and secondary health care and reproductive technologies. They concern the international recognition of the rights of women over their bodies and their sexuality.[15] The attempt to apply the human rights framework to reproductive health is an important innovation. The recent world conferences have been a major landmark in this field. The Declaration and Program of Action of the International Conference on Population and Development (the Cairo Declaration) states that "reproductive health . . . implies that people are able to have a satisfying and safe sex life and that they have the capability to reproduce and freedom to decide, if, when and how often to do so."

Paragraph 6 of the Beijing Platform of Action also states that "the human rights of women include the right to have control over and decide freely and responsibly on matters relating to their sexuality, including sexual and reproductive health, free of coercion, discrimination and violence." Though the term "sexual rights" was included in the draft Platform of Action, it was omitted from the final version, an omission indicating the controversial nature of this suggestion. It must also be noted that the formulation falls short of the right to abortion and sexual preference, an important demand of women's groups and the gay movement. And yet the inclusion of the paragraph, even in this truncated form, and its accompanying vision of sexual autonomy and freedom of choice are important developments in international human rights discourse. It is for this reason that there is an argument for making women's rights, and the accompanying formulations, the fourth generation of human rights. The legal doctrine coming out of international standards on violence against women and those emerging from the discussion of sexual autonomy do not really suit the old provisions contained in traditional human rights law.

CONCLUSION

In conclusion it must be said that human rights discourse is a powerful tool for critiquing states. The discourse has nearly universal acceptance and carries with it an air of universality and legitimacy. And yet when it comes to a woman's private life, we would be mistaken in our belief if we were not to accept the fact that in many societies human rights is actually a weak discourse in the context of family and community relations. While international human rights law is propelled forward to meet the demands of the international women's movement, the reality in many specific societies is that women's rights are under challenge from alternative cultural expressions. It is this weakness that troubles me, because, regardless of all the international standards and accompanying national legislation, unless there is resonance in national civil societies, there is little scope for real transformation. So while international civil society has been active at the national level in the field of women's rights, in many countries civil society is far more conservative when it comes to family and community.

Women's groups working at the national level in many Asian and African countries are facing innumerable obstacles. In this regard I would like to dedicate this chapter to Asma Jehangir and Hina Jilani, Pakistani human rights activists, who have had to face armed thugs in their houses and the threat of death for fighting for women's rights in the national context. The national struggle is the difficult fight, not the international one. Unless human rights discourse finds legitimacy in these areas of a country's national life, women's rights and human rights will remain mere words on paper. Therefore, in Asia especially, this is the paradox that we have to face. International standards of women's rights, which are at the frontier of human rights development, collide with cultural movements at the national level that question the very articulation of women's rights in human rights terms. This contradiction provides the women's movement with the promise of ultimate liberation, but it also contains a darker possibility where women's rights are subsumed by national upheavals that have little respect for the international formulation of women's rights as human rights. The next decade will witness this confrontation. One can only hope that the common values of human dignity and freedom will triumph over parochial forces attempting to confine women to the home. It is only then that we will be able to celebrate the true victory of women's rights being recognized as fundamental human rights.

NOTES

* See Coomaraswamy's reports as the Special Rapporteur on Violence Against Women for the United Nations Human Rights Commission, including her "Violence Against Women: Its Causes and Consequences. A Preliminary Report Submitted by the UN Special Rapporteur in Accordance with [the] Commission on Human Rights Resolution 1994/45," *The Thatched Patio* 7, no. 6 (November–December 1994). *The Thatched Patio* is published by the International Centre for Ethnic Studies, 2 Kynsey Terrace, Colombo 8, Sri Lanka.

1 See Gananath Obeyesekere, *The Apotheosis of Captain Cook: European Mythmaking in the Pacific* (Princeton, NJ: Princeton University Press, 1992).

2 For example, Veena Das, *Critical Events: An Anthropological Perspective in Contemporary India* (Delhi: Oxford University Press, 1995).

3 Hilary Charlesworth, "What are Women's International Human Rights?" in Rebecca J. Cook, ed., *Human Rights of Women: National and International Perspectives* (Philadelphia: University of Pennsylvania Press, 1994), p. 61.

4 Celina Romany, "State Responsibility Goes Private: A Feminist Critique of the Public/Private Distinction," in Cook, ed., *Human Rights of Women*, p. 94.

5 Ibid., p. 94.

6 Donna Sullivan, "Envisioning Women's Human Rights: The Beijing Platform," *China Rights Forum* (New York), Winter 1995, p. 20.

7 Karen Knopf, "Why Rethinking the Sovereign State is Important for Women's International Human Rights" in Cook, ed., *Human Rights of Women*, p. 159.

8 Ibid., p. 155.

9 Velasquez Rodriguez, 28 *International Legal Materials* 294 (1989).

10 Article 4 of the Declaration on the Elimination of Violence Against Women, UN General Assembly Resolution 48/104 (1993).

11 Dorothy Q. Thomas and Michele E. Beasley, "Domestic Violence as a Human Rights Issue," *Human Rights Quarterly* 15, no. 1 (February 1993), p. 36.

12 Rhonda Copelan, "Intimate Terror: Understanding Domestic Violence as Torture," in Cook, ed., *Human Rights of Women*, p. 116.

13 Sunila Abeysekere, "Women's Human Rights: Questions of Equality and Difference," Institute of Social Studies (The Hague, The Netherlands) Working Paper No. 186 (1995).

14 Martha Minow, *Making All the Difference: Inclusion and Exclusion and American Law* (Ithaca, NY: Cornell University Press, 1990).

15 See generally Yasmin Tambiah, "Sexuality and Human Rights," in Marge Schuler, ed., *From Basic Needs to Basic Rights* (Washington, DC: Women's Law and Development Institute, 1995), p. 369.

9

FROM VIENNA TO BEIJING

Women's human rights activism and the human rights community

Manisha Desai

Manisha Desai, *a sociologist, is currently writing about different generations of activists in the women's movement in India and about feminists of Indian origin who live and work in the West. In this essay, she charts the growth and progress of the international women's movement over two decades, from the International Women's Year in 1975 to the World Conference on Women in Beijing in 1995. Opposing both cultural justifications for the abuse of women and liberal, universalistic notions that ignore the issue of gender difference, the women's movement, Desai shows, has sought to negotiate a dynamic and historically grounded standard for women's rights. The main point is to move beyond what she calls the doomed duality of a homogenizing universalism and a paralyzing particularism to achieve practical commitments and enforceable standards for the protection of women's rights.*

THE HUMAN RIGHTS DILEMMA

Indeed human rights, viewed at the universal level, bring us face-to-face with the most challenging dialectical conflict ever: between "identity" and "otherness," between the "myself" and "others" . . . between the universal and the particular, between identity and difference.[1]

The conflict identified by Boutros-Ghali has divided the human rights community into two, usually opposing, camps. On the one hand are foundationalists – most notably governments, some academics, and activists from the First World – who continue to justify universal human rights on the basis of objective reason and morality. On the other hand are the anti-foundationalists[2] – including many Third World governments and Third and First World academics and activists – who emphasize "contingency, construction, and relativity." For the foundationalists it is possible, and indeed necessary, to have universal values and rights shared by all humankind. To the anti-foundationalists, also called particularists or cultural relativists, values and rights should reflect local, cultural norms and practices and not monolithic, western values claiming to be universal.[3]

Such opposition has contributed not only to a theoretical impasse, but, more importantly, to the continuation of human rights violations by state and nonstate actors who question the validity of universal human rights. To move beyond these theoretical and practical consequences, I suggest a third path of critical engagement, one that dynamically moves between historical universals and particulars. This path is evident in the efforts of the international women's human rights movement at the two UN world conferences: the Second World Conference on Human Rights in Vienna in 1993 and the Fourth World Conference on Women in Beijing in 1995.[4]

I will argue that the conflict between universalism and particularism was gradually narrowed during the Vienna and Beijing conferences. Cross-cultural exchanges, or, in Jürgen Habermas' terminology, "practical discourse" in the public sphere,[5] enabled a progressive reduction of that theoretical gap. That trend was reinforced by a growing awareness that finding common ground was a prerequisite for defeating formidable enemies, and translating rhetoric into accountable mechanisms for implementing these rights.

With this aim in mind, I begin with the history of the emergence of the international women's human rights movement. I argue that this movement itself is a tentative resolution of the universalism/particularism debate within the international women's movements prior to the conferences. I then analyze the efforts of the international women's human rights movement at the Vienna and Beijing world conferences, and conclude by discussing the implications of their actions for human rights theory and practice.

THE INTERNATIONAL WOMEN'S HUMAN RIGHTS MOVEMENT

International Women's Year, 1975, marked the beginning of a systematic national, regional, and international coordination among governmental and nongovernmental women's grassroots, academic, and policy groups throughout the world.[6] The UN International Women's Decade (1975–85) with its three world conferences – in Mexico City in 1975, in Copenhagen in 1980, and in Nairobi in 1985 – and their accompanying nongovernmental organizations forums brought together thousands of women from the First and Third World, all engaged in better understanding women's realities and bettering women's lives.[7] Thus, the UN created the possibility of what Habermas would call an "ideal speech situation"[8] within the international women's community.

These gatherings, however, were contentious events. The conferences in Mexico City and Copenhagen were particularly incendiary. There, women from India, Palestine, Brazil, and other Third World countries challenged First World feminists' claims, especially those from the United States, that women were universally oppressed due to their gender and that "sisterhood was global." They countered that for women in the Third World, class, race/ethnicity, nationality, and religion were as important as and woven together with gender in both oppressing them and providing space for liberation. For example, Third World women at the 1975 Mexico City conference, most of whom refused to identify themselves as feminists, argued that racism was a women's issue while the First World feminists were reluctant to focus on such issues. Similarly, in the 1980 Copenhagen conference, Third World women, more of whom now identified themselves as feminists, refused to acknowledge First World feminists' concern over issues of sexual orientation. There were also heated debates about the role of men in women's organizations.

Such critical confrontations were resolved not by "the force of the better argument," but by reciprocal recognition of the validity of the various claims. This recognition, in turn, was fueled by women's grassroots organizing around the various contentious issues. The result was evident at the 1985 conference in Nairobi. There, women from all parts of the world acknowledged that women's issues are manifested differently in different societies requiring varied and multiple strategies of liberation. Learning about the common goals – of freedom, justice, and equality – of apparently different women's movements around the world inspired "reflective solidarity"[9] among women who otherwise were on different sides of the North/South, left/liberal, Black/White, gay/straight, feminist/non-feminist divide.

It was in this process of conflict resolution – at these conferences and the various pre- and post-conference events – that activists became increasingly aware of the United Nations' human rights framework.[10] The adoption by the UN of the Convention on the Elimination of All Forms of Discrimination Against Women (CEDAW) in 1979 further signaled the potential of using human rights instruments to advance women's causes. Furthermore, by the 1985 Nairobi conference, many activists recognized how identity politics could be subverted by reactionary forces for undemocratic ends – such as the use of gender identity by religious fundamentalists to restrict women's lives. Hence, there was a need to move outward, albeit from a position of identity, toward a more encompassing analysis and activism. The human rights discourse provided this overarching framework.[11]

Practically, the mainstreaming of women's issues by governments and international bodies such as the UN increased the availability of resources. Also, due to internal pressures, the general human rights movement began to pay greater attention to women's issues.[12] Organizations like Amnesty International, Human Rights Watch, and the UN Commission on Human Rights began to develop committees focused on women's issues. Despite women's movements' wariness of co-optation, they began to use mainstream resources and discourses.[13]

A turning point for the women's movement was the announcement of the 1993 Second World Conference on Human Rights in Vienna. That announcement sparked a worldwide mobilization by women to redefine the human rights framework. A Global Campaign for Women's Human Rights, coordinated by the Center For Women's Global Leadership at Rutgers University, mobilized the various networks developed during the International Women's Decade.[14] The Center organized a Global Women's Leadership Institute in 1991, where women from all regions explored linkages between women's rights, violence against women, and human rights.[15]

One of the strategies developed at the 1991 institute was "16 Days of Activism Against Gender Violence," which spanned the period between November 25 – the International Day Against Violence Against Women – and December 10 – Human Rights Day. Local action included marches, educational panels, exhibits, street theater, and protest rallies. The campaign also consisted of a worldwide petition drive, calling on the World Conference on Human Rights to "comprehensively address women's human rights at every level of its proceedings" and recognize gender-based violence "as a violation of human rights requiring immediate action."[16] The petition received 300,000 signatures from over fifty countries and was signed by over 800 organizations when it was presented to the world conference in 1993.

In addition to the petition, the global campaign involved holding local and regional hearings on women's human rights violations. Documents of these hearings were brought to the world conference. Participants developed "satellite meetings" in which women from a region would gather to draft a report and recommendations to the world conference. Women in Latin America and Africa held several such meetings to create a platform to use for lobbying at the conference. The Women's Center for Global Leadership likewise held a satellite meeting of women from all regions to prepare a common set of recommendations for the world conference. Finally, the global campaign sent women to the final preparatory meeting of the world conference so their voices could be heard during the formulation of the Vienna Declaration and Platform of Action.

Thus, by addressing internal theoretical and practical conflicts among women's movements, and by effectively utilizing resources from UN bodies and the human rights community, an international women's human rights movement was born. Although this movement included particular critiques from various Third World women's movements, it also emphasized a universal "reflective solidarity" among women. It was with this negotiated solidarity that the movement prepared for the world conference in Vienna.

THE VIENNESE WALTZ

At the Second World Conference on Human Rights in Vienna, the international women's human rights movement had to address explicitly the chasm between universalist and particularist conceptions of human rights, by renegotiating the universal human rights framework in light of women's different cultural and class backgrounds. While women had previously addressed differences among them by mutual recognition, the differences they had with the human rights community were now resolved through "the force of a better argument." The movement's global networks of grassroots groups, representing nearly all sections of women from those countries, were instrumental in that purpose.

Women's groups were the most organized and vocal of the NGO participants at the Vienna conference. Their strategies of gaining visibility and lobbying included: a "rights place for women," which was a centrally located space of two rooms where women activists met to discuss strategies; displays of women's literature, posters, and documentation from around the world; the holding of regular information sessions for mainstream and alternative media; and caucusing everyday so that government and nongovernment delegates could meet and explore collaborative strategies to promote women's issues at the conference and afterwards.[17]

Over sixty of the workshops, seminars, and lectures at the forum focused specifically on women's human rights. The global campaign's button – "Women's Rights Are Human Rights" – adorned the lapels of many official delegates. Women's domination of the conference was evident in the headlines of the major newspapers in the US: for example, the *Dallas Morning News* reported that "It's the year of Women at UN Rights Congress"; the *New York Times* observed that "Women Seize Focus at Rights Forum"; and the *Los Angeles Times* proclaimed that "Women Take Reins – World Sees More Leaders, More Calls for Justice."[18]

This newly recognized strength was what enabled women to engage two sets of adversaries at the conference: western liberals and mostly Asian defenders of cultural rights. The women's movement challenged the truthfulness, rightness, and sincerity of both adversaries' claims.[19] The liberals – less hostile but more formidable – were criticized for supporting a gendered conception of human rights and for the invisibility of women in their organizations.

Conceptually, women cited the following major problems with existing human rights instruments:

1   Most human rights mechanisms seek enforcement of political rights only, while leaving the protection of socio-economic, cultural, and collective rights – the rights which most affect women – to the discretion of individual states.

2   Most human rights instruments are state-focused and have no mechanisms to make nonstate actors, the ones most often responsible for women's rights abuses, accountable for rights violations.

3   All rights, including so-called second- and third-generation rights – informed by socialist and Third World human rights concerns – emphasize

188

rights in the public sphere, thereby overlooking the types of domestic violence routinely inflicted on women.[20]

The women's lobby demonstrated that while claiming gender-neutrality, all instruments in fact assume men to be the bearers of basic rights and do not adequately address women's realities. Thus, women demanded a feminist transformation of human rights. In the words of Charlotte Bunch, this transformation

> begins with what women experience as violations of their humanity and then seeks to connect that to human rights discourse, rather than starting with pre-existing human rights concepts and trying to fit women into them. This transformative approach is the starting point for many feminists in claiming and defining women's human rights as inalienable. Beginning from this view that women have such rights, the question is not whether women's rights are human rights, but why they were excluded before and how to gain wider recognition and implementation of these rights now.[21]

To demonstrate their charge that current human rights frameworks and instruments did not address women's realities, the Global Campaign For Women's Human Rights presented a day-long Global Tribunal on Violations of Women's Human Rights. Thirty-three women from around the world presented testimonies in five areas: abuse within the family; war crimes against women; violations of women's bodily integrity; socio-economic human rights abuses; and persecution related to political participation. At the end of the day, four judges recommended that the specific abuses that women encounter must be seen as human rights abuses, and that the existing human rights documents be modified to include them. These recommendations were ultimately included in the official declaration at the end of the conference.[22]

The Global Campaign also critiqued the continuing invisibility of women in the various UN bodies and sought proportional representation similar to the regional representation that the UN requires for all its organizations. Feminists also critiqued the inadequate resources and compliance mechanisms of all the instruments related to women. For example, it was pointed out that the Commission on the Status of Women, the main body monitoring the various issues related to women, does not have the same status or resources as the Commission on Human Rights.[23] Furthermore, the instruments specifically relating to women are made ineffective by the reservations, usually cultural, from different countries. Feminists at the conference sought more resources for the women's commission and the integration of women's rights in all the general instruments, rather than ghettoizing them in inadequately funded bodies.

The second, and more open, set of adversaries were those (mostly Asian governments) who used the cultural card to question the very concept of human rights. These cultural crusaders' main argument, unwittingly echoed by postmodernist scholarship, was that universal human rights were particularist, Western values masquerading as universal values, and should be regarded as another form of Western cultural imperialism. The most pernicious dimension of that cultural imperialism, they maintained, was the concept of "private" rights; that is, rights to equal inheritance, to choose marriage partners, to divorce, and to have custody of children – that are critical to women's self-determination and dignity. Western economic imperialism – which benefited the elites of most of those developing countries – was not questioned.

Women revealed the political hypocrisy of the cultural card and showed it to be a selective, rigid, and ahistorical interpretation of certain cultural practices, used by elites to maintain their hegemony at home. In the words of Hilary Bowker:

> Women from every single culture and every part of the world are standing up and saying we won't accept cultural justification for abuses against us anymore. We are human, we have a right to have our human rights protected, and the world community must respond to that call and throw out any attempts to justify abuse on the grounds of culture.[24]

Ann Mayer offered an even sharper characterization of appeals to cultural rights:

> If all such "particularisms" mean that violations of women's rights are excused and perpetuated, they are nothing more than disguises for the universality of male determination to cling to power and privilege.[25]

This waltzing with two very different partners, the liberal and cultural crusaders for rights, had a significant impact on the Vienna Declaration and Programme of Action. From the preamble, which expresses concern for violence against women and other forms of discrimination experienced by women, to the various articles and sections, the document emphasized women's human rights. Among the major victories for women were: (1) the reaffirmation of the universality of human rights and the indivisibility and interdependence of political, socio-economic, and cultural rights;[26] (2) the importance of "working towards the elimination of violence against women in public and private life"; (3) the recommendation that all UN bodies integrate gender analysis in their work and incorporate women's rights in all human rights instruments and treaties; (4) the need to facilitate women's access to those bodies; and (5) the expression of support for appointing a Special Rapporteur on Violence Against Women.[27]

The gradual bridging of the universalist and cultural concerns was the product of – to use a Habermasian phrase – "communicative engagement"[28] between women and their liberal and cultural human rights adversaries. At the end of the conference, the movement sought to direct the momentum gathered at the Vienna conference towards the upcoming world conference on women in Beijing. Dorothy Thomas, the founder-director of the Women's Rights Project of the Human Rights Watch, outlined three major challenges for the movement: to move from visibility of women's abuses to accountability for those violations; to avoid ghettoization of women's human rights and to make them part of every level of the UN; and to continue to organize cross-culturally, remaining sensitive to the differences among women.[29] These messages were to reach operatic pitch at the Beijing conference.

THE BEIJING OPERA

If Vienna resulted in a feminist transformation of the existing human rights framework – by addressing the conflict between universalism and cultural relativism – the Chinese conference was oriented towards strengthening the foundation laid at Vienna. Throughout the multiple acts and complex plotting of this Beijing opera, the main task in China was to consolidate the global networks among NGOs, to ensure that the UN and the world governments would be accountable for women's human rights.

At Beijing, one could witness the legacy of the women's human rights movement in Vienna, Cairo, and Copenhagen.[30] Workshops held by different kinds of NGOs – ranging from women's self-help groups working to prevent violence against women to development groups fighting structural adjustment policies and working for sustainable development – all highlighted the utility of the women's rights discourse in their work. As workshop organizer Rita Marin emphasized, the women's rights framework can be seen as providing "power tools" that can be adapted for demanding justice and equality in almost any area.[31] Even Hillary Clinton incorporated this language in her address: "If there is one message that echoes forth from this conference, let it be that human rights are women's rights and women's rights are human rights."

Many human rights organizations, such as the Center for Women's Global Leadership, Amnesty International, and Human Rights Watch, held workshops highlighting how women's groups could use the various human rights instruments for promoting education and achieving justice in their own countries. The focus was on getting legitimacy for women's perspective in the human rights framework within communities worldwide.

In addition to the important work of sharing information and networking with groups, the Global Campaign For Women's Human Rights held a Global Tribunal on Accountability of Women's Human Rights. This time the emphasis was not on making women's human rights abuses visible but on demanding accountable changes. The judges recommended stronger, more concrete implementation of women's human rights. As one workshop organizer observed: "In Nairobi we were tentative, the emphasis was on governments should support the international human rights treaties; in Beijing the demand is, governments must comply."[32]

This assertive tone – a product of over two decades of organizing women around the world – was evident throughout the conference. It was reflected in the questions raised by sessions and plenaries: "What are the UN and world governments doing to fulfill the various promises made at all the world conferences?" "The UN is on trial before the peoples of the world. Will the UN rise to defend its own vision or will we have to go elsewhere?" The Special Rapporteur on Violence Against Women, appointed as a result of commitments made in Vienna, also noted the need to move from expressing grievances and demanding rights to seeking remedies.

The concern over accountability set the stage for a new round of exchanges that would even further narrow the gap between universalist and particularist claims. As an Indian NGO document noted: "We need to seek a community notion of rights that speak of the right to retain our myriad possibilities, our multiple connectedness, our open-ended notions of justice and dissent."[33]

Where did these strategies of networking and calls for accountability lead? At the NGO Forum, the greatest achievements were the solidification and expansion of established networks of women across many differences. The *New York Times* headline echoed this trend: "At UN Women's Meeting, An Outbreak of Harmony."[34] The backgrounding of the previously contentious fault-lines such as North/South, Palestinian/Israeli, Black/White, and gay/straight reflected the search for such harmony. More importantly, unity was a response to the global trends of the breakdown of old paradigms, attempts at reconciliation between old enemies, and resurgence of ethnic and fundamentalist movements. Women now clearly recognized the limitations of identity politics, and realized the need for a global solidarity against the reactionary forces so evident in many parts of the world – forces personified at the conference by delegations of the Vatican and some Islamic and Asian governments.

The resulting "Beijing Declaration and Platform for Action" reaffirmed the Vienna document in its commitment to the universality, inalienability, and interdependence of human rights; the need for governments to support women's human rights despite religious and cultural differences; and in its acknowledgment of violence against women in the home and in armed conflict as violations of human rights. That reaffirmation was especially heartening, representing triumph over renewed efforts by the Vatican and some governments to reverse gains won at Vienna.

The most significant new addition to the document is the acknowledgment of a kind of right to sexuality: "The human rights of women include their rights to have control over and decide freely and responsibly on matters related to their sexuality including sexual and reproductive health, free of coercion, discrimination, and violence."[35] For the first time in the history of the UN

192

there was a debate about sexual preference on the floor of the conference. The document also, for the first time, acknowledged counting women's un-remunerated work.

While the Beijing declaration reaffirmed the commitment to provide new and additional resources toward implementing women's human rights, it did not indicate a willingness to reallocate existing resources to accomplish such a mission. Yet the process of strategizing to develop implementable women's human rights instruments was another step toward the narrowing of the early gap between the universalists and particularists, between theory and practice.

In short, at Beijing, the international women's human rights movement was able to pursue the renegotiated, universal human rights agenda from Vienna within a larger network of women's NGOs from around the world. The move-ment was also relatively successful in avoiding ghettoizing women's concerns by making them part of the general human rights instruments of the UN system. In terms of accountability, however, there still lies a difficult road ahead. This includes holding the UN and the national governments to fulfilling the promises of justice and equality for women.

Many activists involved in the human rights movement now agreed that the fight should be taken back to the local and national levels, so that the gains at the international level could be realized meaningfully. This will require, in the words of one of the judges at the Beijing Tribunal, "going with the spirits of the horse and the dragon." In Chinese cosmology the horse symbol-izes hard work, sacrifice, and patience, while the dragon represents possibilities and power. Both, she emphasized, would be needed to make the governments more accountable.

IMPLICATIONS FOR THE HUMAN RIGHTS COMMUNITY

What lessons does the international women's human rights movement offer to the larger human rights community? At a practical level, the international women's human rights movement has, almost single-handedly, made "human rights" a household word throughout the world. From being a discourse of international agencies, academics, and some committed activists, human rights have become a "power tool" available to thousands of grassroots groups for local organizing. For this the larger human rights community is indebted to the women's movement.

Politically and theoretically, the most important lesson is the need for a participatory, communicative process – evolving out of grassroots organizing – at the local, national, regional, and international levels. Such critical commu-nication facilitates the negotiation of a historically grounded universal – neither arbitrary nor absolute – which is in a dynamic relationship with similarly negotiated, historical particulars. It is this dynamic relationship, at work in various levels of public activity, which can take us beyond the doomed duality of homogenizing universalism and paralyzing particularism.

The international women's human rights movement also raises an important question for the human rights community. How are we to make nation-states and nonstate actors accountable for rights violations? At what levels – local, national, regional, international – and in what ways – legal, social, political, cultural – do we make violators liable? This is yet another dilemma that the community has to confront. One may hope that the dynamism of the international women's human rights movement may yet prompt a new stage in the dialectical confrontation between universalism and cultural relativism, leading toward practical commitments and enforceable standards.[36]

NOTES

I would like to thank Jodi Dean and Micheline Ishay for their critical comments on earlier drafts of this essay.

1 Boutros Boutros-Ghali, "Human Rights: The Common Language of Humanity," in *World Conference on Human Rights: The Vienna Declaration and Programme of Action* (New York: UNDP, 1993), p. 7.

2 Michael Freeman, "The Philosophical Foundations of Human Rights," *Human Rights Quarterly* 16 (1994), pp. 491–514, characterizes the rift in the human rights community in this way. Among the scholars who defend foundations for universal rights are, for example, Jack Donnelly, "Cultural Relativism and Universal Human Rights," *Human Rights Quarterly* 5 (1984), pp. 408–18; Abdullahi An-Na'im and Francis Deng, eds, *Human Rights in Africa: Cross Cultural Perspectives* (Washington, DC: Brookings Institute, 1990); Alison Renteln, *International Human Rights: Universalism versus Relativism* (Newbury Park, CA: Sage Publications, 1990); and Claude Welch and Virginia Leary, *Asian Perspectives on Human Rights* (Boulder, CO: Westview Press, 1990). The anti-foundationalists include, for example, Richard Rorty, "Human Rights, Rationality, and Sentimentality," in Stephen Shute and Susan Harley, eds, *On Human Rights: Amnesty Oxford Lectures* (New York: Basic Books, 1993) and Ernesto Laclau, *New Reflections on the Revolution of Our Times* (London: Verso, 1990).

3 This is not the first conflict faced by the 1948 "Universal Declaration of Human Rights." The first, and less serious, challenge was to the narrow definition of human rights. Thus, from within the Western world, the then Soviet Union and its allies challenged the privileging of civil and political rights which led to the articulation of the second generation of rights, or socio-economic and cultural rights. Subsequently, the newly independent countries in the Third World called into question the overly individualistic nature of rights and championed the recognition of collective or group rights, leading to the formulation of the third generation of rights. See, for example, Hilary Charlesworth, "What are 'Women's International Human Rights'?" in Rebecca J. Cook, ed., *Human Rights of Women: National and International Perspectives* (Philadelphia: University of Pennsylvania Press, 1994), pp. 58–84.

4 I focus on these two conferences because each marks a turning point for their respective communities, namely the human rights community and women.

5 Jürgen Habermas, *The Structural Transformation of the Public Sphere: An Inquiry into a Category of Bourgeois Society* (Cambridge, MA: MIT Press, 1989).

6 This is not to suggest that there was no such coordination among women's groups before. For example, there were various international women's organizations supported by left parties that brought women together. There were also many informal networks. But this was the first time that so many diverse groups, funded by governments and international agencies, began to network on a regular basis.

7 See, for example, Arvonne Fraser, *The UN Decade For Women: Documents and Dialogue* (Boulder, CO: Westview Press, 1987) and Joanna Kerr, ed., *Ours By Right: Women's Rights As Human Rights* (London: Zed Press, 1993).

8 According to Habermas (*Theory of Communicative Action*, Vol. 1, Boston: Beacon Press, 1981), participants communicating in an ideal speech situation work toward an understanding, assuming that their communication will not be constrained by threats of sanctions or unequal power relations. This structure of communication leads to consensus among participants based on "the force of the better argument" (p. 24). Clearly, there were inequalities among women at the various conferences. But given the non-coercive nature of these meetings and the shared aims, such inequalities did not translate into constraints.

9 According to Jodi Dean ("Reflective Solidarity," *Constellations* 2, no. 1, 1995, pp. 114–40), reflective solidarity is "the mutual expectation of a responsible orientation to relationship. This concept of solidarity draws from the intuition that the permanent risk of disagreement must itself become rationally transformed so as to provide a basis for solidarity. This solidarity takes into consideration the historical conditions of value pluralism, the ever-present potentiality of exclusion, the demands of accountability, and the importance of critique" (p. 123). I argue that the international women's movement was able to achieve this solidarity over the two decades of face-to-face communications.

10 See, for example, Charlotte Bunch, "Organizing For Women's Human Rights Globally," in Kerr, ed., *Ours By Right*, pp. 141–9; and Elisabeth Friedman, "Women's Human Rights: The Emergence of a Movement," in Julie Peters and Andrea Wolper, eds, *Women's Rights, Human Rights: International Feminist Perspectives* (New York: Routledge, 1995), pp. 18–35.

11 I am thankful to Susanna Fried, of the Center For Women's Global Leadership, for this observation. Mallika Dutt of the Center also provided critical insights. The human rights framework was both broad enough to incorporate women's issues from around the world and pliable enough to be transformed from a feminist perspective.

12 For example, over 50 percent of Amnesty International's activists and grassroots members are women. Until the mid-1980s, these women had been separating their feminist and human rights work. In the course of the UN decade, however, they saw the opportunity to bring these together and demanded changes within the organization that would allow this to happen (personal communication from Krishanti Dharmaraj, Amnesty trainer).

13 Resources also came from academic feminists, who through their critical analysis of legal systems were providing activists with critical insights about law that could be used in their work.

14 The Global Campaign has become an annual event in which women's organizations from around the world plan many activities at the local, regional, national, and international levels focusing on women's human rights. The theme for the 1997 Global Campaign was "Demand Human Rights in the Home and the World." The 1996 Campaign focused on "Bringing Women's Human Rights Home: Realizing our Visions" (*Global Center News*, No. 4, Summer 1997).

15 Charlotte Bunch and Niamh Reilly, *Demanding Accountability: The Global Campaign and Vienna Tribunal For Women's Rights* (New York: UNDP, 1994).

16 Cited in Friedman, "Women's Human Rights," p. 28.

17 Bunch and Reilly, *Demanding Accountability*.

18 Cited in Friedman, "Women's Human Rights," p. 1.

19 For Habermas (*Theory of Communicative Action*), these three kinds of challenges are associated with the three differentiated spheres of values: the cognitive, the normative, and the expressive, and relate to the objective, the social, and the subjective worlds, respectively.

20 See Gayle Binion, "Human Rights: A Feminist Perspective," *Human Rights* 17 (1995), pp. 509–26; Cook, ed., *Human Rights of Women*; Kerr, ed., *Ours By Right*; Peters and Wolpers, eds, *Women's Rights, Human Rights*.

21 Bunch, "Organizing For Women's Human Rights Globally," pp. 145–6.

22 Bunch and Reilly, *Demanding Accountability*.

23 Elissavet Stamatopoulou, "Women's Rights and the United Nations," in Peters and Wolpers, eds, *Women's Rights, Human Rights*, pp. 36–48.

24 From an interview on CNN, June 22, 1993.

25 Ann Mayer, "Cultural Particularism as a Bar to Women's Rights: Reflections on the Middle Eastern Experience," in Peters and Wolper, eds, *Women's Rights, Human Rights*, pp. 176–88.

26 As written in the document: "While the significance of national and regional particularities and various historical, cultural and religious backgrounds must be borne in mind, it is the duty of states, regardless of their political, economic and cultural systems, to promote and protect all human rights and fundamental freedoms" (*World Conference on Human Rights: The Vienna Declaration and Programme of Action*, New York: United Nations, 1993, p. 30).

27 In March 1994, Radhika Coomaraswamy of Sri Lanka was appointed the Special Rapporteur on Violence Against Women.

28 Habermas, *The Structural Transformation of the Public Sphere*.

29 Cited in Friedman, "Women's Human Rights," pp. 31–2.

30 This section is based on my participant-observations and interviews with women at the NGO Forum in Huairou, China.

31 Rita Marin, Women's Human Rights Workshop, September 1, 1995, NGO Forum, Huairou, China.

32 Ibid.

33 AWHRC, A Dreamscape: Redrafting the Platform of Action (Bangalore, India: Asian Women's Human Rights Council, 1995), p. 17.

34 *New York Times* (September 9, 1995), p. 1.

35 Reported in the *New York Times* (September 11, 1995), p. 1.

36 The Center For Women's Global Leadership, which has emerged as an important player in organizing the international women's movement community around human rights issues, has taken a step in this direction by organizing the Global Campaign for 1998 to celebrate the fiftieth anniversary of the Universal Declaration of Human Rights by reviewing the implementation of the Vienna Declaration and Programme of Action and the Beijing Platform for Action. The campaign emphasizes that "there are no human rights without women's rights" and "building a culture of respect for universal human rights requires that the human rights of women be recognized and protected" (*Global Center News*, No. 4, Summer 1997, p. 1).

Part IV

HUMAN RIGHTS AND INTERNATIONAL RELATIONS

10

HUMAN RIGHTS AND DEVELOPMENT AID

Japan after the ODA Charter

Hoshino Eiichi

Hoshino Eiichi, *a professor at the University of the Ryukyus in Okinawa, specializes in the comparative study of foreign assistance programs. Here, he investigates the role of human rights in the foreign aid programs of the major aid donors of the world, focusing on Japan's foreign aid program, which is now the largest. Addressing the controversial issue of human rights conditionality in foreign aid programs, Hoshino suggests that there might be an alternative model of aid-giving that builds on what he calls the human-rights-in-development perspective. He points to the importance of establishing an infrastructure in each country for the protection of human rights with the help of foreign aid. This model might be another creative way to link the three "generations" of human rights already discussed by previous authors.*

> We desire to occupy an honored place in an international society striving for the preservation of peace, and the banishment of tyranny and slavery, oppression and intolerance for all time from the earth.
>
> "Preamble," Constitution of Japan

INTRODUCTION: HUMAN RIGHTS AND THE JAPANESE ODA CHARTER

This essay examines the relationship between human rights and Japanese foreign economic aid (Official Development Assistance – ODA), especially the impact of the ODA Charter in 1992 on Japan's bilateral economic aid allocation.

For a long time, Japan's ODA to developing countries has been criticized for lacking basic philosophic principles of aid-giving, and for its mercantilistic stance.[1] In April 1991, Prime Minister Toshiki Kaifu announced the "Four ODA Principles." He said that henceforth the Japanese government would pay particular attention to four factors in extending its development assistance: (1) the military spending of recipient countries; (2) their export and import of arms; (3) their development and production of weapons of mass destruction, such as nuclear missiles; and (4) their efforts to promote democratization, secure human rights, and move toward a market-oriented economy. It was the first formal governmental response to public criticisms of Japan's manner of giving foreign aid.

The fourth factor, emphasizing human rights and democratization, has been described as "the new battleground" for West–East confrontation in the post-Cold War world.[2] Inada Juichi describes the end of the Cold War as the international background to this announcement of the Kaifu Four Principles.[3] The "winner" of the Cold War has declared that democracy and human rights are universal principles, and others in different ways have followed suit. In May 1990, the European Bank for Reconstruction and Development made its extension of economic assistance subject to political conditionality, attaching political conditions such as the promotion of multi-party-system democracy, pluralism, and the market economy. A political communiqué of the G7 countries at the 1990 Houston Summit expressed their commitment to supporting development through the promotion of democratization and human rights and via a market-oriented economy.

Oshiba Ryo lists five reasons for this post-Cold War trend toward political conditionality: (1) ideology – the belief that democratization is a worldwide trend; (2) a new development strategy – the understanding that political reform is necessary for successful projects and adjustment programs (cf. good governance); (3) security – the belief that supporting democratization will reduce the chance of serious interstate conflicts (cf. "democratic peace");[4] (4) political – the shift of power balance between the North and the South favors applying political conditionality; and (5) increasing support for political conditionality – especially among nongovernmental organizations and citizens in both developed and developing countries.[5]

Murai Yoshinori has pointed out one good reason not to accept Kaifu's Four Principles at face value. In August 1991, Prime Minister Kaifu flew to Beijing carrying a gift for his host: the announcement that, despite Tiananmen, Japan would return to a policy of full support for China's reform and open door policy through Japan's world-largest commitment of ODA – thus even China was able to satisfy Kaifu's new ODA principles! Murai suggests that what lies behind the Four Principles is great-power chauvinism, Japan's search for "an honored place in an international society" as an economic power. Murai emphasizes the effect of the Gulf Crisis and the Gulf War (1990–1) on Japanese policy. Tokyo had to stop supporting military governments and dictatorships in order to prevent the emergence of another Saddam Hussein, and it could not ignore US pressure on Japan to spend more to support the US global role of "world policeman."[6]

In June 1992, the Japanese government announced the ODA Charter, a new step in attaching political conditionality to Japan's foreign aid policy. The second section of the ODA Charter[7] states:

> Taking into account comprehensively each recipient country's requests, its socioeconomic conditions, and Japan's bilateral relations with the recipient country, Japan's ODA will be provided in accordance with the principles of the United Nations Charter (especially sovereign equality and non-intervention in domestic matters), as well as the following four principles.

> 1) Environmental conservation and development should be pursued in tandem.
> 2) Any use of ODA for military purposes or for aggravation of international conflicts should be avoided.
> 3) Full attention should be paid to trends in recipient countries' military expenditures, their development and production of mass destruction weapons and missiles, their export and import of arms, etc., so as to maintain and strengthen international peace and stability, and from the viewpoint that developing countries should place appropriate priorities in the allocation of their resources on their own economic and social development.
> 4) Full attention should be paid to the efforts for promoting democratization and introduction of a market-oriented economy, and the situation regarding the securing of basic human rights and freedoms in the recipient country.

It is, however, worth noting that there is a serious flaw in this section of the ODA Charter. The Japanese government undertakes to pay full attention to how basic human rights and freedoms are secured in the recipient country, but it does so "in accordance with the principles of the United Nations Charter (especially sovereign equality and non-intervention in domestic matters)." Since the defense of sovereignty is the most common justification for rejecting humanitarian intervention, we would expect that in practice the 1992 ODA Charter might face sovereignty-related difficulties from the beginning.

Understanding ODA as a foreign policy tool, how do Japanese foreign aid allocations actually relate to these principles? What are the real objectives of Japanese foreign aid? With the announcement of the Four ODA Principles, do human rights factors really matter in Japanese aid allocation? How does the Japanese government deal with political conditionality? How do human rights and democratization relate to development assistance? What is the record of Japanese human rights diplomacy to date?

In order to answer these questions, I start the next section with a review of the foreign economic aid literature, followed by a discussion of human rights and development, and a summary of foreign aid and human rights studies. In the second section, I summarize Japanese debates over foreign economic aid, in general and as they relate to human rights conditionality, discussing case studies of Japan's use of positive and negative sanctions. Finally, I shall examine a hypothesis that relates Japan's foreign aid allocation to the incidence of human rights violations in recipient countries.

OBJECTIVES OF FOREIGN ECONOMIC AID AND THE COMMUNITY OF INTERESTS MODEL

Before discussing human rights and development aid, we need to take a look at those studies that attempt to explain general foreign aid-giving objectives. There are two opposing views on foreign aid-giving. Some argue that "aid" is in fact merely an instrument used by donors for their own selfish advantage, for example to dominate and control the recipients. Others argue that the donor governments have already accepted some sort of obligation for the welfare of the less fortunate members of their own societies and, then, would and should (or in fact do) apply the same principle to the welfare of other societies in other parts of the world.[8]

In empirical studies, both arguments have been simplified into two incompatible models: donor interests and recipient needs. In terms of the *donor interests model*, the following are argued to be plausible donor objectives in allocating bilateral economic assistance: (1) to promote exports to recipient countries and to enhance the donor's economic interest; (2) to keep or gain influence in recipient countries, especially to buy support for the policies of the assisting country in the UN and other international forums; and (3) to promote the donor's security objectives.[9] Thus, the donor interests model predicts that donors will allocate their foreign aid according to these self-interests. Alternatively, the *recipient needs model* usually utilizes an index of per capita GNP and other indicators of development needs, and predicts that donors will allocate their aid as supplemental resources according to the recipient's needs for development.

There are, however, no consistent findings to date among investigations of donor behavior. A series of works by McKinlay and Little found that the donor's interests rather than the recipient's needs are salient in economic aid allocation.[10] Although these findings seem to confirm the conventional view of the donor interests argument, there are some inconsistent findings and objections to their tests of the recipient-needs hypothesis.[11]

The key to an alternative explanation is found in an idea that Moon has suggested: the foreign policy behavior of aid-giving is less of an exchange process and more of a community of interests. Moon's *dependent consensus model* implies, for example, "much less confidence in the ability of the United States to fine tune the foreign policies of other nations without a prior and massive penetration of their economic and political systems."[12]

Not only superpowers, however, are engaged in foreign aid-giving, and not only dependency can produce a community of interest. When some analysts argue that the recipient's development also should be classified into the donor interest model, since the donor wants to support the recipient government through contributing to its economic development, they are in fact assuming a community of interests: for example, they could claim that the donor is trying to help the recipient government remain in power or to make its power base more stable.[13]

It is not only plausible, but also desirable, to apply the community of interest argument to non-superpower donors. Though not powerful enough to induce compliance or to win the bargaining game, they are capable of reinforcing desired policies of target countries if there is a community of interest between the donor and recipient. Kondo Tetsuo formally analyzes the notion of power, and argues that, in exercising influence, a country with less resources should use reward rather than punishment, while a country with more resources might typically use punishment rather than reward.[14] Thus, the *community of interests model* claims that a non-superpower donor typically allocates economic aid in response to the development needs of recipient countries within a realm of the donor interests and for efficient use of its limited aid-giving resources.[15]

Human rights in development

Before reviewing the empirical studies on human rights and foreign aid, let me clarify some of the terms I will be using. First, I want to distinguish between "human rights" and "development"; and, then, I want to make a distinction between "human rights *practices*" and "human rights *preconditions*."

As Linda Butenhoff has already described in Chapter 5, the international human rights regime is generally understood to include three generations of rights: civil and political rights (the first generation); economic, social, and cultural rights (the second generation); and group rights (the third generation), such as the right to develop or the right to live in peace. With respect to the relationship between human rights and development, it matters very much which generation of rights one is referring to. Those who emphasize civil and political rights tend to see human rights and economic development as two different things. This is what I will call the *human-rights-*or-*development* perspective.[16] From this perspective, development is concerned with economic growth and the fulfilling of basic material needs, while human rights has to do with issues of political oppression and civil and political liberties:[17] no particular relationship is seen to exist between the two.

Alternatively, those who assume an inevitable interrelationship between the first and the second generation of human rights tend to understand economic development within the context of political issues, and human rights within the context of development. This is what I will call the *human-rights*-in-*development* perspective.[18] From this perspective, development cultivates people's capabilities to judge what kind of development they want and gives them power to pursue it. This in turn tends to lead one to an acceptance of the third generation of human rights, such as seen in the UN Declaration on the Right to Development (1986) adopted at the World Conference on Human Rights at Vienna in 1993.

The second distinction that I want to make clear is that between human rights *practices* (or policies) and human rights *preconditions* (or infrastructure). The human-rights-or-development perspective tends not to see this distinction, especially as far as civil and political rights are concerned. It is believed that improvement of major human rights situations (understood as practices in terms of civil and political rights) requires only the political will of government. Since little is demanded from the government except the individual's right to be left alone, it should be quite easy, it is argued, for a government with the political will not to abuse civil and political rights. Similarly, it is believed that improving economic and social human rights conditions is strictly a development issue and therefore a matter of economic policy not human rights policy. Economic development can improve economic and social rights situations independent of political concerns about equitable distribution, allocation priorities, or political accountability.

The human-rights-in-development perspective, however, tends to see an inevitable interrelationship between development and the capacity of governments to honor civil and political rights. It is believed that improvement in civil and political rights practices and economic and social rights conditions go hand in hand, both requiring political will and economic investment.[19] The 1993 World Conference on Human Rights at Vienna stressed the mutually reinforcing interrelationship of democracy, development, and respect for human rights. Notions of "Good Governance" and "Participatory Development" should also go hand in hand.

A certain level of economic development is a precondition for improving both civil and political rights and economic and social human rights. The necessity of economic development is rather obvious for the improvement of economic and social rights conditions, such as quality education, jobs, adequate medical care, social-insurance programs, housing, and so on. For civil and political rights to be honored, it is argued from this second perspective, economic investments are required to build a human rights infrastructure, including efficient administrations, viable legal systems, public education, and an independent mass media. An improvement in civil and political human rights practices requires legal specialists to draft constitutions and other legislation, and lawyers to provide legal assistance to citizens, and both requirements assume a certain level of economic development. Economic and technical assistance from abroad can be helpful to governments of the least developed countries in their efforts to build this kind of human rights infrastructure.

Political will is also required to improve either civil and political rights or economic and social human rights. The need is obvious in order to secure civil and political human rights, such as the rights to life, liberty, and privacy; the security of the individual; freedom of speech and press; freedom of worship; freedom from slavery; and freedom from torture and unusual punishment. It is equally obvious that achieving economic and social rights is influenced by a government's economic policy. People's participation in the process of development policy-making would seem to be necessary to make the most of development assistance. When the poor face obstacles such as unequal access to land, education, public health care, and other social services, some type of redistributional policies would seem to be required. Such "redistribution with growth" policies or, even more directly, redistributional strategies do indeed require the political will of governments because redistributing power will always face opposition from status quo interests.

Inevitably there will be different assessments of whether a potential aid recipient country has built a sufficient human rights infrastructure.[20] But if in the judgment of foreign aid policy-makers human rights preconditions exist, then one can argue that an improvement of human rights practices in the recipient country is only a matter of political will. In such a case, the use of positive (or negative) sanctions in foreign aid policy can be designed to encourage governments to do the right thing.

But what if it is clear that a potential recipient country does not have a sufficient human rights infrastructure? Reduction or suspension of development aid (a form of negative sanction) could harm the intended beneficiaries because their government cannot complete what is literally a "mission impossible."[21] If a recipient government has agreed to improve human rights practices but lacks the necessary infrastructure, then the first item on the donor government's list of priorities should be to fulfill human rights preconditions such as basic human needs and capital investments in order to help to install a human rights infrastructure.

If a potential recipient country has neither sufficient human rights preconditions nor adequate political will to improve the human rights conditions, the donor government needs to utilize positive (or negative) sanctions to influence the recipient's political will as well as to try to improve the human rights preconditions. Such a policy is on balance the most difficult to conduct, and requires careful evaluations of the situation in the target country.

Human rights or development

A human rights-or-development perspective typically underlies most empirical investigations of the role of human rights conditionality in foreign aid policies. The US was the first donor government to link foreign aid and human rights in a significant way. The Netherlands, Norway, and Canada followed, but their linkages are not yet systematically developed. The proposition that human

205

Table 10.1 Countries criticized by the United Nations for human rights violations in 1978-9 and 1986-7 as recipients of DAC members' ODA

Country	Human rights violations*		Percentage of total ODA disbursements 1980-1†					
	1978	1979	DAC20	Japan20	USA20	Netherland20	Norway20	Canada20
Bolivia	1	1		0.7				
Burma	0	1	0.8	4.1				
Chile	3	3					0.6	
Equatorial Guinea	1	3						
Ethiopia	1	1	3.4	11.2	2.1		0.3	0.5
Indonesia	1	1	3.1		11.5	5.1	0.5	1.6
Israel	2	2						
Kampuchea	1	3						
Malawi	1	1						0.8
Nicaragua	0	2			0.7	0.9		
Paraguay	1	1		0.6	0.6			
Republic of Korea	1	1	1.1	6.9		0.8		
Uganda	1	1						
Uruguay	1	1						

Country	Human rights violations*		Percentage of total ODA disbursements 1988-9†					
	1986	1987	DAC20	Japan20	USA20	Netherland20	Norway20	Canada20
Afghanistan	2	2						
Chile	3	3						
El Salvador	2	2	0.7		3.3			
Gabon	1	0						
Guatemala	2	0			1.5			
Haiti	1	2			0.6			
Indonesia	0	1	4.1	13.1	0.9	8.2		1.7
Iran	2	2						
Israel	2	2	2.6		12.5			
Kampuchea	2	2						
Lebanon	2	2						
Namibia	2	2					0.5	
Paraguay	1	1		0.7				
Philippines	1	0	1.7	5.4	1.8	1.2	0.5	1.0
Sri Lanka	0	1	0.9	2.0	0.5	1.2	1.6	1.0
Turkey	1	0	1.0	1.2				
Zaire	1	1	0.9		0.6			0.8

Notes

* Number of resolutions by UN Commission on Human Rights and the Sub-Commission on the Prevention of Discrimination and Protection of Minorities, and of the Commission's or the Sub-Commission's investigations under the 1503 procedure regarding cases which "appear to reveal a consistent pattern of gross and reliably attested violations of human rights" (Katarina Tomasevski, *Development Aid and Human Rights*, New York: St Martin's Press, 1989, pp. 82–3).

† Percentage of total ODA disbursements among top twenty recipient countries (OECD, *Development Co-operation: 1990 Report*, Paris: OECD, 1990, pp. 239–42).

rights practices should affect the allocation of aid has been the subject of empirical tests, but little reliable evidence has been provided to show consistent linkages.[22]

Cingranelli and Pasquarello have examined US foreign aid to thirty Latin American countries in the light of their human rights records. They conclude that (1) human rights records did not affect the decision of whether or not to extend economic assistance, and (2) once the decision to give aid was made, the US government allocated more aid to governments with better human rights practices in 1982.[23]

Poe too, in his study of twenty-six Latin American countries, concludes that under the Carter administration, human rights violations affected the US decision on whether to grant economic aid in 1980. He also examines foreign aid to Third World countries in general, and finds that once the decision to give aid was made, the US government allocated less aid to governments with higher levels of human rights abuses in 1980 and 1984 (sample of twenty-seven and twenty-six, respectively).[24]

On the other hand, Carleton and Stohl find few significant correlations between aid and human rights in their study of fifty-nine countries in 1978–83. In a study of twenty countries for the 1971–5 and 1977–81 periods, Stohl, Carleton and Johnson find very little significant relationship between the level of human rights violations and foreign aid.[25] They also report a rather unexpected relationship when Israel and Egypt are removed from their sample: recipients with poor human rights records receive more aid.[26] A finding which supports this, a study by Schoultz of twenty-three Latin American countries for the mid-1970s, also concludes that US aid was distributed disproportionally to countries with repressive governments.[27]

Thus, it is not yet clear whether the human rights practices of potential recipient countries really affect the allocation of US foreign aid, or whether "human rights" is merely rhetoric in the foreign aid legislation. If all the cited studies are correct, the only answer is that human rights practices are not systematically linked to the allocation of US economic aid. Some find they are linked in one year but not in another. Some find they correlate in one sample but not in another. In other words, the decisions are arbitrarily made, and in the long run human rights do not have a consistent influence on US foreign aid allocations.

This is probably because donors are preoccupied with their own security, economic, and political interests, or narrowly defined notions of the development needs of their recipients. Especially during the Cold War years, the US thought that it needed to support even nondemocratic or dictatorial governments when they were willing to join the liberal capitalist camp. However, we might expect to see a more straightforward relationship between human rights and foreign aid allocation after the end of the Cold War.

Nonetheless, an alternative explanation can be offered. It is difficult for donor countries to distinguish between human rights practices (a matter of political will) and human rights preconditions (a matter of having the capabilities necessary to sustain the political will to protect human rights). At what point can we say that a particular government has adequate human rights preconditions – that is, that it has built a sufficient human rights infrastructure? This difficulty produces a variety of interpretations of human rights situations in Third World countries, which then might lead to an inconsistent use of conditioning tools by donor governments. Hence, it may be that donor governments cannot finely differentiate levels of human rights abuse, and therefore cannot respond to each human rights violation in an appropriate manner.

This might help to explain why the empirical studies show inconsistent foreign aid policies with regard to human rights violations. In addition, the operationalizations (or indicators) of human rights practices employed in previous studies may not have been appropriate, leading researchers to search in vain for evidence of a systematic influence of human rights on foreign aid allocations.

However, if there were a universally accepted criterion of very serious human rights violations, it could be used for testing the various explanations. There is an emerging consensus on one such criterion: "gross violations of human rights." When a UN human rights committee adopts a resolution charging a particular country with gross violations of human rights, it tends to become a widely accepted norm that other governments should not support such a government and should suspend extension of economic assistance, and at the same time should support (not by official development assistance) the victims of such a regime.[28]

Examining those countries which have been criticized for "gross violations of human rights" in resolutions adopted by UN human rights committees against the top twenty ODA recipients list of the Development Assistance Committee (DAC) can give us a rough test of the usefulness of such a criterion (see Table 10.1).[29] It appears that the conclusion above is supported.

In 1978–9, there were fourteen countries named in this way, in one or more resolutions in the United Nations Commission of Human Rights. Among them, Burma (one resolution), Indonesia (2), Israel (4), and the Republic of Korea (2) are also on the top twenty recipients list of DAC members' total ODA in 1980–1. Bolivia (2) and Paraguay (2) are among Japan's top twenty recipients, while Nicaragua (2) is on the list of both the US and the Netherlands. In sum, ten of fourteen countries were among the top twenty recipients of one or more DAC nations' ODA in 1978–9, and so were eleven among the seventeen countries so designated in 1986–7. Human rights violations during these years did not discourage major DAC countries from offering foreign economic aid.

HUMAN RIGHTS FACTORS IN JAPANESE
FOREIGN AID

Another factor that might explain the inconsistent findings in the current literature on foreign aid might have to do with the heterogeneity of donor countries – different donors might have different aid objectives.[30] In this light, let us look at Japan's allocation of foreign aid, asking the same general questions as we have above. Are donor interests and recipient needs equally important in Japan's selection of aid recipient countries? What are Japan's particular objectives in its allocation of foreign economic aid? Do human rights matter in Japan's extension of its development assistance?

In this section, I will review the Japanese debate about foreign economic aid in general and also specifically with respect to human rights conditionality. I will illustrate Japan's use of positive and negative sanctions with case studies, and in the last part of this section, I will systematically examine a hypothesis that relates Japan's foreign aid allocation to human rights violations.

Japan as the ODA superpower?

Japan's economic aid activities in terms of its disbursements have rapidly increased since the early 1970s. Japan, with a proposed US$10.4 billion budget, in 1989 became the world's largest official development aid donor, a position it has retained since 1991. Organizing its foreign aid allocation in five-year plans, the Japanese government has announced a doubling of midterm ODA targets four times since 1978. Owing to the weaker yen, less funding to international development financial institutions, and more repayment on past loans, Japanese aid disbursement in 1996 was $9.44 billion, a reduction of 35 percent on the previous year. It was below $10 billion for the first time since 1990, and the total ODA of 1993–7 will fall in a range of $55 to $60 billion. It means a 10 to 20 percent increase on the previous five years, but the fourth five-year plan failed to reach the target of $70 billion. Japan's ODA constituted about 17 percent of total ODA (twenty-one DAC countries) in 1996, having been roughly a quarter in 1995. Although the second largest donor (USA) spent almost the same amount ($9.38 billion) in its ODA program in 1996, Japan has nevertheless retained its position as the world's no. 1 aid donor for six consecutive years.

How have Japan's aid objectives changed during its rise to its current top aid-donor position? When Japan was an ordinary major-power donor in the 1970s and early 1980s, its foreign aid-giving might be best explained by the community of interests model; but has that now changed as Japan has become a more important donor? For example, in 1990, there were twenty-eight developing countries whose top donor was Japan, but by 1994, Japan had become the number one donor for forty-six countries and the number two donor for another thirty-one countries. Thus, Japan gained more opportunities to use its ODA as a conditioning tool. Now that Japan has emerged as an ODA superpower, we might expect that the donor interests model would be more appropriate to explain Japanese foreign aid policy. If this is the case, we should observe more situations in which Japan utilizes its economic statecraft as a conditioning tool – in attempts to change a recipient country's behavior using methods such as punishment and inducement.

For what foreign policy objectives might Japan use this economic statecraft? What is the official explanation of Japanese foreign aid policy?[31] For a long time the government claimed that Japanese development assistance policy was based on humanitarianism and the principle of interdependence, widely accepted rationales for extending development assistance in the world.[32] There were, however, different viewpoints. For example, it has been claimed that Japanese aid is intended to serve its own economic interests, by promoting Japanese exports and securing imports of natural resources.[33] It is also asserted that official claims are dubious since the Japanese aid program gives away less and lends more than most other donors. Some have argued that Japan has allocated ODA for security reasons, supporting the US world strategy in the Cold War context.[34] Japan's responsiveness to US demands is also discussed as a factor shaping its ODA allocation and overall foreign economic policy.[35]

Based on an examination of the Yearbook on Economic Cooperation (the Ministry of International Trade and Industry, MITI), the ODA White Paper (the Ministry of Foreign Affairs, MFA), and the Diplomatic Bluebook (MFA), Inada has summarized the objectives and purposes of Japan's foreign aid.[36] He finds that, in the 1950s and 1960s, economic interests such as expanding export markets and securing natural resource imports were important, while in the 1970s the interdependence of international economy was emphasized. In the early 1980s, the priority was comprehensive security; in the late 1980s it was *kokusai koken* (making an international contribution or assuming international responsibility). The term "strategic aid" has been used by researchers since the early 1980s. During the 1980s, humanitarianism and interdependence were still the major rationales for Japan's aid-giving. Murai points to the difference between MFA's diplomatic-strategic rationale and MITI's economic interests-oriented rationale.[37] As we have seen, human rights and democratization as rationales appeared only in the early 1990s.

In addition to the "basic philosophy," the ODA White Paper 1996 (MFA) emphasizes that development assistance is an important instrument for pursuing national interests. The White Paper states that Japanese ODA may help solve problems of poverty and the global environment, promote economic growth, as shown in the "East Asian Miracles," and secure imports of natural resources, all of which would protect the high living standards of the Japanese people. This extends the previous argument of interdependence, while the White Paper argues more clearly than previously that ODA contributes to Japan's peace and prosperity by improving the welfare of people in developing

Table 10.2 Japan's use of positive and negative sanctions

Part 1 Japan's use of positive sanctions (mentioned in the ODA White Papers of 1995 and 1996)

Country		1988	1989	1990	1991	1992	1993	1994
Cambodia	ODA	0.013	0.029	0.863	0.005	0.048	0.666	0.666
	Resolution	CS	C					
	Policy						PM	
El Salvador	ODA	0.032	0.051	0.121	0.084	0.094	0.219	0.217
	Resolution	CS	CS	CS	C	CS	C	
	Policy							PM
Guatemala	ODA	0.068	0.058	0.078	0.168	0.125	0.443	0.444
	Resolution			CS	C	CS	CS AS/ES	
	Policy							
Haiti	ODA	0.234	0.165	0.041	0.095	0.010	0.004	0.004
	Resolution		C		C NM/AS	CS	C	
	Policy							PM/ES
Iran	ODA	0.034	0.052	-0.868	-0.047	-0.580	-0.050	-0.043
	Resolution	CS	CS	S	CS	CS	CS (PD)	(PD)
	Policy							
Mongolia	ODA	0.009	0.019	0.025	0.549	0.521	0.735	0.734
	Resolution							
	Policy			PM		PM		

Country		1988	1989	1990	1991	1992	1993	1994
Nicaragua	ODA	0.006	0.007	0.014	0.542	0.645	*0.571*	0.565
	Resolution							
	Policy			PM				
South Africa	ODA	0.000	0.000	0.000	0.000	0.000	0.000	0.000
	Resolution	CS	C	C	C	C	C	
	Policy							PM
Vietnam	ODA	0.075	0.023	0.019	0.080	*3.354*	0.785	0.821
	Resolution							
	Policy				PM & NM			

Notes

Japan's ODA Figures are a percentage of Japan's total ODA disbursements for the year.

Figures italicized indicate that Japan was the top donor for that country in that year.

Negative figures indicate net repayments by the recipient country.

UN human rights resolutions

    C: UN Commission on Human Rights

    S: UN Sub-Commission on the Prevention of Discrimination and Protection of Minorities

Japanese policy evaluation of recipients:

    NM: Negative move (such as coup) mentioned in the White Paper.

    PM: Positive move (such as general election) mentioned.

Action:

    AS: Aid suspension.

    PAS: Partial aid suspension.

    ES: End of aid suspension.

    PD: Policy dialogue.

countries.[38] This is almost a declaration of the community of interests model, at least in terms of economic interests.

With these objectives clarified, are we going to see more cases where Japan utilizes positive and negative sanctions for human rights and democratization issues? Critics of the ODA Charter attack from different directions. One line of criticism is from those who advocate separating politics from economics. They argue that the government should not politicize its foreign aid programs. A second is from advocates of "Asian values," who argue that the Japanese government should not follow "Western values" such as human rights and democracy in formulating its foreign aid principles. A third line comes from advocates of human rights and democracy, who argue that the government is not serious about these principles: some of them are merely rhetoric, and others have a hidden agenda. They ask whether these principles will really be respected by a Japanese government that has been extending significant amounts of ODA to China, Indonesia, and Myanmar – countries with records of extensive human rights abuse.

The "Asian values" advocates would agree with those political leaders of East and Southeast Asian countries who accuse the US and the Western leaders of trying to impose Western traditions on them. One of the tools for Western imposition of values on traditional Asian cultures is foreign aid. Asian leaders, gathered at the Bangkok Human Rights Conference in February 1993, condemned "any attempt to use human rights as a conditionality for extending development assistance."[39]

Inoguchi Takashi, however, warns there are two straw men in the "Asian values" debate: Ultra-Orientalism and Ultra-Universalism. Inoguchi considers these to be caricatures, far from reality, and suggests that we examine the assertion of Asian values in the context of political economy.[40] He does not agree with advocates of separating politics from economics when he argues that a blind application of Ultra-Universalism would be counterproductive. Quoting from Kishore Mahbubani,[41] Inoguchi characterizes the Japanese ODA Charter as "a national statement borne out by Japan's century-long experiences," and "not a superficial copy of Western values." He argues that "[i]t just needs a careful application, taking into account regional and cultural sensitivities."[42] Kusano Atsushi also emphasizes a passage of the Charter, "[t]aking into account comprehensively each recipient country's requests, its socioeconomic conditions, and Japan's bilateral relations with the recipient country," and argues that rigid application of ODA principles in the form of negative sanction, using ODA as a foreign policy tool, is not a smart move for Japan.[43]

Japanese use of positive and negative sanctions

The 1996 ODA White Paper gives illustrations of both positive and negative sanctions.[44] When favorable moves are observed, Japan will support a country through extending foreign aid (reward or positive sanction). When unfavorable moves appear, Japan will try to influence the government first through diplomatic channels, then freeze delivery of committed ODA, and finally reduce the amount of assistance if the situation has not improved (punishment or negative sanction). Based on his interview with an MFA official, Robert Orr describes three stages of Japan's negative sanctions: first, an attempt to exert influence through diplomatic channels (explaining the ODA principles in the Charter); second, stopping the next year's delivery of ODA if the recipient did not respect the principles; and third, reducing the amount of aid commitment from the next (third) year if the principles are not respected. The third stage continues until either the recipient complies or Japan commits no more aid.[45]

In Table 10.2, I try to summarize Japan's use of positive sanctions and use of negative sanctions. The table consists of three parts: Part 1 lists countries mentioned in the first volume of the ODA White Papers of 1995 and 1996 as examples of *positive sanction targets*; Part 2 lists *negative sanction targets*; and Part 3 lists countries *not mentioned as sanction targets* in the White Paper, but identified as violators of human rights in resolutions of the UN Commission on Human Rights and the Sub-Commission on the Prevention of Discrimination and Protection of Minorities. The table also shows Japan's bilateral aid to each country as a percentage of Japan's total bilateral ODA of that year (negative numbers indicate net loan repayments). When the percentage is italicized, it means that Japan was the top donor for that country during the year. For each country, the table also shows whether or not the country has been labeled a violator by the UN, and whether or not Japan has imposed or lifted sanctions.

Examination of Part 1 of Table 10.2 shows that the positive-sanction target countries were not Japan's major aid recipients: all received less than 1 percent of bilateral aid before any positive moves toward democratization or marketization were observed by the Japanese government. In the early 1990s, three countries in East Asia (Cambodia, Mongolia, and Vietnam) were the primary targets of Japan's use of positive sanctions, which corresponds with the Japanese tendency to concentrate its aid-giving in Asia. Japan quickly became the leading donor for these countries, and extended close to 1 percent of its total bilateral aid to each country.

Iran, seemingly an exception, illustrates an interesting aspect of the Japanese positive-sanctioning attempt: Japan's loan for a water power plant in 1993 is explained as an inducement for Iran to become "realistic" in its economic and foreign policy. According to the White Paper, the Japanese government explained to its Iranian counterpart that its respect for ODA principles was required for the extension of the second portion of the loan. The difficult question of how to choose inducement targets is, though, not answered by the White Paper.

In terms of human rights violations, two cases in Latin America (Guatemala and Haiti) show that Japan could respond to negative moves with aid

Table 10.2, Part 2 Japan's use of negative sanctions (mentioned in the ODA White Papers of 1995 and 1996)

Country		1988	1989	1990	1991	1992	1993	1994
China	ODA	10.491	12.277	10.654	6.598	12.532	15.581	15.282
	Resolution							
	Policy		AS	ES				NM
Gambia	ODA	0.060	0.030	0.095	0.045	0.061	0.116	0.119
	Resolution							
	Policy							NM/AS
India	ODA	2.795	3.795	0.499	10.045	1.493	9.245	9.158
	Resolution							
	Policy						PD	PD
Kenya	ODA	1.787	2.181	1.373	2.230	1.535	1.349	1.332
	Resolution							
	Policy			NM	PAS	PM	ES	
Malawi	ODA	0.625	0.318	0.618	0.198	0.283	1.049	1.036
	Resolution							
	Policy					NM/PAS	PM	ES
Myanmar	ODA	4.042	1.053	0.904	0.953	0.860	1.391	1.382
	Resolution					C	CS	
	Policy	NM/AS		PM/NM				PM
Nigeria	ODA	0.837	2.447	1.160	0.221	0.507	-0.099	-0.097
	Resolution							
	Policy						NM	AS
Pakistan	ODA	4.705	2.618	2.852	1.436	2.067	2.824	2.800
	Resolution							
	Policy						PD	

Country	1988	1989	1990	1991	1992	1993	1994
Peru							
ODA	0.443	0.411	0.588	3.978	1.846	0.570	0.564
Resolution						S	
Policy					NM/PD	PM	
Sierra Leone							
ODA	0.063	0.230	0.088	0.018	0.046	0.108	0.106
Resolution						AS	
Policy					NM		
Sudan							
ODA	0.928	0.617	0.574	0.575	0.327	0.215	0.213
Resolution		NM				C	
Policy					AS		
Thailand							
ODA	5.615	7.212	6.168	4.579	4.937	3.945	3.952
Resolution				NM/PD			
Policy					PM		
Togo							
ODA	0.151	0.230	0.137	0.099	0.023	0.018	0.018
Resolution						NM/AS	
Policy							PM
Zaïre							
ODA	0.365	1.129	0.650	0.237	0.057	0.047	0.046
Resolution				NM/AS		C	
Policy							
Zambia							
ODA	1.411	0.930	0.591	0.932	1.390	1.116	1.098
Resolution						NM	PAS
Policy				PM			

Table 10.2, *Part 3* Countries charged by the UN with human rights violations to which Japan responded with neither positive nor negative sanctions

Country		1988	1989	1990	1991	1992	1993	1994
Afghanistan	ODA	0.000	0.000	0.000	0.000	0.000	0.000	0.000
	Resolution	CS				C		
	Policy							
Chad	ODA	0.001	0.001	0.000	0.000	0.007	0.002	0.002
	Resolution						S	
	Policy			NM			PM	
Chile	ODA	0.233	0.269	0.178	0.201	0.218	0.323	0.324
	Resolution	CS	C					
	Policy		PM					
Cuba	ODA	0.007	0.005	0.008	0.004	0.004	0.007	0.011
	Resolution					C	C	
	Policy							
Equatorial Guinea	ODA	0.012	0.000	0.010	0.011	0.018	0.014	0.014
	Resolution					C	C	
	Policy				PM		PM	

Country		1988	1989	1990	1991	1992	1993	1994
Indonesia	ODA	15.337	16.895	11.931	12.012	16.181	9.176	9.154
	Resolution					S	CS	
	Policy							
Iraq	ODA	−0.158	−0.204	−0.291	0.002	0.002	0.002	0.001
	Resolution			NM/AS	CS	CS	CS	
	Policy							
Israel	ODA	0.006	0.006	0.007	0.007	0.008	0.012	0.012
	Resolution	CS	CS	CS	CS	CS	CS	
	Policy						PM	
Lebanon	ODA	0.003	0.016	0.002	0.001	0.004	0.006	0.006
	Resolution	CS	C			C	C	
	Policy					PM		
Somalia	ODA	0.239	0.259	0.150	0.017	0.002	0.000	0.000
	Resolution					S		
	Policy							PM

suspensions, and to favorable moves by lifting suspensions quickly. The case of aid suspension in Haiti in 1991 was an application of the Kaifu Four Principles; and the end of aid suspension in 1994 was based on the ODA Charter. The case of Guatemala came late after four years of UN resolutions, but the suspension was lifted within one month when the situation improved. In both cases, Japan imposed negative sanctions together with US and other major donors.

In Part 2 of the table, we find that two-thirds of the negative sanction targets have Japan as their top donor, and they received from 0.1 percent to as much as 15 percent of Japan's bilateral ODA. Negative sanctions, threats and punishment, should work better against countries which are more dependent on the sanctioning tool, foreign aid.

The sanctions tool is, however, a double-edged sword. Since aid is based on a community of interests, the sanctioning party also suffers to some extent from a suspension of aid. That is one reason why we do not see many aid suspensions against major aid recipients. Among the eight aid suspension cases, only two countries, China and Myanmar, enjoyed more than 0.5 percent of Japan's total bilateral ODA. The rest of the countries that were targets of Japan's negative sanctions experienced either a partial aid suspension, a softer punishment, or an influence attempt through policy dialogue, that is, a possible threat but not punishment. Among those seven recipients, six countries received more than 1 percent of Japan's bilateral aid.

The cases of China and Myanmar both took place before the Cold War ended, and Japan followed the negative sanction initiatives taken by Western donors.[46] Myanmar (then Burma) was the first Japanese use of negative sanctions. Five months after the coup and before the planned general election in 1990, the Japanese government approved the new government and unfroze projects that had been started before 1988. Aid disbursements to Myanmar after the suspension were said to be for these continuing projects, for emergency humanitarian aid, or to grant aid for debt relief based on a 1978 UNCTAD resolution. Still, 1 percent of Japan's bilateral ODA, as a result, could be seen as support for the SLORC government.

The case of China posed a dilemma in Japanese foreign aid policy: how to respond to human rights violations in a country with close relations to Japan, or at least how to respond to US and Western allies who wanted Japan to join them in economic sanctions against such a country. While halting new economic assistance, the Japanese government had many occasions to suggest that the Chinese government must satisfy the international community in showing a continued commitment to economic reform and liberalization. About one year after June 4, 1989, Prime Minister Kaifu asked the US and other major donors for their understanding for Japan's plan to unfreeze its third yen loan to China (810 billion yen for six years from 1990). Though they did not agree that China had made significant efforts to show its commitment to reform and liberalization, Japan was able to announce its intention to resume official aid to China at the 1990 Houston Summit.[47]

Critics of Japan's ODA argue that behind Japan's resumption of aid projects in Myanmar and the 810 billion yen loan to China are pressures from Japanese industrial circles. It is said that the government's approval of the new Burmese government in February 1989 was influenced by lobbying by Nihon–Biruma Kyokai (Japan–Burmese Society), which sent a letter to the Ministry of Foreign Affairs in January, requesting the resumption of aid projects so that Japanese businesses would not be stuck with huge inventories of materials waiting to be shipped to Myanmar.[48]

In addition to Myanmar and China, there were cases like Thailand and Peru. Japan's response to the Thai military coup in 1991 and Fujimori's closing of parliament in 1992, when some Western donors froze their foreign aid, was to use policy dialogue instead. (See Table 10.2, Part 3 for a list of those countries that were charged by the UN with human rights violations, but to which Japan responded with neither positive nor negative sanctions.) David Arase argues that this non-use or soft use of negative sanctions suggests that Japan is preoccupied with economic interests rather than democracy and human rights in its foreign aid policy.[49]

Five other countries (Kenya, Malawi, Sierra Leone, Sudan, and Togo) are also mentioned in the White Papers as violating human rights, but only four countries (Myanmar, Peru, Sudan, and Zaïre) of all of those identified as targets for negative sanctions in Japan's ODA White Papers appeared in resolutions of the UN human rights commissions. This discrepancy suggests that Japan pays attention to human rights situations in the developing world well beyond the UN resolutions. Since the Japanese government has no systematic monitoring system, nor does it publish annual country reports on human rights practices as the United States does, the cases of human rights violations most likely to come to Japan's attention would be those taken up by the DAC community or cases publicized in the mass media. In three cases (Kenya, Malawi, and Togo) in which Japan imposed negative sanctions on human rights violators by suspending or partially suspending aid as punishment, positive changes resulted in recipient countries. In those cases, sanctions worked!

Part 3 of Table 10.2 lists countries not mentioned as sanctions targets in the ODA White Paper but which were the subjects of human rights resolutions in the UN Commission on Human Rights and the Sub-Commission on the Prevention of Discrimination and Protection of Minorities during the period 1988–94.

The first thing we notice is that, as in the first part, these target countries were not Japan's major aid recipients. Some received no aid from Japan; half received less than 0.01 percent of Japan's bilateral aid. Some of these countries were in civil war, and others had no official diplomatic relations with Japan. When there is no aid relationship, there is no room for sanction, especially negative sanctions. The non-recipient has nothing to lose.

Among ten countries, the only two exceptions were Indonesia and Chile. Indonesia has been one of the top three Japanese aid recipients, receiving

Table 10.3 The effect of recipient need, donor interests, and human rights violations on Japan's bilateral ODA allocation (1990–4)

Variables		ODA90		ODA91		ODA92		ODA93		ODA94	
		Standardized coefficients	(T ratio in brackets)	Standardized coefficients	(T ratio in brackets)	Standardized coefficients	(T ratio in brackets)	Standardized coefficients	(T ratio in brackets)	Standardized coefficients	(T ratio in brackets)
Need	GND (t–1)	0.314	[2.492]**	0.468	[3.337]***	0.421	[3.408]***	0.363	[2.978]***	0.300	[2.819]***
	POP (t–1)	0.206	[1.368]	0.355	[3.466]***	0.502	[5.316]***	0.526	[5.145]***	0.761	[7.193]***
	PQL (t–1)	-0.099	[-0.786]	-0.177	[-1.880]*	-0.132	[-1.505]	-0.127	[-1.346]	-0.126	[-1.406]
Donor interests	MPW (t–1)	-0.162	[-0.986]	-0.004	[-0.038]	-0.282	[-2.769]***	-0.061	[-0.575]	-0.416	[-3.536]***
	TRD (t–1)	0.471	[3.586]***	0.148	[1.216]	0.408	[3.749]***	0.173	[1.530]	0.319	[2.986]***
	RES (t–1)	0.028	[0.251]	0.208	[2.184]**	-0.006	[-0.076]	-0.012	[-0.147]	-0.028	[-0.347]
	MRK (t–1)	-0.023	[-0.206]	0.334	[2.616]**	0.294	[2.735]***	0.240	[2.255]**	0.174	[1.886]*
Human rights violations	HRV (t–1)	-0.014	[-0.123]	-0.115	[-1.327]	-0.054	[-0.681]	-0.053	[-0.607]	0.057	[0.711]
	intercept	-175.977	[-1.863]*	-118.022	[-2.286]**	-108.991	[-2.259]**	-54.639	[-1.615]	-59.588	[-1.694]*
	N	76		84		86		84		75	
	R2	0.241		0.452		0.521		0.482		0.605	
	Adj. R2	0.150		0.394		0.471		0.427		0.557	
	F test	2.659**		7.744***		10.469***		8.737***		12.651***	

Notes: *$p < .10$ **$p < .05$ ***$p < .01$

more than 10 percent of Japan's bilateral ODA. Even after the East Timor incident in 1991, Indonesia still received about 9 percent of Japanese aid. The White Paper, even in the second volume's country-by-country description, does not discuss East Timor, though it mentions positive or negative changes in human rights and democracy in seven other countries. One of them is Chile, but we do not observe much increase in the amount of bilateral aid after Chile's return to democracy in 1989 and its government's efforts to secure human rights thereafter.

The tentative conclusion drawn in the previous section seems to hold here again: foreign economic aid allocation and human rights situations in developing countries are not systematically related to each other. Japan uses positive sanctions in some cases, but they are skewed toward Asia. They are not used with respect to major recipients. Japan uses negative sanctions in some cases, but not in others. There is a bias: African or non-Asian countries as well as small recipient countries have a better chance to be sanctioned by Japan.

Human rights violations and Japanese ODA allocation

Although there are a variety of interpretations of Japanese economic assistance, we do not have many studies that systematically analyze the factors influencing the allocation of Japanese foreign aid. As we have seen in the first section, systematic studies of human rights and foreign aid have been conducted mainly using the case of the United States as an aid donor. The model which examines the decision-making of Japan's aid allocation in this section is that of a rational actor which uses aid as a conditioning tool to promote its foreign policy objectives within a community of interests.[50]

Japanese economic aid allocation is a function of donor interests and recipient needs but is not accounted for by human rights practices in recipient countries: this hypothesis is expressed as an equation relating aid allocation decisions to recipient's development need, donor's foreign policy interests, and human rights violations of possible recipients. Five equations are estimated each year from 1990 to 1994 with following data for the sample of developing countries.[51]

Economic aid or economic assistance is defined as financial flows from a government in one country to a government in another country at concessional rates of interest and repayment, which consists of grants, loans, official export credits, and other long-term capital. It excludes military assistance, private investment, and other means of assistance such as preferential entry into markets. The dependent variable (ODA) is the amount of net disbursement of Japan's official development assistance to a country in a particular year.

Development need is defined in economic terms as an external support and a domestic effort required for a country to achieve its ideal state in constructing its economy and society: the economic requirement "to obtain the good life."[52] It is measured a year before the aid disbursement, in terms of GNP per capita

(GND), population size of a recipient (POP), and physical quality of life (PQL).[53] If a donor allocates its economic aid in response to development need within a realm of the donor interests, some of these three variables should be positive and significant. If there is more "need" in terms of a low GNP per capita, a higher population, and a lower physical quality of life, Japan should allocate more aid to that country.

Donor interest is a utility which is expected to be maximized through foreign economic aid-giving. It is operationally defined along the following four dimensions: security interest (MPW), trade interest (TRD), resource maintenance (RES), and export market access (MRK).[54] They also are measured a year before the aid disbursement. If the community of interests model holds, some of these variables should be positive and significant, along with some positive indications of development need. Since, according to the 1996 ODA White Paper, Japanese ODA is intended to protect the high living standards of the Japanese people, we should expect that Japan's economic trade interests would be significant. The variable for security interests is a mixed bag. If Japan tries to maintain or develop friendship with militarily more powerful countries, the sign of the security interests variable will be positive and significant. Alternatively, if the Japanese government has already been exercising the third principle of the ODA Charter from the beginning of the 1990s (the principle about strengthening international peace and stability through discouraging the development of military power), then the sign should be negative.

As an indicator of human rights practices in the Third World countries, I use a dummy variable of "gross violations of human rights" (HRV) in a particular country. A "1" indicates a resolution in either the UN Commission on Human Rights or the Sub-Commission on the Prevention of Discrimination and Protection of Minorities against a given country during the last two years of Japan's aid disbursement. Our hypothesis suggests that this HRV should be insignificant in explaining Japan's foreign aid-giving.

Table 10.3 shows the results of the regression analysis. First of all, the model developed here explains around 40 or more percent of the variation in Japanese ODA allocation during the period 1991–4, and 15 percent of the variation in 1990. All equations are statistically significant.

Some of the development need and some of the donor interest factors are statistically significant (p value being less than 0.05) at the same time for all five years. The community of interests model, therefore, is appropriate for explaining Japanese foreign aid allocation during this period (1990–4), that is, just before and right after the announcement of Japan's ODA Charter. This means that the world's leading donor is *not* behaving like an ODA superpower in the sense of employing its economic statecraft by means of punishment and inducement in attempts to change recipient countries' behavior.

GNP per capita and population size of the country are constantly positive and significant, except POP in 1990. Trade interest is significant in three years, and so is resource maintenance in 1991 as well as export market access from 1991 to 1993 (and in 1994 to a lesser extent). All these signs support our hypothesis.

The security interests variable, the relative size of military strength, is significant and negative in 1992 and 1994. In our framework of understanding, this means that the Japanese government sometimes pays attention to the third principle of the ODA Charter about discouraging the development of military power when it allocates foreign aid, and sometimes does not. Physical quality of life in the 1991 equation is almost significant but is, unexpectedly, negative rather than positive, which should be examined in future analysis.

Most important of all, coefficients for human rights violation are not significant in any of the equations. Even if we control other factors influencing Japanese aid allocation, Japanese ODA allocation is not accounted for by human rights practices in recipient countries. In other words, Japan's foreign aid is not used as a conditioning tool to reward and punish in a systematic way with respect to human rights. Japan, like the other major DAC donor countries, is not discouraged by human rights violations in extending foreign economic aid – even after the promulgation of the 1992 ODA Charter.

CONCLUSION

While we are aware of the differing "human rights-or-development" and "human rights-in-development" perspectives, most empirical studies assume that the human rights-or-development perspective is an underlying premise of human rights diplomacy. When we control for development needs and donor interests factors in Japanese ODA allocation, the human rights practices of recipient countries are not systematically linked to the allocation of Japanese economic aid. In other words, Japanese foreign aid is not used as a conditioning tool to reward or punish in any systematic way with respect to human rights.

But why? Why is it that the recipients' human rights practices are not systematically linked to the allocation of Japanese economic aid, especially when one of the four principles in the ODA Charter claims that full attention should be paid to the situation regarding basic human rights and freedoms in a recipient country? As we have already suggested, it is difficult for donor countries to distinguish between human rights practices and human rights preconditions, and to judge whether or not a particular government has sufficient infrastructure and political will to protect and promote human rights. These difficulties produce a variety of interpretations of the human rights situations in Third World countries, which can lead to an inconsistent use of conditioning tools by donor governments, which in turn may result in non-systematic foreign aid policies with regard to human rights violations.

Writing policy prescriptions would be easier if donor governments could differentiate between governments with sufficient human rights infrastructure but without political will for the promotion and protection of human rights, on the one hand, and governments with political will but without sufficient infrastructure, on the other. For the former, the answer should be sanctions. However, foreign aid policies toward the latter would call for assistance to support economic development and the establishment of a human rights infrastructure, such as a viable legal system, public education, and a responsible mass media.

But should Japan as an ODA superpower use foreign aid as a policy instrument? The 1992 ODA Charter answers positively, but with the following problematic conditions: (1) in accordance with the principles of sovereign equality and non-intervention in domestic matters, and (2) taking into account comprehensively each recipient country's requests, its socio-economic conditions, and Japan's bilateral relations with the recipient country. Under such conditions, we could not expect any systematic application of foreign aid as a conditioning tool with respect to human rights.

Japan as an ODA superpower as imagined in the 1992 ODA Charter is not ready to use foreign aid as a conditioning tool. For some years to come, we may have to accept a generic foreign aid policy of "flexible approaches for each case." Whether or not people in Japan can hope to "occupy an honored place in an international society" would seem to depend on how much they want their government to work for "the banishment of tyranny and slavery, oppression and intolerance" in its manner of providing foreign aid.

NOTES

1 Asahi Shimbun "Enjo" Shuzaihan, *Enjo Tojokoku Nippon* [Japan: The Developing Country in Aid] (Tokyo: Asahi Shimbun-Sha, 1985). On the Kaifu Four Principles, Alan Rix wrote: "It sprang both from post-Gulf War attitudes that Japan needed to do more to contribute to the maintenance of international security, and from a desire to redress Japan's reputation for commercialism in its aid philosophy." See Rix, *Japan's Foreign Aid Challenge* (New York: Routledge, 1993), p. 34.
2 *Far Eastern Economic Review*, June 17, 1993.
3 Inada Juichi, "Jinken Minshuka-to Enjo Seisaku" [Human Rights, Democratization, and Aid Policy], *Kokusai Mondai* [International Affairs] no. 422 (1995), pp. 2–3.
4 The democratic peace proposition argues that democracies rarely, if ever, enter into war against each other (see Bruce M. Russett, *Grasping the Democratic Peace: Principles for a Post-Cold War World*, Princeton, NJ: Princeton University Press, 1993). For a review of the growing literature on this, Steve Chan, "In Search of Democratic Peace: Problems and Promise," *Mershon International Studies Review* 41 (1997), pp. 59–91. For a policy-oriented argument, see Strobe Talbott, "Democracy and the National Interest," *Foreign Affairs* 75, no. 6 (1996), pp. 47–63.
5 Oshiba Ryo, "Kokusai Kinyu Sosiki-to 'Yoi Gabanansu'" [International Monetary Organizations and 'Good Governance'], *Kokusai Mondai*, no. 422 (1995), pp. 20–1.
6 Murai Yoshinori, ed., *Kensho Nippon-no ODA* [Examining Japanese ODA] (Tokyo: Gakuyo Shobo, 1992), pp. 30–4.

7 MFA, *Waga Kuni no Seifu Kaihatsu Enjo* [Japan's Official Development Assistance] (Tokyo: Kokusai Kyoryoku Suishin Kyokai, 1996), pp. 331–5. An unofficial English translation is in Matsumae Tatsuro and Lincoln C. Chen, eds, *In Pursuit of Common Values in Asia: Japan's ODA Charter Re-evaluated* (Tokyo: Tokai University Press, 1997), pp. 267–72.

8 See, for donor interest arguments, Steven W. Hook, *National Interest and Foreign Aid* (Boulder, CO: Lynne Reinner, 1995); Steve Weissman, ed., *Trojan Horse: A Radical Look at Foreign Aid* (San Francisco: Ramparts Press, 1974); Teresa Hayter, *Aid as Imperialism* (Baltimore, MD: Penguin, 1971). For recipient need arguments, David H. Lumsdaine, *Moral Vision in International Politics: The Foreign Aid Regime, 1949–1989* (Princeton, NJ: Princeton University Press, 1993); L.B. Pearson, *Partners in Development: Report of the Commission on International Development* (New York: Praeger, 1969).

9 See, for example, Vernon W. Ruttan, *United States Development Assistance Policy: The Domestic Politics of Foreign Economic Aid* (Baltimore, MD: Johns Hopkins University Press, 1996); Sarah J. Tisch and Michael B. Wallace, *Dilemmas of Development Assistance* (Boulder, CO: Westview Press, 1994); and John White, *The Politics of Foreign Aid* (New York: St Martin's Press, 1974).

10 See, for example, R.D. McKinlay, "The Aid Relationship: A Foreign Policy Model and Interpretation of the Distributions of Official Bilateral Economic Aid of the United States, the United Kingdom, France, and Germany, 1960–1970," *Comparative Political Studies* 11 (1979), pp. 411–63. Also, see Hook, *National Interest and Foreign Aid*; Alfred Maizels and M.K. Nissanke, "Motivations for Aid to Developing Countries," *World Development* 12 (1984), pp. 879–900.

11 For inconsistent findings, see Louis M. Imbeau, *Donor Aid – The Determinants of Development Allocations to Third World Countries: A Comparative Analysis* (New York: Peter Lang, 1989); B.E. Moon, "Consensus or Compliance? Foreign-Policy Change and External Dependence," *International Organization* 39 (1985), pp. 297–329. For objections, see J.M. Healey and A.G. Coverdale, "Foreign Policy and British Bilateral Aid: A Comment on McKinley and Little," *British Journal of Political Science* 11 (1981), pp. 123–7; Paul Mosley, "Models of the Aid Allocation Process: A Comment on McKinlay and Little," *Political Studies* 29 (1981), pp. 245–53.

12 Moon, "Consensus or Compliance?" pp. 297–8. Other alternatives could be found in Hook's argument on "enlightened" national interest, and Potter's analysis on "accommodation of interests" in the aid relationships. Hook, *National Interest and Foreign Aid*; David M. Potter, *Japan's Foreign Aid to Thailand and the Philippines* (New York: St Martin's Press, 1996).

13 Some argue that economic growth is not the only objective of US foreign aid, but it is a necessary condition for materializing most of the broad objectives of foreign aid. For example, Carol Graham and Michael O'Hanlon, "Making Foreign Aid Work," *Foreign Affairs* 76, no. 4 (1997), p. 96.

14 Kondo Tetsuo, "How to Use Carrot and Stick," *Leviathan* 12 (1993), p. 144. Also see D.A. Baldwin, "The Power of Positive Sanction," *World Politics* 24 (1971), pp. 71–8.

15 See Hoshino Eiichi, "Three Models of the Foreign Economic Aid Allocation: Preliminary Analyses for the Case of China," *Ryudai Law Review* no. 50 (1993), pp. 327–74; Hoshino Eiichi, "Nihon-no Seifu Kaihatsu Enjo" [Allocation of Japanese Foreign Aid and Its Impact on LDC's], *Ryudai Law Review* no. 52 (1994), pp. 425–58.

16 Donnelly classifies development-rights trade-offs into three categories: the needs trade-off, the equality trade-off, and the liberty trade-off (Jack Donnelly, *Universal Human Rights in Theory and Practice*, Ithaca, NY: Cornell University Press, 1989).

17 For example, Jeane Kirkpatrick, "Establishing a Viable Human Rights Policy," *World Affairs* vol. 143 (Spring 1981), pp. 323–34; Irving Kristol, "'Human Rights': Hidden Agenda (1986/7)," in Walter Laquer and Barry Rubin, eds, *The Human Rights Reader* (New York: Meridian Books, 1989).

18 For example, see Cyrus Vance, "Law Day Speech on Human Rights and Foreign Policy (1977)," in Laquer and Rubin, eds, *The Human Rights Reader.* Also see Katarina Tomasevski, *Development Aid and Human Rights Revisited* (New York: Pinter Publishers, 1993); Donnelly, *Universal Human Rights in Theory and Practice.*

19 For example, see Vance, "Law Day Speech on Human Rights and Foreign Policy (1977)," p. 344.

20 It is difficult for concerned donors to judge whether or not a particular government has sufficient infrastructure and political will to promote human rights. This is one reason why the results of empirical studies have provided little evidence that human rights have been an important determinant of economic aid allocation.

21 Governments with sufficient human rights infrastructure but without the political will to protect and promote human rights could use the human-rights-in-development argument. Governments legitimized by developmentalism or development dictatorship also use a similar line of argument. Such governments criticize donors for not understanding the right to development and for violating the principles of sovereignty and non-intervention. (Donnelly, *Universal Human Rights in Theory and Practice*, p. 233.)

22 See, for example, Steven C. Poe, "Human Rights and Economic Aid Allocation under Ronald Reagan and Jimmy Carter," *American Journal of Political Science* 36 (1992), pp. 147–67.

23 David L. Cingranelli and Thomas E. Pasquarello, "Human Rights Practices and the Distribution of US Foreign Aid to Latin American Countries," *American Journal of Political Science* 29 (1985), pp. 539–63.

24 Poe, "Human Rights and Economic Aid Allocation"; Steven C. Poe, *et al.*, "Human Rights and US Foreign Aid Revisited: The Latin American Region," *Human Rights Quarterly* 16 (1994), pp. 539–58.

25 David Carleton and Michael Stohl, "The Foreign Policy of Human Rights: Rhetoric and Reality from Jimmy Carter to Ronald Reagan," *Human Rights Quarterly* vol. 7 (1985), pp. 205–29; Michael Stohl *et al.*, "Human Rights and US Foreign Assistance from Nixon to Carter," *Journal of Peace Research* 21 (1984), pp. 215–26.

26 Stohl *et al.*, "Human Rights and US Foreign Assistance."

27 Lars Schoultz, "US Foreign Policy and Human Rights Violations in Latin America: A Comparative Analysis of Foreign Aid Distributions," *Comparative Politics* 13 (1981), pp. 149–70.

28 Tomasevski, *Development Aid and Human Rights*, p. 117. I would not like to overestimate the utility of this index of gross violations of human rights. It is also true that the Commission is a politicized arena, since it consists of individual countries with contradictory interests. Therefore, it is possible that certain countries could escape from the Commission's monitoring because they are powerful enough or have powerful friends willing to help them. See, for the case of China, Beatrice Laroche, "Dodging Scrutiny: China and the UN Commission on Human Rights," *China Rights Forum* (Summer 1997), pp. 28–33.

29 For a list of violators, Tomasevski, *Development Aid and Human Rights*, pp. 82–3. For data on economic aid, OECD, *Development Co-operation: 1990 Report* (Paris: OECD, 1990), pp. 239–42.

30 McKinlay reported that US foreign aid is sensitive to its security and power political interests, while French aid is related to its trading interest as well as its security

interest; UK aid is related only to its security interest, and German aid only to its trading interest. J.S. Hoadley also established that small state donors such as Australia, Canada, and Scandinavian countries have behaved in different ways in contrast with large state donors. (See McKinley, "The Aid Relationship"; J.S. Hoadley, "Small States as Aid Donors," *International Organization* 34, 1980, pp. 121–37.)

31 The biennial DAC review in 1991 asked the same question: "What is the basic rationale of Japan's aid programme and what are its objectives?" and the ODA Charter was the answer from the Japanese side. See DAC, *Aid Review 1990/1991: Report by the Secretariat and Questions for the Review of Japan* (Paris: OECD, 1991), p. 7.

32 MFA, *Waga Kuni no Seifu Kaihatsu Enjo*, 1989.

33 See, for example, David Arase, *Buying Power: The Political Economy of Japan's Foreign Aid* (Boulder, CO: Lynne Reinner, 1995); Margee Ensign, *Doing Good or Doing Well? Japan's Foreign Aid Program* (New York: Columbia University Press, 1992).

34 For example, see Asahi Shimbun "Enjo" Shuzaihan, *Enjo Tojokoku Nippon*; Kato Kozo, "Kaihatsu Kyoryoku Seisaku-wo Meguru Nihon-to Doitsu-no Taishosei" [Symmetry in Development Cooperation Policy between Japan and Germany], *Leviathan* 18 (1996), pp. 96–118.

35 On foreign aid, see Robert M. Orr, Jr, "Collaboration or Conflict? Foreign Aid and US–Japan Relations," *Pacific Affairs* 62, no. 4 (Winter 1989–90), pp. 476–89; D.T. Yasutomo, *The Manner of Giving: Strategic Aid and Japanese Foreign Policy* (Lexington, MA: Lexington Books, 1986). On overall foreign economic policy, see Kent E. Calder, "Japanese Foreign Economic Policy: Explaining the Reactive State," *World Politics* 40 (1988), pp. 517–41.

36 Inada, "Jinken Minshuka-to Enjo Seisaku", pp. 4–5. His sources are MITI, *Keizai Kyoryoku no Genjo to Mondaiten* [State of Economic Cooperation] (Tokyo: Tsusho Sangyo Chosakai Shuppanbu); MFA, *Waga Kuni no Seifu Kaihatsu Enjo*; MFA, *Gaiko Seisho: Waga Gaiko no Kinkyo* [Diplomatic Bluebook: Review of Recent Developments in Japan's Foreign Relations] (Tokyo: Okura-Sho Insatsu-Kyoku).

37 Murai Yoshinori, "Honto-ni Dare-no Tame-no Enjo-ka" [Who is the Aid Really for?], *ODA Kaikaku* [ODA for Whose Benefit?] (Tokyo: Shakai Shiso-Sha, 1990), pp. 319–22.

38 MFA, *Waga Kuni no Seifu Kaihatsu Enjo*, 1996, pp. 13–15.

39 See, for example, Denny Roy, "Singapore, China, and the 'Soft-Authoritarian' Challenge," *Asian Survey* 34, no. 3 (1994), pp. 231–42; Kishore Mahbubani, "The Danger of Decadence," *Foreign Affairs* 72, no. 4 (1993), pp. 10–14; Bilahari Kausikan, "Asia's Different Standard," *Foreign Policy* no. 92 (1993), pp. 24–41; China, Information Office of the State Council, "Human Rights in China," *Beijing Review* no. 44 (1991).

40 Inoguchi Takashi, "Asian Values and Japanese Official Development Assistance," in Matsumae and Chen, eds, *In Pursuit of Common Values in Asia*, pp. 18–19.

41 Kishore Mahbubani, "The Pacific Way," *Foreign Affairs* 74, no. 1 (1995), pp. 107.

42 Inoguchi, "Asian Values and Japanese Official Development Assistance," p. 20.

43 Kusano Atsushi, *ODA 12,000 Okuen-no Yukue* [Where Does the 1.2 Trillion Yen ODA Go?] (Toyo Keizai Shimpo-Sha, 1993), pp. 174–5.

44 The 1995 ODA White Paper uses terms describing positive and negative approaches and positive and negative linkages (MFA, *Waga Kuni no Seifu Kaihatsu Enjo*, 1995).

45 Robert M. Orr, Jr, "Taigai Enjo-to Nichibei Kan-no Seijiteki Kadai" [Foreign Aid and Political Issues for US and Japan], in Hiroya Ichikawa, ed., *Posuto Reisen Jidai-no Kaihatsu Enjo-to Nichibei Kyoryoku* [Common Vision, Different Paths], (Tokyo: Kokusai Kaihatsu Jahnaru-sha), p. 175.

46 Inada uses these two cases to illustrate his understanding of Japan's "indirect approach" to democratization and support for stability. See Inada Juichi, "Democracy and Stability: Political Considerations in Japan's ODA to Myanmar and China," in Matsumae and Chen, eds, *In Pursuit of Common Values in Asia*, pp. 101–22.

47 Ibid., pp. 112–13. Also see Peter Van Ness, "Understanding Japan's ODA as International Sanctions," in Matsumae and Chen, eds, *In Pursuit of Common Values in Asia*, pp. 208–12.

48 Mainichi Shimbun Shakaibu, *Kokusai Enjo Bijinesu* [International Aid Business] (Tokyo: Aki Shobo, 1990), pp. 23–5.

49 David Arase, "Japanese Policy toward Democracy and Human Rights in Asia," *Asian Survey* 33, no. 10 (October 1993), pp. 935–52.

50 For more formal presentation of the hypothesis, prediction, and model utilized for hypothesis testing, see Hoshino, "Three Models of the Foreign Economic Aid Allocation."

51 The general criteria for selecting the sample of developing countries are: culturally non-European, politically non-Communist, economically non-industrialized, and geographically located in Asia, Africa, or Latin America. Communist countries or national liberation movements are excluded from the sample mainly because of the lack of data. I plan to include Communist countries in the future analysis. For sample and data sources for sample selection, see ibid.

52 D.A. Goulet, "Development for What?", *Comparative Political Studies* 1 (1968), p. 299.

53 GND: Development need in terms of GNP per capita is measured by a proportional difference between the level of target GNP per capita (approximation by the lowest per capita GNP among DAC countries being 100 percent) and the level of real achievement by the country. Data Source: World Bank, *The World Table 1995* (Washington, DC: World Bank, 1995).

   POP: Population size of a recipient. Data Source: UNESCO, *Statistical Yearbook* (UNESCO).

   PQL: Physical quality of life is measured as a proportional difference between the level of the target's physical quality of life (an approximation where the average lowest life expectancy and literacy rates among DAC countries is 100 percent) and the level of real achievement by the country. Data Source: UNDP, *Human Development Report* (Oxford: Oxford University Press); UN, *Statistical Yearbook* (New York: United Nations).

54 MPW: Security interest is a self-preservation concern of sovereignty over land, people, and wealth, which is satisfied by using military measures, showing these intentions, or concluding military treaties with other actors in the international system. It is measured as the level of relative military power of the country: an average of the country's military expenditure as a proportion of the world total military expenditure and the country's size of military personnel as a proportion of the world total military personnel. Data Source: IISS, *The Military Balance* (London: IISS).

   TRD: Trade interest is a benefit which is gained through bilateral export and import. It is the acquisition of foreign exchange and products so vital to internal development. Trade interest is measured by the total amount of the bilateral trade as a proportion of the country's world trade amount. Data Source: IMF, *Direction of Trade* (Washington, DC: IMF).

   RES: Resource maintenance is the level of importance of the country as a resource provider for the donor. It is measured as a proportion gained by dividing the total amount of Japanese import from the country as a proportion of Japanese total import by the total amount of the country's export as a proportion of the world total export. Data Source: Ibid.

MRK: Export market access is the level of importance of the country as an export market for the donor. It is measured as a proportion gained by dividing the total amount of Japanese export to the country as a proportion of Japanese total export by the total amount of the country's import as a proportion of the world total import. Data Source: Ibid.

11

HUMAN RIGHTS PROBLEMS AND CURRENT SINO-AMERICAN RELATIONS

Zhu Feng

Zhu Feng *is a professor at Peking University in China. He pulls no punches in this essay in which he charges the United States with blame for the deterioration of relations between the United States and China. Zhu Feng describes in detail how, in his view, the American emphasis on human rights has undermined the promise and the potential benefits of Sino-American relations. He is convinced that US human rights policy will fail, and, meanwhile, the American commitment to human rights continues to sabotage opportunities for bilateral cooperation. Zhu Feng's answer to the question about how to find common ground is for the United States to drop its criticism of human rights abuses in China. For a different view, see Michael Sullivan's analysis in Chapter 6.*

INTRODUCTION

Since the 1990s, human rights have been a fundamental problem perplexing Sino-American relations. The divergence of the two sides' views over this issue has obstructed the normal process of bilateral relations, as well as increasing the complexity of a whole range of other areas. Trade, arms exports, matters involving Taiwan, and attempts to repair the bilateral relationship by means of high-level political consultations, and so on, have all suffered from this disagreement over human rights. The intensity of disputes over issues of human rights has grown to the point where the whole nature of the Sino-American relationship involves suspicion and instability.

While problems in the bilateral relationship are already numerous, there is at present the possibility of a further escalation towards confrontation and a deterioration in the relationship: Taiwan is one example. Since March 1996, American and Chinese policy towards Taiwan has become a focus of world politics. Yet compared with any other issue in the Sino-American relationship, the conflict over human rights has more potential to make trouble. What is more, the shadow of this conflict can be seen, directly or indirectly, behind all other problems in the relationship. Even in negotiations between the US and China on China's entry into the world market, a matter which is almost purely concerned with economics, we can perceive elements which have to do with human rights.

As things are at the moment, it is hard to see an end to the disagreement and confrontation between the two sides over human rights. If there is to be any improvement in the relationship, there must be a renewal of sober consideration of this serious problem. This essay tries to analyze the manifestations, effects, and influences of the human rights problem in Sino-American relations.

HUMAN RIGHTS PROBLEMS IN SINO-AMERICAN RELATIONS

Human rights problems in the Sino-American relationship are entirely the result of actions taken by the US government. Since the Reagan government, US presidents have all made "concern for human rights" part of their China policy. There are many factors which have helped to bring about the inclusion of human rights in the bilateral relationship. In the 1980s, the main reason was the international background: there was a drop in the degree of confrontation between the US and the USSR after Gorbachev took power, and the new directions implemented by the USSR gave the US reason to push for similar "democratization" in China. Moreover, China had a wave of "liberalization" in the 1980s. The first serious confrontation between China and the US over human rights was in 1987, when China took action to control an incident involving Tibetan splittists. Before the June 4th Incident in 1989, the US exercised a policy of "concern for human rights," which was out of tune with the normal process of the bilateral relationship but certainly did not seriously impede it. [*Editor's note*: The June 4th Incident refers to the violent suppression by the Chinese government of the student-led protests of the spring of 1989 in which several hundred people were killed.] After the June 4th Incident, the Bush administration took the lead in implementing Western political and economic sanctions against China, and the human rights conflict entered the policy domain in the bilateral relationship. In the 1990s, the concern for human rights in China has become increasingly an important, concrete, long-term policy choice. The Clinton administration has clearly laid out human rights as one of the three most important issues in the bilateral relationship, alongside arms sales and the question of Taiwan.

Specific human rights problems in the current Sino-American relationship can be seen in the following five areas:

1 *The US openly supports the activities of Chinese dissidents*, in China and overseas, and asks that China treat these dissidents according to Western human rights

values and standards, and that it implement broader political and civil liberties. To this end, the US has not only provided asylum to dissidents, as well as to criminal elements who vainly attempt to overthrow the Chinese government; it has also given "green cards" to 18,000 Chinese students studying abroad on the grounds that they may "suffer political persecution on their return to China"; and it has used diplomatic occasions to give aid and support to dissidents, grossly interfering in China's legal punishment of a variety of people who have violated Chinese law. In January 1994, for example, John Shattuck, Assistant Secretary of State for Democracy, Human Rights, and Labor, openly met with Wei Jingsheng in Beijing. During his official meetings in China, Shattuck presented a list of names of dissidents with the request that the Chinese government release them or permit them to leave the country. In 1995, the US openly criticized China for Wei's arrest and trial, and asked for his release. In December 1996, Anthony Lake, Assistant to the President for National Security Affairs, and numerous other senior officials of the Department of State met with and openly rendered assistance to Wei's sister. [*Editor's note*: Wei Jingsheng was released from prison and put on a plane for the United States in November 1997.]

2 The US openly attacks China's human rights record in the international arena, and actively belittles and criticizes China through multilateral channels. The Department of State makes unrestrained attacks on China's human rights situation in its human rights report, published at the beginning of every year. Since 1992, the US, along with other Western countries, has tried hard to pass a resolution at the UN Human Rights Commission criticizing China's human rights record and requesting China to abide by international human rights standards. After one such attempt by the US in March 1995 failed, it once again, in January 1996, announced that it would adopt methods similarly hostile towards China, at the 52nd UN Human Rights Commission's meeting. John Shattuck has hinted that this was one of the methods suggested by President Clinton in spring 1994 in an attempt to solve Chinese human rights problems through multilateral channels. The UN Fourth World Women's Conference, held in Beijing in September 1995, was called a "successful" conference by the then US Ambassador to the UN, Madeleine Albright.[1] First Lady Hillary Clinton, however, attacked China at the meeting, without naming it specifically, for activities, such as compulsory abortions and the suppression of religion beliefs, which violate human rights. Since 1990, the US has suspended its donation to the UN Fund for Population Activities, claiming to be unwilling for its donation to be used by the UNFPA, which supports China's family planning policy, to further China's hard work in this area.

3 The US mass media spare no effort in their deliberate and one-sided "exposure" of China's human rights problems, even to the point of distorting the facts. Maltreatment of political prisoners, the removal for transplant of organs from convicts sentenced to death, the oppression and slaughter of Tibetan lamas, purposefully allowing children in orphanages to die, all the above were reported as "facts" and spread like wildfire in the US. It would seem that China's human rights situation is extremely black. The US government also adds fuel to the flames by encouraging these reports. In June 1995, Wu Hongda (Harry Wu) was arrested by the Chinese government for illegal entry into the country, and eventually released and expelled from the country in response to American pressure. The US government reported that China "had made no progress" in the area of human rights.

4 *The US applies a "linkage" principle in its bilateral relations with China.* Although, in May 1994, Clinton announced an unconditional renewal of China's Most Favored Nation trade status (MFN) and "de-linked" MFN and human rights, this certainly does not mean that the US has forsaken the linkage principle.

At present, there are two aspects to the linkage principle. First, there is extensive linkage of human rights with economic relations. James Sasser, the new US Ambassador to China, has declared without reservation that when America does business in China, it is not merely selling goods or opening factories, but bringing along US values, customs, and culture as well. He proposes that, in this way, Chinese will come to understand American thinking about human rights. The US has thus linked its human rights policy towards China with the broad economic contact it has with China today, and business circles are being made a part of the implementation of US human rights policy.

The second aspect of this linkage principle is the continuous linking of human rights with bilateral relations. After the June 4th Incident, the US unilaterally suspended high-level contacts with China. This suspension ended in 1992, but conflict over human rights continues to obstruct the process of bilateral political relations. Moreover, that China's human rights situation "lacks distinct improvement" has become a basis for the US to apply tougher policy. Around May and June 1995, Sino-American relations deteriorated rapidly because of Taiwan's President Lee Teng-hui's visit to the US. In July, the US House of Representatives passed the China Policy Act of 1995, which asked for China's human rights situation to be put under closer surveillance. Since 1996, some members of Congress have appealed for a "relinking" of China's MFN status with human rights to express their concerns about Wei Jingsheng and other jailed Chinese dissidents. Some people in the US government have suggested linking China's human rights record to US support for China's entry into the World Trade Organization.

By the end of 1996, the US had still not lifted many of the economic sanctions put in place after June 4th, such as the suspension of arms sales, postponed transferral of high technology with both military and civilian applications, and opposition to aid to China from international financial organizations. In fact, the principle of linkage in human rights still exists in Sino-American relations.

5 *Channels have been established for bilateral dialogue on human rights problems, but these dialogues have encountered great difficulties from the US side.* The seventh round

of talks was held on January 13–15, 1995 in Beijing, but because of President Lee Teng-hui's June 1995 visit to the US and the subsequent Chinese missile exercises around Taiwan, the human rights dialogue was suspended. Bilateral relations slipped to their lowest point since the establishment of diplomatic relations in 1979. Since the end of the missile exercises in March 1966, however, Sino-American relations have gradually improved. US Vice-President Gore's visit to China, in particular, helped to prepare the way for PRC President Jiang Zemin's state visit to the US in October 1997. The dialogue between the two sides was resumed for the purpose of creating a good atmosphere for the Jiang–Clinton meeting. China's return to the table showed that the Chinese government has adopted an active and constructive attitude towards the disagreements over human rights, aiming to promote mutual understanding and communication and to resolve issues in dispute. The problem is that China's adherence to dialogue instead of confrontation and interference to resolve human rights disputes is not taken into account by the American side. Despite the fact that these government-level dialogues are taking place, the US is still not satisfied. The US has continued to support nongovernmental organizations such as Human Rights Watch and Amnesty International, and Chinese dissident organizations like Human Rights in China in their vilification of China through their media and publications. Meanwhile, the US requests China to stop its jamming of Voice of America, while at the same time it increases its broadcasting time and its power. In addition, the Clinton administration in 1995 established Radio Free Asia with an allocation of ten million dollars, doing its best to make China into a country with no defense against American attacks on its way of thinking and ideology.

Bilateral dialogues on human rights problems have in fact done nothing to ameliorate the conflict over human rights. The Vice-President has met the Dalai Lama informally, thereby giving support to the movement for human rights and freedom in Tibet. Some in the US Congress even threatened to recognize Tibet as an independent country and dispatch an ambassador. In 1992, the Congress passed the US–Hong Kong Policy Act, calling for the President to show his interest in human rights and freedom in Hong Kong. After Human Rights Watch published a report distorting the Three Gorges Dam project in China, the US government announced in October 1995 that owing to environmental and human rights problems, the US would not take part in the construction.[2] The human rights reports issued by the Department of State continue to censure China for "serious human rights problems," and the White House, heedless of protests from its Chinese counterpart, appointed a high-ranking official to be a coordinator for Tibetan affairs in early November, just at the end of President Jiang's visit to the US.

ORIGIN OF THE HUMAN RIGHTS PROBLEMS

Since the 1990s, the US has launched aggressive human rights offensives in bilateral relations and has deliberately suppressed and attacked China. This is the basic cause of the conflict over human rights in current Sino-American relations. China is by and large in a defensive situation.[3] What impels the US, in its bilateral diplomatic relations with China, to be so severe in raising human rights problems? Is US policy towards China inevitably linked to human rights?

A point of view quite widespread in the US is that attention to human rights reflects a traditional morality in American foreign policy. Originating from Christian beliefs, American democracy and democratic institutions, and the spirit of a freely founded state, these values and standards have resulted in a national mission for democracy and freedom.[4] The concrete expression of this mission is a long-standing idealism. This traditional idealist stance in US foreign policy impels the government to "respect and promote" basic human rights, which constitutes a fundamental belief of the American people and of US foreign policy.

One might infer from this that promoting respect for, and guaranteeing, human rights, as well as protecting so-called "legal and moral" principles, would become a "key strength" of US foreign policy. Only if the US government holds high the banner of human rights, and returns to basic beliefs concerning human rights, can its foreign policy be powerful.[5] This sort of theory became the basis for the well-known "human rights diplomacy" of the Carter administration, which tried hard to use it to restore domestic morale weakened by the Vietnam War, gain domestic support for American foreign policy by moral strength, and strengthen strategic opposition to the Soviet Union.

In the late 1980s, Joseph Nye, a well-known professor of political science at Harvard University, further developed this theory with his concept of "soft power." He holds that influences on world affairs are not confined to military and economic forces. The US government can also utilize ideas and values to gain power in carrying out foreign policy. Appealing to ideas and values not only fosters domestic and international support but can also win the confidence of the public. Therefore, it is a "soft power" that stands side by side with military and economic power.[6] Although Nye himself holds the view that human rights problems should be placed after strategic and economic considerations, his idea represents American diplomatic thinking since the 1980s. Not only has Nye's theory been accepted, he also briefly became an important member of the Clinton administration.

Even in the US, though, there is criticism of giving priority to human rights in US foreign policy. Critics argue that an overemphasis on human rights may not be in the national interest, and may even confuse the question of what the real national interest is. Meanwhile, US human rights diplomacy cannot avoid interfering in other countries' internal affairs, which is very dangerous.[7] George Kennan and Henry Kissinger, great masters of realism, have both been unequivocally opposed to placing emphasis on human rights in US diplomacy.

One dominant point of view, however, does at least recognize that American foreign policy is always a combination of idealism and realism. Professor Stanley Hoffmann thinks that two strands of thought can be detected in American foreign policy: "moralism" and "self-interest," which sometimes conflict but otherwise coexist.[8] The specific policy implications of this duality in US foreign affairs are that US policy will clearly manifest moral principles, using human rights diplomacy to "benefit the world"; and that a close watch on America's own interests will be kept, to prevent human rights diplomacy from undermining the realistic pursuit of national interests.[9] Summing up the human rights diplomacy of the Carter, Reagan, and Bush administrations, the policies and realization of human rights diplomacy have been further developed. Following the example of the Carter administration, human rights were given a prominent position in foreign relations, reflecting a stress on moral traditions and responsibility in US foreign policy, while at the same time in the Reagan and Bush administrations, a strongly instrumental character was evident, allowing broader foreign policy goals to be met by means of human rights diplomacy.[10]

Consequently, conflict over human rights in Sino-American relations will inevitably occur. Apart from the US tendency towards hegemony and power politics, the conflict is linked to various specific characteristics of US foreign policy.[11]

In the first decade of normalization of Sino-American relations, there were no sharp conflicts. Human rights seemed to play a neglected and dispensable role in formulating policy towards China. A conspicuous example was that, despite the existence of the Jackson–Vanik Amendment, which restricts the terms under which the US can grant Most Favored Nation trading status, China's MFN status was renewed each year. The June 4th Incident, however, became a turning point for human rights problems in Sino-American relations, due to prejudice and unrealistic reports from the US and Western governments, which then imposed various unreasonable sanctions on China.[12] But it would be a mistake to consider June 4th, a date which many Americans still cannot forget, as basically the only reason that the US got tough towards China on human rights problems.

The Bush administration acted with restraint as far as possible, and thus maintained the stability of the status quo in the bilateral relationship.[13] In May 1991, President Bush vetoed the Congress's resolution on conditionally extending China's MFN status, so that normal bilateral political, economic, trade, and cultural contacts were enhanced. The fact that the two sides reached an agreement on market entry permission in early 1992 provided a rationale for both sides not to place human rights at the center of their relationship.

Nevertheless, late in the Bush administration human rights problems in Sino-American relations changed from "quiet diplomacy" into "quarrel diplomacy." The Bush administration claimed that the cornerstone of American policy towards China was to encourage China's respect for human rights, and undertook a series of steps to put pressure on China. These included requests for the release of political offenders, an end to Chinese jamming of Voice of America broadcasts, and more attention to be paid to the so-called "human rights situation in Tibet." Despite this, Bush still faced domestic attacks on his human rights policy towards China. Bill Clinton criticized Bush for coddling Chinese dictators, and swore to launch stronger human rights initiatives if he was elected president.

Upon taking office, Clinton and his administration ineptly handled the bilateral relationship, and further escalated the Sino-American confrontation over human rights. For example, Clinton provoked Beijing by demanding to search the Chinese ship *Yinhe*, thought to be transporting chemical weapons components to Iran, but which turned out to be carrying nothing of the sort. The administration further assailed China for the use of prison labor to manufacture export goods – a practice, China subsequently demonstrated, engaged in by the United States itself.

On May 26, 1993, Clinton signed an administrative order to attach conditions to the annual extension of China's MFN status, thereby breaking the implicit understanding of all previous American governments since the normalization of bilateral relations not to let human rights affect regular economic and trade relations. This policy did not last long – Clinton reversed it himself a year later, "unlinking" trade and human rights. But his attempt to link human rights to MFN provides an important marker for judging the nature of current Sino-American relations: namely, the former "realist" mainstream has been losing influence, and those factors that had facilitated compromise and the normalization of bilateral relations (peaceful coexistence of states with different systems, cooperation according to strategic interests between big powers, and a stable working relationship between the two sides) have been replaced by new factors. Although these new factors were not yet very clear in 1993, the human rights offensive was undoubtedly one of them.

The problem is that before 1989 there was not a definite human rights agenda. This led the Carter administration to practice a vigorous human rights diplomacy, but since it did not add any human rights issues into the Sino-American relationship, it was criticized for "double standards." Reaganism – the Reagan administration's opposition to leftist dictatorships – did not directly target China. The simple fact is that China and the US have different social systems, historical traditions, economic levels, cultural environments, and values. Thus from theory to practice, it is very difficult to compare the two countries' human rights. The founders of normalized bilateral relations have never forgotten this. Today's Sino-American relations have come about only by seeking common ground while at the same time maintaining difference. Why, then, have human rights problems become a conspicuous "disaster" in bilateral relations since the 1990s?

Professor Jack Donnelly, an advocate of substantive diplomacy, has carefully analyzed the relationship between human rights diplomacy and effective practical means of policy. He suggests that in order to extricate US foreign policy from a predicament of idealism (words without deeds) and realism (deeds inconsistent with words), and reduce the difficulty of coordination between human rights and other foreign policy goals, a series of feasible policy means should be developed.[14] These would include open diplomacy, placing human rights conditions on foreign aid, and what he calls "positive nonintervention." Positive nonintervention – "thorough noninvolvement with regimes guilty of major systematic violations of human rights" – is to enforce a tougher human rights policy and to utilize international economic relations to exert pressure in order to "reduce the frequency with which human rights concerns are sacrificed to other policy objectives."[15] Donnelly's theory can be used to explain the human rights offensives of the 1990s, especially in the case of the Clinton administration.

US HUMAN RIGHTS DIPLOMACY IN THE 1990S

Comparing the US human rights policy towards China in the 1990s with that of the 1970s and 1980s, there are noticeable changes in the choice of realism or idealism in key policies, and in the balance and method of implementing policies. There were several reasons that impelled the US to adjust its human rights policy towards China:

1 The US so far has not formed an accurate, careful, and mature strategy towards China. In the 1970s, a common strategic opposition to the Soviet Union encouraged rapid Sino-American *rapprochement.* With the Cold War over, this has faded away. As far as the US is concerned, the West won the Cold War and hence a dominant position in the world. If common security needs brought China and the US closer, the end of the Cold War has rapidly dissolved their sense of common purpose. A great nation which strives for world dominance and a "disobedient" regional power like China find a huge space between them when considering what their common interests are. Problems like arms sales, trade, Taiwan and Hong Kong issues, human rights, and regional security have appeared and expanded in this space.

China's rapid rise has deepened America's anxiety concerning policy adjustment towards China. China's economic development provides more market opportunities for the US, but China will probably become a strong economic competitor. China's increase of strength is a factor in regional security but also a "threat" to the US security interest. China's domestic stability will benefit peace and cooperation in the Asia-Pacific region, but it does not accord with the rapid democratization desired by the US. These suspicions, in a US that is still strongly ideological, arose from increasingly different interests and perceptions, and in 1995 developed into a clamor demanding that a "containment" policy towards China be put into place. Professor Harry Harding regards the strong suspicion in current Sino-American relations as an important reason for their fragility.[16]

Formerly dominated by the single factor of the Soviet Union, Sino-American relations have become a complicated combination of various conflicts and interests, and are thus more vulnerable to the widespread influence of international change and domestic factors. The intensification of the Taiwan issue is an example. Undoubtedly, the human rights differences were compounded by a long list of other issues troubling the relationship, so it was not merely the human rights offensive that was responsible for worsening the Sino-US relations in the 1990s. However, disputes over human rights have eroded the foundation of trust on which the relationship might have been established, and have made it quite difficult for Americans to determine whether China is friend or foe.

Against this background and the lack of definite direction in post-Cold War US foreign policy, the US government has been unable to formulate a mature and effective strategy towards China. The main indications of this are: (1) its difficulty in establishing a suitable basis for Sino-American relations; (2) vacillation on specific policies in the bilateral relationship; (3) a lack of authority and political resources needed to improve relations; (4) ambiguity in perception of China's image; (5) uncertainty concerning the basic goals of China policy; and (6) a lack of credibility for US China policy, both at home and abroad. Even Joseph Nye, when he was an Assistant Secretary of Defense, admitted that there existed a strategic ambiguity in US policy towards China.

By the middle of 1996, however, the Clinton administration had begun to reevaluate the role of China in international relations and to reassess US China policy. Alarmed by what seemed to be a downward spiral in the Sino-American relationship, Clinton took various measures to limit the damage and to prevent China policy from becoming "a political football" in the 1996 elections. Clinton and leading officials of his government repeatedly emphasized that a policy of engagement with China was the better choice for American national interests, especially when the relationship with China was one of the most important strategic relations in the world. Clinton called for building a partnership with China for the next century.

2 The end of the Cold War fostered an over-optimistic mood of human rights interventionism in America. The end of the Cold War is regarded by many Americans as a victory for Western values and ways of thinking, and the US government has frequently heralded the significance of this ideological victory. The Gulf War in 1991 is also described as a triumph of democracy over autocracy. Both events stimulated domestic enthusiasm for making human rights a goal in foreign policy. President Bush liked to boast that the US had become "the hope of the new world" because of its promotion of freedom and democracy worldwide.

The US has developed a deep-rooted perception of the relationship between democracy, freedom, and security interests proceeding from a view of its own system and historical culture. It believes that there can be no war between democratic states, and that the foundation of America's existence is the combination of a democratic system and a free market economy. Only a worldwide democracy and freedom can produce stability and security. From this point of view, the US human rights mission is a means to this end.

Although the US itself is a pluralistic society, it does not tolerate a pluralization involving political systems and values at the global level. A policy of peaceful evolution directed towards socialist countries is a natural result of this idea; at the same time, it naturally produces a resort to human rights diplomacy in US foreign policy. All previous US administrations have gone along with this to some extent, to gain political strength and authority, and the Carter and Reagan administrations' human rights diplomacy was no exception. In comparison with their predecessors, Bush and Clinton have more understanding of what they are doing, and have had more opportunities and excuses – the "examples" of drastic change in the former Soviet Union and Eastern Europe, and the domestic instability in China caused by "liberalization." They have thus emphasized human rights as a policy objective, as a rationale for government behavior, and to build spiritual strength for an America in relative decline and in the midst of reorganizing its world strategy. In this way the US can turn China into a second Soviet Union and realize its dreams of achieving global democracy and a free market economy, and an end to Communism. In 1992, the Bush administration stressed in its national security strategy that the US would build a world where "political and economic freedom, human rights, and democratic systems could flourish and develop." One of the three national goals Clinton put forward upon assuming office was "to promote democracy and the free market economy" and to pay attention to China's human rights situation.

The disintegration and momentous change in the Soviet Union and Eastern Europe have eliminated any direct security threat to the US. The decline of geopolitics and the balance of power as the guiding ideology of American foreign policy thus became one more excuse for an optimistic human rights interventionism. William Hyland, former editor of *Foreign Affairs*, predicted in the early 1990s that "geopolitical realism is yielding to human rights idealism."[17] Robert L. Bernstein, President of Human Rights Watch, openly advocated "human rights first" and asked the US government to practice a more active and provocative human rights policy towards developing countries, including China.[18]

3 The US Congress takes a hostile stand towards China. Since the 1970s, the US Congress has always been a force behind US human rights policy and interventionism. The strong human rights offensives of the US government are closely tied to the rigid power politics of Congress.

As early as the Nixon administration, the House of Representatives set up a special committee, led by Rep. Ronald Frazer, and held hearings related to foreign policy and human rights, which led to the 1973 Amendment of Article 116 in the Foreign Assistance Act. This amendment forbids the US government from aiding countries that continually violate established international human rights principles.[19] In 1976, Congress again revised the Arms Export Control Act, prohibiting security aid and arms sales to countries that violate human rights. In 1990, Congress passed a law requiring yearly legislative evaluation of Article 582 of the Foreign Assistance Act. The Department of State must annually submit a list of countries that continually and extensively violate human rights, and report to Congress how American foreign aid promotes human rights in recipient countries, as well as how the US itself avoids being involved in human rights violations in these countries.

Moreover, in 1977, the US Congress stipulated that US administrative representatives in international financial organizations should not provide credits or any other kind of international financial support to countries that violate human rights, unless this support can be directly applied to improve the human rights conditions of citizens in recipient countries.[20] It also requested the Department of State to submit open reports on human rights conditions in recipient countries, and later expanded this to include all UN members. All American ambassadors are required to gather information and materials on human rights problems in their respective countries.

The US Congress is pressured by human rights groups which had finally begun to lobby against China in the late 1980s. In turn, it was under the pressure of Congress that President Bush imposed sanctions on the Chinese government in the aftermath of Tiananmen. The US Congress plays an undeniable role in implementing interventionist policy towards China. On the one hand, it has frequently legislated to tie human rights intervention into practical foreign policy; on the other hand, members of Congress often use coercive measures, acting or legislating to strengthen the US interventionist attitude on human rights. Members of Congress judge Sino-American relations in an antiquated, intensely ideological way, and are constantly writing about China's human rights problems. At present, Congress is the most capricious and inflammable area in current Sino-American relations. Support for Taiwan and criticism of China's human rights by Congressional Democrats and Republicans have reminded people of the intense anti-China feelings in the Cold War period.

THE INFLUENCE OF THE HUMAN RIGHTS CONFLICT ON SINO-AMERICAN RELATIONS

Strong offensives from the US in the 1990s on Chinese human rights problems have had an extraordinarily negative influence on Sino-American relations, which up until President Jiang's state visit to the US in 1997 had sunk to their lowest level since 1972. The effects have been as follows:

1 *The conflict aggravates the level of distrust in Sino-American relations.* In the 1970s, the strategic relationship was founded primarily on surmounting the differences of systems and cultures, so domestic political factors did not count as fundamental problems. American human rights offensives towards China have essentially broken through the realist "taboo" against linking foreign policy and internal affairs, undermining the foundation of Sino-American cooperation and correspondingly breaking with the realist mainstream dating from the era of Nixon, Kissinger, Brzezinski, and Haig.

Human rights problems are not the same as ordinary disputes over policy. Trade and nuclear technology proliferation problems can be resolved by consultation on concrete policies because they only involve part of the national interest. Human rights confrontation involves the essential identity of the Chinese national interest, and is the result of two changes in America's understanding of the China issue and in the nature of the bilateral relationship. These two changes reveal a US mistrust of China, and its dissatisfaction with current Chinese policy and its policy-makers. Behind human rights diplomacy can be seen the US suspicion and scorn not only for the legitimacy of Chinese government authority and behavior, but also for the very foundation of its national power.

China's apparent indifference to pressure from the US on human rights problems is seen as a challenge to firmly held American values and the American spirit. Therefore, divergence on human rights between the two countries is not simply a matter of what kind of human rights standards to apply or whether human rights deserve respect; it concerns fundamental differences in the political stands of the two sides. The existing distance between the US and China on human rights problems is hard to overcome, and meanwhile each goes its own way in high-level dialogues.

As a result, both countries now lack an appropriate environment and atmosphere to make policy decisions that might improve bilateral relations, and the emotional component of policy-making continues to grow. China is more and more wary of a "new Cold War" policy from the US. While Chinese estimations of US policy towards China are changing, increasingly the judgment is that the US aims to "contain" China's power, to split China, and to keep it weak for ever. In the US, major debates over China issues have been under way since 1995. In political and academic circles, almost every official, expert, and scholar who has ever been involved with China has participated in the debates.

Various policy proposals have arisen, one after another. These fall into three categories: the first advocates a tougher policy towards China and stresses containment; the second juxtaposes containment and engagement; the third wants to continue the present "engagement" policy while strengthening constructive aspects of the relationship. The US responded to the "Taiwan crisis" in February and March 1996 with a "clear strategy and ambiguous tactics," which shows that in the current political and media climate, the uncertainty of its policy is increasing. In the near future, one can predict that each side will operate more by guesswork, and by trial and error, and this will deepen the existing mistrust.

2 *Conflict further increases the fragility of bilateral relations.* Dr Harry Harding holds that US policy since the end of the Cold War has lacked a comprehensive international strategy, let alone one for China. If the US had any kind of strategy towards China, it would want to draw it into international society, not exclude, contain or attempt to divide it.[21] However, this strategy would have a hard time withstanding the US human rights offensives against China. The fragility of Sino-American relations is especially glaring with respect to human rights differences.

In the first place, the US frequently makes an issue of human rights problems and thus destroys the continuity of policy towards China. There are certainly a variety of voices that can be heard in the current American human rights offensives towards China. Business interests, represented by the Department of Commerce, would like to see consideration of whether human rights should be an important agenda item in the Sino-American relationship. They hold that in expanding economic connections with China, "some of our human rights goals will be accomplished."[22] Diplomats in the Department of State who deal directly with bilateral relations, preferring to avoid endless bickering and to maintain a level of integrity in the relationship, also hope for a degree of easing up on human rights problems.

However, the political force represented by Congress shows signs of being reluctant to moderate the conflict over human rights. This reluctance of Congress is due to its complex environment, motives inspired by a variety of interests, and a rigid insistence on its claim to be the elected representatives of the people, whose will it transmits. A letter signed by forty members of Congress was sent to Secretary of State Warren Christopher in August 1996 after Anthony Lake's visit to China, which expressed their deep concern about the US government's turning away from a human rights critique, and strongly advocated that the administration keep up the pressure on China. The problem is that, to a certain extent, it is Congress that dominates in policy-making towards China. Even though there are various opinions in Congress, Congressional representatives elected through free elections often consider human rights and American values as focal points.[23] In recent years, whenever "Beijing violates human rights," Congress almost always threatens to withhold China's preferential trade rights. Moreover, the US Congress not only keeps a close eye on Chinese domestic human rights situations, but it also disturbs American–Chinese relations by proposing legislation with respect to Hong Kong, Taiwan, and Tibet, showing that human rights have become an excuse by which Congress is able to exhibit its obvious hostility to China. This kind of changeable diplomacy not only obstructs long-term bilateral business relations, but also causes incessant shocks to US policy towards China. Without continuity, American policy towards China cannot be extricated from its current predicament.

Second, the US human rights offensive towards China is not a realistic way to lead China into international society. The main "reason" for US criticism is that the Chinese human rights situation does not accord with generally accepted international standards. Nevertheless, the postwar international human rights movement led by the UN, as well as various international human rights laws, while reiterating a new beginning for universal human rights, at the same time allow every country to adopt specific steps to advance the protection of human rights, according to their own conditions. According to Article 57 of the UN Charter, "All member states promise to cooperate with the UN through common and individual actions" in order to "accomplish universal respect to and observance of human rights and the basic freedom of all mankind."[24] This is an international law which the US takes as the basis for its concern with Chinese human rights. However, this law has never granted any country the right to interfere for whatever reason with another country's sovereign rights. On the contrary, it is the US human rights offensives towards China that have repeatedly "humiliated" China in international society.[25] How does the US expect China to enter the "international society" approved of by the US, given the cost to China of this "humiliation"?

Third, the US human rights offensive towards China is in itself an unbalanced policy. Professor Peter Baehr holds that "the goal of American human rights policy is either to create a better world or to satisfy its own national security and economic interests."[26] The US human rights policy towards China is also intended to meet its security and economic needs. But when this is the case, although the US speaks more sweetly, its national interest motives are more obvious. In essence, the US human rights offensive towards China is an American-style package of appeals for its own interests.

And yet China has carried out reforms and has opened to the outside; it values the Sino-American relationship, and wishes to develop friendly bilateral relations on a basis of equality and mutual benefit. As for human rights, China has its own problems which are not easy for it to talk about. Why does the US still want to adopt policies which damage the sound and steady development of Sino-American relations? The fact is that human rights is one of the three pillars of US national security.[27] The US concept of security and economic interest is closely tied to human rights, and from this standpoint, China is nothing but a dissident. China implements incremental reforms and is unwilling to cozy up to Western-style freedom and democracy, which makes the US exercise its high-pressure human rights policy to force China to "knuckle under." This is why the US repeatedly asks China to accelerate the process of political reforms.

Any foreign policy is strongly motivated by the national interest, yet it must be coordinated with the appropriate policy methods, in order to establish some kind of balance in satisfying both foreign policy goals and feasible policy measures. The US human rights offensive towards China is basically an unbalanced policy in that it cannot make its strong national-interest motives coincide with satisfactory policy effects. Though the US feels good in pursuing this policy, Dr Kissinger has pointed out that whether a policy is good or not depends not on whether one feels good about it or not, but on its effect.[28] China's tenacious opposition to the many facets of US human rights policy has resulted in a mood of "depression" in the US, and this in turn has prompted US policy-makers to look for other problems in the bilateral relationship. The intensification of the Taiwan issue in recent years is directly connected with this. In 1992, although the Bush administration maintained China's MFN status, China's principled stand on human rights problems could not satisfy US human rights diplomacy, and the US then adopted other stern measures against China.[29] These measures included the first visit to Taiwan by a US cabinet-level official since the normalization of Sino-American relations and the ratification of F-16 aircraft sales to Taiwan. Similarly, the Clinton administration wants to maintain the status quo on the Taiwan Straits; and yet, owing to its obvious interests in Taiwan, and its sympathy and support for "democracy" there, it attempts to contain China by raising the position of Taiwan. At the end of May 1995, the US government approved Lee Teng-hui's visit to America. Although from the point of view of the US this demonstrated a more flexible political and economic policy towards China, it contravened basic principles made clear in the three communiqués and severely impaired Sino-American relations. [*Editor's note*: The three communiqués are joint statements concluded by the Chinese and American governments, negotiated and signed by the Nixon, Carter, and Reagan administrations, which constitute the basic principles upon which contemporary Sino-American relations are founded.] Joseph Nye admitted that human rights problems lead the whole Sino-American relationship into a complex and unstable situation.[30]

3 The US human rights offensives towards China make it difficult to orient bilateral relations. US officials have emphasized time and again the paramount importance of the Sino-American bilateral relationship to the US, and thus to the world. The US aims to develop friendly and constructive relations with China. However, the Clinton administration has formally adopted a policy towards China of "comprehensive engagement" that confounds its own human rights policy and is full of contradictions. According to explanations from US officials, the engagement strategy does not mean that the US will ignore its differences with China, but rather that the US will resolve them through active communication.

The biggest divergence in matters of human rights is the vehement and unyielding US human rights offensive, which it has no plans to abandon, at least at present. The 1995 Human Rights Report, issued on March 6, 1996, listed China's human rights record as one of the "worst" in the world. On

February 28, the Clinton administration, ignoring China's strong objection, announced that it, along with the European Union, would sponsor a proposal to condemn the Chinese human rights situation at a meeting of the UN Human Rights Commission. The US also sent a diplomatic note to the fifty-three member-states of the Commission, asking for their support for this proposal.[31] These activities can only further worsen bilateral relations, and cannot diminish the differences between the two. It is also incompatible with the language in the "comprehensive engagement" strategy that calls for expanded common interests and the avoidance or reduction to a minimum of conflict.

The engagement strategy requires settling disputes by dialogue, which China has actively responded to. At a 1996 news conference of the Fourth Session of the Eighth People's Congress, Vice-Premier Qian Qichen noted that Sino-American differences over human rights could be settled by dialogue, and not by confrontation. The unbalanced situation with both sides attacking and defending and the overbearing US stance did not, however, provide an appropriate context for a balanced dialogue. Under the present circumstances, there can be no breakthroughs in the Sino-American human rights dialogue. First of all, there is no basis for such a dialogue, because of the wide disparity in each side's views of what constitutes a human rights problem, and of what the aims of bringing human rights into bilateral relations might be. Second, there is no agreement on content. Both sides hold very different views on human rights standards and protection. Third, there is no practical form for dialogue. Given how US policy towards China is affected by domestic policy, diplomatic-level dialogue has no chance of influencing the decision-making process. Fourth, there is a lack of realistic goals. Neither side agrees on whether it is the US which helps to promote Chinese human rights, or China which helps to improve US human rights. Even so, the existing dialogue is a beneficial and constructive channel. Yet to really resolve differences over human rights, the US must first revise its human rights offensive towards China. Human rights confrontation will otherwise remain as a fundamental factor that causes distrust and destroys the stability of bilateral relations. As Nye said after his visit to China in December 1995, human rights "may undermine our basic political dialogue and obstruct the fulfillment of common and long-term interests between us."[32]

The basic reason for the lack of progress in the human rights dialogue can be explained by a problem in Sino-American relations dating from the late 1980s: whether the US considers China as a friend or a foe. Dr Harding's theory of "neither friend nor foe" is very useful to describe the present situation in the relationship: a situation of policy confrontation despite common interests. Yet it is difficult to make a clear distinction between friend and foe on human rights issues. Leaders and policy-makers on both sides need to redefine the nature of Sino-American relations in this regard. Otherwise it will be impossible to end the conflict over human rights and to end its negative influence on the relationship, because it relates to the most sensitive and immediate kinds of problems.

Before the 1990s, definitions of the nature of the Sino-American relationship, such as a "strategic partnership," a "stable working relationship," and so on, were quite constructive, although they were not especially clear, and they never led to intense bilateral political conflict. Now the relationship has moved into an unstable stage of conflict caused by policy readjustment, a deepening in the relationship, and artificially imposed obstacles. Although most of the conflicts have not worsened the international environment or led to any fierce confrontations, the various conflicts themselves have brought Sino-American relations to an impasse, encountering challenges unprecedented since normalization. The key to a settlement of these conflicts lies not in taking particular concrete steps, but rather in first explicating both sides' attitudes, which have become particularly important in determining the nature of the bilateral relationship.

In China's view, to cooperate people have to become friends, since only friends can really cooperate.[33] If the US truly regards China as a friend, why does it press so hard on human rights problems? China hopes the US will adopt a forward-looking attitude and take mutual long-term interests into consideration. But how does one achieve long-term interests without paying attention to immediate interests, which on both sides are most under attack from the US human rights offensive? What is worse, if the US thinks that its immediate interest in its policy towards China is "to use pressure for change," confrontation will be unavoidable not only on human rights but also on other problems. Frank Ching has pointed out that if the US treats China as a friend, so will China; if as an enemy, so also will China treat the US.[34] This point is worthy of some consideration.

Since the middle of 1996, the American administration has adjusted its policy towards China to be more accommodating and to prepare to establish a partnership for the twenty-first century. Preparatory to the exchange of state visits by President Jiang and President Clinton, bilateral relations gradually improved. Meanwhile, China has become more accepting of human rights criticism and has begun to learn to react to the human rights offensive in new ways. A good example is President Jiang Zemin's speech at Harvard in November 1997 during his visit to the US, in which he compared the different concepts of human rights in China and the United States from cultural, historical, and economic perspectives, instead of from political or ideological ones. Moreover, in October 1997, the Chinese government signed the International Covenant on Economic, Social, and Cultural Rights after many years of delay. The exchange of official visits by President Jiang Zemin and President Bill Clinton has provided an opportunity for a fresh start in Sino-American relations.

CONCLUSION

Human rights issues are a hurtful and depressing problem in Sino-American relations: hurtful both because they erode the basis of a cooperative bilateral relationship that has promising long-term prospects, and because they dampen the warm feelings which since the 1970s the Chinese people have developed, with some difficulty, towards the US. This has weakened the Chinese people's enthusiasm for reform in the process of modernization. US opposition to China's bid for the 2000 Olympic Games and its repeated attacks (such as on human rights problems, the Taiwan issue, and China's entry to the WTO) have stirred up Chinese nationalism and made the image of America less attractive for increasing numbers of Chinese. A poll conducted by *China Youth Daily* of young people in Beijing found that 87.1 percent of Chinese youngsters regarded the United States as the most unfriendly country. The newspaper concluded that the results of the poll were "a natural response to US unfriendliness toward China, implying a wakening and development of Chinese self-consciousness."[35] What is depressing is that the US puts itself forward in matters of human rights as a Savior, when its lack of understanding of China is so evident, as are its lack of due respect for China, and its many "hidden" agendas – all of which give cause for reflection and a need to maintain vigilance.

The US is single-handedly responsible for the intensification of the bilateral human rights conflict in the 1990s, reflecting its changed understanding of China since the end of the Cold War and the resulting policy adjustments. This kind of change and adjustment is clearly not yet finished, creating much perplexity and uneasiness in the US. The uneasiness comes from uncertainty about what a rising and powerful China might mean for the US, and what worrisome challenges China's future action might present it with. The perplexity comes from not knowing which of its assumptions and guesses to act on and which to reject, and what policy should be applied in dealing with China. As a result, its human rights offensive towards China has become the only explicit policy measure with a demonstrably large domestic base of political support: it conforms to US foreign policy traditions, takes no really sizeable risks, and moreover has the support of both political parties and of the US public.

All US citizens, whatever their background, needs, or desires, can reach unanimity on matters of human rights and make whatever use of them they want. Given the current unstable and confused state of US policy and American understandings of China, the human rights offensive is of particular value to the US: seen from whatever angle, this policy suits long-term US interests. Moreover, maintaining this offensive can increase its strength in negotiations with China. Therefore, the US human rights offensive will doubtless become part of long-term policy. In December 1995, after China's legal trial of Wei Jingsheng, John Shattuck said that human rights issues held a "very important place" on the agenda of Sino-American relations, and that the US would "double its efforts" to focus on China's human rights.[36] The problem is that current US China policy, which is perplexed and unstable to the point of being prejudiced and overwrought, has an increasingly strong influence on Chinese policy towards the US. Yet this is not the beneficial interaction that the bilateral relationship requires. On the contrary, it will cause distrust which will be difficult to reconcile, and will escalate policy conflict.

The US human rights offensive will never achieve success. It neither integrates the shape and effect of policy, nor can it keep a balance between policy goals and means. The US offensive has only strengthened Chinese rejection and resistance, and the tougher the offensive becomes, so will China's resistance become more intense. US human rights diplomacy resembles its erroneous policy on Taiwan, in severely undermining bilateral relations. Defense Secretary William Perry admitted that an engagement strategy with a core of human rights does not completely succeed, "because China does not want to pursue those reforms implemented in Russia."[37]

The US human rights offensive towards China is in itself inconsistent, and can be no more than a hesitant and vacillating policy. A developing China provides many market opportunities to which the US government cannot be indifferent. In order not to hurt and enrage China excessively, and to construct a positive direction for development, the US must sometimes tone down its line on human rights problems. Congress insisted that President Clinton should boycott the UN Fourth Women's Conference held in China, yet finally Clinton allowed his wife Hillary to make the trip there; Shattuck also clearly stated after Wei Jingsheng's trial that China should not be isolated because of human rights. At present, human rights diplomacy as represented by government departments of business and trade is comparatively "moderate" towards China, asking for an expansion of economic and trade relations and a more central place for them in the US focus on Chinese human rights. But the US government's quieter line on human rights may draw vigorous attacks from ultra-rightists at home. Human Rights Watch, in its report at the end of 1995, attacked the US for sacrificing attention on humanitarian problems to protect its business interests. There is always some member of Congress reminding Clinton of his human rights stand towards China. The ultra-conservative presidential candidate Pat Buchanan attacked Clinton as an immoral salesman for the top Fortune 500 companies. The Clinton administration must proceed according to the situation, often seeking an equilibrium between its national interests and domestic anti-China forces. However, there can be no change in the US government's policy of insistent suppression of China on questions of human rights, and incessant trouble-making in bilateral relations. Clinton's 1996 State of the Union Message quite clearly stated that the US will lead the world in the two areas of "economics and values." Considering that a presidential election was due in 1996, the US could not soften its human rights offensive towards China. There can be no doubt that the quarrels and conflicts between the countries will not easily be calmed as long as the policy continues.

Professor Walter LaFeber, a well-known historian of US–Soviet Union relations, has pointed out in his summary of the history of the Cold War that US foreign policy in the 1990s is faced with the great challenge of how to extricate itself from Alexis de Tocqueville's "problem" dating from 160 years ago.[38] De Tocqueville's research led him to believe that although US democracy was suited to the settlement and development of the American continent, it was not suited to the implementation of foreign policy, which needs continuity, high-level confidentiality, and sufficient concern for the national interest. Democracy in the US has produced considerable inconsistency of public opinion, a people who like to speak out what is on their mind, and individuals who are basically concerned about their self-interest and not the national interest. Consequently, he thought that American democracy might be the world's poorest system for dealing with foreign affairs. Professor LaFeber quoted de Tocqueville to explain that US foreign policy should not be further dominated by domestic factors. The US ought to guard against making too much of its victory in the Cold War, and even less should it think that it may act as it wants, with no restraint, to dominate world affairs. The current US policy towards China shows, unfortunately, that Professor LaFeber's words have gone unheeded.

NOTES

This essay was translated from the original Chinese by Zhang Yan and Anne Gunn.

1 Madeleine Albright, speech on September 18, 1995 at the National Committee on US–China Relations, *Cankao ziliao* [Reference Material] (September 22, 1995), p. 1.
2 "The Three Gorges Dam in China, Forced Resettlement, Suppression of Dissent and Labor Rights Concerns," *Human Rights Watch/Asia Newsletter* 7, no. 2 (Febuary 1995).
3 Andrew J. Nathan, "Human Rights in Chinese Foreign Policy," *China Quarterly* no. 139 (Spring 1994), pp. 622–5.
4 Louis Rene Beres, *Reason and Realpolitik: US Foreign Policy and World Order* (Lexington, MA: Lexington Books, 1994), pp. 79–81.
5 Cyrus R. Vance, "The Human Rights Imperative," *Foreign Policy* no. 63 (Summer 1986), pp. 2–6.
6 Joseph S. Nye, Jr, "Soft Power," *Foreign Policy* no. 80 (Fall 1990), pp. 153–71.
7 Roberta Cohen, "Human Rights Decision Making in the Executive Branch, Some Proposals for a Coordinated Strategy," in Donald P. Kommers and Gilbert D. Loescher, eds, *Human Rights and American Foreign Policy* (Notre Dame, IN: Notre Dame University Press, 1979), p. 217.
8 Stanley Hoffmann, *Primacy or World Order: American Foreign Policy Since the Cold War* (New York: McGraw-Hill, 1978); and *Duties Beyond Borders: On the Limits and Possibilities of Ethical International Politics* (Syracuse, NY: Syracuse University Press, 1981).

9   Peter R. Baehr, *Human Rights and Their Roles in Foreign Policy* (London: Macmillan, 1994), p. 82.
10 Jamar Jacoby, "The Reagan Turnaround on Human Rights," *Foreign Affairs* 64, no. 5 (Summer 1986), pp. 1066–86. David P. Forsythe, "Human Rights in U.S. Foreign Policy: Retrospect and Prospect," *Political Science Quarterly* 105, no. 1 (1990), p. 447.
11 The characteristics of idealism and realism in US foreign policy have been extensively researched by Chinese scholars. See Zi Zhongyun, "Brief Review of Some Characteristics of Postwar US Diplomacy," *Meiguo yanjiu* [American Studies] no. 1 (1988); Wang Jisi, "A 'Strategic Triangle' in US Foreign Policy towards China," *Meiguo yanjiu* no. 2 (1992); Huo Shiliang, "American Idealism and East Asia," *Meiguo yanjiu* no. 2 (1992).
12 James D. Seymour, "Human Rights and the World Response to the 1989 Crackdown in China," *China Information* 4, no. 4 (Spring 1990), pp. 1–14. This article analyzed concrete sanctions in detail.
13 Disputes between the Bush administration and Congress on policy towards China are analyzed in detail in Harry Harding's book, *A Fragile Relationship: The United States and China Since 1972* (Washington, DC: Brookings Institute, 1992).
14 Jack Donnelly, *Universal Human Rights in Theory and Practice* (Ithaca, NY, and London: Cornell University Press, 1989), pp. 241–6.
15 Ibid., p. 246.
16 Harry Harding, "US–China Relations in 1995: How Fragile, How Enduring?" a paper for a conference on Sino-US Economic Relations, sponsored by the Center for Asia-Pacific Studies, Lingnam College, Hong Kong, June 21–3, 1995, pp. 12–16.
17 William G. Hyland, "America's New Course," *Foreign Affairs* 69, no. 2 (Spring 1990), p. 7.
18 Robert L. Bernstein and Richard Dicker, "Human Rights First," *Foreign Policy* no. 94 (Fall 1993), pp. 43–7.
19 Tom Harkin, "Human Rights and Foreign Aid: Forging an Unbreakable Link," in Peter G. Brown and Douglas MacLean, eds, *Human Rights and U.S. Foreign Policy: Principles and Applications* (Lexington, MA: Lexington Books, 1979), p. 17.
20 David P. Forsythe, *Human Rights and U.S. Foreign Policy: Congress Reconsidered* (Gainesville: University of Florida Press, 1988), pp. 1–23.
21 Harding, "US–China Relations in 1995: How Fragile, How Enduring?" p. 9.
22 See the essay by Jeffrey E. Garten, Under Secretary of Commerce, "Power Couples," *New York Times* (January 15, 1996), p. A17.
23 Gerald Solomon, Republican Congressional representative, speech in July 1995, *Cankao ziliao* (October 17, 1995).
24 *An Overview of World Human Rights Law* (Sichuan: People's Publishing House, 1990), p. 938.
25 Nathan, "Human Rights in Chinese Foreign Policy," pp. 635–7.
26 Baehr, *Human Rights and Their Roles in Foreign Policy*, p. 92.
27 Yuan Ming and Fan Shiming, "Post-Cold War American Understanding of the Shape of Chinese Security," *Meiguo yanjiu* no. 4 (1995), p. 17.
28 Henry Kissinger, "On American Policy Towards China: Don't Gamble with National Destiny," *Sunday World News* [Germany] (July 23, 1995). *Cankao ziliao* (July 26, 1995), p. 3.
29 William J. Barnds, "Human Rights and US Policy towards Asia", in James T.H. Tang, ed., *Human Rights and International Relations in the Asia Pacific* (London: Pinter, 1995), p. 79.
30 Joseph Nye before the East Asia and Pacific Affairs Sub-Committee of the US Senate Foreign Relations Committee, *Cankao ziliao* (October 15, 1995), p. 2.

31 Paul Dogfrey, "UN Human Rights Proposal Seems Likely to be Passed," *Dongfang kuaixun* [Eastern Express], Hong Kong (Febuary 29, 1996).
32 Joseph Nye, Jr, speech to the Asia Society, Washington Center, *Cankao ziliao*, (December 16, 1995), p. 7.
33 Jiang Zemin, speech on US–China Relations to the National Committee, October 22, 1995, New York, *Renmin ribao* [People's Daily] (October 23, 1995).
34 Frank Ching, "Welcome China into the World: Washington Should Build a Relationship of Trust with Beijing," *Far Eastern Economic Review* (March 7, 1996), p. 32.
35 See *Zhongguo qingnianbao* [China Youth Daily] (July 22, 1995), p. 1.
36 John Shattuck, at a news conference on December 13, 1995, *Cankao ziliao* (December 13, 1995), pp. 2–3.
37 *Cankao ziliao* (Febuary 2, 1996), p. 3.
38 Walter Lafeber, *America, Russia and the Cold War, 1945–1992* (New York: McGraw-Hill, 1993), p. 354.

12

FROM JUDGE TO PARTICIPANT

The United States as *Champion* of human rights

Daniel W. Wessner

Daniel Wessner *is a lawyer, a social scientist, and an ordained minister. Currently, he is in Hanoi doing research for his PhD dissertation on social and political change in Vietnam. In this final chapter, Wessner, himself an American, assesses the US role as a champion of international human rights. He describes a process of change from the role of "judge" of the human rights performance of other governments to one of "participant" in multilateral human rights covenants. His essay is in part one man's answer to the question: how can the United States presume to criticize the human rights practices of other governments when its own history is marked by the atrocities of slavery, genocide against Native Americans, CIA covert operations, and Vietnam?*

INTRODUCTION

The United States has engaged in international human rights practice in two significantly different ways. This mix is not so much a sign of schizophrenia as one of maturing. Initially as an international judge, the United States traditionally declared human rights legal standards through its foreign policy. This declaratory posture has been both positive and negative. Positively, it has contributed to a growing body of international legal human rights standards and instruments. But as the US government itself has generally abstained from ratifying international human rights covenants, its partici-patory role has been minimal. A double standard incites counterjudgments from various parts of the world, as others question the consistency, responsibility, and reciprocity in US standards, practices, and opinions.[1] Such foreign-policy debates wallow in harangue and rhetoric that create more intransigence than progress.

A remarkably different role for the United States is its more recent posture as a participant and judge in the objective scrutinizing of human rights dialogue. In the past, the US role in drafting international human rights standards was more the work of select international lawyers than a reflection of US governmental and popular processes. By contrast, this newer role of participant-judge acquires meaning from broader participation by the United States in the 1992 ratification and 1994–5 implementation of the International Covenant on Civil and Political Rights (CPR). By cooperating with international reporting criteria, scrutiny, and dialogue the United States has stepped down a rung or two from lofty international judgeship to a plain of covenantal multilateralism. In the future, the United States is, therefore, more apt to play the concomitant and complementary roles of judge and participant. Although customary international law and domestic incorporation of international law are evolving in the meantime, the above changes in the US role are the essential subject matter of this chapter.[2] Three historical US shifts demonstrate its evolution: from a history of primarily setting standards and judging performances; to a transitional phase of double standards in foreign policies, domestic legislation, and international covenantal commitments; and finally to the present multilateral role of participant-judge.

A HISTORY OF JUDGING

Historically the US proclivity has been to locate human rights abuses elsewhere rather than delve into its own past and present. US history has its high points, not the least of which are its constitutional protections. But there is another side. The history of the United States includes the near annihilation of a native population, profit from institutional slavery, harsh exploitation of natural resources and human labor, the use of atomic bombs and production of unbounded nuclear weaponry, and intervention in other states' affairs via covert and overt military and economic actions. In so doing, the United States has often sought to remove itself from objective human rights scrutiny. At the same time, the United States has declared its better side while judging the abuses of others. This view of human rights allows for legal and civil issues close to home, but places "human rights problems" on foreign soil, or in other parts of the United States deemed "foreign." The US Civil War and US involvement in World War II, for instance, show the evolution of US human rights judging. These events suggest the first of several why-and-how elements in the maturation of the United States as a champion of human rights practices. Reasons for confronting slavery and wartime barbarism had as much to do with economics and politics as they did morality. Moreover, the methods of human rights advocacy were one-sided. While judging the travesties of others, US leaders concealed US culpability.

The Civil War and human rights

During the *antebellum* years there were Northern critiques of the South, and Southern diatribes against the North. Neither side honestly confronted its own human rights problems. Rather, each projected its moral and societal inadequacies upon the other. This created paradoxes that both shame and illuminate US human rights practices. Robert Fogel explains why and how the moral, economic, and demographic disequilibrium of this period led to competing claims of superiority and promise while masking immense abuses close to home.[3] He examines how US historians have propagated myths of Northern morality and the inevitable Southern economic collapse, even though the *antebellum* South made efficient and profitable use of mulatto procreation, gang labor, and economies of scale. In contrast, the Northern economy was in distress as massive immigration and aggressive industrialization devastated the native worker population, fueled racist and nativist fraternities, triggered recession and inflation, transformed commercialism and technology, and justified a genocidal westward expansion to keep a lid on the boiling cauldron of socioeconomic tension.

In this Northern flux the religiously and morally guided Abolitionists condemned the South's "unmitigated evil." But their message of slavery's travesty upon human rights fell mostly on deaf ears. Only one out of every three hundred Northern voters in the 1840s supported the Abolitionist line.[4] Realizing this, Abolitionist methods to secure human freedom ironically became demeaning. The antislavery appeal compromised, strategized, and secularized. The movement's judgmentalism whipped up hysteria against the "moral lepers" of the slave South power structure, propagated dishonest fears of the Southern economy, advocated lowering the human valuation of the slaves from three-fifths of a person to zero in order to decrease the Southern electoral count in Congress, and trumped up "negrophobia" in the North.[5]

These tactics to secure for some people the right of human freedom came at the expense of dehumanizing others. The strategy worked in that a new Republican Party won the 1860 presidency, but it included a widely cast net of Free Soilers, Know-Nothings, racist nativists, Northern sectionalists, job opportunists, and only a few morally convinced Abolitionists.[6] Mixing roles of judge and politician, this human rights story includes moral compromise, impatience, deception, pandering to fears, and 600,000 lost lives. Still slavery had to die. The United States is rightly recognized as a champion of this cause. Democracy and human rights, as valued today, hung in the balance. Fogel argues that this hard path "preserved and reinforced conditions favorable to a continued struggle for the democratic rights of the lower classes, black and white alike, and for the improvement of their economic condition, not only in America but everywhere else in the world."[7] In 1848 William E. Channing lamented the slowness of this first serious consideration of human rights in the United States, given the fact that slavery stood "in direct hostility to all the grand movements, principles, and reforms ... of an advancing world."[8] Slaves were caught in the middle of a judgmental human rights debacle that politicized and marginalized them, if only barely humanizing them.

World War II and human rights

Was the human rights struggle any more or less noble by the middle of the twentieth century? Many historians, international lawyers, and political theorists date the maturing of US human rights consciousness to the end of World War II.[9] Richard Lillich posits that World War II catalyzed revolutionary developments in international human rights legal methods, such as when the Genocide Convention responded to Nazi atrocities.[10] With these changes in international laws, the work of the United Nations, and respective countries' domestic incorporation of international law, individuals could find direct and indirect protections via a growing body of laws, monitors, and limitations on a state's reach of human lives.[11] The war effort, in part, vindicated human rights as expressed in President Roosevelt's Four Freedoms, the Nuremberg and Tokyo war tribunals, the Universal Declaration of Human Rights, and the United Nations Charter. Articles 55 and 56 of the charter called upon member-states to promote, observe, and respect human rights. Moreover, various organs of the United Nations started to hone the human rights debate on the floor of the General Assembly, in the International Court of Justice, on the Trusteeship Council, and before the Economic and Social Council, the Security Council, and the Human Rights Committee. But, like the Abolitionists, the Allied leaders at Potsdam and drafters of the UN Charter at San Francisco commingled economics, security, and political might with morality.

If modern-day attention to human rights abuses is believed to have begun with global shock over world war, or over Japanese germ pathogen testing, the rape of Nanjing, and armies of comfort women, or over Nazi eugenics, a massive war machine, and genocide, then one must study parallel cruelties. How honest are conclusions about the birth of modern human rights concerns in the broader context of Allied carpet-bombing of civilians, US pioneering in sterilization and eugenics, the incarceration of 110,000 Japanese-Americans, the use of atomic bombs in a war that had essentially expired, and postwar collaboration with Axis scientists of biological destruction?[12] With troubling parallels in mind, Secretary of War Stimson told President Truman two months before the atomic bombing of Hiroshima and Nagasaki that he did not want to have the United States get the "reputation of outdoing Hitler in atrocities."[13]

It is true that throughout this century and especially after World War II the United States actively promoted humanitarian efforts and drafted early international legal instruments. Even before the war the United States had helped Jews in Eastern Europe, interceded on behalf of Armenians in the Turkish massacre, and advocated a "minorities treaty" and the Slavery

Convention.[14] Furthermore, President Roosevelt's pronouncement of Four Freedoms placed human rights in the center of international relations. Freedom, for him, meant "the supremacy of human rights everywhere," especially through freedom of speech, expression, and religion, and freedom from want and fear.[15] Around the time of the 1945 San Francisco Conference, which adopted the UN Charter, Secretary of State Stettinius and President Truman proclaimed the US hope that an international Bill of Rights, mirroring the US one, would be incorporated into each state's system of law.[16] US lawyers and Eleanor Roosevelt figured prominently in this postwar commitment to human rights covenants. They submitted articles, draft legislation and amendments, proposals and alternative language for numerous clauses, and well-reasoned briefs. Hence the 1954 final drafts of the Covenant on Civil and Political Rights and the Covenant on Economic, Social, and Cultural Rights (CESC) reflected more than anything a US position.[17]

Unfortunately US efforts toward furthering international covenants were hamstrung by Cold War fears, rhetoric, and national interests. As a victor in a world war that thwarted totalitarian regimes and conquest, and as the emerging economic and military hegemon, the United States presumed that its Constitution, Bill of Rights, and way of life were the international benchmark of human rights practices. So even though the United States judged and scrutinized every word, phrase, and nuance of the emerging human rights covenants, and won approval of its preferred wording for all but a couple of clauses, it steadfastly refused to ratify them. During the Cold War the United States often judged that its anti-Communist stance, in and of itself, was an uncompromising position in support of human rights. It was argued that its containment of Communism would protect people from tyrannous governments that denied basic human rights. This ideology melded moralism, humanitarianism, military strategy, and economic policies in propagating the American Way.[18]

Although it was evident at the Nuremberg and Tokyo war tribunals that there was a budding postwar international consensus that human rights are legally inviolable, the United States refused to be an equal participant in the process. The tribunals became a victor's court that purgatively projected collective shame on a vanquished Axis foe. The proclivity to lead and judge, but not participate in self-scrutiny, matched Truman's own ambivalence after the atomic bombings. On the one hand, he judged the Japanese as bestial, and did not question the earlier incarceration of innocent Japanese-Americans. On the other hand, he shuddered at the immense loss of civilian life and halted the atomic bombing even though more payloads were ready to be flown.[19] Stimson's earlier caveat underscores the need to pay attention to fine moral lines between the victorious and the vanquished. Problem-solving must consider both internal and external issues, both domestic and international factors, both humanitarian and political concerns.

Generally speaking, the postwar institutionalization of human rights protections was still a critically progressive step. It steered some countries away from purely political use of human rights issues, and crafted constructive roles for multilateral, covenantal participant-judges. The legal guts for the Universal Declaration did not come until the drafting of the CPR and CESC in 1954, which were approved and opened for signature by the United Nations in 1966 and became legally enforceable in 1976.[20] With the enforceability of the CPR came the formation of the Human Rights Committee and the beginning of its investigations, oversight, and reports. Still it took nearly two decades before the United States finally ratified the CPR on June 8, 1992, becoming its 127th adherent.[21] In September 1994 the State Department belatedly submitted its initial report of US human rights activities to the UN Human Rights Committee, as required by Article 40 of the CPR. However, the US Senate has not acted to ratify the CESC, nor has the United States signed the CPR's Optional Protocol, which would otherwise empower individuals to hold their government directly accountable for a breach of the CPR. By comparison, a broad cross-section of countries has ratified both CESC and CPR, with an additional fifty-nine countries accepting the power of individuals to petition and scrutinize their own government's performance under the CPR Optional Protocol.[22] Even today the United States hesitates to ratify and implement multilateral covenants to protect the rights of children, women, victims of torture, migrant workers, racial minorities, indigenous peoples, and regional and issue-specific treaties.[23] This pattern of hesitancy stretches back to antebellum federal–state sovereignty tensions, and has been steadfastly maintained through much of this century by a combined lobby of anti-Communists, states' rights activists, isolationists, and segregationists.

The United States judged its sovereignty as standing beyond the purview of multilateralism, particularly with the introduction of the first of several constitutional amendments by Senator John Bricker in 1951. The decades of Senate debate over the Genocide Convention show how Bricker Amendment supporters, who were almost successful in passing a constitutional prohibition on international treaty-making, waged a ten-pronged attack on US participation in nearly all human rights covenants.[24] First, Bricker supporters were unabashedly racist and ethnocentric in their coloring of the US human rights debate. Second, they argued that multilateral adherence to rights treaties played into the hands of Socialism, Communism, and world federalism. Third and fourth, they were concerned that US citizens and private property might fall subject to unjust jurisdictions and seizure abroad if the United States adhered to covenants or extraterritorial courts. Fifth, they feared that World Court rulings might conflict with domestic decisions and legislation. Sixth, they were wary that international human rights covenants themselves would instigate disagreements and fuel international entanglements. Seventh, they wanted to maintain the protection of rights already embodied in the US Bill of Rights. Eighth, they argued that multilateral covenants would circumscribe effective US international security measures and the containment of communism.

The final two concerns were domestic and disclosed deeply ingrained fears of enhanced federal power. These states' rights advocates insisted that neither executive signing of a treaty nor Senate ratification could constitute self-executing legislation. They argued that federal interests in advancing human rights covenants were merely a veneer for attacks on states' rights. Segregationist phobia portrayed images of a federal government colluding with international organizations to form a global federalist culture. Just as the South believed it had sacrificed sovereignty in the 1860s and the Reconstruction period, these states' rights advocates suspected further federal encroachment through international covenants. As was made clear through the course of lengthy Congressional hearings on the Genocide Convention, several states would not tolerate any international or federal scrutiny of activities that might be construed as racist or genocidal, especially at a time of federal affirmative action during the Civil Rights Movement. Concomitantly, decades of covenant opponents judged human rights abuses abroad. With self-scrutiny so unsettling, it was apparently easier to project some of the United States' own domestic human rights problems through US foreign policy and military engagement in Southeast Asia.

IN TRANSITION TO A NEW ROLE

The second reason why the United States became involved in the international human rights debate stems from the social trauma of the post-Vietnam, post-Watergate years. Whether or not people knew of Secretary Stimson's 1945 caveat to President Truman that the United States not match Hitler's atrocities, the devastating human rights abuses of a US-waged war in Southeast Asia provided troubling parallels.[25] There arose a collective search for moral integrity and decency in the wake of millions of Vietnamese casualties, 58,000 US combat deaths, and perhaps as many suicides among returning US veterans.[26] These costs suggest comparisons to the Nazi Holocaust.[27] As the perpetrator of much loss and pain, the United States shied away from multilateral checks on the behavior of nation-states. It viewed them as intrusions on its own national interests and state sovereignty. Unlike the Abolitionists in the Civil War era, however, this second reason for renewed interest in human rights was not a bastardization of the advocates' ideology and belief system. It was instead the natural consequence of collective shame and the painful result of unmitigated, unchecked confidence in how the United States practiced human rights and political hegemony. Although the locus of human rights problems remained abroad, there was still a growing recognition of the need for internal domestic scrutiny and a willingness to consider meaningful US participation in multilateral discussions.

If President Roosevelt gave human rights prominence on the international stage during World War II, it was President Carter who placed the issue squarely on the US agenda in the late 1970s. Although several human rights procedural checks were already in place before Carter was elected, his administration linked human rights and foreign policy and adroitly focused public attention on the matter.[28] Before Carter's term, in 1973 Congress had already promulgated legislation directing US policy-makers to apply human rights considerations in bilateral foreign affairs. There were provisions for a new bureau and an assistant secretary of state for human rights and humanitarian affairs, plus incremental federal legislation requiring an annual human rights report on practices in foreign countries.[29] Moreover, a "sense-of-the-Congress" provision recommended denial of economic or military assistance to foreign governments that interned or imprisoned its citizens for "political purposes," and enacted statutes linking foreign assistance and trade benefits to a country's human rights status. The Jackson–Vanik Amendment to the Trade Reform Act of 1974 prohibited Most Favored Nation status to non-market-economy governments denying or restricting the right of their citizens to emigrate. From 1974 to 1976 Congress introduced increasingly strong language in Sections 116 and 502B of the Foreign Assistance Act of 1961, mandating that the president terminate military and economic assistance to any government engaging in a "consistent pattern of gross violations of human rights."[30]

President Carter honed the focus of this new major political agenda item. Combining first human rights experts and the executive policy-making community, then bringing in the wider two-party political system, and finally engaging the general population in human rights issues, Carter creatively built on the questions of an aroused, post-Vietnam public. He generated interest in renewed moral integrity as a nation, acted as a policy entrepreneur, and channeled post-Vietnam malaise toward incremental, functional policy-making.[31] The executive branch secured procedures and implemented funds to continue monitoring human rights abuses. These statutes imbedded federal responsibility for dealing with these issues. With the help of Congress, nongovernmental organizations, churches, and academics, Carter "galvanize[d] latent support for human rights in the general public" by engaging myriad local, state, federal, and international actors in longer-term human rights policy.[32]

In Carter's inaugural address he stressed that human rights was "the perfect unifying principle" for reinforcing US foreign policy with moral integrity. He declared that the US

> commitment to human rights must be absolute. . . . Because we are free, we can never be indifferent to the fate of freedom elsewhere. Our moral sense dictates a clear-cut preference for those societies who share with us an abiding respect for individual human rights.[33]

In part, this human rights stance signaled an ideological competition with the Soviets. But even more, it argued that the long-term national interests of the United States included the restoration of moral legitimacy and credible human rights practices among Western allies.[34] Thus Carter's foreign policy began to link military and economic aid with positive human rights records.

Shortly thereafter Carter suggested before the United Nations a shift for the United States from the role of judge to a committed and scrutinized participant:

> The basic thrust of human affairs points towards a more universal demand for fundamental human rights. The United States has a historical birthright to be associated with this process.
>
> We in the United States accept this responsibility in the fullest and the most constructive sense. Ours is a commitment and not just a political posture. . . . [O]ur own ideals in the area of human rights have not always been attained in the United States, but the American people have an abiding commitment to the full realization of these ideals. And we are determined, therefore, to deal with our deficiencies quickly and openly. We have nothing to conceal. . . .
>
> . . . . In our relationships with other countries, these mutual concerns will be reflected in our political, our cultural, and our economic attitudes. . . .
>
> I believe that this is a foreign policy that is consistent with my own Nation's historic values and commitments. And I believe that it is a foreign policy that is consonant with the ideals of the United Nations.[35]

At least in word, human rights issues began to find a place on US shores. These were no longer problems found exclusively abroad. Nevertheless Carter's enunciation of human rights policy presumed US global championship. These US commitments remained largely within the realm of foreign policy. Even though Carter signed and submitted to the Senate four human rights covenants, it would be years and even decades before ratification and participation through multilateral covenants.[36]

Carter also echoed the *antebellum* caveat of Channing, noting the limits of moral suasion. He tempered assurances of national greatness with the United States' need to regain lost moral integrity:

> I understand fully the limits of moral suasion. We have no illusion that changes will come easily or soon. But I also believe that it is a mistake to undervalue the power of words and of the ideas that words embody.
>
> In the life of the human spirit, words are action, much more so than many of us may realize who live in countries where freedom of expression is taken for granted. The leaders of totalitarian nations understand this very well. The proof is that words are precisely the action for which dissidents in those countries are being persecuted.

Nonetheless, we can already see dramatic worldwide advances in the protection of the individual from the arbitrary power of the state. For us to ignore this trend would be to lose influence and moral authority in the world. To lead it will be to regain the moral stature that we once had.

. . . . I believe it is incumbent on us in this country to keep that discussion, that debate, that contention alive. No other country is as well qualified as we to set an example. We have our own shortcomings and faults, and we should strive constantly and with courage to make sure that we are legitimately proud of what we have.[37]

Skeptics deemed Carter's shift in human rights policy an attempt to renew a belief in basic decency for a post-Vietnam, post-Watergate country. But his policy was also judged to be naïve, moralistic, misleading for foreign citizens, overly individualistic, pompous, lacking realist pragmatism, and hypocritically inconsistent.[38]

Under Carter's approach, implementation of human rights policies was directed not so much at the Communist bloc or at the East as it was against hard authoritarian regimes that were members of Western military alliances. The effort was to get the entire US-led Western house in order.[39] Hence by 1977, for example, the United States reduced levels of military aid by two-thirds for Argentina, Chile, and Uruguay, and later eliminated it altogether. Nonetheless bilateral human rights concerns still figured haphazardly and minimally. For instance, in US–Argentine relations, President Carter, Vice President Mondale, and State Department personnel met with Argentina's ruling junta to denounce political atrocities. Human rights activists in Argentina were received publicly by Washington. Moreover, Congressional votes denied twenty-three international development loans to Argentina, and opposed another eleven to Uruguay and five to Chile. At the United Nations and the Organization of American States the United States supported activities against these juntas. Arguably the human rights policies had at least a temporary restraining effect on the military excesses of the Southern Cone juntas. But all of these loans were eventually released upon assurances that torture and terror by the juntas would abate. There was, however, a chasm between word and deed. Military rule continued,[40] and Argentina's "Dirty War" still targeted the "political Left, trade unions, intellectuals, mainstream autonomous social organizations, and dissidents of all sorts, as well as numerous ordinary, apolitical citizens who were forced into or became accidentally enmeshed in the politics of torture and disappearances."[41]

So long as the US human rights stand remained bilateral and part of foreign policy, its intent would be mixed. There would be recurrent inconsistencies in US human rights practices and humanitarian interventions abroad. The champion of rights would be viewed sometimes positively, sometimes negatively, but never as a credible judge or solid, objective participant. Shying away from multilateral scrutiny, the United States remained prone to messianic and ideological swings: from idealist savior of human rights activists under Carter, to abrupt "realist" defender and benefactor of anti-Communist, authoritarian juntas in the Southern Cone under Reagan. Consequently, the US government, and particularly the executive branch, was charged internationally and domestically with uneven, unjust, and selective human rights practices. Yet the fact that this critique could occur at all was due to the gradually increasing regimes of human rights consciousness and monitoring that matured appreciably under Carter's agenda.[42]

An outstanding example of the value of this regime of human rights consciousness is the body of legal, empirical, and theoretical literature that has criticized the egregious "mixed motives" of US humanitarian intervention.[43] Without sure commitment to multilateral covenants, there were in the 1970s and 1980s no objective conditions to identify genuine humanitarianism on the part of the United States, as opposed to coercive and ulterior foreign-policy motives in the name of human rights protection,[44] whether by military, economic, or legal forms of intervention.

Military intervention is rarely legitimate or effective if its intent is intrusion for the sake of humanitarian, ideological, or political restructuring, and if the move is uninvited or relies upon force without the consent of the inviting state.[45] Yet this very form of unilateral intervention is evident in much diplomacy and covert activity. In such cases, "when human rights conflict with even minor security, political, economic, or ideological objectives, human rights usually lose out."[46] For example, David Forsythe and Jack Donnelly catalogue fourteen post-World War II instances of US military and CIA interventions (mostly in Central and South America) that cloaked obstructions of fundamental human rights with false humanitarianism.[47] Nearly every intervention by the United States during the Cold War espoused the protection of people from nonhumanitarian Communism – the Kirkpatrick Doctrine – but ended up supporting "the reactionary side" in the Third World, "frustrat[ing] people's right to self-determination," let alone lives – two very fundamental human rights.[48]

More recently, in Haiti the issue of US intervention rests on the restoration of democracy, which itself is a matter of human rights and self-determination. Moreover, US incursions into Grenada and Panama leave little doubt that the United States is willing to use force openly in the Caribbean to restore democratic ideals and protections. Yet many would read the UN Charter's underlying goal of peace and protection of human rights as not countenancing an intervener's desire to spread "democracy," to stabilize the internal politics of neighboring states, or to effect its own hegemonic control over others.[49] Even if "the intervening side has overwhelming military superiority" and is driven by genuinely altruistic, compassionate reasons, military humanitarian intervention rarely works. Richard Falk argues that the failure of such intervention "invariably leaves the target society worse off than if the internal play of forces had been allowed to run its course, however destructive and brutal."[50]

Humanitarian intervention also takes the form of economic coercion and embargoing as well as material aid. Each of these affects humanitarian and political changes within a target state, and bears upon the people's receipt or denial of basic rights to food, health, and sustenance. In the Gulf War the United Nations and assorted US allies claimed their mission was one of human rights, for they sought to oust the authoritarian, aggressive regime of Saddam Hussein, who was known to repress Kurds, marsh Arabs, Shi'ites, and Kuwaitis. During that war UN Security Council Resolution 661 was in accord with several international legal prohibitions against any economic embargo of food and medicine; the resolution clearly exempted "supplies intended strictly for medical purposes and, in humanitarian circumstances, foodstuffs."[51] This recognizes the moral repugnancy of denying food to the point of near starvation, in which case innocent civilians needlessly suffer and die in the scramble to reach "humanitarian aid" drops. But any ostensible humane economic intervention that permits near starvation before extending "help" perverts the meaning of humanitarianism and human rights.

By contrast, the substantial multilevel international effort behind economic humanitarian intervention against Rhodesian and South African minority practices of apartheid, together with the concerted indigenous support of Black majorities and collaborating Whites, remarkably ameliorated abuses.[52] Several UN-led initiatives, both voluntary and mandatory, read "threat to the peace" broadly under chapter 7 provisions of the charter, concluding that it requires findings of neither a direct violation of international law nor the existence of aggression. Economic humanitarian intervention through embargoes surmounted domestic jurisdiction and self-determination defenses. Still the United Nations process relied on the United States and other member states to adopt foreign policies and domestic laws to implement UN-ordered sanctions. Unfortunately, underscoring the obstacles to implementing human rights practices via foreign policy, it took years for the United States to comply with effective legislation. It became a contest of domestic US wills: enforced, monitored humanitarian embargoing in collaboration with Africans versus the economic independence of multinational corporations and US national security arrangements.

Direct material aid comprises yet another form of humanitarian intervention. The US marine mission in Somalia supposedly arose from "a growing conviction that many thousands more people would starve to death within weeks in the absence of strong action," and from "a Pentagon calculation that the military risks would be minimal."[53] The project was also intended to portray a benign image of US post-Cold War leadership. It soon became clear through UN and US statements that the marines were also to disarm political factions, train a police force, clear mines, and restore domestic order. This agenda of political restructuring marked a radical change from the initially stated human-itarian objectives.[54] The goal was not so much peace-keeping as intrusive peace enforcement to include "re-establishment of national and regional insti-tutions and civil administration in the entire country"; this "nation-building" became essentially "political warfare" aimed at General Aidid and other Somali targets.[55] To accomplish these larger ends, the UN mandate permitted heavy foreign firepower to quell resistance in Mogadishu. A lopsided international media presented scores of UN and US casualties but ignored several hundred Somali deaths in these same incidents. Moreover, the international coalition's "willingness to kill indiscriminately" undermined the mission's humanitarian claims.[56] Such foreign policy, rather than multilateral covenanting, hinders effective US human rights practice.

The anomalies in US human rights practices during this transitional phase from judge to participant-judge underline the need for a new paradigm to bridge the goals of foreign policy and human rights. Problem-solving must consider both internal and external issues, both domestic and international factors, both humanitarian and political concerns. The United States cannot presume it is the benchmark of international human rights practices. There are times that it must observe the progress and regress of others, as well as itself, with the aid of multilateral scrutiny. The very struggle for human rights implementation is often the path to realizing substantive and sustainable human rights. Furthermore, this scrutiny of human rights abuses may continue, even during administrations that do not choose to keep this issue on a political front burner. Thus the Reagan administration had to answer for its courting of abusive, albeit anti-Communist, regimes, and the Clinton administration has been pressed to explain flip-flops on human rights policies *vis-à-vis* China. The fact that domestic questioning ensues shows the lasting effect of longer-term agenda-setting and institutionalized procedures put in place in the 1970s.

This process is incomplete. Despite increasing checks on US human rights practices, the abuses in El Salvador worsened through the 1970s with the advent of paramilitary death squads; the kidnapping and killing of politicians, labor leaders, peasant activists, and academics; and attacks and assassinations of church leaders and parishioners. US aid grew from less than $100 million in 1979 and 1980 to $4 billion in the decade of the 1980s.[57] During this same time the United States also orchestrated an assault against Nicaragua by ille-gally mining its harbor, training Contras, destroying its economy, and continuing huge amounts of aid in the midst of massacres of civilians.[58]

A MORE PARTICIPATORY ERA

US human rights history began with the United States being a standard-bearer and international judge of human rights. It later entered more participatory and constructive roles, but since these were wrapped within unilateral and bilateral foreign policy actions, the human rights practices of the United States remained confusing, inconsistent, nonreciprocal, and irresponsible.[59] The United States' ability to judge was enmeshed in positions of adversarial politics. In the early 1970s, an important step away from this subjective milieu was the initial institutionalization of human rights procedures, which were enhanced by the Carter agenda. These steps incrementally led to increased external and internal scrutiny of US human rights practices from the 1970s to the present.

A significant stride toward a new participant-judge role was Carter's signing of the Covenant on Civil and Political Rights and submitting it to the Senate for its advice and consent. The CPR was eventually ratified and implemented by the United States in 1992. Here began a third reason why and method by which the United States practices human rights in the post-Cold War era. The demise of competing Cold War ideologies, along with the advent of complex interdependencies and diverse leadership in military, economic, and regional roles, has called the United States to a more participatory posture in an undefined new world order. The roles of states, the United Nations, and multinational corporations have recast the concept of sovereignty. A longer-term context suggests the United States and others will benefit from participation in an objective, scrutinizing, and mutual international human rights debate and practice. This is preferable to the frustrations and condemnation of any one country trying to sit as the judge, arbiter, or policeman.

In sharing the lead with several others, the United States has gained a deeper, more affordable, and broader sovereignty by engaging in the agenda-setting, policy adoption, and constructive implementation of international standards as agreed upon among states party to the CPR and to reporting procedures before the UN Human Rights Committee. This is the first of several steps that the United States could take in a more participatory role. Down the road it should submit to the jurisdiction of the International Court of Justice and ratify many helpful covenants that the United States still resists. Its overall foreign policy might reflect multilateralism more than bilateralism and unilateralism. If reasons and methods for human rights dialogue were to evolve, the United States could hang up its judge's robe and become accountable to the UN Human Rights Committee pursuant to Article 40 of the CPR.

Standards of judicial competence

If the United States is ever to attain the stature of being an international judge of human rights practice, it would need to answer two questions: who placed the United States on the bench, and did it meet the criteria of good judgeship? In answer to the first question, no one other than the United States placed it on the bench. On the contrary, the United Nations pronounces mutual recognition of sovereignty among states, with no single state sitting in judgment over others. As for the second question, a judge is held to a higher standard of behavior. A judge must conduct affairs and reach decisions in an evenhanded manner free from bias, partiality, impropriety, and inconsistency. A judge's own conduct and thought processes are scrutinized at least as keenly as the judge's examination of others. A judge cannot, therefore, rest in the realm of partiality, weak evidence, cultural relativism, polemics, prejudice, opinion, or simplistic paradigms. This is not to say that countries generally, if ever, behave so objectively. But when a particular country, by word or deed, holds itself up as *the* judge, it begs the burden of a higher standard of duty. Failing to meet that standard tarnishes its credibility in the eyes of others.

The Shattuck Report

The procedural scrutiny of the UN Human Rights Committee has elicited polar responses from critics and proponents of US participation. Whereas there was little debate over the US Senate's 1992 consent to join 126 other countries party to the CPR, the actual submission of reports under the covenant in 1994 and 1995 drew sharp domestic criticism. On September 19, 1994 Assistant Secretary for Democracy, Human Rights, and Labor John Shattuck explained that this report would generally testify to the excellence of domestic US human rights practices, even while acknowledging discriminatory episodes in the United States' past and present. Critics complain that this procedure senselessly supplies ammunition to internationally known abusers of human rights. Indeed, China commented that the United States was finally admitting publicly that it had "cruelly violated human rights" through enslavement and disenfranchisement of African-Americans, destruction of Native American lives and culture, maltreatment of immigrants, and discrimination against women.[60] Shattuck and proponents of the reporting procedure counter, however, that candidness presents "cruelty and injustice alongside vision and courage."[61] Going well beyond China's critique, the report concedes further problems and debates concerning urban racial unrest, judicial and educational inequalities, teenage capital punishment, juvenile incarceration, prison labor, hate and war-propagating speech, certain poor working conditions, inadequate security for children, and drug, alcohol, and tobacco abuse. Rather than a fault, this is precisely the intent of the report.[62] Such disclosure and discussion are signs of maturity. Whereas the Carter agenda spoke vaguely, this report is specific. Naming precise human rights problems is a surer step toward correcting them.

The second leg of this reporting procedure occurred on March 29 and 31, 1995 when Shattuck and other government personnel appeared before the Human Rights Committee to respond to questions and criticisms based on the 1994 report. The press described the session as the United States swallowing "a big dose" of its own human rights medicine. The *Washington Post* and *International Herald Tribune* reported that forceful criticisms came from several international and domestic nongovernmental organizations (NGOs)

269

that "unleash[ed] a barrage of criticism" focusing on the US practice of capital punishment of teenagers under the age of 18, the absence of an Equal Rights Amendment, the passage of discriminatory state-level measures such as California's Proposition 187, and widespread police brutality and ill-treatment of prisoners. The UN committee also argued that the large number of US conditions placed on the covenant amounted to "treaty cosmetics" that would have the effect of weakening it.[63] In addition, the *Washington Post* found this public hearing needlessly redundant since corrections of US human rights practices come from US citizens, who are free to test and challenge US policies. The paper posited that a state's human rights record does not proceed from the "prodding of critical outsiders."[64] It reasoned inconsistently that US participation might still contribute to the policing of *others* whose records fall short.[65] This line of argument is blind to the constructive learning curve within US human rights practices. It presumes, as did the United States for so long, that the United States is the rightful champion or judge, so why alter a record of unparalleled advocacy?

Entering a new role instead, the United States now adds legislative and administrative checks and balances that admonish and punish human rights violators through decisions regarding economic aid, technology transfer, diplomatic support, international loans, and military assistance and exercises. It takes the further step of a more transparent human rights policy and answers the charge of double standards and hypocrisy in criticizing the performance of others while refusing scrutiny of itself. Ratifying the CPR goes halfway in correcting this duplicity, for as the report notes, the US government deems it necessary to push for Senate ratification of the CESC, an inseparable complement to the CPR. The report rightly acknowledges that Cold War divisions between proponents of the CPR (allies of the United States) and the CESC (allies of the USSR) were superficial and politicized. Moreover, in the work of the Human Rights Committee the United States is now welcome to participate fully. It may argue and clarify its understanding of human rights theories and practices. Acceding to both the CPR and CESC would also mean an acceptance of documents that largely reflect, though not perfectly, the values of the United States and its Constitution and the Bill of Rights. This shift reaffirms the United States' "somewhat bruised image as a country dedicated to the rule of law, and to admit that US society may have something to learn from others."[66] This shift brings a participant-judge into the international mainstream.

A reserved, though candid, disclosure is an abiding feature of the report. Underscoring the unique features of US protections of rights, it speaks of continuing difficulties and conflicts. The text's underlying theme is domestic, not foreign: there continues to be substantial progress in correcting human rights abuses in the United States. Echoing Roosevelt's Four Freedoms and the early days of Carter's human rights agenda, the report argues that while human rights concerns are global, they most importantly direct the United

States to overcome injustice and strengthen democracy at home. The report, therefore, broaches good and bad data about US citizens, including the significantly high rates of births out of wedlock, poverty among non-Whites, and disproportionate levels of education among various races.[67] It also explains the place of human rights within a constitutional, federal, two-party system with independent branches of state and federal governments.[68] And it notes the avenues of litigation open to US citizens seeking remedy for alleged abuses.

The report also seeks to justify the US government's several reservations, declarations, and understandings that condition its ratification of the covenant. Unfortunately the number of conditions placed on the CPR by the United States is high. Specifically, the *reservations* to the CPR limit or exclude the effect of its articles dealing with limitations on the death penalty, the definition of cruel, inhuman, or degrading treatment or punishment, segregation of adult and juvenile offenders, the reduction of penalties for criminal offenders, and prohibitions on war propaganda and hate speech.[69] The US *understandings* to the CPR interpret the scope of state obligations of nondiscrimination, compensation for wrongful arrest and imprisonment, segregation of accused and convicted persons, the underlying purposes of incarceration, the due process rights to counsel and presentation of witnesses, the prohibition of double jeopardy, and federal–state relations.[70] Finally, the four US *declarations* concern the non-self-executing nature of the covenant, and the US government's acceptance of the Human Rights Committee's competence to receive interstate complaints against the United States. The report stresses that despite these conditions US law and practice comply with nearly every fundamental requirement of the covenant.[71] The report thus challenges the criticism of NGOs and the UN committee that these conditions threaten the effectiveness of the covenant itself.

Regarding domestic implementation of the covenant's provisions, the report distinguishes between the US federalist political system and the centralization of other states that are party to the covenant. The US system requires that parts of the covenant be protected and implemented by federal legislative and judicial jurisdiction, and others by state and local authorities.[72] This qualification is neither a reservation nor a modification of US international obligations under the covenant, but rather a domestic concern that the constitutional balance of authority between federal and state governments not be altered. Also, it is intended to allow the federal legislature to oversee domestic implementation of the CPR, rather than have federal and state judiciaries contend over the precise meaning of "often vague language" within the covenant that could generate immense litigation.[73] This is consistent with judicial precedent in US courts, which generally defer to Congress when clarifying the intent and meaning of international law. Finally, this understanding of the CPR notifies other covenant parties that the US government will remove any federal obstacle to the abilities of US states to meet their obligations under the covenant. This approach seeks common ground between states' rights and federalism in such a way that casts no doubt on the constitutional power of the federal government to accept treaty obligations, even if they affect the laws of the states.[74]

Certain substantive differences between the covenant and the several US reservations concern insistence on the death penalty, exceptional circumstances under which juveniles are to be treated as adults, the protection of hateful and bellicose speech, and the self-executing modality of domestic implementation. But as important as these reservations, understandings, and declarations are, the substantive issues and difficulties are at least mentioned in the report with candid honesty. Remarkably, the Senate at last concedes the need to consider the appropriateness of change, while still believing that this will be best effected by normal legislative process.[75] The Senate speaks of reaching "full compliance" with international standards of human rights practice, which is an important recognition that the CPR and CESC contain broader human rights guarantees than US law, and that improvements in US laws may be necessary.

CONCLUSION

As a *champion* of human rights, the United States at various times has played leading international roles, emphasizing judgeship or participant status or a sensible and just combination of both. In the course of this role-playing there have been times of seeming US schizophrenia: between being a champ who takes the side of human rights and marginalized peoples and being a chump who politicizes human rights and further harms the unprotected.

There are limits to how far current CPR reporting and scrutinizing procedures will affect and correct US role-playing. Although the covenant's scope does not touch many parts of US foreign policy, it does institute a critical and disciplined state practice.

Now by reporting objectively, and hearing both an internal critique and that of an international board of rights experts, the United States genuinely enters a debate over its own human rights practices and those of others. Covenantal participation furthers transparency and enlarges the substantive and geographic scope of human rights dialogue. These responsibilities call upon an entire state and not just on the skills and convictions of certain international lawyers, scholars, and groups of human rights activists. In this current phase of US human rights practice, the country learns to judge itself and hear outside criticisms. It anticipates the light of dialogic truth, by which it may mature and change for the better.[76]

NOTES

The author is indebted to the editor of this volume, Jack Donnelly, Ved Nanda, John McCamant, and three anonymous reviewers for their advice and critique. This research was assisted by an award from the Social Science Research Council (SSRC) of an SSRC–MacArthur Foundation Fellowship on Peace and Security in a Changing World.

1 Peter Van Ness, "What Ever Happened to Bill Clinton's Human Rights Policy?" *Current Affairs Bulletin* (June–July 1994), p. 40; see also Van Ness, "Who is Making US China Policy?" *Business Times, Weekend Edition* (July 30–1, 1994).

2 Regarding domestic incorporation of international human rights law, see generally Richard B. Lillich, "The Role of Domestic Courts in Enforcing International Human Rights Law," in Hurst Hannum, ed., *Guide to International Human Rights Practice*, 2nd edn (Philadelphia: University of Pennsylvania Press, 1992), pp. 228–48; see also Lillich, *International Human Rights: Problems of Law, Policy, and Practice*, 2nd edn (Boston: Little, Brown, and Co., 1991), pp. 87–163. For the US government's understanding of this task of domestic legal incorporation, see John Shattuck, Assistant Secretary for Democracy, Human Rights, and Labor, "Introduction to a Report to the UN Human Rights Committee," *Department of State Dispatch* (September 19, 1994), Nexis printout, p. 5. On the impact of evolving customary international human rights laws, see Theodor Meron, *Human Rights and Humanitarian Norms as Customary Law* (Oxford: Clarendon Press, 1989).

3 Robert William Fogel, *Without Consent or Contract: The Rise and Fall of American Slavery* (New York: W.W. Norton and Company, 1989).

4 Ibid., pp. 323–39.

5 Peter Kolchin, *Unfree Labor: American Slavery and Russian Serfdom* (Cambridge, MA: The Belknap Press of Harvard University Press, 1987), p. 371; and Fogel, *Without Consent or Contract*, pp. 343, 349.

6 Fogel, *Without Consent or Contract*, pp. 362–86.

7 Ibid., pp. 416–17.

8 Ibid., p. 416, quoting William E. Channing.

9 See, for example, Hurst Hannum and Dana D. Fischer, "The Political Framework," in Hannum and Fischer, eds, *US Ratification of the International Covenant on Human Rights* (New York: Transnational Publishers, Inc., 1993), pp. 7–8; Richard B. Bilder, "An Overview of International Human Rights Law," in Hannum, ed., *Guide to International Human Rights Practice*, pp. 4–6; Jack Donnelly, *International Human Rights* (Boulder, CO: Westview Press, 1993), pp. 6–7; Henry Kissinger, "Continuity and Change in American Foreign Policy," *Society* 15, no. 97 (1977), quoted in Lillich, *International Human Rights*, p. 968; and Kathryn Sikkink, "The Power of Principled Ideas: Human Rights Policies in the United States and Western Europe," in Judith Goldstein and Robert O. Keohane, eds, *Ideas and Foreign Policy: Beliefs, Institutions, and Political Change* (Ithaca, NY: Cornell University Press, 1993), p. 139.

10 See "Convention on the Prevention and Punishment of the Crime of Genocide," signed December 31, 1979, given to the Senate for advice and consent with two reservations, five understandings, and one declaration on February 10, 1986; passed with proposed implementing legislation on February 19, 1986. Congress, however, delayed enacting the executive's proposed implementing legislation, thus postponing the convention's enforceability until February 23, 1989; see 78 *United Nations Treaty Series* 277 (1948); see also 6 *Wisconsin International Law Journal* 43–74 (1987); and Natalie Kaufman, *Human Rights Treaties and the Senate: A History of Opposition* (Chapel Hill: University of North Carolina Press, 1990), pp. 37–63.

11 Lillich, *International Human Rights*, pp. 5–7.

12 Regarding the use of atomic weapons, see Barton J. Bernstein, "The Atomic Bombings Reconsidered," *Foreign Affairs* 74, no. 1 (January–February 1995), pp. 135–52; Barton J. Bernstein, "Understanding the Atomic Bomb and the Japanese Surrender: Missed Opportunities, Little-Known Near Disasters, and Modern Memory," *Diplomatic History* 19, no. 2 (Spring 1995), pp. 227–73; and J. Samuel Walker, "History, Collective Memory, and the Decision to Use the Bomb," *Diplomatic History* 19, no. 2 (Spring 1995), pp. 319–28. On the logic and consequences of Nazism, see especially Robert Jay Lifton, *The Nazi Doctors: Medical Killing and the Psychology of Genocide* (New York: Basic Books, 1986); Robert N. Proctor, *Racial Hygiene: Medicine Under the Nazis* (Cambridge, MA: Harvard University Press, 1988). In reference to US collaboration with Axis scientists, see Sheldon H. Harris, *Factories of Death: Japanese Biological Warfare, 1932–45, and the American Cover-Up* (London: Routledge, 1994), pp. 173–233; see also Proctor, *Racial Hygiene*.

13 Secretary Stimson, quoted in Bernstein, "Understanding the Atomic Bomb," p. 146.

14 See "Slavery Convention," signed September 25, 1926, entered into force on March 9, 1927, 182 *United States Treaty* 479 (1926); "Protocol Amending the Slavery Convention," signed and entered into force December 7, 1953, 7 *United States Treaties and Other International Agreements* 479 (1956); "Supplementary Convention on the Abolition of Slavery, the Slave Trade, and Institutions and Practices Similar to Slavery," signed September 7, 1956, entered into force April 20, 1957, 18 *United States Treaties and Other International Agreements* 3,201 (1967).

15 Franklin D. Roosevelt, State Department, 1 *Foreign Relations of the United States* 25–6 (1942), quoted in Hannum and Fischer, "The Political Framework," p. 13, n. 21.

16 Secretary of State Edward Stettinius, 12 *Department of State Bulletin* 928–9 (1945), quoted in ibid.

17 Kaufman, *Human Rights Treaties*, pp. 66–7, 74–93.

18 David P. Forsythe, *The Internationalization of Human Rights* (Lexington, MA: Lexington Books, 1991), p. 103.

19 Bernstein, "The Atomic Bombings," pp. 148, 152.

20 "International Covenant on Civil and Political Rights," adopted December 16, 1966, entered into force March 23, 1976, entered into force for the United States on June 8, 1992, 999 *United Nations Treaty Series* 171 (1966); "International Covenant on Economic, Social, and Cultural Rights," adopted December 16, 1966, entered into force January 3, 1976, 999 *United Nations Treaty Series* 3 (1966).

21 United States Department of State, "Civil and Political Rights in the United States: Initial Report of the United States of America to the UN Human Rights Committee under the International Covenant on Civil and Political Rights" (Shattuck Report) (Washington, DC: Department of State Publication 10200, Office of the Legal Adviser, 1994), p. i.

22 Although President Carter signed and submitted this covenant to the Senate in 1978, and a hearing was held in 1979, the US Senate Committee on Foreign Relations did not ratify the CESC, nor act upon the CPR and two other treaties submitted, including the International Convention on the Elimination of All Forms of Racial Discrimination and the American Convention on Human Rights. See *Message from the President of the United States Transmitting Four Treaties Pertaining to Human Rights*, 95th Congress, 2nd Session (Exec. E), February 23, 1978; "International Covenant on the Elimination of All Forms of Racial Discrimination," adopted December 21, 1965, entered into force January 4, 1969, 660 *United Nations Treaty Series* 195 (1965); and "American Convention on Human Rights," signed November 22, 1969, entered into force July 18, 1978, 36 *Organization of American States Treaty Series* 1 (1969), Organization of American States Off. Rec. OEA/Ser. L/V/II.23, doc.21, rev.6.

23 See Jean-Bernard Marie, *Human Rights Law Journal* 15, nos 1–2 (March 31, 1994), p. 67.

24 Kaufman, *Human Rights Treaties*, pp. 42–92.

25 Tony Smith, *America's Mission: The United States and the Worldwide Struggle for Democracy in the Twentieth Century* (Princeton, NJ: Princeton University Press, 1994), p. 265.

26 Kissinger speaks to the search for integrity in "Continuity and Change," p. 966. Regarding veteran suicides, the estimated range runs from 9,000 to well over 100,000. At the Forum on Viet Nam, Cambodia, and Laos at the State University of New York at Stony Brook in June 1993 spokespersons for the US Veterans Administration and the Viet Nam Veterans Foundation cited 81,000 suicides. Additional reports on suicide rates include Daniel A. Pollock, Philip Rhodes, Coleen A. Boyle, Pierre Decoufle, and Daniel L. McGee, "Estimating the Number of Suicides among Vietnam Veterans," *American Journal of Psychiatry* 1,247, no. 6 (June 1990), pp. 772–6; "The Wall Within," *CBS Reports* (New York: CBS News, June 2, 1988); "Vietnam 101," *60 Minutes* (New York: CBS News, October 4, 1987); David Spencer, *Facing the Wall* (New York: Macmillan, 1986); John Langone, "The War that Has No Ending," *Discover* (June 1985), pp. 44–54; and R. Anderson, "Vietnam Legacy: Veterans' Suicide Toll May Top War Casualties," *Seattle Times* (March 18, 1981), p. 1.

27 Richard H. Minear, "Atomic Holocaust, Nazi Holocaust: Some Reflections," *Diplomatic History* 19, no. 2 (Spring 1995), pp. 347–65.

28 Sikkink, "The Power of Principled Ideas," pp. 151–2; and Smith, *America's Mission*, pp. 239–65.

29 Sikkink, "The Power of Principled Ideas," pp. 152–4; and Jack Donnelly, "Post-Cold War Reflections on the Study of International Human Rights," *Ethics and International Affairs* 8, nos 99–101 (1994).

30 Richard B. Lillich, "US Foreign Policy, Human Rights, and Foreign Trade and Investment," in Lillich, *International Human Rights*, p. 953.

31 See Michael T. Hayes, *Incrementalism and Public Policy* (New York: Longman, 1992), pp. 134, 137; and Andrew Weiss and Edward Woodhouse, "Reframing Incrementalism: A Constructive Response to the Critics," *Policy Studies* 25, nos 255–73 (1992), p. 268.

32 Donnelly, *International Human Rights*, pp. 98ff.; Jack Donnelly, "Human Rights, Humanitarian Crisis, and Humanitarian Intervention," *International Journal* 48 (1993), p. 639; and Sikkink, "The Power of Principled Ideas," p. 161.

33 Lillich, *International Human Rights*, p. 954, quoting President Carter, 1 *Published Papers of the President* 2, 3 (1977).

34 Sikkink, "The Power of Principled Ideas," p. 164.

35 Lillich, *International Human Rights*, pp. 954–5, quoting President Carter, *Address to the United Nations*, 76 *Department of State Bulletin* 329, 332–3 (March 17, 1977).

36 Carter, *Message from the President*. All four treaties – the American Convention on Human Rights, the International Convention on the Elimination of All Forms of Racial Discrimination, and the CPR and CESC – remained pending when the Carter administration left office.

37 Carter, "Humane Purpose in Foreign Policy," in Lillich, *International Human Rights*, p. 960, quoting 76 *Department of State Bulletin* 621, 622–3 (1977).

38 Smith, *America's Mission*, pp. 251–2, 264–5; Ernst Haas, "Panel, Human Rights: A New Policy by a New Administration," 1977 *American Society of International Law Proceedings* 68, pp. 72–6, quoted in Lillich, *International Human Rights*, pp. 965–6.

39 Sikkink, "The Power of Principled Ideas," p. 157.

40 Donnelly, *International Human Rights*, p. 118; Sikkink, "The Power of Principled Ideas," p. 153; and Smith, *America's Mission*, pp. 241–8.

41 Donnelly, *International Human Rights*, p. 117.
42 Kenneth M. Himes, "The Morality of Humanitarian Intervention," *Theological Studies* 55 (1994), pp. 103–4; and Lillich, *International Human Rights*, pp. 980ff, 1005, 1025, 1028.
43 Lillich, *International Human Rights*, pp. 564–637; and Donnelly, "Human Rights, Humanitarian Crisis," pp. 610–14, 622, 627–8.
44 Jarat Chopra and Thomas G. Weiss, "Sovereignty is No Longer Sacrosanct: Codifying Humanitarian Intervention," *Ethics and International Affairs* 6, nos 95–117 (1992), p. 96.
45 Richard A. Falk, "Intervention Revisited," *The Nation* (December 20, 1993), pp. 756–77.
46 Donnelly, *International Human Rights*, p. 104.
47 Ibid., pp. 99–135; and David P. Forsythe, "Human Rights and Peace: International and National Dimensions," in *Human Rights in International Perspective Series* 1 (Lincoln: University of Nebraska Press, 1993), pp. 34–52.
48 Falk, "Intervention Revisited," p. 755; Donnelly, *International Human Rights*, pp. 100–4; and Forsythe, "Human Rights and Peace," p. 49. For the Kirkpatrick Doctrine, see Jeanne Kirkpatrick, *Dictatorships and Double Standards: Rationalism and Reason in Politics* (New York: Simon and Schuster, 1983).
49 Joshua Muravchik, "Beyond Self Defense," *Commentary* (December 1993), p. 22.
50 Falk, "Intervention Revisited," p. 757.
51 See Article 54, "Protocol I Additional to the Geneva Convention Relative to the Protection of Civilian Persons in Time of War," entered into force by the United Nations on December 7, 1978, UN Document A/32/144. annex 2, reprinted in 16 *International Legal Materials* 1,442; not ratified by the United States.
52 Thomas Borstelmann, *Apartheid's Reluctant Uncle: The United States and Southern Africa in the Early Cold War* (New York: Oxford University Press, 1993).
53 *Washington Post*, quoted in Muravchik, "Beyond Self Defense," p. 19.
54 Falk, "Intervention Revisited," p. 760.
55 Ibid. and Muravchik, "Beyond Self Defense," p. 20.
56 Falk, "Intervention Revisited," p. 760.
57 Ibid., pp. 115–16.
58 Ibid., p. 115; and Mark Danner, "The Truth of El Mazote," *New Yorker* (December 6, 1993), pp. 50–133.
59 Van Ness, "What Ever Happened to Bill Clinton's Human Rights Policy?"
60 Yu Quanyu, "China Leads the US in Human Rights," *Beijing Review* (October 3–9, 1994), p. 24; and see Shattuck, "Introduction to a Report to the UN Human Rights Committee," p. 3.
61 Shattuck, "Introduction to a Report to the UN Human Rights Committee," p. 5.
62 Ibid.
63 *International Herald Tribune* (March 31, 1995), p. 7; Kaufman, *Human Rights Treaties*, pp. 148–74; Dinah Shelton, "Issues Raised by the United States: Reservations, Understandings, and Declarations," in Hannun and Fischer, eds, *US Ratification*, pp. 269–77.
64 *Washington Post*, editorial reprinted in the *International Herald Tribune* (April 1–2, 1995), p. 4.
65 Ibid.
66 Hannum and Fischer, "The Political Framework," p. 288.
67 Department of State, Shattuck Report, pp. 2–4.
68 Ibid., pp. 7–25.
69 Ibid., at discussion of Articles 6, 7, 10 (2b) and (3), 15(1), and 20, respectively, at pp. 33–207.

70 Ibid., at discussion of Articles 2(1) and 26, 9(5) and 14(6), 10(2a), 10(3), 14(3b, d and e), 14(7), and 50, respectively.

71 David Stewart, assistant legal adviser for human rights and refugees, Department of State, "US Ratification of the Covenant on Civil and Political Rights: The Significance of the Reservations, Understandings, and Declarations," *Human Rights Law Journal* (April 30, 1993, pp. 77–83). His commentary on the conditions mirrors the justifications given in the Shattuck Report on pp. 31–2, 55–6, 61–2, 66, 73, 90, 96, 99, 122, 133–5, 137, 140, 159–60, 202, and appendix 3.

72 Department of State, Shattuck Report, pp. 31–2.

73 Ibid., p. 79.

74 Ibid., pp. 79, 83.

75 "United States: Senate Committee on Foreign Relations Report on the International Covenant on Civil and Political Rights," *US Senate Executive Report* 102–23 (102nd Cong., 2nd Sess.), January 30, 1992, p. 4, reprinted in 31 *International Legal Materials* 645 (1992), quoted in Shelton, "Issues Raised by the United States," p. 271, n.2.

76 Thomas Merton, *Conjectures of a Guilty Bystander* (New York: Image Books, Doubleday, 1989), p. 81.

CONCLUSION

Peter Van Ness

It is not by chance that this debate about human rights has emerged at the end of more than forty years of Cold War. Citizens, scholars, activists, and government officials everywhere are puzzling about what kind of world we now find ourselves in, and how we might shape that world into something better than what we have had. No one, East or West, North or South, wants to return to the nuclear nightmare and the ideological crusades of the past.

Opportunities abound, but imagination in establishment circles seems to be in very short supply. Realists busy themselves with searching for "new enemies," behind every door and under every bed; idealists hope for international harmony but often find, instead, horrors like Bosnia and Rwanda; and pessimists are convinced that the New World Order will collapse into a global anarchy.

It is a unipolar moment in world history.[1] The United States today is perhaps even more predominant than at the end of World War II. After the collapse of its principal strategic opponent, the USSR, and with many of America's economic rivals from East Asia facing financial crisis, the new situation provides a superb opportunity for the United States to play an imaginative leadership role. Yet, like all countries, the United States continues to be hypocritical in the implementation of its human rights policies. Washington's main task is to get its own house in order.

Even the best of governments are duplicitous and inconsistent when it comes to questions of morality in foreign policy, because a big part of their job is to accommodate a broad range of diverse concerns and to formulate a composite "national interest." But they can be moved; they can be pressured and influenced from within and without – even the worst of them – at least to some extent. They can sometimes be embarrassed and shamed into doing what is right. Thus far, human rights NGOs have been the most successful in pressuring governments to practice what they preach. The international women's movement is a good example of what can be achieved against substantial odds.[2]

Let me suggest three basic principles that I think are vital to establishing a viable human rights policy for any government, East or West: consistency, reciprocity, and responsibility.

1   *Consistency* in human rights diplomacy means practicing what you preach by ratifying the major international human rights treaties, including the International Covenant on Civil and Political Rights and the International Covenant on Economic, Social, and Cultural Rights. The US record on ratification of such treaties is one of the worst when compared with other Western industrialized countries. China's record has been even worse. But both the United States and China are moving step-by-step to become parties to the major UN agreements.[3] Consistency also means developing one set of standards for evaluating human rights conditions that is applied to all countries, friends or foes, including one's own country as well.

2   *Reciprocity* requires that, just as you presume to examine the human rights conditions in other countries, you also invite the same sort of investigation by others of your own human rights practices. Australia, for example, which sent the first official human rights delegation to China in 1991, invited the Chinese to visit Australia to study the situation there, including the conditions of the Aborigines.[4] Reciprocity also means that, just as the United States, for example, urges other countries to come to terms with human rights abuses in their past (e.g. Japanese World War II atrocities in China and Korea), it should also acknowledge the abuses of its own past (such as genocide against the Native American population, and US covert operations around the world).[5]

3   *Responsibility* in human rights diplomacy obligates foreign-policy-makers to commit their governments to observe and to protect human rights as a foundation stone of their country's foreign policy, just as economic and strategic objectives are given priority. Responsibility to the international community entails a willingness to comply with the international human rights treaties that one has ratified and to participate in international institutions to undertake collective efforts to protect human rights.

Putting these principles into practice would show a seriousness of purpose on human rights as well as good faith in relations with other states, UN institutions, and NGOs committed to protecting human rights. For the United States, practicing these three principles would help to enhance the moral authority that is so vital to world leadership.

For the immediate future, Asian governments will naturally be preoccupied with trying to save their economies, which will inevitably involve paying greater deference to the US – so in this sense, we have probably seen a peak of East Asian self-confident assertion of its values and visions for the future, at least for the time being. In those Asian countries most adversely affected by the financial crisis, there is likely to be a rise in anti-American sentiment as the bankruptcy of companies, loss of employment, sharp decline in salaries, and the collapse of family savings are blamed on austerity programs forced on Asian societies by the IMF and the United States.

The IMF economic reforms may be conducive to structural changes that encourage the evolution of more open and accountable political regimes (for example, the 1997 changes in leadership in Thailand and South Korea, and the fall of President Suharto in Indonesia in 1998, are particularly promising), but when the full impact of the economic collapse is felt in sharp declines in standard of living and lost hopes, the grassroots reaction may be extreme – as we have learned from the rise of extremist politics associated with the Great Depression of the 1930s. Throughout history, periods of sharp economic decline following years of increasing prosperity have proven to be politically volatile, increasing the likelihood of outbreaks of ethnic conflict, xenophobia, and fascist politics. As the Indonesian military has already said it would, governments can be expected to respond with force to defend political stability and their positions of power, making the short-term outlook for human rights in East Asia more pessimistic.

In the West, human rights as a priority issue is not likely to disappear. The US Congress, for example, has its own diverse priorities with respect to international human rights, and the Republican Party majority seems determined to press forward on a broad range of policy initiatives.[6] In Asia, leaders and citizens, despite the financial crisis, are no less determined to shape their futures in their own way.[7]

The task for all of us, inhabitants of a shrinking planet, is to devise ways to work together to protect the human rights of all: shaping and reshaping global standards; encouraging ratification of existing agreements; monitoring compliance; and holding governments accountable for the commitments that they have made. Working to achieve these objectives together, we can find common ground.

NOTES

1   See, for example, Michael Mastanduno, "Preserving the Unipolar Moment: Realist Theories and US Grand Strategy after the Cold War," in Michael E. Brown *et al.*, eds, *America's Strategic Choices* (Cambridge, MA: MIT Press, 1997), pp. 123–62.
2   Women's Environmental and Development Organization (WEDO), *Mapping Progress: Assessing Implementation of the Beijing Platform* (New York: WEDO, 1998).
3   Moreover, China has now released from jail and sent into exile in the United States both Wei Jingsheng and Wang Dan, China's two best-known dissidents jailed by the Beijing government for their human rights activities (see Wei Jingsheng, *The Courage to Stand Alone: Letters from Prison and Other Writings*, New York: Viking, 1997; and Matt Forney, "Beijing Spring," *Far Eastern Economic Review*, April 2, 1998, pp. 20–2). However, Human Rights in China, when announcing Wang Dan's release, listed the names of 158 other Beijing citizens still held in prison by Chinese authorities in connection with the demonstrations of 1989 ("One Release Is Not Enough," April 19, 1998, Human Rights in China press statement <hrichina @hrichina.org>).
4   Ian Russell *et al.*, *Australia's Human Rights Diplomacy* (Canberra: Australian Foreign Policy Papers, 1992).

5   The American CIA still refuses to declassify thousands of files on US covert operations undertaken more than thirty-five years ago (during the Truman, Eisenhower, and Kennedy administrations). Without this information, it is not possible for American citizens to know fully and to evaluate what agencies of government have done in their name abroad. (Tim Weiner, "C.I.A., Breaking Promises, Puts Off Release of Cold War Files," *New York Times*, July 15, 1998, p. A13.)

6   Jeffrey Goldberg, "Washington Discovers Christian Persecution," *New York Times Magazine* (December 21, 1997), pp. 46–52, 60, and 64–5.

7   *Our Common Humanity: Asian Human Rights Charter, a People's Charter* (Hong Kong: Asian Human Rights Commission and Asian Legal Resource Center, 1998).

INDEX

282